A Rising Middle Power?

A Rising Middle Power?

German Foreign Policy
in Transformation, 1989–1999

Max Otte
with Jürgen Greve

St. Martin's Press
New York

A RISING MIDDLE POWER?
Copyright © Max Otte with Jürgen Greve, 2000. All rights reserved. Printed in
the United States of America. No part of this book may be used or reproduced
in any manner whatsoever without written permission except in the case of brief
quotations embodied in critical articles or reviews. For information, address St.
Martin's Press, 175 Fifth Avenue, New York, N.Y. 10010.

ISBN 0-312-22653-5

Library of Congress Cataloging-in-Publishing Data
Otte, Max, 1964– with Greve, Jürgen
   A rising middle power? : German foreign policy in transformation, 1989–1999
/ by Max Otte.
      p.   cm.
   Includes bibliographical references and index.
   ISBN 0-312-22653-5
   1. Germany—Foreign relations—1990- 2. Germany—History—
Unification, 1990. 3. Germany—Foreign relations—1945- 4. North Atlantic
Treaty Organization—Germany. 5. Germany—Military policy. I. Title.
DD290.3.O89   2000
943.087'9—dc21   99–055259

Design by Letra Libre, Inc.

First edition: July, 2000
10 9 8 7 6 5 4 3 2 1

Contents

Preface

Max Otte

This project, in many ways, spanned more than a decade—the same decade the book is about. It started in 1989, when I began my doctoral studies at Princeton University and extended through my dissertation proposal in 1993, the final submission of the dissertation in 1996, the submission of the book manuscript in 1998 and the completion of the book in 2000. Had I known the labors that would be involved, I might have shied away from the whole endeavor. Now that the fruits of my labor are before me, I cannot hold back a certain sense of accomplishment and pride.

Throughout the 1990s, I wandered between the Old World and the New, successively living in Princeton, Cologne, Dar es Salaam, Aspen, Jackson Hole, Hamburg, Berlin, and again in Cologne before "settling" into a dual existence in Boston and Cologne. My dissertation was by no means my only project. I was working as a management consultant to major corporations, universities, governments and international organizations, and later also as an investment banker. Two books emerged in that period before I finally finished this one. But this is the one I am proudest of, because it was by far the hardest.

As a permanent resident of the United States and a German citizen, one sees some of the events covered in this book with two sets of glasses. When the Berlin Wall fell, I was in the graduate-student bar of Princeton University, the infamous so-called debasement bar. The volume on the TV was turned off, but suddenly, I saw people dancing on the Brandenburg Gate—and I could not believe my eyes. I thought it was a trick. It took quite a while until the reality of the moment sank in. My friends were very happy for me and extended their congratulations. But I had to leave the room—this is how much I was touched by the moment.

I did then and do now have an agenda with this book: contemporary Europe warrants American attention, maybe even more so than before. Europe may be a funny place that is sometimes hard to interpret, but Europeans often hold the same view about America. (In fact, I wrote a book about this, too.) I sincerely hope that with this book I can contribute to continuing American-European-German understanding, something the world needs even more now than in the past. The United States and Europe have drawn as close economically as they were before World War I, and the world needs their continued cooperation and collaboration. Understanding is the first step for this collaboration to grow and prosper.

I am indebted to many people. First, my three dissertation advisers Aaron Friedberg, Hanns Maull, and Richard Ullman provided stimulation and encouragement, but also criticism and direction. Each of them, including the co-readers, engaged me far beyond the call of duty. This is not to say that sometimes I would not have preferred a little less "engagement," but a dissertation at a major university is supposed to be hard work, and the final product was much, much better because of the guidance I received.

I was fortunate to have Jürgen Greve, a German student of history, work with me since early 1999 to update the period from 1997 to 1999 and provide insights for other parts of the book. The section on reunification and the chapter on the new Schröder government are largely his. Without Jürgen, this book would not have come into existence. I am also indebted to C. Fred Bergsten, Ben Bernanke, Kent Calder, Gerhard Fels, Robert Gilpin, Erik Goldstein, William W. Grimes, C. Randall Henning, John Ikenberry, Karl Kaiser, Suzanne Keller, Thomas Kielinger, H. Joachim Maitre, Uri Ra'anan, John Silber, and Hermann Simon.

I sincerely thank my editor, Karen Wolny, as well as Ruth Mannes, Gabrielle Pearce, and an anonymous reviewer for seeing me through this project with great enthusiasm and professionalism.

Friendship and love provide the ground from which productive works can emerge. My gratitude goes to Barbara, who accompanied me for an important part of the way. Jörg and Harald: thank you for being important discussion partners about life, work, and everything.

Finally, my sincere gratitude goes Max and Lore Otte, my parents. Thank you for instilling in me a passion for truth and a yearning for knowledge that will never fade.

Max Otte
Cologne, March 2000

Foreword

Wolfgang Gehring

General Manager, Continental Airlines Germany

A decade after the breakdown of Communism, the contours of the new Europe are still vague. It was obvious that after the end of the Cold War, Europe would change significantly. But to many Americans, this change did not seem to warrant the same level of attention as did the Cold War. After all, the United States was left in the position of sole superpower, and Europe seemed to be on the right track, largely speaking. Moreover, the developments in the new Europe, were contradictory and difficult to interpret.

With this careful account of German foreign policy from 1989 to 1999, Max Otte provides a skillful interpretation of the new Europe, seen from the perspective of Germany, new Europe's most important power. The result is a refreshingly original insight and a complex, but ultimately reassuring assessment of Germany and Europe.

In Otte's analysis, German power may have risen, but the parameters of German foreign policy have changed little. Germany is still dependent on the U.S. security shield, and the European Union as an economic area. These, then, have been and will be the two foremost security interests of the "new" Germany. A third interest, stability in Eastern Europe, was already present in preunification Germany and has received added emphasis.

Based on a moderately "realist" view of international relations, Otte analyzes the policies of Germany as they relate to the major players in the new Europe—the United States, Russia, France, Great Britain, and other European states. For Otte, the emergence of a European Union is unlikely. At the same time, Europe has transcended "politics among nations": the European states realize that they need each other—both economically and politically. Their respective potential is simply too small to go it alone. Still, national sovereignties in core areas continue to be guarded jealously, making a true European defense and foreign policy unlikely.

Surprisingly, Otte sees Germany as the major defender of the status quo in Europe. Germany's policymakers realize that Germany is a middle power and does not have the potential to become a truly global power. In the early nineties, Gray spoke of Germany as a "reluctant power," Kielinger and Otte called Germany the "pressured power." Otte now provides the theoretical underpinning: he convincingly argues that Germany has achieved all its objectives, and then some. Germany is content to pursue its three major interests—a strong security relationship with the United States, economic integration in Europe, and stability in Eastern Europe and Russia. If change comes to Europe, it will most likely come from the outside, from either an ambitious United States or a revisionist Russia.

Otte is a strong believer in "Transatlantica," a concept Hermann Simon and Otte pioneered in an article in the *Harvard Business Review*. Transatlantica completes what was interrupted by two World Wars in a tumultuous and often tragic century. America and Europe are best positioned to benefit from the New Economy. Transatlantica consists of an America and a Europe of roughly equal economic strength, coupled with a further Americanization of the European economy and the continuing security leadership of the United States.

Within Transatlantica, the United States and Germany will play pivotal roles. Increasingly, Germany will replace Great Britain as America's most important partner in Europe. This is for the better of Transatlantic relations, because Germany needs the United States even more than it needs Europe. With American backing, Germany has the power and political maturity to act as a stabilizer in Europe.

Max Otte, of course, is a model citizen of Transatlantica. A German citizen and a permanent resident of the United States with degrees from Princeton and the University of Cologne, he lives in Boston, Massachusetts and Cologne, Germany and travels the Atlantic at least a dozen times per year. It is therefore especially fortunate that he has devoted his energies to such an important subject.

We at Continental Airlines are of course very happy with the emergence of Transatlantica. We wish the book the success it deserves. Even more importantly, we hope that it will further strengthen the understanding between the United States and Germany.

Wolfgang Gehring
Frankfurt, April 2000

I
-
Introduction

I

T hree times in the twentieth century, the political map of the world changed radically. In all three episodes, Germany was in the epicenter of events. Twice (1914–1919; 1939–1945) these changes were accompanied by wars of unprecedented scale; the third time (1989–1991) a peaceful revolution swept away the order that had been in place for more than 40 years.

Unlike the two world wars, the revolution from 1989 to 1991 has not yet acquired a proper name. Yet its effect on the international system—if less painful—is in no way smaller than that of the world wars. Within a brief period of time, the Warsaw Pact and the Soviet Union collapsed, obliterating the ordering principles of almost half of the political world. Suddenly, the Western model seemed to be undisputed. At the beginning of the new century, there is again hope for universal progress and the creation of a "new world order." There seems to be a distinct possibility that the twenty-first century will be a long period of relative stability similar to the one that lasted from 1815 to 1914.

But as before, states are struggling to adjust to a new global situation in which many of the assumptions of the past have to be thrown overboard. The hope for a universal dominance of Western principles is already fickle, punctuated by the harsh realities of numerous local conflicts and undermined by the seeming impotence of large powers to affect those conflicts. Moreover, states seem to have lost their sense of direction and their ability to mobilize resources on a larger scale. There is, at times, a striking discrepancy between the eagerness on the part of world leaders to demonstrate unity and agreement and their inability to commit themselves and their domestic constituencies in earnest to the task of building a world system that will last well into the twenty-first century.

Times of major change in the international system always pose great challenges to states. Cherished principles of the past, upon which one or more generations of leaders have based their policies, have been thrown overboard or at least have been radically questioned.

After the First World War, neither the United States nor England was ready to adjust to the changes in the international system. The war had stalled Germany's ambitions for hegemony, significantly weakened England's global role, and established the United States as the dominant world power. The world had transcended the Pax Britannica. But this change was not reflected in the roles that states carved out for themselves. The United States remained inward-looking and was not willing to assume the burden of leadership. This absence of leadership by the United States, the inability of Great Britain to continue to provide such leadership, Germany's grievances, and the Great Depression produced a fateful situation, and eventually Germany and Japan launched a Second World War.

This war resulted in the partitioning of Germany and the defeat of Japan, completed the transformation of power from Great Britain to the United States of America, and established the Soviet Union as a second superpower. Contrary to 1919, in 1945 the United States came not only with blueprints for the new world order, but with the firm commitment to lead and put those plans in practice. From the experience of the First World War and its aftermath, America had drawn the lesson that decisive leadership would be an essential component of the post–World War II international system.

The triumph of the West between 1989 and 1991 poses similar questions of leadership, if—as always in history—under different circumstances. The euphoria of 1989 quickly evaporated, leaving in its place sobriety and exhaustion. The West had organized in response to a threat. When that threat collapsed, the West itself was confronted with difficult questions. There had been no blueprints for the post–Cold War world. Nobody had foreseen that the structures that had dominated international relations for more than a generation would vanish overnight. Even now, ten years after the end of the bipolar system, the structure of the new world order remains unclear.

The core institutions of the West—NATO, the European Community, the G-7, the IMF, and the World Bank, to name a few—are facing challenges they are not prepared for. In some cases, such as NATO, the very legitimacy of institutions is called into question. Moreover, for many, the very fabric of international politics seems to have undergone a change. Increasingly, states seem to be at the mercy of economic forces beyond their control. Technology, as the argument goes, is creating a global economy, and nonstate actors such as transnational corporations and interest groups are international actors in their own right. In this environment, all major states were—and still are—searching for principles to guide them through a maze of uncertainties.

II

This is an analysis of the reaction of one nation, Germany, to the changes that radically transformed the country's security environment within two short years. After 1989, nothing for Germany was as it used to be. A formerly divided, semi-sovereign state, over which the Allied Powers formally still had the last say, had regained its full sovereignty. The highest concentration of modern military and nuclear forces in any one area of the world, divided into two hostile blocks and separated by the inner-German border, was largely dispersed. The Soviet forces were leaving the country. The ever-present threat of immediate extinction had lost most of its terror.

Germany's security was further enhanced by the dissolution of the Warsaw Pact and the Soviet Union. Germany chose to remain anchored in the North Atlantic Treaty Organization (NATO), the Western European Union (WEU) and the European Union (EU). For the first time in its history, Germany was surrounded on all sides by friendly nations seeking cooperation and assistance on a wide variety of issues.

Moreover, reunification had made Germany by far the most powerful state in Europe, with an economy far superior to that of any other European nation. United Germany, with a population of 80 million, was suddenly one-third larger than France or Britain. Germany's GDP was almost one-third greater than that of France, the second-largest European economy, and almost twice that of Britain.

We now have excellent accounts of the diplomatic processes that surrounded and enabled German reunification, the most notable ones by Philip Zelikow and Condolezza Rice for the allied perspective and Karl Kaiser, Werner Weidenfeld and Horst Teltschik for the (West) German side.[1] We are able to see how diplomacy changed historical realities that once seemed to be cast in cement almost overnight. These studies leave us in awe of this dense period of international relations, in which so much was achieved peacefully in such a brief time. A fateful confluence of broader historical trends, a particular set of personalities, and fortunate policies led to an acceleration of history itself, culminating in German re-unification and a seeming confirmation of the West.

The "German question" was settled, and the new Germany has contin-uously demonstrated that it is a responsible member of the international community. Germany is also a cornerstone of the institutions that main-tained four decades of stability and prosperity in Europe—namely NATO and the European Union.

Yet the new age has spawned many new challenges, not least for Ger-many.[2] As those challenges—the need for political and economic reform in the European Union, the need to foster stability in Russia, to control rampant illegal migration, to prevent small-scale wars at the borders of the European Union, to control nuclear terrorism, and the general need to maintain stability in Europe and beyond—mount, how will Germany react? What will the grand strategy of the most powerful European state look like?

By tracing the often subtle, sometimes sudden changes in German pol-icy, strategy, and doctrine in the years from 1989 to 1999, this study at-tempts to shed light on those important questions. This analysis can lead us to a better understanding of three issues. One, how did the German polit-ical system react to large-scale change in the international environment? Two, has Germany itself changed? Three, if Germany has changed, was this change largely completed by the mid-1990s, or is it likely to continue? In other words, is the Germany that we are seeing now the one we are likely to see ten years from now, or will there be more major changes?

There are, by and large, three perspectives that inform the study of in-ternational relations and can help us to answer those questions: "realism," "institutionalism," and "constructivism."[3] Realism is the dominant per-spective underlying American foreign policy today. It played almost no role as an intellectual underpinning to German foreign policy before 1989.[4] Here, institutionalism and liberal constructivism were powerful forces, in-forming the policy elites and the populace alike.

Realists believe that history is still ultimately driven by nation-states, that self-interested states strive for power and autonomy, that military power reigns supreme, and that international stability derives from an equilibrium of forces. States that strive for peace are less likely to achieve a stable in-ternational order than states whose primary concern is equilibrium.[5]

An international order arises when strong states are able to assert cer-tain principles that suit them. Realists believe that for an international order to be stable, it must be legitimate. All major powers must agree to or at least accept the principles instituted by the strong states. The institutions, treaties, and arrangements that arise out of such agreement are not necessarily equitable. But no major state is so dissatisfied with the existing order that it attempts to overthrow those institutions and arrangements or question the fundamental principles underlying them. A legitimate order does not preclude change or conflict, nor does it guarantee peace. It does allow, however, for conflicts to be managed within an established framework. In other words, a legitimate order creates an environment in which conflicts are resolved, rather than avoided.

For legitimacy to endure, states and other political actors must inhabit roles roughly commensurate with their aspirations and power. Strong states lead and set most of the rules, middle states try to use their influence, and small states find niches in which they are comfortable. Conflicts occur, but the survival of major actors or their vital interests are not threatened. If either the self-perception or the capability of states changes, the system must be able to accommodate those changes. If it is not possible to address emerging disequilibria within a given order, war and revolution will threaten to shake the very foundations and legitimacy of that order.[6]

Twice, Germany has attempted to overthrow the European order. The preeminent realist Kenneth Waltz believes that Germany's power is again on the rise and that Germany will increasingly act like a world power, including the acquisition of nuclear weapons.[7] Ultimately, this attempt might lead to conflict, because "states have always competed for wealth and security, and the competition has often led to conflict."[8] John Mearsheimer sees the risk of Europe reverting "back to the future"—to a system of states struggling for preeminence in shifting alliances because the conditions that guaranteed stability in Europe, especially superpower supremacy, have vanished.[9]

Institutionalists believe that national power is important, but only one of the many forces that determine national policy. International institutions and arrangements can create and sustain order, even in the absence of strong states that set and enforce rules. Institutions can make states modify their quest for power and autonomy in order to cooperate.

Moreover, many institutionalists believe that states increasingly operate in an era of complex interdependence, where states, international institutions, large corporations, and other transnational actors all have an important role in international relations.[10] States therefore do not have a monopoly on power—often, they are not even the most important actors. In many areas of "low politics," overall military power and strength take a backseat to economic power and power in specific areas. Smaller states might prevail over larger ones in specific areas. Institutionalists are also less concerned with large-scale conflict and change, because they assume that at least in the West, states share many common assumptions, and that conflict will play itself out within a given framework.

Karl Kaiser, for example, sees an ongoing process of integration and cooperation in Western Europe.[11] German unification might change some factors of this process, but not the process itself. A more independent Germany with larger responsibilities would be better able to "assert and ensure its own particular interests and, thereby, its own democratic stability and tolerance for multilateralism."[12] It will also dampen false expectations about its own role.

Philip Gordon argues that Germany will be forced into a much greater international role than in the past. This will somewhat weaken Germany's obsession with international consensus.[13] Smyser, Gray, and Schöllgen see a return of the German *Mittellage* (middle position) between East and West.[14] All three authors point to a high degree of institutional cooperation: Europe is qualitatively different from the balance-of-power politics of previous times, because the (Western) European nations have become mature democracies unlikely to use force against each other.[15]

In this new environment, "German policy is beginning to weave a wide web of cooperation that stretches from Paris to Moscow through Berlin and Warsaw." This "transcontinental chain of cooperation is unprecedented and amounts to a German reshaping of the continent." Smyser expects this transformation to be achieved by "diplomacy, money, and carefully calculated transformations of existing organizations" with military means playing no role. This "makes the effort all the more extraordinary."[16]

Constructivists, finally, assert that states need not pursue their narrowly defined self-interest, because "self-interest" as used by realists is only one of many possible social constructs. States might as well assume an enlightened role in promoting international law, nonintervention, a division of labor among states, and world progress (or any other role they construct for themselves). For constructivists, norms are thus constructed and spread through social interaction. Realist thinking is only one way of looking at international relations, and it is dependent on the special circumstances that created it.

Constructivists are often (but not always) "liberals." They are interested in whether states can cooperate out of "enlightened self-interest," even if the search for power and prestige would dictate otherwise. In other words, states might be as interested in the common welfare as they are in their own power and prestige.

For Hanns Maull, Germany's defeat in World War II caused a radical change in Germany's domestic structure and foreign policy orientation. A new type of nation has emerged, a "civilian power."[17] The objectives of civilian powers are radically different from the motives realists ascribe to states. They include: "a) the acceptance of the necessity of cooperation with others in the pursuit of international objectives; b) the concentration on nonmilitary, primarily economic, means to secure national goals, with military power left as a residual instrument serving essentially to safeguard other means of international interaction; and c) a willingness to develop supranational structures to address critical issues of international management."[18]

Richard Ullman extends this interpretation to all of Western Europe.[19] For Ullman, Western Europe has transcended "politics among nations" and has moved to a stage where universal norms and joint aspirations define national goals.[20] Thomas Berger has shown that during the postwar decades, antimilitarism has become so deeply engrained in the German and Japanese national cultures that traditional military power politics, even to the extent that France or the U.S. would engage in it, is highly unlikely in both Germany and Japan.[21]

III

In this study, we will apply a realist perspective to German foreign policy between 1989 and 1999. We hope to show that this perspective offers a coherent and consistent approach for explaining the changes that occurred after 1989. But contrary to realist authors such as Waltz and Mearsheimer, we will argue that Germany is a cornerstone of the status quo in Europe, and that disturbances to that status quo, if they ever arise, will likely come from outside. Germany is a middle power with limited resources, not unlike Metternich's Austria, which Henry Kissinger so brilliantly analyzed.[22] Its security is inextricably linked to the stability of the status quo and the principles that underlie it. This cannot be said about either Russia or the United States, two nations that, for different reasons, may pose challenges to the status quo. Russia, of course, may develop revisionist aspirations. But even the United States, dissatisfied with the status quo, may withdraw from Europe or push the vehicle of NATO toward new objectives. Both developments would severely upset the delicate balance of European institutions.

During the first 25 years of its existence, the Federal Republic of Germany developed a particular foreign policy doctrine that in many ways differed from those of the more traditional powers, leading Hanns Maull to call it a "civilian powers" and a "prototype of a promising future."[23] Germany's foreign policy doctrine consisted of integration within NATO and renunciation of military force for purposes other than self-defense, European integration (and partial conflation of German and European interests) and, later, détente and reconciliation with the East. Germany developed a military whose highest purpose was never to fight. Postwar German politicians mistakenly assumed that German and European interests were synonymous. And Germany strove for multilateral solutions whenever possible.

Unconventional as they might have been, all these elements of Germany's foreign policy doctrine can be explained using a realist perspective and national interests as a basis for analysis. After World War II, Germany was a defeated, divided middle power, unable to provide for its own security or even economic survival. First and foremost, the Federal Republic needed U.S. support to guarantee its existence during the years of the East-West confrontation. A hypothetical neutral and united Germany, which had been discussed during the founding years of the Federal Republic, would have found it hard to stay outside the Soviet sphere of influence. Any use of military force in Central Europe could have quickly escalated to a threat against the very existence of Germany. Hence, Germany had to be interested in downplaying the use of force while maintaining a strong and protective military. Also, Germany could not hope ever again to dominate Europe. But as a medium-sized, highly industrialized power it needed European markets. Its neighbors were highly suspicious of Germany's powers and ambitions. It was therefore a logical step to stress European over German interests in order to promote cooperation and integration, rather than balancing among Germany's neighbors. Finally, as long as Germany's security structures were clear, détente and cooperation with the East could help to ease tensions and further enhance Germany's security.

From 1949 to 1989, European security structures were basically "locked in." For the United States, "bipolarity" was the decisive feature. For Germany, in addition to the East – West confrontation, a second dimension overlays bipolarity, that of European integration. The United States and Germany both wanted a strong and secure Germany to counter Soviet power. Ultimately, Soviet missiles threatened New York as much as Berlin. Of course, Germany had a larger interest in linking threats to its territory to threats to the United States, whereas the United States made some attempts to localize conflicts in Europe. By and large, however, the Atlantic alliance was very cohesive. France had an interest in developing a European Community (which it hoped to dominate) to bolster its status as a world power alongside the United States. And Germany had an interest in a European Community that would create a secure economic zone and establish close cooperation within Europe. Only by giving up some sovereignty could Germany hope to win influence in Europe.

Germany's security calculus depended on a number of scenarios. Germany was vulnerable mainly to three developments: (1) a withdrawal of U.S. troops and protective shield, (2) a breakdown of Germany's trading sphere (the EU), and (3) adversarial developments in Eastern Europe in general and Russia in particular. This basic structure of vulnerabilities has remained relatively unchanged even after the breakdown of the communist system. The whole of German foreign policy—before and after unification—can be understood as diplomacy focused on trying to prevent any of these developments. What may change is the relative weight given to any of those objectives, or the style in which the domestic debate is being conducted. But basically, Germany's essential security calculus has changed less that that of either the United States or Russia.

The new international situation that Germany encountered after it had become a sovereign state on October 3, 1990, was considerably more complex and had become "unlocked." The end of bipolarity had created a whole number of conceivable international constellations. In certain ways, Germany found itself in a *Mittellage* again, a middle position that Adenauer's diplomacy had tried to prevent. Germany has remained a middle power, and any attempts to overplay its middle position could backfire, because Germany still lacks the resources to be a wanderer between the worlds. Aware of this fact, Germany's governments have so far stressed the continuity of the international system rather than change. Above all, Germany's partnership with the United States has been upheld by all postunification governments. The United States remains the best guarantor of Germany's military security: an independent German military would not be welcomed by Germany's neighbors, and a multilateral European military is not yet on the horizon. Germany has also tried to preserve and develop the status quo of the European Union, thus giving deepening precedence over widening.

The events of 1989–1991 did not change Germany's basic security calculus. Germany's military and even economic might has not grown all that much. We will show this by analyzing different measures of German power in detail. Germany, now more than ever, remains a pillar of the status quo. Barring unforeseeable international events, we should not expect major surprises. The new Schröder government—the first federal government in which the Green Party is a coalition partner—will not reverse the changes toward a more independent Germany. But neither will it risk the institutional fabric on which Germany's security rests—NATO and the European

Union. For this reason, it will refrain from a significant withdrawal of financial contributions to the EU, and it will continue its policy of cautious participation in military efforts.

Germany's foreign policy doctrine, however, has changed more radically than many people realize. In the decades before the demise of the Warsaw Pact, the domestic debate in the Federal Republic strongly leaned toward institutionalist or even constructivist values. International cooperation and integration were important concepts; "national interests" were often regarded as anachronistic. As the new Germany evolves, elements of realism are becoming more prevalent. Germany is ready to send troops abroad in allied mission, something that had been unthinkable before. The notion of Europe as a substitute fatherland began to recede as "national interests" emerged more clearly in the mid-1990s. The study of grand doctrine and geopolitics, all but forgotten in the postwar Federal Republic, have begun to emerge anew. Germany is becoming low-key leader and legitimate broker in the post-postwar Europe.

The United States, in particular, should welcome the new Germany. It can rely upon Germany as a junior partner and stable ally with complementary interests under one condition: that the United States itself does not try to radically change or redefine the European security environment, either by withdrawing from the Atlantic alliance or by trying to give it a mandate it was never intended to have.

In 1993, Thomas Kielinger and this author wrote: "If there is any 'special relationship' between the United States and a European country, it should be with Germany. In contrast to Britain, which has often used its own special interests to weaken Europe, and in contrast to France, which has used Europe to weaken the United States, a Germany bolstered by the United States would be a cornerstone of a Europe both stronger and more supportive of American interests. That kind of Europe would be in a better position to shoulder some of America's many burdens."[24]

In 1994, Bill Clinton made a statement that can be interpreted in the same way. Asked by a journalist in Germany whether the relationship with Britain or Europe was more important, he replied that "the United States and Germany have a more immediate and tangible concern with . . . [many] issues even than our other friends in Europe."[25] Embarrassed, German government officials played down the comment. This author believes that America would be served well by emphasizing the American - German relationship, and that a "special relationship" is indeed in the interest of both.

Some readers will not share our outlook for the future, or our policy prescriptions. This is, however, primarily an empirical study of past events.

The process of adjustment through which Germany went between 1989 and 1999 is independent of the lessons for the future that one derives from it. Throughout the study, we have tried to present facts and processes as they were evolving between 1989 and 1999, focusing on the interaction of German domestic politics, norms, international institutions, and diplomacy. This should leave readers with enough material to draw their own conclusions.

II

A Tradition of Limited Sovereignty: The Foreign Policy Doctrine of the Federal Republic of Germany, 1949–1990

I

From its founding in 1949 until the collapse of the Soviet system after 1989, the Federal Republic of Germany was part of a static and rigid bipolar international system. Although its independence was extremely limited in this political constellation, West Germany accepted the situation. As a smaller, semisovereign and highly vulnerable power, it sought a close alliance with the West. Despite the radical threats to West German survival that emanated from the East-West confrontation, the U.S. nuclear umbrella provided the best guarantee for the security of Germany and Europe.

The fact that Germany occupied a middle position, or *Mittellage,* was almost irrelevant. Because both German states were closely integrated into their respective treaty systems, the fear of "encirclement" that German politicians had developed before World War I was absent. Unlike the Kaiserreich, the Federal Republic was not a semihegemonic power on the European continent. The Federal Republic did not necessarily demand counterbalancing.

Moreover, both Germanys were loyal parts of the respective systems, so that their neighbors did not fear a return to the "swinging policy"— *Schaukelpolitik*—between East and West that Germany had conducted in the interwar period. The 1922 Treaty of Rappallo is a synonym for this tendency of "swinging."[1] Though some of the early German postwar politicians, such as Jakob Kaiser, favored a Germany in a middle position, Germany's first chancellor, Konrad Adenauer, pursued close German association with the West. Adenauer also wanted to bar future German governments from returning to a "swinging policy."[2] This also implied that reunification, though theoretically still a goal of German foreign policy, had very little implications for practical policy.

The East-West confrontation fostered coherence within the two most important treaty systems of the West, NATO and the European Economic Community, later renamed the European Community and even later renamed the European Union. Over the decades, Germany's low profile and conciliatory policies within those treaty systems helped to decrease ressentiments. Moreover, divergences of opinion within the West remained at a low level.

In his classic work on Metternich's policy during and after the Congress of Vienna, Henry A. Kissinger demonstrated that a foreign policy based on norms and principles is conducive to the interests of a middle power. At the time, Austria could play a role much larger than its power alone allowed it. By establishing Austria as a guardian of conservative monarchic values, Metternich could gain the goodwill of mighty Russia for securing Austria's position in Italy, the Balkans, and Germany. Yet Austria also needed to actively involve England in continental affairs to pursue this policy.[3]

There are some parallels to the postwar situation of the Federal Republic of Germany—here, too, a policy based on norms and principles helped to stabilize the status quo, foster Germany's security, and promote Germany's objectives. Those norms were: the renunciation of traditional power politics, multilateralism, integration with the West, nonaggression, defense orientation, democracy, and reconciliation with the East. Among those, the renunciation of power politics by German politicians and the population at large deserves special attention. Any use of power in Germany's environment would have meant the worst possible outcome for Germany, including a likely escalation to large-scale conflict and possible annihilation.

In few states was the study of national power as thoroughly banned from public discourse as in the old Federal Republic of Germany between 1949 and 1989, or the Bonn Republic, as it became known. "National interest," "grand strategy," and "power politics" became anathema. Even "foreign policy doctrine" was always used in mantra-like conjunction with "integration in NATO" and "European unification" to show that there was really no such thing as an independent German foreign policy doctrine. Those pillars of the Germany security doctrine were equated with Germany's national interest, not seen as policies that followed from those interests. The "German question"—the unification of the divided country—was still (barely) alive, but it had little implications for daily policy.

In the 1980s, Adenauer biographer Hans Peter Schwarz wrote a book entitled *The Tamed Germans: from Obsession with Power to Oblivion*.[4] Schwarz argued that the style of German foreign policy was one of dependency, solidarity in alliances, need for harmony, multilateralism, moralism, delegitimization of power politics, and a forgotten reason of state *(Staatsräson)*. Even books written after unification signaled the same underlying thesis. Gregor Schöllgen wrote a book entitled *Afraid of Power: the Germans and their Foreign Policy,* and Christian Hacke entitled his history of German foreign policy since World War II *World Power Against its Own Will: the Foreign Policy of the Federal Republic of Germany*.[5]

Multilateralist defense structures under an American nuclear umbrella, European unification, and, later, rapprochement with the East were the three pillars of German foreign policy. Integration in NATO and U.S. nuclear protection was one core pillar of the security doctrine of the old Federal Republic of Germany. This entailed a military whose only mission was the defense of the home territory, integration in NATO command structures, the renunciation of nuclear, biological, and chemical weapons, and the renunciation of independent C3 (command, control, and communications) capabilities. Moreover, there was an understanding that German forces were never again to serve outside Germany's territory.

European integration was another core pillar of the foreign policy doctrine of postwar Germany.[6] The preamble of the German constitution of 1949[7] included the statement that Germany "would serve world peace as an equal part of a united Europe."[8] The postwar generation, epitomized by Chancellor Helmut Kohl, had strong hopes for the unification of Europe. Many Germans saw Europe as a substitute fatherland, believing that closer integration would eventually lead to the political unification of Europe. Timothy Garton Ash called this a "habitual conflation of German and European interests," but there is ample evidence that many German policymakers believed in such an identity of interests.[9]

Détente was somewhat more problematic. For the first 20 years of its existence, the Federal Republic did not acknowledge the existence of a second state on German soil and did not maintain diplomatic relations with states that recognized the German Democratic Republic (GDR). This hardened position at the height of the Cold War put the United States and other Western nations in a comfortable position, allowing them to handle East-West relations mostly by themselves. When the Federal Republic of Germany made its first attempts at détente during the Brandt government, the Nixon administration, itself an advocate of détente, eyed such steps with suspicion. Yet, close German integration with the West remained a cornerstone of the Federal Republic's doctrine.

Despite challenges, the core elements of Germany's foreign policy doctrine—complete integration in Western defense structures and renunciation of independent military capabilities, Europe as a substitute fatherland, and détente with the East—lasted throughout the postwar era. But doctrines do not last forever, and under the influence of a new geopolitical situation, they have changed between 1989 and 1999. Germany is now a sovereign power. We intend to show, however, that Germany is still a middle power, and that many of the fundamental structures of its environment have remained intact. In the future, a status quo-oriented, norms and principles-based foreign policy will be as important as ever for Germany.

II

In May 1945, the last German government under great Admiral Dönitz signed its unconditional surrender to the allied forces. The German state had ceased to exist. After the failed battle of the bulge in 1945, Hitler himself had wished for Germany to be annihilated. To him, a country that was not able to reign was not worthy of existence. In February 1943, Goebbels had declared an all-out war in his notorious speech at the Berlin *Sportpalast,* and Germany had engaged in it. As a consequence, Hitler's policy of no retreat and scorched earth had prolonged the fighting in many areas, and the Allied bombings had reduced many cities to rubble. The German infrastructure was devastated.

The victory of the Allies was complete. The war effort had unified them in the struggle against the Third Reich. American, French, and British forces occupied the western half of Germany, Russian forces the eastern half. Allied plans for the postwar period had remained vague.[10] Of course, it was to be ensured that a war of aggression would never again emanate from German territory. Some in the West recommended dismantling German industry and creating an agricultural territory—the U.S. secretary of the treasury Henry Morgenthau was one of the most outspoken advocates of this position.[11] But the United States, Britain, and France had no clear and common strategy.

The Soviet Union, on the other hand, did have consistent and immediate objectives: Stalin wanted to preserve the gains from the war and expand and solidify his country's power. After the October revolution, the Soviet Union had been a weak country, torn by upheaval and threatened by external forces. Terror, the murder of up to 20 million people, and the solidification of a repressive regime had consolidated Stalin's power within the Soviet Union. Stalin also wanted to solidify international power for his country, which had born the brunt of the land war and had suffered more than 14 million casualties in the fight against Germany.

In 1939, Germany and the Soviet Union had agreed on the partitioning of Poland by signing the Molotov-Ribbentrop pact. When Germany's invasion of Poland started World War II, Stalin was quick to occupy the eastern half of Poland. After the war, Stalin was not ready to return to Poland the parts he had taken in 1939. Soviet forces occupied roughly one-half of the German prewar territory, including the provinces of East Prussia, Silesia, Pommerania, and the Eastern part of Brandenburg. Stalin annexed the northern half of East Prussia including the city of Königsberg, which was renamed Kaliningrad. He also retained the parts annexed from Poland, giving Poland the southern half of East Prussia and Silesia instead. The areas annexed from Germany were ethnically German, and so its inhabitants, among them this writer's family, were expelled by force. Stalin told the British foreign minister Ernest Bevin not to worry, because "there were not many Germans left in the territories which had been taken from Germany."[12]

Although the three Western Powers did not agree with these steps, they conceded Soviet and Polish administration of the de facto annexed territories under the condition that "the final delimitation of the western frontier of Poland should await a peace settlement."[13] Thus was born the issue of Germany's eastern frontier, which remained open until 1990. The annexed territories comprised one-quarter of Germany's pre-World War II territory. Its population was relatively smaller, since those areas had been mostly agricultural. Nevertheless, the league of expelled Germans was a powerful force in West Germany in the 1950s and 1960s, demanding German reunification within the borders of 1937. Until the 1970s, German national TV showed political maps with the old border delineation.

Four zones of military administration were established after the victory. The Western (American, British, and French) zones would, in the future, comprise the Federal Republic of Germany; half of the Soviet zone would be the German Democratic Republic, and the other half was annexed by the Soviet Union and Poland. Berlin was put under joint administration. The Four Powers, united in their wartime effort, could not agree on a postwar strategy on Germany. In the United States and Britain, attention was directed toward domestic questions, and France was still too weak to play a significant role.

The Soviet Union, intent on being compensated in full for the losses suffered during the war, began a program of reparations and repatriation of forced labor to help in the reconstruction of its industry. Factories, machines, and disposable assets were dismantled and brought to the Soviet Union. By the spring of 1946, at least one-third of the industrial installations had been thus relocated. German prisoners of war were kept in Soviet labor camps—some until 1955. The Western Powers also dismantled some factories, and France kept some German prisoners in labor camps, but soon their focus was to shift to the devastated conditions in Germany.

As soon as 1946, the Truman administration began to abandon its perception of a harmonious partnership with the Soviet Union and began to see Soviet behavior as part of a strategy to achieve Soviet and communist domination in Europe. Britain had been more suspicious from the beginning. Churchill had warned openly about the communist danger in March 1946 and proposed a defense treaty between the United States and Great Britain.

In September 1946, U.S. secretary of state James Byrnes stated that the Germans should "now be given primary responsibility for the running of their own affairs."[14] This entailed, of course, a continuation of the military occupation, but the Western Powers were ready to have some form of economic self-administration. In the same month, Winston Churchill demanded a "United States of Europe" (without Great Britain) in a speech in Zurich, arguing that France needed a partnership with a strong Europe to regain its moral leadership in Europe.[15]

The new American secretary of state George Marshall was ready to extend American economic assistance to Europe and Germany. At the council of foreign ministers' meeting in Moscow in March and April 1947, he sought to achieve a treaty that would keep Germany disarmed for at least 25 years in return for American assistance. The Soviet side rejected Marshall's offer of complete German disarmament. Stalin apparently placed greater value on the consolidation of his immediate power sphere—even at the cost of having American troops in West Germany. In March 1947, President Harry Truman announced what was later to become known as the Truman Doctrine—the commitment of the United States to help free and democratic peoples to maintain their independence, primarily through economic and financial assistance. The first objective was the support of the Greek government against a communist insurgency.

In June 1947, Marshall introduced the European Recovery Program— or the Marshall Plan, as it became known later. Eastern European countries were invited to join, but declined under the influence of the Soviet Union. Germany was one of the main beneficiaries of the plan. The United States and Great Britain joined their zones for the purpose of economic administration and gave a German economic council responsibility for economic affairs.

Events accelerated in 1948. In the spring, the communist party seized power in Czechoslovakia. The London conference of the three Western victors ended, recommending the integration of the Western parts of Germany into Western structures. In March, the Soviet representative left the allied control council for Germany. In June 1948, the three Western occupation zones began a currency reform. The Soviet Union, in turn, imposed an economic blockade on West Berlin. America organized an air relief effort to guarantee the survival of the city. In July the German *Ministerpräsidenten* (governors) received the "Frankfurt documents," containing a mandate for the preparation of a constitution, from the three Western military governors. On September 1, the German Parliamentary Council began drafting a constitution for the Federal Republic of Germany, or a basic law *(Grundgesetz),* as it was called.

In January 1949, the Soviet Union and other communist states founded the Council for Mutual Economic Assistance (COMECON). The North Atlantic Treaty Organization (NATO) was founded in Washington, D.C. in April. On May 12, France, Great Britain, and the United States declared an occupation statute for their military zones in Germany. On May 23, the parliamentary council enacted the basic law of the Federal Republic of Germany (FRG). On September 7, the German Bundestag convened for the first time. The Federal Republic of Germany came into existence as a state, subject to the limitations imposed on it by the occupation statute. On October 7, the Soviet zone was given a constitution, establishing the German Democratic Republic. Four years after the end of World War II, the division of Germany was all but complete.

The Federal Republic of Germany deliberately called its constitution a "basic law" in order not to preordain any constitution that a united Germany would give itself. This basic law contained a federal order with individual states retaining many powers, among them education and police. Its preamble stated that

> in the knowledge of its responsibility before god and the people, driven by the will to preserve its national and state unity and to serve world peace as an equal member in a unified Europe . . . to give state life and order for this transition period, the German people have adopted this basic law with their

constitutional power. They have also acted for those Germans who were not allowed to participate. It remains for all German people to complete the unity and freedom of Germany in free self-determination.[16]

The emerging East-West rivalry had created two states on German soil.[17] Both states had only limited sovereignty The Allied Powers, represented by their high commissioners, retained powers over foreign relations, military policy, and many other aspects of the young state.[18] The same was true, of course, for the Soviet Union in its own sphere of influence. The Federal Republic was in a peculiar situation. As Hacke observes, it was a state in which the national interest (German unification) and the reason of state for the Federal Republic of Germany (strengthening and solidifying this state) were rather different.[19] Most Germans initially saw the Federal Republic as a provisory state that would soon give way to a unified Germany. Legally, the German Reich had not ceased to exist. The borders of 1937 were still the legal borders of Germany, although they had lost all practical relevance.

III

The development of the Federal Republic cannot be understood without the figure of Konrad Adenauer. Already in his mid-seventies when he became chancellor in 1949, Adenauer remained in office for one-and-a-half decades, during which the old man dominated the political processes of the young state. "In the beginning, there was Adenauer," wrote Arnulf Baring.[20] A convinced Catholic, Adenauer had grown up in the francophile Rhineland, which had partly been incorporated into Protestant Prussia in the nineteenth century. Adenauer did not believe in the German nation; he was deeply rooted in his home town of Cologne, convinced "that Cologne was really the cultural center of the occident."[21] His own leanings were toward the West and Southwest, toward French and Catholic life-styles and philosophies rather than the Protestant ethic of Northern Germany. Thus, while Bismarck (who believed in Prussia, not in Germany) perceived Berlin to be the center of Europe from Berlin, Adenauer considered Cologne to be the center. It is no coincidence that, as lord mayor of Cologne, Adenauer convened a conference of other Rhenish mayors in 1919 to study the possibilities for a Western German state. The initiative, at the time, was without consequences.

A consummate politician for the clerical *Zentrumspartei* (Party of the Center) even at a young age, Adenauer had been an influential member of the upper house in Wilhelminic Germany, the president of the Prussian State Council, and lord mayor of the city of Cologne in the Weimar Republic. After the national socialists relieved him from power, he spent his time in obscurity in his home in Rhöndorf. Adenauer never affiliated himself with the resistance against the Nazis, but he did not collaborate either.

After World War II, members and committees of the parliamentary council met in Bonn, a sleepy little resort on the Rhine, with Allied officers to discuss their issues. In September 1948, Adenauer ensured that the parliamentary council and not the conference of *Ministerpräsidenten* would receive Allied communications. As President of the Parliamentary Council, Adenauer was in an excellent position to establish close ties to the three allies that occupied Western Europe, creating a network of influence in the emerging state. For men aspiring to positions of influence, he became the sought-after contact.

Adenauer was by no means the best-known public figure. In October 1948, one month after the creation of the parliamentary council, 65 percent of West Germans could not identify "the most able German politician." Preoccupied by the quest for survival in a devastated Germany, and still politically numb from the Third Reich, the average German was not particularly attuned to politics. Among those who had an opinion, three times more (15 percent) opted for Kurt Schumacher, the leader of the SPD (Social Democratic Party), than for Adenauer (5 percent).

The federal elections of summer 1949 did not produce a clear winner. The Christian-Democratic/Christian Social sister parties, the CDU/CSU, as a successor to Adenauer's *Zentrumspartei,* had become the strongest faction, with 139 seats in the parliament. The SPD came in a close second, with 131 seats. The Free Democratic Party, the FDP, gained 52 seats. In this situation, three options were possible—the continuation of a grand coalition, a CDU/CSU coalition government with the FDP, or an SPD coalition government with the FDP. The Social Democrats clearly saw themselves as morally entitled to form the new government.

In this critical period, Adenauer invited leading CDU/CSU and FDP figures into his Rhöndorf home on August 21, 1949. Adenauer was not authorized to decide about the coalition question—that question would have properly belonged to the plenary of the CDU/CSU members in the Bundestag, which had not yet constituted itself. But Adenauer, himself only chairman of the CDU in the British zone, assumed the chairmanship of the discussion, proposing a coalition with the FDP. He offered Theodor Heuss, chairman of the FDP, the office of president, which in the new German *Grundgesetz* was largely ceremonial. The small conservative party *Deutsche Partei* (DP) joined the emerging coalition.

To dispel any doubts, the old man had even solicited the opinion of his physician, who had stated that Adenauer could assume this office for no longer than two years. Thus, the decision was preordained. As later, when he was retained as a chancellor after voting for himself instead of abstaining, Adenauer displayed a penchant for power politics underneath his soft Rhenish accent and his humorous way of speaking. After the first parliamentary elections the German Bundestag constituted itself on September 7, 1949. Heuss was elected president of the Federal Republic on September 12; Adenauer was elected chancellor on September 15, paying his inaugural visit to the three high commissioners on September 20.

In his first government declaration, Adenauer established the lines of his policy: the gradual re-establishment of sovereignty by close international cooperation with the West, even at the expense of a temporary alienation with the East. "There is no doubt that according to origin and mentality we belong to the Western peoples."[22] Adenauer invoked the creation of a United States of Europe. He explained Article 24 of the German *Grundgesetz,* which allowed the Federal Republic to transfer sovereign rights to supranational institutions in order to create a lasting and peaceful order in Europe and the world. He held up the promise of reunification and stressed the fact that the annexation of Germany's eastern territories was not recognized.

Adenauer did not create a foreign ministry, "because foreign relations had remained the prerogative of the allied powers." However, "although foreign relations are the prerogatives of the Allied High Commissioners, each activity of the federal government contains some foreign relations. Germany . . . [is] more closely intertwined with other countries than ever before."[23] This allowed Adenauer to concentrate foreign relations in the federal chancellery, maintaining a monopoly over contact with the high commissioners, which still held the ultimate power in Germany. But Adenauer had a strategy not only for integrating Germany with the West but also for regaining German sovereignty step by step: "The only way to [German] freedom is if, in accordance with the allied High Commissioners, we enlarge our freedom and competencies step by step."[24]

In the early years of the Federal Republic the major choice was between close integration with the West, and the stepwise recovery of sovereign rights at least for the Federal Republic, or the pursuit of a unified, neutralized Germany, even at the risk of conflicts with the Western allies. Influential figures within Adenauer's governing CDU/CSU, such as Jakob

Kaiser, opposed the doctrine of West-integration at the cost of abandoning hopes for fast reunification. The Berlin-based Kaiser proposed a neutral Germany that was to have a "bridge function" between East and West. SPD leader Kurt Schumacher pursued a social democratic policy and cooperated with the socialist movements of the West. Schumacher also was a strict anticommunist. This distinction between socialism and communism may be difficult to understand from today's perspective, but at the time, it was essential. In the immediate postwar era, all major parties leaned toward some kind of social democracy. Even the CDU, in its Ahlener program of 1947, tried to reconcile socialist and Christian values. A decade later, the social market economy had become the official German policy, and the SPD incorporated elements of market policies in its 1957 Godesberg program.

In addition to leaning somewhat toward social democracy as an economic form of government, most Germans were also leaning toward a unified Germany, if need be neutral. For many, the idea of two separate German states was inconceivable. Germany should be disarmed and neutral, the only logical consequence of World War II. This was, in essence, an extrapolation of Stresemann's policies in the Weimar Republic. Germany would be a mediator between East and West, between the United States and the Soviet Union. Moreover, Schumacher and Kaiser had been actively resisting Nazi Germany, whereas Adenauer had been in inner exile in his house in Rhöndorf. This gave Schumacher and Kaiser considerable moral legitimacy. Schumacher, for example, had lost an arm in World War I, and had spent almost a decade in Nazi concentration camps.

Adenauer's position as chancellor, leader of his party, and major contact partner to the high commissioners, however, provided him with a strong position from which to promote his idea of a westward-oriented Germany—even at the cost of unity. Moreover, Kaiser overestimated the position of Germany at the end of World War II. There was simply no Germany that could assume the bridge function between East and West, nor were the victors interested in Germany assuming that role.

Both Kaiser and Schumacher were lions; Adenauer was a fox. Both Schumacher and Kaiser were charismatic personalities. In the new situation, however, skillful negotiation, tenacity, and diplomatic language became valuable assets, all of which Adenauer possessed. Both Schumacher and Kaiser assumed a natural air of superiority (Adenauer could do that, too, and was very harsh in instances), but he knew how to treat the allied powers. As early as 1946, Kaiser tried to negotiate with Soviet representatives, fundamentally misunderstanding his position. Schumacher's worldview was based on the position that, of course, the social democratic party was the legitimate heir for government in Germany, and that all other parties had been compromised. His shock was great when the CDU/CSU was able to form the first coalition government.

Creating a neutral Germany would certainly have been difficult. The Korean War of 1950 had further increased Germany's strategic value for the United States and the Western allies. France and Great Britain were quite happy to see Germany divided and would probably have strongly opposed any attempt to create a neutral, unified Germany, even if unarmed. West-integration, on the other hand, was also costly. After all, there was only one Germany, and millions of refugees from the eastern provinces had settled in the west—temporarily, as they thought. Russia, too, was much more concerned with solidifying its sphere of influence and benefiting from the spoils of war than with devising a long-term strategy that would eventually exclude the United States from Europe. By 1946, they had taken out in reparations what was worth taking out, and were looking for further reparations from the West, whereas the United States, in particular, was already considering ways to make Germany economically viable again. A plan by George Marshall that would guarantee complete German disarmament and some additional reparations to the Soviet Union was rejected. At this point in 1947, the United States started to concentrate on the Western zones. In the words of Zelikow and Rice, "It seems odd in retrospect that the Soviets rejected Marshall's offer of complete German disarmament and some reparations. Michael Howard has observed that 'one of the most remarkable aspects of the whole period is the astonishing stupidity of Soviet policy. All the cards were in the Soviet hands if they had only cared to play them. What is more, their opponents were playing with marked cards because of Soviet espionage."[25]

Once, briefly, Adenauer's policy seemed in danger. By 1952, the initial advantage of the Soviet Union had shrunk. Negotiations between the Federal Republic and the Western Powers for a European defense community had progressed far, and it seemed likely that such a community would come into existence. On March 10, 1952, Stalin offered to conclude a peace treaty with the Western Powers and Germany with the result of a neutral reunified Germany. (Thirteen years earlier, to the day, Stalin had signaled to Hitler his willingness to cooperate at the eighteenth convention of the Soviet Communist Party.) Adenauer reacted quickly and without consulting the cabinet or his party: seeing his policy of integration into the West threatened, he urged the three Western Allied Powers to decline this offer. To illustrate the limited extent to which the Federal Republic had regained sovereignty and underline the willingness on the part of Adenauer to first tie the country to the West and then open further negotiations, it must be noted that at the time, the southwestern state of the Saar was still under French occupation, and that Adenauer declared in April 1952 that his negotiations with France had failed.

The "missed opportunity" of the Stalin note has been the subject of many legends and myths in postwar Germany.[26] Most likely, speculation about it can never be proven or disproven. However, the relevance of the episode has greatly decreased since 1989–90, when Adenauer's policy was finally vindicated. Up to 1989–90, however, the division of Germany into two states seemed a fact, and the goal of unity a distant utopia. Against this backdrop it is understandable that the discussion about Stalin's offer moved the hearts and minds of historians and Germans interested in those aspects of foreign policy right until reunification.

IV

Like the emergence of the Federal Republic itself, the reemergence of a German military power was rushed by external developments. It was also inextricably linked to the idea of European unification. The Korean War that started in June 1950 set in motion a train of events leading to German rearmament much faster than most Germans had desired—or feared. This rapid rise to the level of an (almost) equal member of the family of nations was marked by a number of steps: the Petersberg treaty of 1949; the first revision of the occupation statute of 1951; the treaty governing the relations between the Federal Republic and the Allied Powers of 1952; the proposal for a European defense community; its rejection in the French national assembly; and, finally, Germany's membership in NATO in 1955.

World War II had led to a radical break with the preceding century of military expansionism. Politicians of almost all parties dissociated themselves as clearly as possible from military ambitions. During the 1949 election campaign, for example, the conservative CSU member Franz Josef Strauß, later defense minister and advocate of a European multilateral nuclear force stated that any German who would ever pick up a gun again should lose his hand.[27]

After Adenauer had formed his government, the Allied Powers declared an occupation statute in which they retained control over the foreign policy of the newborn republic.[28] Only two months later, Adenauer succeeded with a first step toward formal recognition—the Petersberg Treaty.

Germany was allowed to join some international organizations and establish consular relations.[29] This, of course, entailed a recognition of the interests of the Western Allies and a step further away from reconciliation with the Soviet Union. Kurt Schumacher, leader of the SPD, consequently called Adenauer a "Chancellor of the Allies" in November 1949.

East–West tensions were rising. Berlin suffered from a blockade by Soviet forces. Western statesmen and planners began to look for new ways to defend the West. In December 1949, Adenauer began to think publicly about a military contribution of the Federal Republic to Western forces. He continued to actively promote German rearmament at every possible juncture.[30] France and England, however, were still opposed to the idea, and Adenauer had to move with great caution.

In March 1950, Winston Churchill, then in opposition, also proposed West German rearmament. In June, North Korean troops invaded South Korea. The West became acutely aware of its weakness in conventional weapons. In July the Allied high commissioner for Germany John J. McCloy declared that the Allied Powers would protect Germany against a foreign attack. In August, the consultative assembly of the European Council approved Winston Churchill's proposal to create a joint European army with German participation. A few weeks later, Adenauer sent an official memorandum to John McCloy, signaling the readiness of the Federal Republic to provide a German contingent for a future European army.[31] In July, the German Bundestag passed a resolution that a supranational Europe be created that also would assure the defense of its members. In August, Germany became an associated member of the European Council.

On November 8, 1950, the Bundestag saw its first major debate on rearmament and military policy. Adenauer argued that a front was needed to protect the democratic nations against the totalitarian nations, namely, the Soviet Union. Adenauer named as a condition that Germany should have the same rights as other nations. The opposition leader, Schumacher, emphasized that the plans for a joint defense would be unbalanced, favoring allied over German interests, and that the German debate should make clear that military force in Germany could have only one objective: the preservation of peace.[32]

The way to German rearmament and the creation of European forces, however, was to be more complicated than this rapid start may have suggested. Although the United States pressed for a German military contribution, France and England were reluctant to give up their opposition to German rearmament. The communiqué of the three Western allied foreign ministers of September 1950 did not end the occupation status and did not recognize Germany as a sovereign state, two goals for which Adenauer had cautiously but persistently campaigned. The United States succeeded neither in the conference of the foreign ministers of the three Allied Powers nor in the conference of the foreign ministers of the twelve NATO states to overcome French resistance to rearmament.

The specific shape of a German army within the joint defense force also posed considerable questions. The Americans wanted German divisions under NATO command. (Since the highest military commander of NATO was an American, this effectively meant American command.) The French resisted, but saw that some form of German rearmament was probably necessary in the face of ongoing communist expansionism and the Cold War. Thus the French prime minister René Pleven presented a plan for the creation of a European army in October 1950. The so-called Pleven plan entailed a truly European army, in which a European officers corps and a European defense minister led smaller national military units— preferably of company and battalion size. All German troops were to be included in this truly multilateral defense structure, whereas France, Britain, and other countries would be allowed to retain some national forces. Germany would also be forbidden the production of certain weapons.

The United States and Great Britain did not support this project, because they saw operational difficulties and a need for a fast buildup of forces. Adenauer, too, did not like a plan that clearly implied an inferior status for Germany. Throughout 1950 and early 1951, negotiations proved to be difficult. An additional factor complicated the situation. In November 1950, the Soviet Union, alarmed by the talks for strengthening NATO and the Western European forces, had proposed another Four Power conference with the objective of creating a neutral, disarmed Germany. Adenauer firmly opposed a disarmed Germany, but he was afraid that leftist forces in France, Great Britain, and Germany itself would give the proposal enough weight. This would endanger the fledgling process of tying the Federal Republic of Germany closer to the West.

By early 1952 France had modified its original plan to include some German concerns. This, in turn, had led the United States to support the plans for a European Defense Community that would complement NATO. Germany, however, was still to be a member of only the European Defense Community. In practice, this could have meant that German troops would have to go to war without any German approval. Adenauer's position was weak. The conference of the three Allied foreign ministers proposed a closer connection between NATO and the European Defense Community. Although Germany was still not an equal partner, Adenauer had to defend the compromise. Despite rather tenacious efforts to establish the Federal Republic as an equal partner, this was all he could get without risking a breakdown of the whole process.

The Treaty on the European Defense Community was signed in May 1952, together with a "treaty governing the relations between the Federal Republic of Germany and the Three Powers" *(Deutschlandvertrag)*.[33] The occupation statute was ended and the high commissioners were replaced by ambassadors. The Federal Republic was given full power over its internal and external affairs, subject to conditions in the treaty. The conditions included the right of the Allied Powers to station troops in the Federal Republic and the prerogative of being solely responsible for the defense of the Federal Republic. The treaty also stated that they would strive for a freely negotiated peace treaty for all of Germany, and that the question of Germany's borders could only be dealt with in such a treaty. A united Germany would have to fulfill the obligations of the Federal Republic incurred in this treaty. Germany was now a sovereign nation—with the exception of certain questions concerning defense, the Saar state (which was still occupied by France), the status of Berlin and its freedom to enter international treaties that would infringe upon the powers of the Allied Powers.

In the translation of Zelikow and Rice, Germany signed a treaty that contained the following stipulations: "in view of the international situation, which has so far prevented the reunification of Germany and the conclusion of a peace settlement, the three powers retain the rights and responsibilities . . . relating to Berlin and to Germany as a whole, including the reunification of Germany and a peace settlement." Article 7 assured Germany that the three Western Powers would seek "a peace settlement for the whole of Germany, freely negotiated between Germany and her former enemies, which should lay the foundation for a lasting peace. They further agree that the final determination of the boundaries of Germany must await such a settlement. Pending the peace settlement, the Signatory States will cooperate to achieve, by peaceful means, their common aim of a reunified Germany enjoying a liberal-democratic constitution, like that of the Federal Republic, and integrated within the European Community."[34]

Thus, Germany did not receive sovereignty over the ultimate question of the German nation. A peace treaty would have to be concluded with the Four Powers. Germany's eastern provinces—Prussia, Pomerania, Silesia, and the part of Brandenburg east of the Oder river, though now inhabited by Poles and Russians, were legally still part of the German nation. The German Reich within the borders of 1937 was still the relevant definition, although the Federal Republic, as a state, was much smaller than that. The Four Powers were also responsible for Berlin, which was not part of the territory of the Federal Republic. (The German Democratic Republic had recognized its borders with Poland in 1950.) Zelikow and Rice summarize: "This complicated legal situation meant that the FRG was, in fact, an interim state whose final structure and boundaries would be determined in a "peace settlement." The Four Powers remained legally indispensable to the reestablishment and determination, someday, of "Germany as a whole."[35]

The European Defense Community seemed to make good progress in 1953. The Bundestag ratified the Treaty about the European Defense Community in 1953 with 224 to 162 voice (2 abstentions). However, the French national assembly rejected it on August 30, 1954. Since the negotiations about the European Defense Community and NATO had been conducted in parallel, most elements were in place to make Germany a member of NATO. This is, in fact, what happened. Due to the diplomatic skill of the British foreign minister, Eden, who made the proposal to accept Germany, the NATO states did indeed do so in October 1954. Germany was to become a fully sovereign member of NATO, with a national defense force integrated into NATO command structures. Germany incurred the obligation not to produce nuclear, biological, or chemical weapons. After a 40-hour-long debate, the Bundestag voted for NATO and WEU membership on February 27, 1955. The treaty was accepted with a 324 to 151 margin of votes.

Only six years after its foundation, the Federal Republic of Germany was (almost) a sovereign nation. Churchill had welcomed Adenauer to England in October 1954 with the words: "I congratulate you, that the European Defense Community is in shambles." According to Hacke, this was indeed fortunate for Germany. It prevented a special French-German treaty with French dominance and accelerated the emancipation of Germany. Hacke observed that with the failure of the European Defense Community in 1954, "Adenauer's maximum goal, a supranational Western Europe including the Federal Republic, had not been achieved but that his minimum goal, the integration of the Federal Republic in the West, had been reached."[36]

From that time on, until reunification and beyond, Germany's military doctrine encompassed five core components: civilian restraint, defense-orientation, integration and semi-sovereignty. Moreover, its army was built on the model of the "citizen in uniform," introducing as many democratic features as possible into military life.

1. Civilian Restraint

The German security and military doctrine was based on the assumption that military force was not a legitimate means of promoting national interests.[37] Thus, military power was not to be used to further political objectives, even if they were worthwhile causes. In 1965, the federal government also adopted a policy of not sending weapons into crisis areas outside the NATO area, regardless of whether allies or other nations were the recipients. This policy satisfied three objectives: it would minimize the danger that Germany would be involved in military conflicts outside Europe, it would de-emphasize the use of military force, and it would present Germany as a moral example.[38]

2. Defense Orientation

German security doctrine was based on the assumption that the only mission for German forces was a defense of NATO territory against attacks. The specific situations of the East-West conflict further implied that the Bundeswehr would only serve in the defense of the home territory. Until the Persian Gulf War of 1990, Germany never seriously considered the use of its military except for the defense of the NATO treaty area against open aggression (although some experts began to broach the topic in 1987). The idea that the Bundeswehr was a purely defensive army (and that NATO was a truly supranational organization) became deeply entrenched in popular and elite opinion. Many Germans believed that the German constitution forbade any use of the Bundeswehr.

In August 1990, the respected Allensbach Institute implied in one of its surveys that the Grundgesetz forbade military missions abroad.[39] At the time, only 32 percent of the surveyed population favored the implied necessary change in the Grundgesetz, while 53 percent opposed a change of the basic law, demonstrating that a doctrine of territorial defense and non-involvement out-of-area had become deeply entrenched in the population.

In January 1984, a poll by the Allensbach institute showed that 84 percent of the German population viewed the German army as a purely defensive army *(Verteidigungsarmee)*.[40] During basic training, Bundeswehr recruits, among them this writer, were regularly told that the sole mission of the Bundeswehr was a political one: to deter an attack. Many soldiers were convinced that if war broke out, it would mean that the Bundeswehr had failed. The following dialogue circulated among soldiers: "What does the German soldier do if a war starts?" "He will go home, because he has failed." The dialogue was only half joking.[41] Though ultimately not based on constitutional law, the perception of the Bundeswehr as an army designed solely for the defense of the home territory reflected the realities of the Cold War. The only conceivable scenario was a large-scale aggression against German territory, and the use of German soldiers in other regions would have involved grave risks.[42]

Article 26 of the German constitution makes the conduct or preparation of a war of aggression a criminal act. Article 24 states that the Federal Republic may transfer sovereign rights to a collective system of security in order to maintain peace. Article 115 specifies that in the "defense case," command over the German forces will be transferred to the chancellor. For this to occur, however, the "defense case" must be declared by the parliament with a two-thirds majority of those present and at least 50 percent of total votes. If this is not practical, the defense committee of the Bundestag must declare the defense case with a two-thirds majority. As a last resort, the law states some conditions under which command power is transferred automatically.[43]

3. Military Integration and Semisovereignty

The debate about NATO and the European Defense Community showed that Adenauer was not willing to accept a legally inferior status for German forces and would fight tenaciously for a full integration of Germany into NATO. Germany was to have its own defense ministry, and the defense minister and the chancellor were to be the supreme commander. In case of an attack on NATO territory, however, command would be transferred to the Supreme Allied Commander Europe (SACEUR), an American military official. All German forces, geared to the defense of a large-scale conventional attack, were fully integrated into the NATO treaty organization. Forces of many allied nations were permanently stationed on German soil. Parts of the (inner-German) front would be defended by Allied forces, parts by German forces. Germany did not have a general staff or an independent command and control structure. As a consequence, Germans perceived NATO as a supranational organization, while in fact it was an intergovernmental treaty.[44]

4. A New Type of Army

During the early years of the Federal Republic, Adenauer had to regain political sovereignty step by step through small concessions from the allies. The new German army was to be completely different from any earlier German army. First, the German forces were limited to a total of 500,000 personnel. Second, in 1954 the Federal Republic renounced the possession if nuclear, chemical, and biological weapons. Third, all units were to be put under NATO command—the Bundeswehr did not maintain independent command and control capabilities. There was to be no general staff, just inspectors in generals' rank for the three forces. The highest military office was the general inspector *(Generalinspekteur)*. The general inspector was not the supreme commander. This function was to be exercised by the defense minister. Fourth, the Bundeswehr was subject to strong civilian control. Its structure should be as "civilian" as possible given its military task. This objective was paraphrased in the term "citizen in uniform," contained in the soldiers' law of 1956, and the concept of "inner leadership" *(innere Führung)* introduced by Wolf Graf Baudissin. For example, in 1958 one member of parliament was permanently commissioned to audit the leadership and organization of the Bundeswehr and its accordance with the principles of a democratic state and to receive complaints by soldiers *(Wehrbeauftragter)*. The soldiers' law prescribes duties, but also explicitly specifies rights of soldiers.

The government white book of 1971/72 dealt at length with the civilian nature of the Bundeswehr, emphasizing that "discussion among soldiers and obedience are not mutually exclusive, rather they supplement each other." "There is no homogeneous leaderships corps anymore, because the social development of our society is reflected in the Bundeswehr." The book states that "The nation is the school of the army, not vice versa," thus turning around an old Prussian proverb according to which "the army is the school of the nation." The white book also suggested that active service was changing, because the authority of the specialist was increasingly replacing the authority of rank: "The team of specialists has replaced the uniform group of former times." The Bundeswehr was to exercise a cooperative style of leadership.[45]

Until the Persian Gulf War, officially Germany referred little to those five major tenets of German military doctrine, implicit though they may have been. All major debates after the creation of military forces and NATO membership revolved around the question of whether certain steps were defensive, whether disarmament would increase the security of the Federal Republic, or whether the Federal Republic should strive for a more neutral position between East and West. There were three large public debates on military policy in preunification Germany: (1) potential nuclear rearmament in 1957/58; (2) the creation of a joint multilateral nuclear force in 1963/64 and the debate between the Atlanticists and the

Europeanists; (3) the NATO double-track decision in the early 1980s. In addition, some debates more limited to military experts took place, most notably: (1) on the double-zero solution and the third-zero solution with regard to intermediate and short-range nuclear forces in central Europe in the mid—to late 1980s; and (2) a potential contribution of Germans to military action in crisis areas in the same period. However, a use of the German military for purposes other than the defense of the home territory was never seriously considered until 1990.

In the large public debates, the CDU/CSU traditionally stood for NATO integration, "peace through strength" and the Atlantic alliance, whereas major parts of the SPD (and from the early 1980s on the Green Party) stood for far-reaching disarmament and tendencies toward neutralization. The FDP, on a pro-NATO basis, maintained a profile of reconciliation between both positions, which became known as Genscherism.[46] "Peace through strength" and a commitment to the Atlantic alliance always prevailed, although in particular the double-track decision in the early 1980s created deep schisms in the country.[47]

V

European integration constituted the second core pillar of the doctrine of postwar Germany.[48] When the German constitution was formulated in 1949, its preamble included the statement that Germany "would serve world peace as an equal part of a united Europe."[49] Germany's constitution, more than any other constitution, explicitly allows for supranational integration: Article 24, Section 1 says that "the union can transfer sovereign rights to interstate bodies by law." Section 2 says that "the union can place itself under a system of collective security to maintain the peace; it will accept limitations on its sovereign rights that will create and secure a peaceful and lasting order in Europe and among the peoples of the world."[50] Many Germans saw Europe as a substitute fatherland, believing that functional integration and political unification were Europe's future. These hopes were especially strong for the German postwar generation, epitomized by Chancellor Helmut Kohl. Garton Ash has called this a "habitual conflation of German and European interests," but there is ample evidence that many German policymakers believed in such an identity of interests.[51]

Two concepts were in conflict from the beginning: the "United States of Europe" (a phase coined by Winston Churchill and describing supranational integration—without Great Britain),[52] and the "Europe of the Fatherlands" (a phrase coined by Charles de Gaulle and describing intergovernmental co-operation). Germans largely wanted the United States of Europe. In March 1950, Adenauer proposed a political union between France and Germany. In July of the same year, the German Bundestag demanded the creation of a supranational federal power in Europe. When Germany received an invitation to become a member of the European Council in 1950, Adenauer wrote:

> The unification of Europe on a federal basis is necessary and in the interest of all European countries, especially Germany. The European Council is the beginning of such a unification. The Federal Republic must join the invitation in the deep conviction that this is the only way to secure peace in Europe. . . . There can be no doubt that the German people have honestly and gladly welcomed the thought of a European union from the beginning. European unification was seen as the sign of new times and great hope.[53]

France was much more reluctant. Even after the creation of the first European institutions, French president Charles de Gaulle spoke out against a supranational Europe and supported a confederation of states.[54]

Constitutional lawyer Bardo Faßbender observed that the German basic law, more than any other constitution at that time, declared the openness of the state to its environment. Faßbender called this particular German trait "integration-open statehood," and commented, "it is amazing to see how the members of the constitutional assembly have turned their dependency on the allied victors into a positive trait, prepared to give away something that their state didn't have: sovereignty."[55] While Japan remained fairly isolated despite its global trading reach, German became one of the engines of trading, financial, and political integration in Europe. While Japan was protected by a bilateral treaty with the United States, Germany pursued full economic, political, and military integration in the West. The EC gave (West) Germany close economic and political links with Western Europe and a substitute for national aspirations after the idea of a greater Germany had been discredited.

European institutions did emerge only slowly after the war. In 1949, the Allied Powers had issued a Ruhr statute, which put the heavily industrialized Ruhr area, home to such firms as Krupp, Thyssen, Mannesmann, Borsig, and Rheinmetall under international control. Germany accepted this statute in November 1949 by joining it. Germany also became a member in the Organization for European Economic Cooperation (OEEC), a body that had been created to facilitate cooperation between the war-ravaged countries of Europe, speed reconstruction and foreign trade, and administer Marshall Plan assistance. France had put the Saar area, an ethnically German region with a strong coal and steel industry bordering France, under French control. The Saar area was allowed to rejoin Germany only in January 1957, and Adenauer had to tenaciously pursue this goal. This showed that France was very reluctant to yield advantages won out of World War II.

Another French proposal, however, showed far-sightedness and proved to be one of the crystallization points for European unification: in May 1950, the French foreign minister Robert Schumann proposed to put the European coal and steel industry under supranational control, thus creating a unified European industry in those sectors. In doing so, he fell back upon proposals made by the German chancellor. On November 7, 1949, Adenauer had stated in an internal government paper that close economic cooperation with France could dampen fears in Paris.[56] The same day, the chancellor stressed that idea in an interview published by the *Baltimore Sun*.[57]

Of course, one objective was the prevention of independent national arms industries, but the plan also had a forward-looking element in the creation of integrated European institutions. In 1951, the foreign ministers of Belgium, France, Germany, Holland, Italy, and Luxembourg signed the Treaty on the European Community for Coal and Steel. The Bundestag ratified this treaty in January 1952, and the community came into existence in July of the same year, with Jean Monnet as its first president.

In June 1955, the foreign ministers of the European Community for Coal and Steel decided to create a common European market. In the same year, a European currency agreement went into effect. It allowed for certain clearing functions among the six members of the European Community. In March 1957, those nations signed the Treaties of Rome, establishing the European Economic Community (EEC) and the European Nuclear Community (EURATOM). Those treaties came into effect in January 1958. The institutional structure of the European Community had essentially been established. Until the Treaty of Maastricht, only three major developments took place: (1) the European institutions gradually accepted more members; (2). in 1978 the European Council decided that a European parliament be elected in 1979; and (3) later in the same year, the European Council agreed upon the creation of the European Monetary System.

The 1960s, however, would see little progress in Germany's foreign policy environment. After a period of relaxing East-West tensions following

Stalin's death in 1953, the Cold War intensified again in the late 1950s and early 1960s. This development culminated in the erection of the Berlin Wall and renewed tensions about Berlin's status. European progress, too, seemed to stall. Charles de Gaulle had reentered the political arena, first as prime minister in 1958, then as president in 1959. Germany's economic might was already resurgent. Germany had also achieved almost equal status. Due to the U.S. engagement, it was not dependent on French security guarantees. For the following decade, Charles de Gaulle did everything possible to strengthen France's position in Europe and beyond, even at the risk of aggravating allies.

In November 1958, the plan for a European free trade area had to be shelved due to French objections. At the same time, the first trade barriers between the members of the European Community were dismantled. This block-building was not without consequences—Denmark, Great Britain, Norway, Austria, Portugal, Sweden, and Switzerland formed a European Free Trade Area (EFTA) in 1960. In the same year, the EEC nations agreed to include agriculture in the Common Market, thus laying the ground for a problem that has been plaguing the European Union until today and is consuming roughly two-thirds of the total EU budget. Despite these steps, de Gaulle argued against supranational integration and for a European confederation. Consequently, the proposals of the Fouchet-Commission for a European political statute went nowhere despite the pro forma agreement of the EEC states to strengthen political cooperation. The negotiations were terminated in 1962. In 1961, Great Britain applied for membership in the EEC. The Federal Republic of Germany repeatedly supported this desire. In January 1963, de Gaulle openly opposed British membership, thus blocking a widening of the EEC and a dilution of French influence.

The years 1961 and 1962 were also years of increasing East-West tensions. 1961 saw the building of the Berlin Wall, 1962 the Cuban Missile Crisis. In November 1962, the United States and Great Britain agreed upon the delivery of American nuclear "Polaris" missiles for British submarines, which were eventually to be placed under a common NATO Multilateral Force (MLF). In early 1963, the American under secretary George Ball promoted this force in Germany and invited Germany to participate. De Gaulle declined to participate. (France subsequently stressed the importance of a national nuclear *force de frappe*.) In the same month, France and Germany signed a far-reaching cooperation agreement, the Elysee Treaty. Germany was eager to reassure the United States that this treaty would not have any negative consequences for NATO.

In the following years, the French policy of "France first" put Germany in a precarious position. Both NATO and U.S. support as well as French friendship were needed to stabilize and consolidate the position the Federal Republic had achieved by the early 1960s. As a consequence, an internal debate between "Europeanists" and "Atlanticists" within the CDU/CSU coalition and the other parties erupted. Adenauer, a Europeanist, resigned in 1963, to be replaced by his long-term economics minister Ludwig Erhard, an Atlanticist. The government of the Federal Republic confirmed its readiness to participate in a multilateral force, even without France. In April 1965, the France, Germany, Italy, and the BENELUX states agreed to merge the European Community for Coal and Steel, Euratom, and the European Economic Community into the European Community. French policy, however, remained problematic. In July, France boycotted the Council of Ministers and the European Commission because the negotiations on agricultural policy were in deadlock. France also wanted to veto certain decisions. The Bundestag, a few months later, vehemently opposed national veto power in the Council of Ministers and a weakening of the European Commission. Nevertheless, France achieved a compromise that de facto allowed national veto.

Hardly two months had passed since the crisis of the European Community was resolved when the next crisis erupted. In February 1966, the NATO nuclear planning group constituted itself in Washington with German participation. In March, France notified the NATO members that it would leave the joint military organization (but still participate in the political arm of NATO). This policy became known as the "policy of the empty chair." The Bundestag reaffirmed the German commitment to remain integrated in NATO. By 1966, the conflict between Europeanist and Atlanticist solutions had thus left a patchwork of solutions. Germany's commitment to continuing friendship with both France and the United States had been severely tested, but survived, even in the face of renewed East-West tensions.

However, De Gaulle's "France-first" policies—"his de-facto re-introduction of the veto in the council of ministers, France's withdrawal from the military organization of NATO and de Gaulle's repeated veto against British membership in the EEC led to deep resignation in the EEC concerning the prospects of further integration."[58] This did not weaken support for the EU in principle: In a note dated March 25, 1966, the German government declared "Nowhere has the thought of a unification of Europe found such strong resonance as in the Federal Republic of Germany, which even foresees the transfer of sovereign powers to international organizations in its constitution."[59] Rather, the concrete road to further progress seemed difficult to detect.

German grand strategy in the later 1960s and early 1970s shifted toward reconciliation with the East. After chancellor Willy Brandt's vision of reconciliation with East Germany and other Eastern states had been accomplished, his successor Helmut Schmidt asserted in his first government declaration in 1974: "The goal of a political union of Europe seems more urgent than ever. . . .We pursue the political unification of Europe, in partnership with the United States of America."[60] Schmidt found a congenial counterpart in the French president Valery Giscard d'Estaing, and German-French cooperation in European unification flourished. The 1970s were an era of global economic crises, with rampant inflation and two oil shocks. Economic tensions between Europe and the United States had been rising since Richard Nixon had "closed the gold window" and suspended the convertibility of the dollar in August 1971. Further unilateralist American policies during the Carter administration prompted Germany and France to create the European Monetary System, the precursor to monetary union as agreed upon in the Maastricht Treaty.[61]

In his first government declaration, Helmut Kohl continued this policy and set the goal of opening new ways for the unification of Europe.[62] The programs of most major parties also emphasized European integration. The CDU party program of 1978, for example, included the creation of a democratic federal European state as a major foreign policy goal.[63] The SPD party program of 1989 stated that "The United States of Europe, demanded by the Social Democrats . . . in 1925, remains our goal."[64] The FDP program for the federal elections in 1994 stated that "there is no alternative to the European Union. This union shall not become a centralist super-state, but a modern and democratic federal state."[65]

VI

The postwar structures of the Federal Republic had essentially been put in place between 1948 and 1957. Adenauer had achieved his goals of Western integration. He had also regained many rights for the German state. Germany was almost, but not completely, sovereign. In questions of reunification, borders, Berlin, and defense, the Allied Powers retained ultimate rights, although they had bound themselves to settle issues, should they arise, in agreement with Germany. Germany had rearmed, firmly integrated into NATO. The European Communities had been created. From 1949 until approximately 1969, Germany's foreign policy framework was essentially bipolar and very stable. The only issue that posed a serious challenge to the prevailing framework was France's increasing unilateralism in the 1960s, which put Germany in the uneasy position of having to choose between the United States and France or of having to bridge an increasing gap. Despite some prolonged and heated debates between Europeanists and Atlanticists in Germany, the young state managed to indeed bridge the gap between both positions.[66]

Toward the end of the 1960s, however, another issue became increasingly urgent. The de facto division of Germany had now lasted for two decades. The Cold War had had a number of peaks, in the late 1940s and early 1950s as well as in the early 1960s. At those times, the steady stream of refugees from the GDR to the West had amounted to a serious bloodletting. Out of a population of approximately 18 million, 200,000 were leaving in peak years. The GDR reacted by fortifying its borders and imposing strict travel restrictions. When this did not help, the GDR erected the Berlin Wall in 1961, thus closing the last possibility for travel between West and East Germany.

In the 1950s, the Federal Republic of Germany began to establish and expand its diplomatic contacts. In 1951, the Federal Republic was admitted to international organizations such as the GATT (General Agreement on Tariffs and Trade), WHO (World Health Organization), and UNESCO (United Nations Educational and Scientific Organization). (Membership in the United Nations would have to wait until 1973.) In May 1955, the Allied high commissioners were replaced by ambassadors. A few months later, upon the invitation of the Soviet Union, Adenauer also traveled to Moscow. Ten years after the war ended, the Soviet Union released the last remaining prisoners of war. The Federal Republic of Germany established diplomatic relations with the Soviet Union.[67]

As far as diplomatic relations with Warsaw Pact countries were concerned, this was to be first and last diplomatic bridge to the east. Only a few months later, the so-called Hallstein doctrine stopped any diplomatic contacts with the East. According to the *Grundgesetz*, the Federal Republic of Germany viewed itself as the sole representative of the German people. The government of the German Democratic Republic was not viewed as a legitimate representative of the people in the eastern part of Germany. Since there had been no free elections in the East since the inception of the GDR, this view was plausible and sustainable. In December 1957, foreign minister Von Brentano declared to diplomatic representatives present in Bonn that the Federal Republic would sever diplomatic relations with any state that recognized the German Democratic Republic. The West

German government saw "the other" German state as an illegitimate structure, and well into the 1960s and 1970s, it was common to speak of East Germany as the Soviet Sector.

This, of course, had many reasons. Elections in the East were a farce, with regular approval rates of 98 percent and higher for the government. UN commissions to supervise free elections had routinely been turned down. The preamble of the German Grundgesetz, however, stated that the "German people are to regain unity and freedom in free self-determination."[68] In 1950, the German Democratic Republic had recognized its eastern borders with Poland, thus legitimizing the expulsion of roughly 7 million Germans from ethnically German provinces (East Prussia, Pomerania, and Silesia) that had belonged to the prewar Reich. The majority of the refugees—among them this author's father's family—had resettled in West Germany. Well into the 1960s, the league of the expelled Germans (Bund der Heimatvertriebenen) remained a powerful force in Germany. The German constitution was an interim solution, and most politicians were eager to assure citizens that the German Reich within the borders of 1937 still existed. Since there had not been a peace treaty, the illusion that Germany could be reconstituted within its legal borders was a powerful one.

In the first 15 years of the Federal Republic, Adenauer, too, took great care not to establish any diplomatic relations with East bloc countries, if for different reasons. He wanted to have the Federal Republic firmly integrated into the West and steadfastly resisted any attempts to draw the East and West closer together in order not to endanger Western unity and the emerging orientation toward the West in his fellow countrymen. In 1956, for example, invitations to parliamentarians to visit Beijing and Czechoslovakia were perceived by the government as part of a process of accommodation and were stopped.[69]

By the end of the 1960s, the self-imposed isolation of the Federal Republic began to become counterproductive. It seemed increasingly difficult to keep third states from recognizing the German Democratic Republic, and foreign policymakers in the Federal Republic could not be sure when the dam would burst and a general wave of recognition would ensue. There were new signs of détente between the United States and the Soviet Union. If this understanding were to become too intimate, the Federal Republic could easily be left out of developments that concerned its vital interests. Moreover, important humanitarian and practical concerns had taken a backseat: many families had been torn apart and not been allowed to communicate and transit to Berlin had repeatedly been blocked.

Other urgent issues were not dealt with due to the inability of both German governments to speak to each other.

After 17 years of CDU leadership, 14 of which had been under Adenauer, a grand coalition of the CDU/CSU and SPD formed a government in 1966 under chancellor Kurt Kiesinger (CDU). The government was short-lived, to be replaced by a coalition government of the SPD and FDP, with Willy Brandt (SDP) as chancellor and Walter Scheel (FDP) as foreign minister. The late 1960s had been a time of reform and turmoil in most Western democracies, with student protests against the prevailing social order and the Vietnam War reaching a peak in 1968. Germany, too, had been shaken by these developments.

The Kiesinger government, in which Brandt had served as foreign minister, had initiated some cautious corrections of course, both with regard to relations with the Federal Republic's Eastern neighbors, and with regard to domestic reforms. During the mid-1960s secret contacts between FRG and GDR government figures were sporadically sought through middlemen. One of those was the director of the Berlin office of the news magazine *Der Spiegel*.[70] In 1963, a convention on passengers *(Passierscheinabkommen)* had been signed between East and West Berlin (as the first official document in which both sides participated).

The *Ostpolitik* of the Brandt-Scheel government between 1968 and 1973 was the first major revision of the German postwar doctrine. The debate between Atlanticists and Europeanists a few years earlier had been deep and profound, but it had not changed any practical aspects of German foreign policy. The United States had remained the main underwriter of German security. Germany had to balance between the United States and an increasingly unilateral France, thus conducting a difficult, but ultimately successful balancing act. The domestic division on *Ostpolitik* was much deeper than during the Europeanist—Atlanticist debate, because many Germans were personally affected by the new *Ostpolitik*.

In contrast to the Europeanist-Atlanticist debate, the *Ostpolitik* of the Brandt-Scheel government really changed Germany's doctrine and policy. The refugees, who had until now harbored illusions of a return to their lands (Germany within the borders of 1937), and who had been reassured by all politicians that this was the goal of German policy, now saw that illusion gone. Germany recognized the postwar status quo, though it did not forego the option of peaceful reunification and recognized that all agreements were subject to a freely negotiated peace treaty. Having done so, Germany regained considerable room for maneuver in East-West relations.

The new *Ostpolitik* contained a number of bilateral treaties between the Federal Republic and the Soviet Union, the German Democratic Republic, and Poland as well as an agreement among the Four Allied Powers on the status of Berlin. In those treaties, the Federal Republic recognized existing borders and pledged not to violate them by force or work toward their revision. The Federal Republic also recognized the fact that there were "two states in Germany." It did, however, keep open the option of German unification in agreement with the Four Powers and the free will of the people. By recognizing the postwar status quo, this series of treaties paved the way for a much more active international diplomatic stance of the Federal Republic. The Federal Republic was now an almost normal state.

At the time, however, the new *Ostpolitik* had to overcome considerable challenges. First, there was the domestic opposition. The Brandt-Scheel government had come into existence with only a narrow margin of votes of 251:235 (with 4 invalid votes and 5 abstentions). Scheel had had great difficulties in uniting his small FDP to form this new government. A large conservative wing was leaning toward the CDU, and in the following years, a number of parliamentarians laid down their mandate or changed to the CDU. Thus, the domestic margin grew smaller and smaller. In 1972, the CDU even tried to replace Brandt with their own chancellor-candidate Rainer Barzel by a vote in the Bundestag and lost only narrowly. With this narrow political majority, it entailed considerable risks for the SPD-FDP coalition government to alienate the conservative wings of the FDP or the powerful *Bund der Vertriebenen*.

The diplomatic challenges were as large as the domestic challenges. Brandt had sent his representative Egon Bahr to Moscow in January 1970, early after the formation of the new government. In doing so, he did not consult with, but rather informed the Western Allies. This, too, was a novel step, and the Western Powers viewed it with considerable suspicion.[71] Initially, the Soviet Union, though interested in the negotiations, was not very accommodating. The Federal Republic wanted to normalize relations with the East, not endanger the Western alliance, and also keep open the option of eventual reunification. At a number of junctures, the negotiations seemed to fail, sometimes because of the Soviet Union, sometimes because of the Western Powers, sometimes for domestic reasons. But tenacity and diplomatic skill prevailed. The Brandt government achieved its objectives, albeit at high domestic costs.

One outcome of this process of normalization and détente was the Conference for Security and Cooperation (CSCE) in Europe. Thirty-five

European States, the United States, and Canada signed its final declaration in August 1975 in Helsinki. This declaration contained principles to guide the participating nations and a document about confidence-building measures in the military sphere. The CSCE was the first comprehensive postwar forum to address the issue of European security. Renamed the Organization for Security and Cooperation in Europe (OSCE) in 1994, it provided the kernel for a future collective system of security in Europe. German critics of the Western alliance and proponents of collective security often emphasized the OSCE as the forum in which European security should legitimately be handled. After reunification, there were certain indications that foreign minister Hans-Dietrich Genscher also saw the OSCE as the forum of the future.[72]

VII

In the late 1970s and early 1980s, détente gave way to a more confrontational climate. The Brandt-Scheel government had raised high hopes and had indeed brought about a fundamental correction of the foreign policy doctrine of the Federal Republic. It was now free to maintain relatively normal diplomatic relations with its eastern neighbors and move more freely in international diplomacy. At the same time, the government had not given up on the possibility of eventual reunification by the free will of the people. It had just pledged not to actively undermine existing structures.

But after the 1972 high points of German *Ostpolitik*, and certainly after the conclusion of the Conference for Security and Cooperation in Europe in Helsinki in 1975, the daily business of coexistence assumed priority. The high hopes of *Ostpolitik* expressed by parts of the SPD, among them Brandt and Bahr, gave way to normalcy. This was especially clear after Helmut Schmidt became chancellor in the spring of 1974. Schmidt was a former officer and defense minister, and he had been closely involved with NATO's Harmel report of 1968, which contained a commitment to defense and détente for NATO.

The East and the West still were fundamentally different systems. Moreover, the Soviet Union increasingly tried to use superpower détente and the SALT (Strategic Arms Limitation Talks) process to decouple Western Europe from the United States. While the superpowers were engaged in limiting strategic nuclear weapons, the Soviet Union began to build up its intermediate and short-range arsenal in Europe. This implied questions and problems of deterrence. Would the United States use its strategic arsenal to deter a limited nuclear attack on Western Europe? Official NATO strategy implied so, but the credibility of this threat was questionable.

Many in Germany, especially in the SPD, believed that Germany had emancipated itself as an independent state and could now proceed with a separate détente in Europe. Helmut Schmidt, parts of the SPD, and the CDU/CSU opposition held a different view. They believed that after the big steps of Ostpolitik and a normalization with the East, Germany's priorities still continued to be with the West, as a pillar of the Western alliance.

Schmidt was also afraid that superpower relations could lead to a decoupling of European security if an agreement was reached at the global and strategic level, without including Europe. In a historic speech at the London Institute for International Strategic Studies in May 1977, Schmidt expressed his concerns: "SALT II will stabilize relative parity in strategic nuclear weapons. This will inevitably lead to a reduction of the political and military importance of strategic nuclear weapons; the strategic component will increasingly become a means of last resort to safeguard the survival of the owners of such weapons."[73] In the spring of 1978, U.S. president Jimmy Carter stopped the production of the neutron bomb against the advice of his defense minister and head of the national security council. Schmidt, too, was not ready to come out strongly in favor because of strong opposition within his SPD. Egon Bahr, for example, had called the neutron bomb "a perversion of human thought."[74]

In December 1979, the NATO states agreed upon the so-called "double-track decision": the disarmament negotiations with the Soviet Union were to be continued, but in case a solution for intermediate-range nuclear forces could not be reached, such weapons would be stationed in the territory of the Federal Republic by 1983. But the West still appeared weak. In 1979, the United States was humiliated by the hostage crisis in Iran, and in 1980 the Soviet Union invaded Afghanistan.

When Ronald Reagan became president of the United States, he reversed Carter's course and embraced a strategy of full confrontation with the Soviet Union comprising a military buildup, economic sanctions, and ideological confrontation. This was not Helmut Schmidt's idea. While Schmidt had always supported Western firmness in vital security matters and had perceived Carter as an insecure and volatile president, he was also a pragmatist opposed to the ideologization of security affairs.

Even in the face of a deteriorating security climate, Schmidt tried to strengthen economic relations with the East, thus continuing the "change by rapprochement" strategy of his predecessor. Moreover, Schmidt was the government head of a state that had handled the economic crises of the 1970s very well, compared to other industrialized nations, including the United States. Schmidt knew that the Federal Republic did well economically, and he often lectured other statesmen on economic affairs. This was not appreciated by Carter, and the climate between both deteriorated to the point of personal animosity over time. Schmidt, however, was behind a host of economic initiatives: the G-5 summits (which began in 1975), the European Monetary System (which he and Giscard d'Estaing agreed upon in 1978), and numerous export promotion efforts of the Federal Republic.

As the NATO double-track decision approached, a growing fraction of the SPD and the general population began to ardently oppose it. Many Germans hoped that détente could be saved, and feared that a stationing of additional nuclear weapons in Germany would make matters worse. Germany experienced a broad popular antiwar and peace movement with broad support from major parts of the SPD and intellectuals. Schmidt stood firmly behind the agreement, but he was increasingly isolated in his own party. In the fall 1982 the FDP, the junior coalition partner, decided to change affiliations, thus making possible the formation of a CDU/CSU-FDP government under Helmut Kohl. The official reasons for this change were a correction in economic policy—the Federal Republic was in the midst of a recession. The government was eager to demonstrate continuity in foreign policy; thus Hans-Dietrich Genscher remained foreign minister.

The new government was reelected in March 1983. From the beginning, Kohl had strongly and clearly supported Ronald Reagan publicly, without "ifs" and "whens." In the confrontational climate of the early 1980s, this led to major domestic opposition, but earned the Federal Republic valuable goodwill that Kohl was able to use during reunification. In substance, Kohl was not so far away from Schmidt. He too preferred economic ties to the East to continue and opposed ideological confrontation. But he saw it as more important to reassure the United States before making his points. In the fall of 1983, new cruise missiles and intermediate-range forces were stationed in Germany. The antiwar movement had peaked, and so would East-West tensions.

In 1985, Mikhail Gorbachev became secretary-general of the Soviet Communist Party, bringing with him perestroika and glasnost, a program of comprehensive reform for the Soviet Union. Though this was not clear in the West, armament, the protracted war in Afghanistan, and continuing economic mismanagement had brought the Soviet Union and the East bloc to the verge of disaster. Gorbachev tried to integrate the Soviet

Union more closely with the Western system to obtain the means for economic reform to strengthen the Soviet Union. Ronald Reagan's idea of a competition with the West had proven right.

In early 1989, Bush began to advocate moving "beyond containment" and integrating the Soviet Union into the world system.[75] In May Bush raised hopes that the division of Europe might be overcome soon during a speech in Mainz, and explained that the United States would support a unified Germany. Bush also welcomed Germany as a "partner in leadership."[76] Of course, at the time nobody seriously expected German unification to take place within the next decade. In June, Gorbachev traveled to Germany and received a hero's welcome. Hundreds of thousands of people flooded the streets, demonstrating that Gorbachev had struck a certain chord. Nevertheless, the collapse of the Berlin Wall and the communist block from late 1989 to 1991 was a more or less complete surprise.

VIII

Germany's unification was the result of a fateful confluence of broad historical trends, the interplay of certain personalities, and skillful and determined diplomacy. The process, as the accounts by Zelikow and Rice, Teltschik, Kaiser, and Weidenfeld show, is a vindication of the concept of traditional diplomacy over multilateralism.[77] A focus on national interests explains the positions of the major actors well, and the interplay of a handful of national governments is sufficient to explain and analyze the outcome of the process. If "realism" is a precedence of "national interests" over "multilateral and supranational solutions," then realism is well suited to interpret the episode. At the same time, the major actors followed a course of enlightened self-interest and developed a perspective of moderation and cooperation. This enabled the resolution of even touchy issues.

A weak and accommodating Soviet Union, a supportive United States, a largely positive popular opinion in Western Europe and decisive leadership by Helmut Kohl eventually enabled reunification. The United States supported German unification from the beginning. Some of the larger European nations, especially Britain and France, initially assumed a more critical position.[78] Margaret Thatcher openly opposed unification and later called it her biggest failure not to have prevented unification.[79] The French president François Mitterrand, irritated by the fact that Kohl had not discussed his 10-point plan for German unification with him, visited the GDR in late December 1989 and tried to defend the existence of two German states.[80] However, he also made clear that he did not fear German unification and would not block it. What was more important, the French population did not seem to have the same worries as the French policy elites: two-thirds of the population supported reunification. The people of most other European countries were similarly supportive.[81]

The West German government, led by Kohl, was the driving force behind unification, using accepted norms and principles of self-determination and diplomacy to strengthen its position. Since the Ostpolitik of the Brandt-Scheel government, Germany's official line had been one of reconciliation with the East and the improvement of living conditions there. Though the goal of unification was still officially upheld, it had become irrelevant to foreign policy making. Opinions within Germany were initially divided. In November 1989, it was not clear whether Germany was to be reunified, and if so, if it should happen on Western terms. An influential minority, both left and right, believed that even if unification under Western conditions was in the national interest, it was totally unrealistic. Both sides would have to make compromises. Countess Dönhoff, co-publisher of the influential *Die Zeit,* had summarized this position in early 1989, when unification was still a hypothetical question, as follows: "Unification under a European roof sounds good, but how should we imagine it? As an *Anschluß* of the GDR under Western conditions to an FRG integrated in Europe? Total (Soviet, M.O.) capitulation in peacetime? This cannot seriously be believed by anybody."[82]

The concept of a neutral Germany received some initial support from parts of the SPD and the Green Party. In early 1990, Germans were asked whether they would welcome the unification of Germany if the precondition was a neutral Germany. Forty-six percent of the population favored such a solution versus 27 percent that disfavored it.[83] This result might have been influenced by the timing and phrasing of the question: if unification within the Western alliance and unification with the precondition of neutrality had been posed as alternatives, the figures might have looked different. A 1991 poll by the RAND corporation confirms the pro-Western orientation of the population: 54 percent of Germans supported a continuation of NATO, 35 percent favored a Western or all-European solution, and only 10 percent favored neutrality.[84]

Others went further and supported the existence of two German states. Though the German constitution listed reunification as a main goal, significant parts of the SPD, the Green Party, and a small part of the FDP had not only accepted the division of Germany, but saw it as Germany's lasting contribution to a peaceful order in Europe. Parts of the policy elite thus perceived the German division to be in the national interest. (The population, on the other hand, largely supported unification.)[85] In the weeks after the fall of the Berlin Wall, Willy Brandt, the former German chancellor, mayor of Berlin, and honorary chairman of the SPD, united the SPD behind the goal of unification.[86] By the spring of 1990, unification was supported by the overwhelming majority of the German policy elite.

The Federal Republic reacted in a foreseeable and established manner when the crisis in the German Democratic Republic became openly visible in August 1989. Thousands of GDR citizens, frustrated by the refusal of their leadership to follow the reform course that Gorbachev had propagated, fled through the permeable Hungarian border and on to Austria.[87] The government tried to stabilize the situation and preserve the status quo by warning GDR citizens against indeliberate actions. Faithful to Ostpolitik, West Germany stood by its objectives of stabilization of the situation in the GDR and humanitarian improvements for its citizens.[88] Walter Priesnitz, under secretary in the ministry for inner-German relations, declared that the flight across the Hungarian border was no easy feat, and that most of the refugees were captured by East German border guards. He appealed to GDR citizens to remain in their state. The Federal Republic would do everything in its power to improve living conditions in the GDR.[89] Rudolf Seiters, minister of the chancellery, appealed to the GDR leadership to allow reforms in its country in order to reduce the stream of refugees.[90]

But only a short time later, the German position began to change. Epitomizing his generation, Kohl strongly supported West European reconciliation and unification and an alliance with the United States, but also held deep-seated convictions about German unity, convictions that were much weaker in the younger generation. On August 25, Hungarian prime minister Nemeth and foreign minister Horn arrived in Bonn for consultations about the East German refugees who were trapped inside Hungary. Germany offered economic assistance. A short time later, the Hungarian government issued a statement that it would not send back those refugees. On September 9, Hungary allowed the refugees to leave for West Germany. Under the leadership of Helmut Kohl, the German government had begun to destabilize the situation for the German Democratic Republic.[91] Subsequently, the stream of refugees swelled. National unity was on the agenda again. Indeed, Helmut Kohl made clear that "in the past weeks it had become clear that we Germans belong together and that the will for unity is not some will, but a deep-seated moral force."[92] Even earlier, he had declared that the question of unity was still on the international agenda.[93]

Quickly, the major powers realized that the existence of the second German state was threatened and that the status quo in Europe might change radically. This could not be in the interest of the Soviet Union, France, or Great Britain, whose influence would inevitably be diminished. While the Soviet government had remained silent about the developments in East Germany—maybe hoping to use them as a lever for domestic change—on September 26, foreign minister Eduard Shevardnadze made clear that the Soviet Union did not support the destabilization of the GDR. While self-determination was a right in principle, "national egotism" was not permissible. Attempts at reunification would be outright revanchism with the objective of overthrowing the postwar order.[94]

But events in the GDR began to accelerate. In September and early October, tens of thousands of East Germans joined in the first large-scale demonstrations in more than three decades, demanding far-reaching reforms. Egon Krenz, who had replaced Eric Honecker as party chairman, painted a bleak picture of the economic situation in his first official visit to Moscow. For example, interest payments on foreign debt, mostly to Western nations, accounted for 62 percent of export earnings.[95] For a short time, the East German government was paralyzed. There were no massive police interventions against demonstrations, even when protesters began to climb the Berlin Wall. On November 11, 1989, the German Democratic Republic opened its borders. This lead to a truly massive stream of refugees, and fatally weakened the second German state. In November alone, 133,000 Germans relocated from the GDR to West Germany.[96]

Now the West German government had to master a difficult diplomatic situation. The goal of reunification had a solid foundation in international law. Germany's Western allies had paid lip service to this goal, many undoubtedly hoped it would not materialize. France and Great Britain, and certainly the Soviet Union, necessarily saw it as a diminution of their influence. The United States welcomed unification as long as Germany would remain in NATO, thereby strengthening the American-led alliance. In this situation. Germany's choice was quickly made: Kohl tried to win early support from its most important ally, the United States. This crucial partnership helped to engineer unification against the will of the Soviet Union, France and Great Britain, who all stood to lose from it to various degrees. Of course, Germany also tried to reassure its other partners, but without U.S. support, unification would have been impossible. It helped that in the case of reunification, international law and the German national position were largely congruent, something that could not be said of the major countries that initially opposed or tried to delay unification—the Soviet Union, France, and Great Britain.

In his state-of-the-nation report of November 8, before the Bundestag, Kohl stressed self-determination for the people in the GDR, the rule of law, and their right to a democratic government. But he also pointed out that the events of recent times had shown that the division of Germany was unnatural. In a press conference of November 11, Kohl again stressed that the East German people should have the right of free decision and that he did not doubt they would opt for unity.[97] Kohl also put this in the context of European unification and the creation of a new peace order in Europe. The completion of the Common Market would foster European integration and would further promote European unity. Moreover, the process of change initiated by Gorbachev gave hope that the East-West conflict could be overcome. The goal of the Federal Republic was a peace order that was not dictated by a few large powers but "which would be designed by the peoples of Europe in free self-determination." This right, according to Kohl, was recognized in the UN charter. To denounce it as "revanchism" would violate a basic law of the international community. The goal of German policy was "a free and united Germany in a free and united Europe."[98]

U.S. national interest and international norms both were foundations for early and decisive U.S. support. Different from the European powers, the superpower United States did not see a Germany reunited on Western terms as a significant disturbance in the balance of power. To the contrary, a stronger Germany could further U.S. objectives.[99] Reunification was engineered as a classic masterpiece of diplomacy among nations. There was no common approach of the West based on common values and norms, a notion that Kohl had evoked on November 8, 1989. International law nevertheless helped: in June 1989, the governments of the Soviet Union and the Federal Republic had signed a declaration that reaffirmed the rights of all peoples to determine their own fate and to choose their own political and social system. Self-determination received a prominent place in the declaration.[100] In November, the Soviet Union found it hard to extricate itself from this position. Of course, at the time it was hard to foresee the acceleration of events a little while later.

On October 23, Kohl had sought the support of George Bush, assuring that the Federal Republic would remain tied to NATO and the EU. Bush replied that a unified Germany within the established treaties would be no threat. One day later, Bush went public, stating that he foresaw new developments in the German question, but saw no danger because of the Federal

Republic's unshakable commitment to the alliance.[101] Immediately after the fall of the Berlin Wall, Kohl signaled the other powers that, regardless of future developments, the Federal Republic would act only after careful consideration and take a step-by-step approach. At the same time, he once again stressed self-determination for the people in the GDR and emphasized the right to free speech, free unions, free association, and free, equal, and secret elections. Both German states would belong to one nation.

It was in the interest of both Germany and the United States to keep the number of actors small and to give the Federal Republic the decisive role. Throughout 1998, the United States helped the Federal Republic to thwart initiatives that were designed to allow a larger number of powers have a say in German reunification. Immediately after the fall of the Berlin Wall, the Soviet government proposed making the German question the subject of a Four Powers conference. The Federal Republic, which was not informed by Gorbachev, was not to be included. The United States immediately informed the German government. Ultimately, the United States could not prevent such a Four Powers Conference (which was also desired by France and Great Britain), but it could render it ineffective by limiting the content of the conference to questions of Allied rights and powers in Berlin. Another Soviet proposal to make German unification the subject of a KSCE conference—a forum with 35 member states—was also stopped because it would have meant the death of the idea of fast reunification.[102] Kohl also avoided discussing the subject of German reunification at the Paris special summit of the European Union in mid-November to avoid making the impression of giving other European powers a say in reunification.[103]

On November 28, Kohl presented a 10-point-plan for German reunification.[104] This plan contained two sections. The first section dealt with the relationship between the German states. It stressed easier travel and technical and economic assistance in exchange for political reforms and the development of confederate structures, based on the condition of free elections in the GDR.[105] These points did, of course, pursue the objective of national unity and were directed against the new East German proposals of a treaty community, which would have stabilized the East German state.[106] The second part of the plan tried to assuage the other powers interested in the process.[107] It demonstrated the will of the Federal Republic to tie Germany into multilateral structures. The Federal Republic would base its policy on Western norms and values. All further steps should take place in coordination with the multilateral structures of the EC and the KSCE and the creation of an overarching security system in Europe.[108]

Kohl also cited a NATO resolution from 1967 in which the NATO members declared that a final and stable solution in Europe was impossible until the core of the tensions in Europe, the German question, was resolved.[109] In reality, of course, the actual diplomacy of the Federal Republic aimed at (and succeeded in) strongly limiting the number of actors involved in the process of German reunification.

The plan had not been coordinated with the Western Allies. Margaret Thatcher promptly declared that German unification was not on the agenda. First, there would have to be democratic structures in the East before this issue could be discussed.[110] While French president François Mitterrand stayed in the background, foreign minister Dumas publicly warned against undue haste in the German question and brought up allied prerogatives.[111]

Immediately after the announcement of the plan, Kohl reassured Bush in a phone conversation that the Federal Republic would remain a loyal ally.[112] Bush was tolerant of Kohl's initiative. Kohl acted to fulfill this commitment. The German constitution, the basic law, allowed for two ways of unification. Article 146 foresaw a constitution to be agreed upon by all German people. With the new constitution, the basic law would become ineffective. The other alternative was a simple accession of additional states to the area of the Federal Republic according to Article 23. Kohl followed the second option against considerable domestic opposition. This, of course, implied not a new beginning and a new Germany, but a continuation of the Federal Republic of Germany with all its traditions and treaty obligations. The GDR would cease to exist, and the states in the GDR would have to be constituted according to the West German basic law.[113] This, of course, was largely congruent with American interests.

But Kohl's policy of weakening the second German state and accelerating the unification process may or may not have been in keeping with U.S. interests. The chancellor therefore repeatedly explained to Bush that he was not following a set timetable. He also pointed out the dimension of the crisis in the GDR and suggested that a fast integration of the GDR may be the only solution to mastering the crisis. In addition, one should not underestimate the emotions that were attached to reunification. Kohl, though certainly a promoter of this process, presented himself as a victim of external forces.[114]

On a second issue that could run contrary to U.S. interests, the chancellor had to actively intervene. The United States wanted all of a united Germany as a member of the Atlantic alliance. This position was documented in the Four Points of November as well as in the new political guidelines of January.[115] In a speech from January 29, 1990, Genscher reaffirmed the Federal Republic's membership in NATO, but also emphasized that a special status would have to be found for the territory of the former GDR. His suggestion to change from confrontation to cooperation in European security structures was interpreted in the German press as a call to dissolve NATO and the Warsaw Pact.[116] He also stated that the Soviet Union could not possibly accept an eastward expansion of NATO.[117]

Kohl reacted with heavy criticism, leading Genscher to retract his call for a change of security structures.[118] Genscher did, however, maintain the position that the NATO area should not be expanded to East German territory. From January to March, Genscher continued to test the waters. Kohl tolerated Genscher's position that NATO should not expand, thereby testing the Federal Republic's room for maneuver in the West. Kohl's silence on some issues was noted by the American side. In an interview of mid-January, Kohl left the question whether a unified Germany would be a member of NATO unanswered.[119] A short time later, he reaffirmed his firm commitment to having U.S. soldiers stationed on German soil but did not mention NATO.[120] Even at a high-level meeting at Camp David in late February, Kohl argued that no NATO troops should be stationed on the territory of the former GDR. But in the final press conference, Bush declared that a united Germany was to be a full member of NATO. Kohl had yielded to Bush's position.[121] In March, Genscher again openly demanded that the existing alliances be replaced by cooperative security structures. Kohl reprimanded him in a sharp note.[122]

This established a typical pattern of German foreign policy that was to regularly surface in the period covered in this analysis. Not only the interests of the Western Allies, but also the interest of the Soviet Union, and later Russia, had to be taken into account by the Federal Republic. Often, different parts of the German government maintained slightly different positions, especially on the issue of all-European security structures versus Western security structures. The different positions were a means to test international reactions. This can be seen in the case of NATO enlargement and the efforts to end the Kosovo crisis.

Germany needed U.S. support. Already in January, the American side had developed the concept of two-plus-four negotiations, in which the two Germanys as primary negotiators, together with the Allied Powers, were to decide upon Germany's unification process. It was in the interest of both Germany and the United States to keep the number of actors small. Both wanted to have the option of making rapid progress, and both acted from a strong position. In mid-February, James Baker pushed through this concept against the strong opposition of the smaller NATO members.[123] But the United States also had to stop initiatives by France, Great Britain, and the Soviet Union to expand the interpretation of Allied Powers, which could block reunification.

Bush had promised Kohl in Camp David that there would be no second Yalta. He also promised his support for a fast conclusion of unification by the fall. When the EC foreign ministers proposed a CSCE summit against the opposition of the German delegate, the United States played for time to give the Federal Republic an opportunity to press ahead with de facto unification. The American government also assisted Germany in setting a late date for the two-plus-four negotiations against Soviet wishes. When the negotiations started in early May 1990, the first free parliamentary elections had already established a situation that was unfavorable for the Soviet Union. The Christian Democrats had emerged victorious in the GDR and had formed a grand coalition with the Social Democrats. The new government under Lothar de Mazière vigorously pursued unification—and let the Federal Republic largely set the conditions.[124]

In the two-plus-four negotiations, James Baker resisted Soviet attempts to delay the process and to expand allied powers. America asserted that only a minimalist agenda was the subject of the negotiations—only the status of Berlin and certain powers concerning border questions would be included. United Germany was to have sovereign say over its policy toward ABC weapons, which were only to be discussed in the two-plus-four forum. All other important issues were to be decided by the German states.[125]

The policies pursued by West Germany and the United States show a preponderance of classical diplomacy, or "power politics." A united Germany was not seen as a threat by the United States, but as a strong and helpful partner. Moreover, the Soviet Union would be greatly weakened. Germany's role as a loyal ally over the past decades certainly helped to create this perception. It is highly unlikely that the United States would have supported an uncertain and wavering Federal Republic with the same intensity. The Federal Republic, too, pursued its national interests with an eye toward power structures. As shown, Helmut Kohl was ready to push issues unilaterally when he saw an advantage. In this process, Kohl did outmaneuver the Soviet Union, France, and Great Britain more than once. Legal norms like the right of self-determination, which Kohl often mentioned, strengthened Kohl's position. Multilateralism as an ideal of German foreign policy was often circumvented. Quite a few of Kohl's steps and initiatives were not coordinated with Germany's partners. A basis for this, however, was the overall support extended by the United States.

In France and Great Britain, a reunited Germany was not seen as an essential threat—so reliable had Germany's policy been over the past decades—but both countries were certainly acutely aware of the fact that their weight in Europe would necessarily be reduced if Germany was reunified. In January 1990, Margaret Thatcher gave an interview to the Wall Street Journal in which she tried to generate understanding for Gorbachev's position and termed Kohl's and Genscher's policy "egotistic" and "nationalist." Both risked the overthrow of Gorbachev, with unforeseeable consequences for the international system, with their policy of rapid unification.[126] In a phone conversation with Bush in late January 1990, Thatcher voiced even stronger concerns, saying that she had "the greatest mistrust against a united Germany." The German government would now achieve what Hitler had tried in vain. She also recommended keeping Russian troops stationed in Germany for an indefinite period to prevent dangerous nationalist tendencies.[127] Yet Thatcher, who was already isolated, could not resist American and German positions forever. Britain accepted an early reunification during the Ottawa conference of the NATO foreign ministers.[128]

France's policy was less open, but attempts to slow down reunification and to diminish German influence were still visible. One the one hand, France needed Germany much more than Britain to achieve its ambitions in Europe. On the other hand, of course, a strong Germany would also endanger these ambitions. There were early signals from Paris that reunification would be supported if Germany's commitment to Europe was not to suffer. The spokesperson of the French president, Hubert Vèdrine, declared that a strengthening of the European Community would have to have priority. Foreign minister Roland Dumas declared that the East Germans' wish for reunification was legitimate; however, one should not neglect international commitments.[129]

Mitterrand, who also was the acting president of the EC in the second half of 1989, called a special summit of the EC heads of state and government for November 18, 1989, without coordinating this step with Germany.[130] This ran contrary to Germany's policy, which aimed at discussing reunification only with a small circle of powers. As a consequence, Kohl avoided discussion questions concerning reunification during the summit, which was partially conducted in an "icy atmosphere."[131]

But this was not the only step France took to slow reunification. Mitterrand met bilaterally with Gorbachev in early December and paid a state visit to the GDR in late December, thus trying to bolster the East German government.[132] Moreover, France was not disinclined to follow Soviet proposals for a Four Powers conference on German unification, although the German government strictly opposed such a conference without an equal participation of the German states. During the European summit from December 8–9, 1989, the French president declared that France could not resist the Russian plea for a meeting of the Berlin ambassadors of the four Allied Powers.[133]

Nevertheless, France saw the signs of the times early on and tried to use unification to promote its own goals. At the Strassbourg summit of early December, one of Mitterrand's pet projects, a European monetary and economic union, was discussed in depth.[134] Mitterrand was determined to advance this project during his EC presidency.[135] France did indeed win Germany's support for this project, which Kohl had treated with great reserve before.[136]

Germany's strategy of coupling monetary and economic union with supranational political integration, however, was greeted with only moderate support by Mitterrand. In principle, he opposed a political union for Europe. According to Werner Weidenfeld, one of the best observers of the period and a close adviser to Helmut Kohl, even the German-French initiative of April 1990 was founded in the desire to prevent "federalist excesses" in the EC. The strategy of controlling Germany through supranational integration was only a secondary consideration. With monetary and economic union, on the other hand, France hoped to harness Germany's economic power for its own objectives without having to give up too much national autonomy.[137]

Great Britain and France, though both opposed unification, did not manage to create a united front. Britain's strong opposition to German reunification was a potential threat to Mitterrand's objectives for the EC.[138] Monetary and economic union could be more easily achieved in bilateral negotiations between France and Europe. Britain had made clear during the European summit of June 1988 that it opposed economic and monetary union.[139]

The Soviet Union, of course, strongly opposed reunification, because it stood to lose most from the process. Gorbachev finally agreed to reunification on Western terms in June 1990 during a visit by Kohl to the Soviet Union. In the press conference, the parties declared that after reunification, the rights of the Four Powers would cease to exist and that Germany was to decide freely which treaty organizations it was to join.[140]

The reasons for this change of course were certainly multifaceted. For one, Gorbachev and Kohl had signed a common declaration during Gorbachev's visit to Bonn in June 1989 which stressed all peoples' right to self-determination. Moreover, the Soviet Union was plagued by large political and economic problems—and would cease to exist in December 1991. A certain gratitude for German economic assistance also helped. When Gorbachev urgently asked for German economic and food assistance in January 1990, Kohl acted fast and decisively. Within eight weeks, 25,000 metric tons of meat, 50,000 tons of pork, 20,000 tons of butter, 15,000 tons of milk powder, and 5,000 tons of cheese were delivered to the Soviet Union.[141] In May 1990, a delegation of German economic experts visited the Soviet Union. Although not a single high-ranking government member was part of the delegation, it was received by both Shevardnadze and Gorbachev, indicating the high importance the Soviet Union gave Germany as an economic partner. As a consequence, Germany granted credit guarantees in the amount of DM 5 billion.[142] The German side repeatedly stressed that it saw this economic assistance as part of a bargain about reunification.[143] Later, Germany also paid DM 12 billion to allow the Soviet troops stationed in Germany reintegration in the Soviet Union. A further DM 3 billion were granted as a non-interest bearing loan.[144]

IX

The distinguishing feature of German foreign policy from the late 1960s until after reunification was its continuity. Despite some domestic upheavals, Germany continued a policy of close alliance with the United States, European integration, and détente with the East, in that order. This continuity was partially determined by the external constraints Germany was subjected to. At some points, however, German statesmen might have taken different courses. Schmidt might not have initiated or might have waived the double-track decision. The economic might of Germany could have led to overconfidence in its ability to handle its own security affairs, leading to a U.S.-German rift. Realism, modesty, and continuity enabled unification, the greatest success of German postwar diplomatic history.

The events of 1989–1990, however, did change the security framework for Germany. The core of this book will be devoted to the question of how strongly this framework changed and how strongly German foreign policy itself has changed between 1989 and 1999. The book concludes with some predictions about future changes we should expect, and which future changes are needed for Germany to perform its role in the new international system.

III

National Power and Influence: What Did Unification Change?

I

The foreign policy doctrine of the Federal Republic of Germany evolved under very specific postwar circumstances. By 1955, the major elements with the exception of détente and Ostpolitik were all in place. The events of 1989–1991 changed the established framework of German foreign policy. Did this fundamentally affect Germany's strategic situation? In particular, has German power increased significantly after reunification? In the realist view, this would prompt Germany to become a revisionist power and to strive for institutions and arrangements that better reflect its new international position. Since we argue that Germany is a pillar of the status quo, we must—and will—demonstrate that Germany's relative power has *not* changed significantly.

Despite its centrality in many theories of international relations, "power" is an elusive concept. For this study, we distinguish between "power capabilities" and "realized power," "tangible power" and "influence" or "soft power," "asymmetric vulnerabilities" and "asymmetric sensitivities." Ideally, the computation of power would be a straightforward exercise based on various indices. This would allow us to express national power in a single measure, comparing Germany's power before and after unification.[1] But in reality, power has to be measured for specific areas, because different forms of power are not always easily fungible and different tasks might require different forms of power.[2] The possession of nuclear weapons, for example, may carry little weight in trade negotiations among allies.

There is also a difference between "power" and "influence."[3] "Power" is the ability to impose one's will in adversarial situations (conflict), whereas "influence" may be used in cooperative situations to change the other's behavior. "Power" has a coercive character, "influence" may be used noncoercively. "Hard power" is based on quantitative economic, territorial, or military measures, "soft power" can be based on perceptions, persuasion, or ideology. Power also derives from asymmetries in sensitivities and vulnerabilities, with vulnerability being the more important dimension.[4] Sensitivities denote degrees of state responsiveness within a given international order; vulnerabilities rest on the availability and costs of alternatives to the existing order.

The analysis of German power after 1989 produces some surprises: First, we intend to demonstrate that German global capabilities have changed relatively little since 1989. The country is a middle power that cannot be interested in establishing a major global role. Germany *is* the dominant power in Europe. But it is first and foremost the smallest element in a triangle comprising the United States, Russia, and Germany. This realist view provides a fruitful perspective for analyzing German foreign policy. While it should be in Germany's interest to slowly reshape Europe according to its own preferences, that reshaping will stop short of major changes that would disturb the overall structure of security relations.

Second, far from being a rising economy, Germany has passed its economic peak. Germany should therefore be seen as a nation that will increasingly safeguard its resources and that will be less likely to use checkbook diplomacy. Germany's diplomacy may become more defensive and status-quo oriented rather than revisionist over time.

Third, Germany has the same structure of vulnerabilities as it had in 1989, although those vulnerabilities are now at a much lower level. The major threat to Germany—a nuclear attack from Russia—is still there. Although it is much less likely, Germany must continue to safeguard against the worst. (The second major threat—a conventional attack from the East—has all but vanished.) Germany also needs the European Union to safeguard its trade. At the same time, German sensitivity to adversarial developments in its orbit has actually *increased*. The bipolar world of the Cold War effectively shielded the old Federal Republic from civil strife and unrest. Today, with permeable eastern borders, Germany is much more sensitive to civil strife, unrest, uncontrolled migration, transnational crime and terrorism, and economic crises than it was before.

Fourth and finally, power also rests in the perceptions and attitudes that others harbor. A nation's policy or ideology can therefore exert considerable influence.[5] We will argue that the strongest increase in German power is indeed in the area of "soft" power. Other countries increasingly see Germany in the role of honest broker or advocate without strong ambitions beyond the status quo. This accumulated goodwill enables Germany to leverage its power resources more effectively.

II

By most measures of power capability—territory, population, military and even economic strength—Germany remains a middle power. With regard to territory and population, unified Germany is a small middle power not in the same league as the most resource-rich global players.[6] Germany's territory has increased by almost 50 percent through unification. Large countries such as the United States, Russia, China, and Canada, however, are many times larger. Even France, Spain, and Japan outsize united Germany. With an area of 137,700 square miles, unified Germany is well behind France (212,000 square miles) and Japan (146,000 square miles).[7] The united Federal Republic's area is smaller than that of the state of Montana (145,400 square miles) and significantly smaller than was imperial Germany or even the Weimar Republic.

Germany's population has increased by one-third through unification, from 62 million in 1989 to 81.2 million in 1994. This number reflects significant net immigration in the intervening years. Still, Germany is a smaller middle power. The population of China is 14 times larger, the United States three times as large, Russia twice, and Japan is 50 percent larger. However,

Table III.1 Manpower and Defense Budgets of Selected Nations, 1997

	Personnel Strength	*Defense Budget ($bn)*
U.S.	1,447,600	267
Russia	1,240,00/381,000 conscripts	n/a
Germany	347,100/152,560 conscripts	27
France	380,820/156,950 conscripts	37
United Kingdom	213,800	36
Japan	235,600	43
China	2,840,000/1,275,000 conscripts	n/a
Iran	518,000	n/a

Source: Compiled from The International Institute for Strategic Studies, ed., *The Military Balance 1997–1998*, (London: Brassey 1997).

Note: n/a: budgets would give a misleading picture

Germany's population is 23 percent of the EU population. It is one-third higher than either France's or Great Britain's population.[8]

Military strength has traditionally been an important measure of national power. Here again, Germany is a middle power. The figures are comparable to the U.K., France, and Japan and are far smaller than those of such military superpowers as the United States and the former Soviet Union or even contemporary Russia. Germany lacks nuclear weapons—the ultimate military resource—and has renounced the acquisition of such weapons. Currently, total manpower and defense budgets of some nations are as follows:

Before unification, West Germany, Japan, France, and the United Kingdom spent roughly the same amount on their respective militaries. The various disarmament treaties of recent years have set in motion a far-reaching restructuring of military forces, especially in Europe. Germany is one of the countries most strongly affected by the restructuring. It now spends less on defense than either the United Kingdom or France.

Many argue that Germany's true power rests in its economy. An analysis of economic power, however, shows that even in economic terms, Germany is a middle power and not a giant. Even if productivity in East

Table III.2 Exports in Billions of U.S. Dollars

	1987	1989	1991	1993	1995	1997
U.S.	254	363	421	464	585	689
Germany	294	341	402	380	523	512
Japan	231	273	314	362	442	421

Source: Compiled from IMF, ed., *Direction of Trade Statistics 1995* (Washington, D.C.: IMF, 1995), *International Financial Statistics Yearbook 1998*.

Table III.3 Trade Balances of G-3 Nations

	1987	1989	1991	1993	1995	1997
U.S.	−172	−130	−88	−139	−186	−210
Germany	66	72	13	32	60	70
Japan	81	65	78	121	160	83

Source: Compiled from IMF, ed., *Direction of Trade Statistics 1995* (Washington, D.C.: IMF, 1995), *International Financial Statistics Yearbook 1998*.

Germany catches up to Western levels, Germany's economy will still be one-third the size of the U.S. economy, and less than half the size of the Japanese economy.[9]

Exports and imports are often used as another measure of economic power. Kenneth Waltz argues that because of its high volume of exports, Germany rivals U.S. international economic power and is stronger than Japan.[10]

It is the trade balance that is often used to argue that Germany and Japan occupy a prevalent place in the international economy.[11] Since the mid-1980s, Germany has indeed shown a persistently positive trade balance.

Exports and trade balances, however, are strongly dependent on an existing international order. For Germany, this is primarily the European Union. Should Germany's trading sphere, the EU, break down, the country would have very few means of sustaining its level of exports. Exports do give Germany power, but it must also be careful to sustain the institutional framework that supports this trade.

III

The preceding analysis has revealed that Germany's power resources are relatively small. This is not the whole story. Most indicators of future economic development show that Germany's tangible power has peaked and that the global weight of the German economy is declining. The long-term performance of the German economy is lackluster. The German

Table III.4 Growth Rates: GDP

	60–68	79–90	89–95	60–95
U.S.	4.5	2.6	1.9	2.9
Japan	10.2	4.1	1.9	5.5
Germany	4.0	2.0	2.0	2.9
France	5.4	2.1	1.3	3.3
U.K.	3.0	2.1	1.0	2.3
Italy	5.7	2.4	1.3	3.4
Canada	5.0	2.7	1.2	3.8

Source: Compiled from OECD, ed., *Economic Outlook—Historical Statistics,* 1960–1990 (Paris: OECD 1992). OECD, ed., *Economic Outlook—Historical Statistics, 1960–1995* (Paris: OECD 1997).

share of OECD output peaked at approximately 0.14 in 1980 and experienced a moderate but steady decline to 0.12 in 1990.[12] West Germany's postwar dynamism seems to have leveled off.

In each of the three decades from 1960 to 1990, the growth rates of the German economy have been slightly below the average of the other G-7 nations. Between 1960 and 1995, Germany (and the United States) had the second-smallest long-term growth rate, only ahead of the United Kingdom. More recently, however, the U.S. economy seems to have gone through a successful restructuring, whereas Germany's economy remains hampered by many barriers to growth.

Even reunification and the opening of markets in Eastern Europe are not likely to reverse this trend. The level of investment, productivity, and spending on research and development as well as the composition and quantity of trade are indicators of the dynamism of an economy. Each of these indicates a slowing, rather than an accelerating, economy.

A healthy domestic economy is characterized by strong domestic investment. Germany still maintains a middle position among the three largest industrialized economies—in 1993 gross investment was 22 percent of GDP, versus 30 percent for Japan and 16 percent for the United States. But Germany's investment situation is not as favorable as it might seem. Over the past 30 years, Germany has experienced the largest relative decline in investment rates of the three nations, falling by almost 50 percent.

Domestic investment, in the wake of unification, should have drastically increased: both the stock of private capital and public infrastructure in former East Germany were largely obsolete. In a dynamic economy, this would have necessitated large-scale replacement and upgrading. Gross capital formation (which includes replacement of obsolete infrastructure) did indeed go up briefly from DM 448 bn in 1989 to DM 593 bn in 1991. But after this small increase following unification, net domestic investment leveled off and resumed its long-term decline.

In a slowing economy, long-term capital will migrate abroad. This is an indicator of declining domestic investment, industrial innovation and dynamism. It happened to post-1850 Britain, and it is happening to Germany today. Between 1987 and 1991, foreigners invested only $5.6 bn in Germany, but $48 bn in the United States, $24 bn in Great Britain, and $10.5 bn in France. Even smaller economies such as the Netherlands, Spain, Belgium, and Australia were ahead of Germany.[13] At the same time, Germans invested heavily abroad (DM 107 bn between 1989 and 1992, or twice as much as in the period before).[14] As a result, Germany's net foreign direct investment is increasing.

Table III.5 Western Assistance to Reforming Countries

| Donor | Central and Eastern European States Commitments 01/01/90–12/31/92 | | | Commonwealth of Independent States, Date 06/18/93 | | Total | Percent of Total |
	Commitments	Of which: credits	Of which: export credits	Commitments	Of which: credits		
Germany	8300	5492	2837	39779	28037	48083	36.60
France	1809	1588	1282	1995	1920	3805	2.90
Great Britian	740	651	0	1050	828	1791	1.36
EU-countries	11412	9776	5834	49996	37769	64508	49.10
From EU budget	3023	562	81	3576	1750	6602	5.03
EBRD	5083	5036	0	85	51	5168	3.93
Japan	2532	1975	543	3890	3397	6422	4.89
U.S.	5546	1964	1859	8442	6118	13995	10.65
G-24 total	37786	23640	10428	0	0	0	
IMF	7071	7071	0	853	853	7924	6.03
World Bank	6298	6298	0	563	563	6886	2.24
Grand total	52800	38606	10428	78591	57896	131391	100.00

Source: Jörg Winterberg, *Westliche Unterstützung der Transformationsprozesse in Osteuropa,* 13, "Unterstützung der Reformprozesse in den Staaten Mittel-, Südost- und Osteuropas (einschließlich der baltischen Staaten) sowie in den neuen unaabhängigen Staaten auf dem Territorium der ehemaligen Sowjeunion," *Deutscher Bundestag, Drucksache* 12/6162, 12 November 1993.

Three indicators support the conclusion that Germany will see a further deterioration of its economic and competitive position—a weak position in research, a rent-seeker society with high labor costs, and a weak position in future technologies.[15]

First, though Germany spends a relatively high percentage of its GDP on education, the quality and quantity of cutting-edge output, especially in research, has declined. In his analysis of the American-Japanese challenge, Konrad Seitz warns that German universities, which were leading until the 1930s, have become second or third class.[16] The number of international patents registered by German individuals and firms relative to those registered by U.S. and Japanese individuals and firms has declined rapidly.[17]

Second, Germany has become a highly unionized rent-seeker society with high labor costs and social benefits and little flexibility. German labor costs are currently the highest of any country. In 1993, labor costs and fringe benefits per hour averaged DM 42.67. Switzerland was in second place with DM 39.55, Japan third with DM 37.30 and the United States thirteenth with DM 27.84—or 65 percent of the German cost level.[18] In addition, Germans are now working fewer hours than employees in any other EU nation, the United States, or Japan.[19] Since 1983, labor costs per

Figure III.1 GDP in Comparison, 1997, ($ billion)

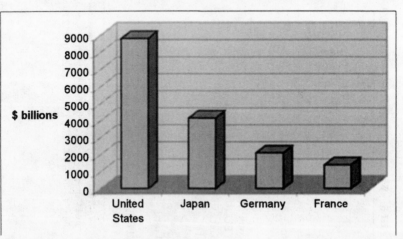

Source: Compiled from IMF, ed., *International Financial Statistics Yearbook 1998* (Washington, D.C.: IMF, 1998).

unit have risen by almost 40 percent compared to Germany's most important competitors, thus strongly diminishing the competitiveness of German products.[20]

Third, the sectoral composition of GNP and trade is a further indicator for long-term economic development.[21] In the early years of this century, economist Joseph Schumpeter developed the theory that economic development is ultimately dependent on the emergence of new industrial sectors, which disrupt old economic processes and fundamentally change the way production is organized.[22] An analysis of the sectors in which a nation is internationally competitive can shed light on its economic growth potential. If the nation has a solid foothold in emerging and future industries, it may be expected to have a dynamic economy.

Michael Porter identifies four clusters in which the German economy is particularly competitive—petroleum and chemical products, multiple business (machine tools and instruments), textiles and apparel, and health care.[23] With the exception of health care, all of these clusters came out of the second wave of industrialization that Germany spearheaded in the second half of the nineteenth century. Of course, products and production processes within the clusters were modernized, but Germany's competitive industries themselves are broadly the same as they were 100 years ago.[24] By contrast, the United States is competitive in five clusters—semiconductors and computers, transportation, office equipment, telecommunications, and defense—of which at least two (semiconductors and computers, telecommunications) are "future industries."[25]

Figure III.2 International Patents Registered

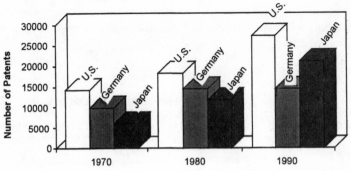

Source: "Standort Deutschland," 100.

According to Porter, Japan also has five broadly competitive sectors: semiconductors and computers, office equipment, telecommunications, health care, and entertainment/leisure.[26] Of these, three are in future industries (computers, telecommunications, and entertainment).[27]

German industry is strong in mechanical products (or mechanical products with some electrical components) and chemicals. None of the genuine future technologies—biotechnology, computers, telecommunications, or consumer electronics—is significant. If economic growth depends on innovative sectors, German industry is badly positioned for the next round of economic development: German companies have largely failed to capture a lead in emerging future technologies.

Financial Power

During 1989–1992, financial power reinforced Germany's strong position in Europe, facilitated reunification, and enabled global engagements. Germany mobilized massive amounts of capital for the reconstruction of former East Germany. It was by far the largest individual contributor to the EU budget. It helped to finance the Persian Gulf War. It also contributed the largest share of financial assistance to Eastern Europe and Russia. This massive display of financial power is likely a thing of the past. There is ample evidence that Germany has exhausted its room for financial maneuver.

In the years before and after reunification, Germany used its financial capabilities so extensively that during the Persian Gulf War it was accused of "checkbook diplomacy."[28] Germany also spent large amounts to support an economic buildup in the former East Germany. In 1991, public transfers to the new federal states were DM 113 bn (roughly $ 71 bn), in 1992 DM 145 bn (roughly $ 91 bn), and in 1993 DM 140 bn. These figures surpassed the total amount of Marshall Plan assistance to Europe in each individual year.[29]

Table III.6　German Government Deficit 1991–1993 (DM bn)

1989	1990	1991	1992	1993	1995	1996
−28	−72	−108	−118	−134	−110	−121

Source: Compiled from Deutsche Bundesbank, ed., Annual Report 1996 (Frankfurt/M.: Deutsche Bundesbank, 1996).

In addition, Germany was the most important financial supporter of Central and Eastern Europe and the countries of the former Soviet Union. From 1989 to mid-1993, Germany contributed more than $50 billion in aid to the former Soviet Union. During the same period, the United States and Japan committed only $9 bn and $3 bn, respectively.[30] Even the much heralded Clinton initiative in early 1993 offered only $3.4 bn (of which much was previously committed money or consisted of tied resources that flow back to the donor). Japan offered $1.8 bn, while Germany contributed $20 bn to Russia in 1993 alone.[31] Germany's assistance was seen as a quid pro quo for unification or as a safeguard against adversarial developments in the East as well as a humanitarian gesture.[32]

Germany is by far the largest contributor to the EU budget. In 1993, German payments accounted for ECU 18,700 bn out of a total EU budget of ECU 65,000. France, the second largest contributor, paid 12,000 ECU.[33] Germany is also the largest net contributor to the EU, paying more than three times the amount of the second-largest net contributor (Britain).[34]

Various indicators suggest that the recent impressive display of German financial power is not sustainable in the medium and long term. An important, if not fundamental, source of a state's financial power is its capacity to raise taxes or to obtain credit.[35] Germany has strained its financial power. Its ability to tax, or to use domestic and international capital markets, has declined markedly.

After unification, Germany, by design or default, followed the same strategy as the United States in the early Reagan years. It used the international capital markets to finance deficit spending at home.[36] Although the government raised taxes somewhat, the increase was not sufficient to finance the buildup of Eastern Germany and the assistance to Eastern Europe.

High interest rates helped to attract the necessary capital from the international capital markets. In early 1994, foreign investors held 40 percent of all German government bonds. Overall, foreigners bought twice as many German government bonds as Germans.[37] This use of capital markets may be termed "power consumption": Foreign holdings of German government bonds make Germany more dependent on foreign investors.

As a result of massive resource transfers to former East Germany and the fulfillment of other obligations, the German government deficit has exploded. In 1993, Germany's government deficit amounted to DM 275 bn. Public transfers to the East in 1992 amounted to 6 percent of the West's GDP.[38]

As a result, more federal debt was added in the five years after the fall of the Berlin Wall than between the creation of the Federal Republic and 1989.[39]

Germany was only barely able to stay below the debt ceiling of 60 percent, a precondition of the Maastricht treaty for monetary union.[40]

An abatement of the strain on public finances is not in sight. The *Institut der deutschen Wirtschaft* conducted a scenario analysis to forecast necessary transfers to former East Germany for the ten years between 1994 and 2003. In the most optimistic scenario, total transfers are still DM 685 bn, or DM 68.5 bn annually. In the most pessimistic scenario, this figure soars to DM 1,725 bn—or DM 172.5 bn annually.[41] Not only do transfers to the East continue, but transfers to the EU will rise from DM 43 bn in 1994 to DM 54 bn in 1998.[42]

IV

Power also derives from asymmetric sensitivities or vulnerabilities. Sensitivity refers to the degree of dependence within a given order; vulnerability denotes the cost of changes in an existing order and the alternatives available to states.[43]

The analysis of German vulnerabilities and sensitivities in two areas—military security and trade (economic power)—yields partially counterintuitive results: while Germany's *overall level of vulnerability* has clearly decreased, Germany has become *more*—rather than less—*sensitive* to security disturbances.

In the post–Cold War security environment, Germany's security calculus is complex and depends on a number of scenarios that are determined by the three major German vulnerabilities: a withdrawal of U.S. troops and their protective shield, a breakdown of Germany's trading sphere (the EU), and adversarial developments in Eastern Europe and Russia. The changes

Table III.7 **German Public Debt 1965–1996 (DM bn)**

1965	*1970*	*1975*	*1980*	*1985*	*1990*	*1995*	*1996*
113	163	323	535	847	1218	2292	2129

Source: Compiled from Deutsche Bundesbank, ed., *Annual Report 1996* (Frankfurt/M.: Deutsche Bundesbank, 1996).

Table III.8 Openness of G-3 Economies (Exports and Imports as Percentage of GDP)

	1960	1970	1980	1990	1991	1992	1995	1997
U.S.	9.3	11.3	21.0	22.1	21.5	21.8	24.3	25.6
Germany	35.4	40.2	53.3	58.0	61.2	59.9	46.9	52.1
Japan	20.9	20.3	28.2	20.9	18.9	17.9	17.3	19.8

Source: Compiled from OECD, ed., *National Accounts 1096–92, Vol. I.*

after 1989 clearly and dramatically increased Germany's overall level of security. Germany's vulnerability to a direct conventional attack from the East became much smaller after 1989. A major conventional threat is now highly unlikely. Russia, the only major conventional power in the East, is greatly weakened and would have to pass two tiers of adversarial states to reach German soil. The potential nuclear threat, however, has not disappeared completely. Instability in Russia might bring to power forces toying with nuclear brinkmanship, and Germany, a very small state, can easily be devastated by less than a dozen nuclear explosions.

But the basic *structure* of vulnerabilities—to a withdrawal of the U.S. security shield, a breakdown of the EU, and adversarial developments in the East, particular Russia—remains the same. Germany is still vulnerable to a nuclear threat. Against such threats, NATO and the U.S. umbrella still provide the best safeguard for Germany. Russia's nuclear potential can best be countered by the United States. The U.S.-German partnership has withstood the test of time. Any alternative security regime—a European (e.g., French-German) nuclear defense,[44] or Germany's acquisition of nuclear weapons—are inferior, though not inconceivable.

The relative weight of items two and three, however, may slowly be changing. Whereas the maintenance of the EU is now second in this rank-

Figure III.3 Germany's International Competitive Position

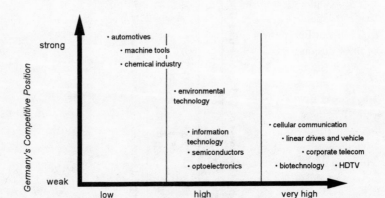

Source: "Standort Deutschland," 100.

ing and considerations in Eastern Europe are third, Germany's economic importance to the EU could become so large that a breakdown of this trading system would become all but inconceivable—the other EU states might need Germany more than Germany needs the EU. This changing nature of Germany's perceived vulnerabilities could foster important changes in Germany's foreign policies.

Let us analyze the two other dimensions—relations with the United States and Russia—first. The U.S. and Russian positions—either friendly or adversarial—are depicted in a matrix.

Obviously, a simultaneous continuation of the U.S. security shield, the creation of a European defense identity, and a cooperative Russia constitutes the best possible outcome. An adversarial Russia and a simultaneous withdrawal of the United States constitutes the worst possible outcome.

Scenarios III and II contain different risks, while scenario I should clearly be avoided. Scenario III entails the risk of a return to the Cold War structure, albeit with changed power constellations (a West far superior to Russia). Scenarios IV and III also entail the risk of additional NATO missions in Northern Africa and the Persian Gulf and an increasing likelihood of Germany becoming engaged in limited military operations. Scenario II would be a radically new structure, with a Europe (and Germany) responsible for its own security, entailing the risk of a renationalization in Europe. Scenarios IV and II entail different gains. Scenario IV emphasizes stability. To a nation that placed a premium on creating its own security system, scenario II might also be highly attractive. Of course, scenario II is more likely, if Europe develops a stronger defense identity. This, then, is one of the unresolved strategic issues in German foreign policy: will Germany try to create a more independent European security architecture? If Germany is indeed a power of the status quo, this development would be rather unlikely.

While the structure of German *vulnerabilities* has remained *essentially unchanged,* German *sensitivities* to adversarial developments in Eastern Europe and Russia have *increased.* The disappearance of the iron curtain and the rigid East bloc structure made Germany much more sensitive to crises below the level of an open attack on German territory, especially uncontrolled migration, crime and nuclear terrorism. During the era of the East-West conflict, the situation in Europe was extremely stable, and developments in the East—with the exception of a full war—could have little impact on Germany. The iron curtain effectively shielded Germany from economic, interstate, and social developments in the region.

Today, social and political upheaval could bring waves of refugees to Germany. One example has been the Yugoslavia crisis. The potential emergence of adventurous regimes in Central Europe would probably not constitute a vital threat to Germany but would have severe implications nonetheless. Crime—heightened by the welfare differences between East and West—is being exported to Germany. A total of 27.1 percent of all crime suspects in Germany are foreigners.[45] The smuggling of nuclear contraband—plutonium as well as complete weapons—is possible under current conditions and directly threatens Germany. In the summer of 1994, for example, plutonium and uranium of Russian origin was confiscated in Germany. (There are some signs, however, that the smuggling of plutonium had been "engineered" by the *Bundesnachrichtendienst,* the German secret service.)[46] The rise in security threats below the level of full war is an incentive for Germany to become a net exporter of security to the East—but without upsetting traditional security structures.

Hanns Maull concludes that the increase in German power is based on shifts in the international system outside Germany—namely, the disintegration of the Soviet Union—and that Germany remains a highly vulnerable country.[47]

Economic asymmetries have widened in favor of Germany. Trading power is a major basis of Germany's economic influence in Europe—both in the West and in the East, where Germany has gained a significant number of "client" states. Germany's trade is widely diversified, yet sufficiently concentrated to enable Germany to be of paramount importance to its neighbors. Moreover, Germany is largely isolated from trade with the other large industrialized nations.[48] Germany could thus emerge as the leader of a powerful European trading bloc.

Germany's trading power, however, depends on the continuation of the European Union. The costs of any potential alternatives (partial breakdown of the EU and a German trading bloc extending eastward) would be very high. Germany can therefore be expected to remain supportive of the European institutions. With imports and exports amounting to 60 percent of its GDP, Germany is more of a "trading state" than the United States and Japan, whose economies are still predominantly based on domestic economic activity.[49] Without the EU, Germany would be far more vulnerable than either the United States or Japan.

Trading power derives from asymmetries in bilateral relationships.[50] A state may be highly dependent on imports from another state, but it might also be highly dependent on exports to this state. If the mutual dependencies are roughly equal, one might speak of "interdependence." If they are somewhat out of balance, the result might be termed "asymmetric interdependence." If they are very disparate, the result could be called "dependence."[51]

Table III.9   Germany's Trade with Particular Countries as Percentages of German and Country GDP

	Trade as percent of German GDP	Trade as percent of country GDP
U.S.	1.76	0.86
Japan	1.57	0.84
France	6.73	7.32
Italy	4.99	6.63
U.K.	3.94	5.63
Bel.-Lux.	3.88	25.95
Netherlands	4.82	23.56
Spain	1.86	4.39
Denmark	1.13	12.00
Austria	2.80	23.23
Switzerland	3.27	15.73
Sweden	1.18	7.30
Poland	0.06	10.65
Former Czechoslov.	0.72	18.89
Former USSR	1.18	8.33

Source: Compiled from IMF, ed., *Direction of Trade Statistics 1993* (Washington, D.C.: IMF, 1993), and Leon Podkaminer, *Country Reports: Bulgaia, Croatia, Czech Republic, Hungary, Poland, Romania, Russia, Slovakia, Slovenia, Ukraine* (Wien: Wiener Institut für internationale Wirtschaftsvergleiche, 1995), *National Accounts 1960–92, Vol. I.*

The sum of bilateral exports and imports, expressed as percentages of German GDP, denotes German dependencies on other countries. Expressed as percentages of the partner country's GDP, it denotes other countries' dependencies on Germany. The majority of Germany's trade—roughly two-thirds—is concentrated in Europe.[52] In all of these relationships (and thus in a majority of its trade), Germany is the dominant partner.

V

So far, we have found little evidence that German power has increased significantly. Tangible German power resources have not grown, and the long-range outlook for the German economy is not very bright. Germany's vulnerabilities have certainly decreased, but this cannot be translated into an independent military policy. Security partnership with the United States is still very important.

Yet, as I will argue below, Germany's influence is likely to increase. This seeming paradox can be explained by the conversion of tangible power resources into soft power. To a large extent, power is a social construct and reveals itself through interaction among various actors. A's ability to get things done will not only depend on A's tangible power resources, but also on the general willingness of B to accept A's leadership and the power B ascribes to A.[53] If B perceives an increase in A's power as undesirable, B will try to counterbalance moves by A.[54] If B expects things to be done by A because it ascribes the requisite capabilities to A, and if B is generally supportive of A's objectives, A has greater power than if B sees A as lacking in power, pursues different objectives than A, or mistrusts A.[55]

Germany's power is often overestimated. Partially because of Germany's impressive, but temporary display of financial power in East Germany, Eastern Europe, the Persian Gulf War and the EU between 1989 and 1993, other actors ascribe to it a financial prowess that the country simply does not have. This has led to rising expectations for Germany's contribution to European and world affairs. On a global scale, Germany does not have more power resources than it did, say, in 1978. Yet high expectations can be a source of political clout, even if realities have changed.

Traditional reservations and apprehensions about Germany have largely vanished, enabling Germany to play a larger role and to use its power more effectively. Other nations increasingly perceive Germany's power as being in their own interest. The positions of five key countries or groups of countries—(1) the United States, (2) France, (3) Russia, (4) Western Europe as a whole, and (5) the Central European states—indicate this development.

United States

Even after 1990, the United States remains the primary underwriter of German military security, with a considerable influence on Germany. And the United States seems to be ready to transfer more tasks to its ally. Previously, Germany had been treated as a junior partner destined to help execute U.S. strategy—important but junior nevertheless. Any independent moves by Germany during the Nixon,[56] Carter, or Reagan presidencies had been treated with resentment. Actual policies contained a strong element of unilateral U.S. decision making coupled with power-sharing rhetoric.[57]

George Bush was the first president to adopt the notion of a strong, independent Germany in a strong, independent Europe. In early 1989, Bush welcomed Germany as a "partner in leadership."[58] During the collapse of East Germany and the Eastern bloc, the Bush administration steadfastly supported German self-determination in the process of unification, even against the expressed concerns of the Soviet Union, Britain, and France.[59]

American-German collaboration during reunification strengthened the trust between both countries, setting the stage for the elevation of the U.S.-German relationship to the next level. According to Clinton, Germany would become a regional partner with full rights and responsibilities.[60] The United States moved further in the direction of a political division of labor. This elevates Germany to a new level of importance, and also of independence, in U.S. strategic thinking.[61]

Before and during his visits to Germany, President Clinton explicitly endorsed German leadership in creating a stronger European defense capacity, promoting unity in Europe, and assisting Eastern Europe. He explicitly stated that his administration had given "stronger support to these

Figure III.4   Germany's Security Calculus

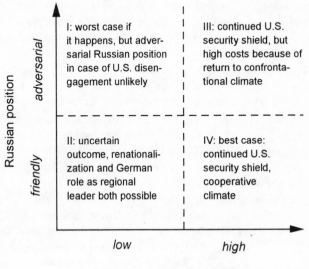

goals than previous administrations."[62] At the same time, he refrained from concrete proposals regarding how Germany would carry out its leadership role, referring instead to his "great confidence in the larger purposes and direction of this country. . . . Anything that can be done to enable Germany to fulfill the leadership responsibilities that it is plainly capable of fulfilling is a positive thing."[63]

Asked by a journalist whether the relationship with Britain or that with Germany was more important, Clinton made a statement that allowed the interpretation that Germany had replaced Britain as America's "special partner" in Europe: "The United states and Germany have a more immediate and tangible concern with these issues (helping Eastern Europe), even than our other friends in Europe."[64] Clinton's enthusiasm even caused some uneasiness in Germany, which also had to safeguard good relations and a low-key posture vis-à-vis France and Britain.

France and (Western) Europe

Reconciliation with France and close integration into Western Europe gave Germany acceptance and legitimacy in Europe and beyond, making France one of the two most important security partners for Germany. French motives toward Germany, however, are more mixed than American motives. Since World War II, France has regarded Germany with ambivalence. On the one hand, there has been a deep-felt need for reconciliation and integration to secure Europe's (and therefore France's) place in the world. On the other hand, there has also been an element of controlling Germany by integrating it.[65]

French policymakers have been acutely aware of the increase in German power—"what for the first time could mean an equal position to many in Germany is perceived as a strong imbalance in Germany's favor on the French side."[66] Whereas before, French elites had assumed that France's special position in NATO and its nuclear capabilities allowed it to deal with Germany on an equal (or superior) basis, the new geopolitical situation after 1989 and German unification has sometimes raised fears that French influence would decline.

This perception of a stronger Germany has led to a number of policy initiatives, which have often been driven by forward-looking as well as defensive objectives. The deepening of the EU would increase European identity and capabilities. But it was also seen as a way to neutralize Germany's increased power. Political scientist Ingo Kolboom quotes a German diplomat as describing the French policy toward Germany as a new "Rhine Union policy,"[67] which has been adapted to the changing circumstances.[68]

Common security interests may not be as easy to define as in the Cold War era. Although both nations share most concerns, Germany's priorities lie in Eastern Europe (i.e., the stabilization of the reform countries), while France's are in Northern Africa (i.e., the containment of fundamentalist Islamic forces, migration, and military adventurism in the area). German and French interests also diverge regarding NATO and the United States— Germany supports continuing U.S. engagement in Europe, while France would prefer a separate European defense identity.[69] Finally, France is pressing for a more protectionist trade policy in the European Union, while Germany is a (relative) champion of free trade. This has created conflicts with the United States, leaving Germany in the uneasy position of mediator.[70]

Should French policymakers come to the conclusion that German interests are diverging from French interests too strongly, counterbalancing behavior might ensue and German power would be adversely affected.[71] Though there are some signs of counterbalancing, the basic structure of French-German cooperation seems likely to remain intact as long as Germany is willing to make significant financial contributions to the EU. French-German cooperation after World War II has been deep and comprehensive. Organizations such as the German-French youth exchange program have served as models for recent German cooperation with Poland. Germany and France are each other's largest trading partners. While the French elites were still ambivalent about German reunification, French popular opinion widely supported a German reunification based on self-determination and a peaceful revolution.[72] In a survey in 1992, 56 percent of the French population stated that Germany was France's most reliable partner (versus 42 percent for the United States).[73] The Eurocorps and the strengthening of the EU have further strengthened institutional ties. When German units of the corps paraded on the Champs-Elysées on the occasion of the revolutionary celebration of July 1994, French opinion was largely sympathetic.[74] But if Germany opted to press for a fundamental reform of the EU, German-French cooperation might suffer greatly.

Other EU and EFTA Nations

As a group, the other EU and EFTA states are also very important to Germany. Most of Germany's trade is concentrated in this area, and German foreign direct investment is largely situated in Western Europe. Germany's unification and newfound international position have mostly been received positively in these nations. Tendencies of counterbalancing are much less pronounced than in France, because most of these nations (with the exception of Britain) are more concerned with their economic and social well-being, rather than their political status.

Germany's EU and EFTA neighbors form a fairly heterogeneous group: There are founding members of the community of six (the Netherlands, Belgium, and Luxembourg), who remain at the core of European integration and are loyal NATO members. There is a larger power with a strong transatlantic orientation (Great Britain), a NATO member whose population opted not to join the EU (Norway) and other EFTA states who opted to join the EU but to remain neutral (Austria, Sweden, Finland). Denmark is a NATO member that acceded to the EC together with Britain in 1972, but it opted against the Maastricht treaty in 1992. Switzerland is neither a member of the EU nor of any of the European defense communities. Italy, with an economy larger than Britain's, lacks the concern for international power and prestige that Great Britain and France have displayed at various times. Finally, there are the south European states of Spain and Portugal, longtime NATO allies who joined the European Community in 1986.

Despite their diversity, most of these nations largely accept and welcome the increase in German power. German unification only briefly evoked the ghosts of the past. Some leading politicians, for example in Denmark and Italy, made initial negative comments about German unification. However, the realities of interdependence had transcended concern over national power: popular opinion was largely supportive of unification in most Western European nations. In 1990, 52.4 percent of the Dutch population supported unification (23.2 percent "against"), 71 percent of the Belgian population supported unification (15 percent "against"), as well 56 percent of the Danish and 58 percent of the Austrian people.[75]

The smaller EU and EFTA nations have long accepted the web of interdependence woven by Germany. Germany is by far the most important trading partner for most of the smaller EU and EFTA nations. Some of Germany's neighbors have effectively tied their currencies to the German mark without much public debate and without official treaties (Netherlands, Belgium-Luxembourg, Austria).

There are still concerns about the political and cultural clout of an enlarged Germany. But Germany is seen by many as a champion of the smaller nations, unlike France and Britain. Germany's federalist political system, which transfers large powers to individual German states, can be a guarantee that the EU itself will be attentive to the needs of its smaller members.[76] As long as Germany continues to play by the rules of the EU, that is, as long as it subjects its foreign policy to highly multilateralized procedures, counterbalancing behavior by these nations is extremely unlikely.

Great Britain

Great Britain had the strongest initial reservations against a stronger Germany. But even Germany and Britain share a number of vital interests—a commitment to the American presence in Europe and NATO and an interest in the widening of the EU, though partially driven by different motives.[77]

Russia[78]

Germany has played an important role in Russia's foreign policy. In a short time, Germany has turned from potential enemy to major advocate of economic and political integration with the West. Under the leadership of President Boris Yeltsin, Russia has used Germany to gain access to international institutions, to demand assistance from the Western community and as a direct provider of assistance. Germany has been a key ally to Russia in all of these processes.[79] Germany is Russia's largest trading partner, accounting for 15 percent of Russia's imports and approximately 10 percent of its exports. German-Russian trade is twice the volume of U.S.-Russian trade.[80] The United States may be more important to Russia than Germany because of reasons of prestige and cooperation in global security affairs. The issue is not entirely clear, however. Some Russian voices ascribe priority to the Russian-German relationship.[81]

At the Houston economic summit of July 1990, Kohl asked the other G-7 nations to follow Germany in providing more economic assistance to the Soviet Union. Later, Kohl pressed for Russian participation in the summit, which was first realized in the form of a special meeting in 1992, with full participation in the political part of the summit of 1994. In October 1992, the German and Russian foreign ministers started a process of far-reaching political consultation.[82] In December 1992, Kohl promised additional financial assistance to Russia. Kohl was the first Western statesman to visit Russia after the reformist Gaidar had been voted out of office.[83]

In an interview with *Le Figaro,* Yeltsin openly acknowledged that Germany had done more than any other country to support the reforms in

Russia.[84] At some point, Russian foreign minister *Andrei Kozyrev* even referred to a German-Russian "Axis"—a phrase that was promptly rejected by the German foreign minister.

German-Russian relations have a solid underpinning of popular opinion. In a 1991 survey, only 14 percent of Russians interviewed in nine cities responded that united Germany could be a security threat to Russia, whereas 66 percent said it would not be a threat.[85] A growing network of political and economic cooperation, treaties, and personal ties bolsters German-Russian relations. The Federal Republic's security and economic guarantees during the reunification process laid the foundation for acceptance by the (then) Soviet Union.[86] During Yeltsin's visit to Bonn in May 1994, Kohl committed to promoting Russia's integration into the G-7, a process that, according to Kohl, "would lead to the G-8."[87] Subsequently, Yeltsin participated as a full partner in the Naples summit of 1994. Kohl also strongly supported Yeltsin in the difficult year of 1993, reassuring him at every important juncture either through personal visits or telephone calls.[88]

The relocation of the Russian troops stationed in Germany was conducted smoothly and characterized by trust and cooperation.[89] President Yeltsin noted that "the withdrawal of the Western Army became a test of the durability of the relations between Russia and Germany. . . . The common work of thousands on both sides became a large school for practical Russian-German partnership and cooperation."[90] A direct phone line has been installed between the Kremlin and the Federal Chancellery.[91] Transnational cooperation is increasing.[92] The German and Russian militaries have made some tentative steps toward closer cooperation.[93] During the controversy surrounding NATO enlargement, Germany also proposed a special status for Russia vis-à-vis NATO to take into account Russian sensitivities.[94]

Despite those positive developments in Russia, the situation might change in case of domestic upheaval and change in Russia or a revisionist foreign policy. Russia's treatment of the "near abroad" may lead to destabilization and is not commensurate with Germany's interpretation of international law.

Central and Eastern Europe (and Central Asia)

Germany's eastern neighbors consist of two tiers. A first tier consists of (mostly) immediate neighbors comprising the Visegrad states (Poland, the Czech Republic, the Slovak Republic, Hungary), Slovenia, Croatia, and the Baltic states; a second tier comprises the southern Central European states—Romania, Bulgaria, Bosnia, Serbia, and states constituting the Russian "near abroad"—Belarus, the Ukraine, and the states of Central Asia. As with Russia, with these states Germany changed from opponent to partner virtually overnight. Different from Russia, states in the first tier not only see a very important economic partner in Germany, but also wish Germany to play a larger role in their military security. In particular, they see in Germany an advocate of NATO enlargement.

For most of the states in the first tier, Germany is already the most important trading partner.[95] Most are actively seeking membership in the EU and in NATO and want active integration in the Western community. In 1998, Poland, Hungary, and the Czech Republic were formally accepted as members of NATO. Often, Germany was a leader in these processes, although Russian sensibilities also had to be weighed carefully by Germany. Defense minister Volker Rühe promoted an early NATO membership for states of the region.[96] Germany also led in forming the North Atlantic Cooperation Council.[97] Foreign minister Klaus Kinkel supported the Baltic states' concerns for closer association with the West.[98]

Past traumas dating back to World War II and before, though not forgotten, have been quickly overcome by pragmatic concerns. The cases of Poland and the Czech Republic may serve as an example for the whole group. Poland had suffered greatly under German occupation in World War II. After the victory over Germany, Stalin retained the territories claimed from Poland in World War II. The country was "moved" westward by resettling the population of its eastern provinces into Germany's eastern provinces (East Prussia, Silesia, Pomerania). Millions of Germans were expelled from their homes. Germany effectively lost one-quarter of its core territory.[99]

Until unification, Germany did not recognize its territorial losses, although it had pledged not to violate existing borders by force. Immediately before unification, Kohl refused to issue a clear statement about the border issue to placate the Silesian League and the League of Expelled Germans. This created considerable anxiety in Poland. In early 1990, over 70 percent of Poles feared a security threat from Germany.[100] During the two-plus-four negotiations, however, Poland was invited to join the discussion on the border issue, and both German states pledged to recognize the Oder-Neiße (Odra-Nysa) line as the permanent legal border. United Germany realized this pledge and Polish fears subsided quickly.

The Polish government is seeking close cooperation with Germany. An internal report by the German Federal Press Office was entitled "Reconciliation, Trust and Good Neighborly Relations—the German

Polish Relationship."[101] In 1994, Poland and Germany signed an environmental treaty whose level of detail is equaled only by the French-German treaty.[102] A Polish-German national organization for youth exchanges was modeled after the French-German organization.[103] In 1993, both states agreed on closer military cooperation. The German Henning von Ondarza, former supreme commander of the NATO forces center, became senior adviser to the Polish army.[104] German tourism is enriching the Polish border towns, and many Poles have found temporary work in Germany.[105]

The invitation of German president Roman Herzog to the celebrations commemorating the anniversary of the Warsaw uprising by Polish President Lech Walesa stirred much controversy in Poland. The subsequent approval that Herzog's thoughtful speech received by most Poles is symptomatic of fundamentally sound relations.[106] Hans-Adolf Jacobsen states that "The fundamental conflict [the border issue, M.O.] has been resolved, while common interests dominate."[107] In an article entitled "Facets of the German-Polish Partnership," the Swiss *Neue Züricher Zeitung* wrote in 1994: "The relations between Germany and Poland fifty years after WW II are better than anyone could have hoped in 1945."[108]

Czech-German relations, though not burdened by direct territorial claims, are hindered by conflicting interpretations of the 1938 Munich Treaty.[109] Despite highly courageous and conciliatory statements made by Czechoslovak president Vaclav Havel after the fall of the Berlin Wall, both nations are taking much longer to resolve their open issues than Poland and Germany.[110]

For historical reasons, the Czech Republic and Poland represented the most difficult cases of German cooperation with Eastern neighbors. Yet in both nations official policy and (to a lesser, but still solid, extent) popular opinion has supported close cooperation with Germany. The Slovak Republic, Hungary, Croatia, and Slovenia are all historically closer to Germany. Support has been stronger from the beginning.[111] The Baltic states have often sought security reassurances from Germany.[112]

The states of the second tier have also strongly solicited German support. Bulgaria campaigned for membership in the EU in Germany first.[113] Romania sees a partner in Germany with regard to EU membership and return of the Moldovan territories.[114] Ukrainian president Leonid Kravchuk campaigned very openly for German support during his first official visit.[115] Kazakhstan actively seeks economic support.[116] Germany and the United States were the first states to open embassies in Georgia.[117] The Ukraine, Kazakhstan, and Georgia all are interested in closer security cooperation with Germany.[118] The same is true for Azerbaijan and Belarus.[119]

VI

The German economic system, its foreign policy doctrine, and its federal constitution equip it with considerable soft power.[120] If Germany is indeed the "prototype of a promising future" or "economically, politically and intellectually a country, whose time has come," Germany should be able to exert considerable influence, be it because foreign governments adopt part of the German doctrine or be it that their respective populations view the German system and policies favorably.[121] Germany's acceptance of international limitations on its sovereignty and its active pursuit of multilateralism should become increasingly attractive.

The German model of postnational military policy may point the way to Europe's future. There was widespread popular protest in Germany when France resumed nuclear testing in 1995. (The German government, for good reasons, did not join in.) Contrary to what one might have expected, German popular protests did not create a unanimous wave of resentment in France, but found resonance in large parts of the French population. French president Jacques Chirac even offered to put French nuclear weapons under European command to legitimize the testing. Even if this was only a political maneuver, the multilateralization of security policies according to the German model seems to be an idea with considerable appeal, at least in Europe.[122]

The German federal system is another point of attraction, especially for the small states in the European Union. The second legislative chamber in Germany, the Bundesrat, has an equalizing effect between larger and smaller states. Smaller states have a proportionately much higher vote than larger states. Thus

> The Germans, with considerable powers already distributed to jealous Länder (in a way that was not artificially imposed on them by World War II victors but was an outgrowth of centuries of splintered principalities) will adapt nicely to the new regional-based dynamics of Europe. . . . Neither Paris nor London has yet reconciled itself to such decentralization.[123]

Along with the decentralization of power, German federalism is a highly effective example of a vertical division of labor. This type of federalism might also be a promising model for Europe.

The German economic and legal system, characterized by the social market economy, has had a considerable attraction for reformers in Central and Eastern Europe. In many nations, the harsh reforms proposed by the World Bank were viewed with skepticism. A more "social" capitalism took hold instead, for example in Poland, Hungary, and the Czech Republic. In Russia, both Yeltsin and Victor Chernomyrdin had conceded by the end of 1992 that in economic affairs, Germany was the most important Western partner.[124] Other reforming nations from Central Asia to Central Europe increasingly turned towards Germany.

German legal experts and think tanks have helped to reshape the legal systems of many reforming countries. In Estonia they assisted in the writing of a constitution, in Hungary they made possible in the adoption of the entire German civil code.[125] Germany has supported legal reform through private and political foundations, such as the German Foundation for International Legal Cooperation, which is active in Bulgaria, Estonia, Latvia, Lithuania, Poland, Russia, the Czech Republic, Ukraine, Hungary, and Belarus.[126] The states of Central Asia are within the domain of the German Ministry for Economic Cooperation. Though there is a lively competition with American experts and the American legal system, a legal order modeled after German law to enable a smooth adaptation of EU laws is highly attractive to many states.[127]

Language and Culture

Germany's cultural clout is becoming more noticeable: out of the 16 million students learning German worldwide, 12 million are living in Eastern Europe and the former Soviet Union.[128] Germany has also sent an increasing number of language teachers to the reforming countries.[129] (Despite this growing influence, English is still by far the most important language.) German minorities exist in some countries, particularly Russia, Kazakhstan, Romania, and Poland. Contrary to former times, these minorities are not a reason for concern anymore, but contribute to closer links between the nations. Some 326,000 Poles have claimed membership in the cultural-educational society of the German minority and up to 1.5 million Polish residents may be eligible for dual citizenship under German law.[130] The Polish government, which for a long time had denied even the existence of a German minority, now affords a relaxed policy vis-à-vis the German minority.[131] The German minority issue in Russia has been treated in a similarly relaxed manner.[132]

Immigration and Political Refugees

In 1992 and 1993, acts of violence committed by Germans against foreigners were a focus of German and international concern. From January to November 1992, 1,912 such acts of violence against foreigners took place.[133] David Keitly speaks of "over fifteen thousand acts of hatred."[134] The international press reported in detail about Germany's problems with xenophobic violence. President Richard von Weizsäcker made it the central issue of a speech on November 8, 1992.[135]

Despite these events, a rapidly rising stream of immigrants and political asylum-seekers turned to Germany in the early 1990s, testifying to the continuing attractiveness of Germany. From a low of 20,000 in 1983, the number of asylum-seekers rose to a high of 438,000 in 1993. Between 1980 and 1990, 44 percent of all asylum-seekers coming to Europe selected Germany as their destination. In the 1990s, this percentage surpassed 50 percent.[136] By 1993, Germany was home to 6.5 million immigrants, representing some 8 percent of the total population. Only such small and attractive states as Switzerland had to cope with a higher number of asylum-seekers per capita than Germany.

Germany's liberal law for political asylum, born out of the experiences of the Third Reich, had helped to create this situation. Article 16 of the constitution granted every applicant the right to a full legal process, and, if political persecution is recognized, the automatic right to stay in Germany. During the long period (often, many years) that such a process could take, the German social system would pay generous subsistence to the applicant, while perversely not allowing him or her to work. After long political debates, the Bundestag passed a modified immigration law in 1993, which promptly reduced the stream of asylum-seekers and made it somewhat easier to deal with misuse of the system. Persons who enter Germany through so-called "safe third countries" (e.g., the EU, Poland, the Czech Republic) can be sent back without process. As a consequence of reduced immigration, acts of violence and the number of right-wing sympathizers decreased markedly. Even after 1993, German retains a liberal asylum law by international standards and is the destination of many asylum-seekers.

Since the influx of migrant workers from EC countries and Turkey in the 1960s, Germany has been an immigration country. Not all major political parties have accepted this fact; especially in the conservative CDU/CSU there have been repeated discussions between the proponents of a "multicultural society" and the opponents of making Germany an immigration country.[137] The right-wing influence, however, has been isolated and has been shrinking since 1993. All major social forces, police included, unconditionally support the rights of immigrants. In November 1992, hundreds of thousands of Germans silently demonstrated for the rights of foreigners, thus showing that the majority of Germans opposes xenophobia. Despite a more restrictive immigration law, Germany continues to attract many foreigners, which also bolsters its "soft" power.

IV

The Loss of Innocence: Germany and Military Missions Abroad, 1990–1995

The Bundeswehr is an instrument to secure peace in the hands of the political leadership. It is a treaty army. Because of its dependency on the forces and means of the treaty nations, it cannot be an instrument of purely national action. The task of the Bundeswehr is defensive, in peace, during tensions, and in wartime. This is the content of the constitution, which in article 87 provides the forces exclusively with a defense mission.

—*Government White Book 1970/71*[1]

I

Between 1990 and 1995, Germany's military and security doctrine underwent radical changes. From 1949 to 1990, Germany declined to use its military for any task other than self-defense. This, in effect, meant that the military was not used at all. Within a short period, military missions abroad again became a viable option for German military policy. In July 1994, the German supreme court issued an opinion on Article 24 of the constitution: German forces could participate in collective peacekeeping and humanitarian missions as long as they were sent by a collective mandate to enforce or ensure peace. Only a year later, German airplanes became involved in actual combat missions over the former Yugoslavia.

An outside-in model explains this radical change well. Demands by the Western Allies were unequivocal: Germany was to make stronger contributions to joint military efforts. Many in Germany's foreign policy establishment were initially shocked that the country was to lose its innocence. But that shock quickly subsided. Germany was obliged to its allies, and it had always placed a high value on consensus. Outside pressures and expectations caused the government to redefine national interests, which in turn had consequences for public opinion and the development of a new domestic consensus. The process experienced some delays and setbacks, but overall this simple model captures the period. With the exception of the Socialist Unity Party, the SED, all German parties and the German population grew increasingly activist.

With strong international pressure to participate in military missions abroad, two conflicting objectives had to be reconciled by the German government: the need for Germany to act in consensus with its partners and the need to maintain a defensive, mainly nonmilitary security doctrine. These conflicting values ensured that there would be internal debate. A united domestic front against the change in military doctrine could never be created despite popular opinion opposing a more activist military policy.

This radical change in Germany's security doctrine fits our basic "realist" model. Though the absolute level of Germany's security had certainly increased after reunification, Germany's basic security dependencies did not change all that much.[2] Germany remained heavily dependent on the Western alliance for its security. A policy of restraint during the years from 1990 to 1994 could have eventually endangered Germany's security alliances. As to the alternatives: a neutral, nonnuclear Germany would not have been able to provide for its own security. A nuclear and well-armed Germany, on the other hand, might have increased Germany's autonomy, but not its security—counterbalancing and mistrust in Western Europe would outweigh the gains from an autonomous security policy. Ultimately, it is the paradox of the period that Germany acquired more capabilities for military action in order not to pursue a more autonomous military policy, and that such a nonautonomous security policy is in the "realist" interest of a middle power such as Germany.

II

At the outset of the Persian Gulf crisis, German interests, including security interests, were complex, ill-defined, and difficult to disentangle. Kaiser and Becher write that they included the maintenance of a close relationship with the United States, the conclusion of the two-plus-four negotiations, prevention of disturbances in the unification process, a special responsibility for Israel, strengthening of multilateralism by strengthening the UN, and a demonstration that Germany would be a reliable partner in crisis management.[3] Moreover, Germany was in the final phase of the two-plus-four negotiations, which were dramatically changing the balance of power in Europe. An agreement about the withdrawal of all Soviet troops from German soil was imminent. The German leadership feared that any sign of resurgent German military strength outside Europe could change the Soviet position.

To add to this complex situation, the international security environment itself was in transformation. The years from 1989 to 1991 were a particularly dense period in international relations. Within two years, the division of Germany was overcome, most states in the former East bloc adopted democratic constitutions, the CFE Treaty was negotiated, and the Warsaw Pact and the Soviet Union were dissolved in April 1991 and December 1991, respectively.

After 1989, the heretofore dominant East-West conflict and the division of much of the political world into two stable alliances quickly faded into the background. The post-1990 international system was characterized by a paradox: small wars and major domestic upheaval became increasingly likely at a time when the risk of a large nuclear confrontation or a world war was greatly reduced.[4] It became easier for smaller powers to start wars for ethnic, religious, or nationalistic reasons without the risk of an international escalation of the conflict. Thus, "contradictory, asynchronous and ambivalent processes of militarization and civilization" have characterized the global system.[5]

These changes presented considerable challenges to the international community, which have not been overcome to date. How could states contribute to the development of a peaceful and prosperous international order? Should states intervene in smaller conflicts for reasons other than self-defense or vital strategic interests? If so, under which conditions should this happen, which means should be selected, and what should be the general guidelines for the exercise of national force in the new international system? The second Gulf war provided the first example of potential post-Cold War cooperation in crisis management and a landmark for the security policy of the new Germany.

The Persian Gulf crisis erupted before Germany had completely negotiated its unification treaty and a bilateral treaty with the Soviet Union. Even so, its Western partners pressed it for a military contribution to the Persian Gulf War. Germany was confronted with a serious dilemma. It was seen as a key actor in the new international environment. Its allies pressed it hard to play a more active role in peacekeeping and within the UN. To what extent should Germany continue its particular postwar military doctrine (that is, a limitation to self-defense), and to what extent should it contribute to international efforts at crisis management by military means?

During the two–plus–four negotiations, Germany had achieved all of its major strategic and security objectives: Germany would remain a full NATO member. German NATO forces could be stationed on the territory of the former East Germany.[6] The threat of large-scale conventional and nuclear war in central Europe was considerably reduced, and Germany was allowed to freely choose its security alliance. Germany accepted some limitations on its sovereignty. Only Allied forces and nuclear weapons were not allowed in the eastern part of Germany.[7] Germany confirmed its renunciation of ABC weapons. The strength of its forces was to be limited to 370,000.[8] Article 2 of the treaty rules out a war of aggression.[9] Those limitations, however, were fully welcomed by Germans as being in their own interest. For a brief moment, it seemed to Germans that they could continue their "civilian" postwar policy of focusing on defense and economic growth.

This perspective proved illusory before it even had time to fully develop. The Persian Gulf War surprised a nation that was neither psychologically nor militarily prepared for military missions abroad and that was in the middle of an exceptionally complex international situation. But united Germany was perceived as a major power by its allies and was expected to contribute to the joint military effort. Thus, self-perception and international perceptions were in stark contrast.

After the invasion of Kuwait by the Iraqi army on August 2, 1990, the United States reacted quickly in making clear that it would not tolerate the aggression and that it was prepared to fight for a "rollback," if necessary. One day after the invasion, President Bush began to build the anti-Iraq war coalition. On August 5, he sent the first major contingent of troops to Saudi Arabia. On August 8, he publicly announced large-scale military support for Saudi Arabia, bolstered by approval ratings of 80 percent.[10] President Bush asked for allied assistance at an early stage. England and France, among others, supported the effort by contributing military forces.

The German government agreed to these demands in principle but tried to keep a low profile, providing mostly financial and logistical assistance. This caution was based on concerns about the Soviet Union, but also on the recollections of a nation that had experienced deep domestic splits during the NATO double-track decision. The German government indicated that it would work for German participation in future joint efforts after the constitutional questions had been resolved.

On August 16, German mine sweepers were ordered to the Mediterranean, but they were also ordered not to participate in any operations until the war had ended. In a report to the Bundestag, Hans-Dietrich Genscher said on August 23, 1990, that the German constitution currently forbade a German participation in the war, and that he had explained this to the other states.[11] This official position was based on a compromise between the FDP and the CDU, who did not want to jeopardize the first all-German elections in October and the final phase of the two-plus-four negotiations. One day before the deadline Iraq had been given for a withdrawal from Kuwait, chancellor Kohl declared his solidarity with the allies, "who carry the main burden in this conflict."[12] Germany worked on a far-reaching spectrum of support measures for the alliance short of active military support. Helmut Kohl decided to keep the plans secret and to present them personally to James Baker on September 15.[13] The short period of German silence, however, was sufficient to invite decidedly negative international press reactions.[14]

Though Germany did not send combat troops, the Persian Gulf War did lead to the "largest mobilization of Germans abroad since World War II"[15] and became a test case for fundamental principles of German foreign policy since 1945. For the first time since 1945, the Federal Republic sent weapons into crisis zones. It stationed 18 Alphajets and 270 troops in Turkey, close to the Turkish-Iranian border. Israel received a battery of Patriot missiles and the promise of two long-desired submarine vessels. "These actions effectively made Germany a part of the war coalition" wrote *Der Spiegel*.[16]

During 1990–91, Germany provided the alliance with financial and logistical assistance and equipment to the tune of over DM 17 billion. This amounted to more than one-third of Germany's annual defense budget.[17] It included DM 9.1 billion in direct financial contributions to the United States, financial contributions of DM 2.2 billion to Israel, Great Britain, France, and Turkey, provision of military equipment to Turkey, the United States, Israel, Great Britain, the Netherlands, France, and Egypt, and economic assistance of over DM 2.5 billion to Egypt, Turkey, Jordan, Israel, Syria, Tunisia, and international organizations to help offset the effects the embargo against Iraq had on these countries. A large part of the logistics for U.S. forces was handled on German soil, and the German government made sure that trains and air transport were handled with priority. Nevertheless, Germany was seen by many as "the reluctant ally" and a "free rider."

Throughout and after the Gulf War, there was considerable international pressure on Germany. The criticism by its main ally, the United States, was moderate but discernible. George Bush urged united Germany to "take responsibilities for leadership in our commonwealth of nations." To "conclude that these challenges are not everyone's concern" would mean putting "at risk everything we have achieved."[18] The CDU/CSU ministers in the government and the respective parties were in consensus that there was to be no second episode in which Germany would stand aside. This would entail grave risks for Germany's international position, endangering even such foundations of Germany's security as NATO.[19] Foreign minister Hans-Dietrich Genscher therefore declared before the UN general assembly in September 1991 that Germany was ready to assume larger international responsibilities.[20] But it was to be a complicated process until Germany was formally ready to contribute to military missions abroad.

III

Between 1991 and 1994, Germany's situation remained unclear. It was not entirely certain whether the constitution allowed military missions abroad. Large parts of the population remained opposed to such missions. Nina Philippi counts at least five major positions in the debate.[21] According to the first opinion, missions abroad were permitted in all cases except for the preparation and conduct of a war of aggression. The second opinion admitted Bundeswehr missions in all cases that were covered by the UN charter. One expert thought that peace enforcement was possible, while peacekeeping was not admissible. Opinion four wanted to allow only peacekeeping and peace enforcement missions under UN command. Fighting missions authorized by the UN but under a different command (such as in the Persian Gulf War) were inadmissible. Self-defense under Article 51 of the UN charter without UN authorization was inadmissible outside the framework of NATO and the WEU. Opinion five finally stated that Bundeswehr participation in UN missions and missions outside the defense of the NATO and WEU treaty area were inadmissible. In 1994, the supreme court legitimized international missions with only moderate conditions.

Against this domestic backdrop, the German government acted decisively: it created new realities step by step by sending soldiers to humanitarian missions in Somalia and Cambodia and by participating in the air-lift and sea reconnaissance operations in former Yugoslavia, risking that some of actions would be ruled unconstitutional in retrospect. Before the decision of the supreme court, the Bundeswehr participated in nine different UN operations, in: (1) Turkey and Iran; (2) the Persian Gulf; (3) Iraq and Bahrain; (4) Cambodia; (5) the former Yugoslavia; (6) the Adriatic Sea; (7) Somalia, Kenya, and Djibouti; (8) Georgia; and (9) Rwanda, Burundi, Kenya, and Zaire. Given these actions, the German government could hardly be called "cautious." As early as 1992, it was clear that the government had broken with its previous military doctrine. In a speech before the thirty-third Bundeswehr officer's congress on May 12, 1992, Chancellor Kohl declared: "Security means more than the ability to defend oneself against a common attack," and demanded a "preemptive security policy." The Bundeswehr was to support NATO in crisis management. None of the international partners would accept a limitation to peace-keeping missions.

The issue of missions abroad had surfaced before in the 1980s, but it had quickly been buried again. Some experts and decision makers had begun to reconsider the situation when the United States repeatedly called upon its European allies for more burden-sharing in the early 1980s. In reaction to these requests, Helmut Schmidt had commissioned a legal study to evaluate the possibility of sending German military missions abroad. The study, presented in June 1982, concluded that the constitution allowed strict self-defense, and defense of and assistance to treaty partners in the framework of NATO and WEU, but did not allow missions to defend purely economic interests. It dealt only vaguely with participation in UN missions.[22] The study became the basis of two decisions by the Federal Security Council, through which the Federal Republic effectively limited its ability to contribute to international crisis management. Foreign minister Hans-Dietrich Genscher played an important role in these decisions. This also explains the prevailing interpretation that persisted when the CDU/CSU-FDP coalition assumed power in 1982.

In April 1992, Volker Rühe succeeded Gerhard Stoltenberg as defense minister. In his inauguration speech, Rühe stressed that the mission of the Bundeswehr had expanded[23] and wasted no time in demonstrating his resolution to fulfill the changing requirements. In May, Rühe sent 150 medical personnel of the Bundeswehr to a UN mission in Cambodia.[24] For the moment, there were no major protests by the SPD. Shortly thereafter, Rühe sent the destroyer *Bavaria,* three reconnaissance planes, and 377 soldiers to the Adriatic sea to support an embargo against Serbia under a

WEU mandate.[25] Their mission was "to monitor ship movements to collect information and to transmit this to the UN." There was to be no application of force.[26] According to Rühe, "Germany would have isolated itself without this minimum contribution."[27] The SPD called upon the supreme court to stop the operation.

In 1993, a domestic controversy over German participation in NATO air surveillance of the flight ban over Bosnia escalated to a "political-satire."[28] Foreign minister Kinkel and justice minister Sabine Leutheuser-Schnarrenberger announced that they would resign if German soldiers mounted the AWACS planes before the supreme court made a decision.[29] The FDP strictly opposed combat missions, demanding a clarification or change of the constitution as a precondition. When it became clear that the court would not consider the case before the fall of 1993, the members of the governing coalition agreed on an unusual procedure. The FDP would sue its own government to bring about a clarification. *Der Spiegel* concluded: "One coalition partner sues the other one, although both want the same result. Seldom has German national policy been this contradictory."[30] The SPD, too, addressed a complaint to the supreme court.

The supreme court declared on April 8, 1993, that the complaints were justified but declined to impose an injunction against the AWACS missions. It argued that forbidding the missions at this early stage would entail grave risks: "The hearings have shown that a withdrawal of the German soldiers from the planes would considerably weaken the AWACS unit and endanger the enforcement of the flight ban. This would damage the trust the Federal Republic had built with its allies through steady cooperation." The disadvantages if an injunction was not imposed, but participation was later found unconstitutional, were thought to be less grave by the judges.[31] The final decision had yet to be made.

On April 12, 1993, UN secretary-general Boutros Boutros-Ghali requested a German battalion for the UNOSOM II operation in Somalia to provide "logistical support in pacified areas."[32] Volker Rühe quickly announced the participation of German soldiers in this humanitarian mission. A transport battalion, protected by two companies of light infantry, was to support the effort in Somalia.[33] The SPD addressed a new complaint to the supreme court with the goal of having a temporary injunction against the Somalia mission. SPD chairman Björn Engholm explained the party position: "The SPD cannot tolerate arbitrary violation of rules by stretching the constitution."[34] The SPD did not succeed before the supreme court with its petition to call back the German soldiers.[35] The judges, however, demanded cooperation between government and parliament and requested that the approval of the Bundestag with a simple majority be solicited as a "constitutive act" for such missions.

The long-awaited judgment of the supreme court on July 12, 1994, finally clarified the situation. "The second senate of the court decides that the mission on which the government had decided in Somalia, the Adriatic Sea and in AWACS planes over the former Yugoslavia have their legal foundation in Article 24, paragraph 2 of the constitution. On the basis of this article, the federal government had subjected itself to systems of collective security. With this decision, it also has accepted the obligations that typically go hand in hand with such a system." The judges made missions conditional on the approval of a simple majority of the Bundestag. According to the judges, the constitution did not give the power over missions exclusively to the executive, but integrated the legislature. Thus the government had violated the constitution by sending troops to the Adriatic and in flight over the former Yugoslavia without consulting the Bundestag.[36]

Most parties welcomed the decision. The voices of the victors, even of such outspoken proponents of military missions as Volker Rühe, were guarded. Rühe called for "restraint, to not to give the impression that the decision is the starting point for an inflation of missions."[37] Foreign minister Kinkel warned of a relapse into power politics and declared that Germany would continue its "culture of restraint."[38] If the question arose whether and when to send German soldiers, each case should be judged according to whether "special German interests were affected, and whether our special, value-oriented foreign policy requires our engagement." The FDP demanded a "deployment law to prescribe the action to be taken in different cases and the necessity for Bundestag approval."[39] Kinkel also demanded that the Adriatic and Yugoslavia missions be retroactively sanctioned by the Bundestag. For this purpose, the Bundestag met for a special session on July 22, 1994, for which many members had been called back from summer vacations. In a personal (that is, nonanonymous) vote, 424 of 488 members approved both missions. Some hard-liners, such as the leader of the CDU/CSU parliamentarians, Wolfgang Schäuble, interpreted the court decision more actively: "We would deny realities if we continued to regard strict restraint as the general virtue of German foreign policy."[40] Schäuble's position, however, was not representative of the mainstream.

The SPD interpreted the decision most restrictively. SPD leader Günther Verheugen claimed, for example, that UN missions had to be under UN leadership and command. Thus the Persian Gulf War had not been a UN mission, but an American mission with UN sanctioning. This would not constitute a collective system of security, and German participation had therefore not been justified. NATO and WEU would therefore not be able to conduct missions out of area without a UN mandate.[41]

Despite this battle by the SPD, it was clear that the opportunities for any German government to engage in military missions abroad had vastly increased. The *Süddeutsche Zeitung* commented: "The court decision put the final period behind one of the most ardent foreign policy debates of the past years. The judges have decided upon a very loose interpretation of the constitution: Article 24, which deals with the participation of Germany in collective security systems, according to the judges allows everything that had been highly contested heretofore, it allows military assistance to allies in the whole world." Only a war of aggression and unilateral action continued to be ruled out by the constitution. Within four short years, one of the two major pillars of Germany's security doctrine had radically changed.

IV

Bureaucratic politics explains some of the more intricate dynamics of the process. The defense and foreign ministries were the major catalysts of change. The defense ministry showed great interest in expanding its mission and securing a new legitimization. The foreign office emphasized international law, UN missions and humanitarian tasks, resulting in a more restrictive course. Both actively propagated international solidarity, although the emphasis was slightly different. The defense ministry was primarily Atlanticist and NATO-oriented (despite the missions in Cambodia and Somalia), whereas the foreign ministry was globalist and UN-oriented. This implied a difference in the perception of the role of states: whereas the foreign ministry had supranationalist ambitions, planners in the defense ministry viewed international cooperation more as a process among sovereign states.

In this controversy, statements by the chancellor often remained vague. After a long tenure, Helmut Kohl had increasingly begun to transcend bureaucratic controversy. This established a pattern that was later repeated during the discussion on NATO enlargement: Kohl let the foreign and defense ministers take various initiatives, assuming the role of ultimate arbiter. Whereas he leaned toward Rühe's position in the case of missions abroad, he was closer to Kinkel concerning NATO expansion. Helmut Kohl did actively support a more activist German role in line with his party's position and Germany's increased responsibility in the world. His main foreign policy project in the period between 1991 and 1993, however, was the creation of the European Union, in which he invested extensive personal effort. Kohl was also the creator of the so-called (and short-lived) Kohl doctrine, according to which German soldiers were not to be sent into areas where the Wehrmacht had been as an occupation force. (The doctrine died in 1994–95.)

In the defense ministry, support for crisis management began to evolve rapidly. Dieter Wellershof, the outgoing inspector general of the Bundeswehr, strongly advocated international crisis management. *Der Spiegel* wrote, "The nonparticipation of German troops in the Persian Gulf War had left many officers, especially in the international planning staffs, with an inferiority complex."[42] Those officers, according to *Der Spiegel,* "were afraid that Germany would be degraded to a second-class NATO member."[43] By mid-1991, the inspectors of the three forces had begun to elaborate concepts for out-of-area missions. In 1991, the Bundeswehr journal *Informationen für die Truppe* devoted one-third of its 74 pages to UN missions and fighting missions out of area. This initiative by military officers was especially sensitive in Germany, which placed a high value on civilian leadership of the military. Defense minister Gerhard Stoltenberg continued to utter general comments to the effect that the Bundeswehr would have to consider risks and challenges outside Europe.[44]

It took over a year before the political leadership of the Bundeswehr reacted with a formal position paper. In early 1992, Gerhard Stoltenberg presented "military-political and military-strategic guidelines for the restructuring of the Bundeswehr." The paper specified new tasks for the Bundeswehr: maintaining access to strategic raw materials, securing free world trade, and participating in collective missions beyond NATO.[45] The paper stated:

> After the end of the specific and direct military threat of the East-West confrontation, a latent and partially acute and varied conflict potential is at the fore of a preventive security policy. . . . A solely German or European perspective is not adequate for the security of Germany and future challenges. . . . The evaluation of risks must be done with a European and alliance view, but always with a global perspective. Germany must consider a wider horizon in the frame of the various collective systems of crisis and conflict management.[46]

The cabinet rejected the paper in a rare agreement of FDP, CDU, and CSU colleagues.[47] Afterwards, Genscher commented that "defense of the home territory" had received much too little consideration in the paper.[48] The maintenance of access to strategic raw materials, securing free world trade, and the participation of the Bundeswehr in collective missions beyond NATO were perfectly legitimate goals in a traditional security framework. But this traditionalist interpretation of security policy ushered in Stoltenberg's quick decline. A short time later, Stoltenberg resigned (though for different reasons). Preservation of access to raw materials was deleted from subsequent strategy papers.

When Volker Rühe became defense minister, he initially warned the military not to create the impression that "it was the main task of the Bundeswehr to stroll between Mexico City and Calcutta. The (pacifist) instincts of the German people, which had grown in over 40 years, could not simply be commanded away."[49] The Germans would be prepared neither materially nor psychologically for missions abroad. Soon it became clear, however, that Rühe's strong words had the primary purpose of asserting his position as defense minister against his own bureaucracy. With the exception of the military's enthusiasm for a unified military command staff (the old general staff), he shared the military's desire to prepare Germany for missions abroad and quickly began to press the issue. The Bundeswehr was to be ready for peacekeeping missions in 1993.[50]

In November 1992, Rühe issued "defense-political guidelines" for the defense ministry, which had almost the same content as the Stoltenberg-Naumann paper of January. The Bundeswehr was to be prepared for crisis management out of area.[51] The guidelines also referred to specific and legitimate German interests. Those interest were based on the German constitution, the UN charter, and the CSCE charter, but not necessarily always congruent with the interest of German partners. This section allowed the conclusion that the Bundeswehr was to acquire capabilities for power projection.[52] The enlarged mission of the Bundeswehr was defined as follows: "The Bundeswehr protects Germany and its citizens against political blackmail and foreign danger, promotes the military stability and the integrity of Europe, defends Germany and its allies, serves world peace and international security in accordance with the UN charter and helps in the case of catastrophe, saves in cases of need and supports humanitarian actions."[53]

The guidelines thus met the obligations for crisis management that the federal government had incurred vis-à-vis NATO and the WEU in the "Petersberg declaration" of June 1992.[54] Rühe took a considerable risk by issuing the guidelines on his own authority and not bringing paper before the cabinet. Public opinion could have backfired. However, despite criticism from the left, there was no storm of public opinion.

Only a small step separated from Rühe's defense-political guidelines from the White Book on the Security of the Federal Republic of Germany and the Situation and Future of the Bundeswehr, issued in April 1994.[55] Both the chancellor and the defense minister signed the white book, which presented an encompassing redefinition of German security, again before a supreme court judgment had cleared the constitutional situation. Integration into the Western democracies and the restoration of unity and sovereignty in freedom had been achieved. Germany would now have to define its security policy more independently. Germany had learned the lessons of history and would continue its policy of active integration and broad international cooperation. However, "[c]oncrete security policy must be based on (national) interests. They determine priorities. They are the manifestation of the policies of a sovereign state, the point of departure to evaluate risks and necessities for action, basis for reconciliation of interests, cooperation and international stability."[56]

The book identified five central interests of German security policy:

- protection of freedom, security, and welfare of German citizens and the protection of German territory;
- integration with the democracies in the European Union, because democracy, rule of law, and economic welfare in Europe increase peace and security for Germany;
- the lasting transatlantic alliance with the United States, based on common values and interests, because the global power of the United States is indispensable for international stability;
- the integration of Eastern neighbors in Western structures based on reconciliation and partnership and the creation of a new security order encompassing all European states;
- the global recognition of international law and human rights and a just economic order based on market principles, because the security of individual states is guaranteed only in a system of global security and peace, rule of law and economic well-being for all.[57]

In conclusion, the defense ministry had reacted quickly to the changing situation by readjusting the mission of the Bundeswehr, sometimes unilaterally and without specific feedback by the other parts of the government. The defense-political guidelines of November 1992 and the Bundeswehrplan '94 anticipated the political (or legal) decisions taken later. Moreover, the defense ministry took a more traditional view of national interests: German national sovereignty and security were to be defended.

Even so, German military doctrine was more internationalist and than that of many of its allies.

The foreign ministry placed a larger emphasis on global security institutions and the rule of universal global law (as opposed to specific German interests). The FDP was less traditionalist than the CDU. Moreover, whereas NATO was the primary domain of the defense ministry, the tasks of the foreign ministry included the UN, the CSCE, and the European Union.

Soon after taking office in 1992, Klaus Kinkel began to demand that Germany return to "normalcy" in international relations. One of the main projects of the new foreign minister was a permanent German seat in the UN security council. After Japan had addressed the issue of a seat for Japan unofficially, Kinkel followed suit in his speech before the General Assembly of September 1992:[58] If "the reform of the UN Security Council will be discussed, Germany will present its wish to have a permanent seat in this body."[59] Kinkel reconfirmed his request in his speech before the General Assembly a year later, arguing that "the world situation has changed and that the decisive questions of security and foreign policy are being discussed in the Security Council today. That's where the music plays. Without grandeur and a 'Germans to the front' attitude, I have to say clearly: it is German interests that require a stronger German participation within the UN and in the Security Council."[60] Kinkel confirmed that the emphasis of German foreign policy would be in the area of peace making—economic cooperation, protection of human rights, humanitarian assistance, and environmental protection.

The 1992–1993 reform discussion, however, did not result in specific reform steps for the Security Council. Most permanent members of the Security Council jealously guarded their privileges; in addition to Germany and Japan, the south demanded better representation, and a reform and democratization of voting procedures.[61] Ultimately, the discussion led nowhere.[62]

Germans also viewed the project with ambivalence. For some, the German request for a permanent seat meant strengthening multilateral structures. Kinkel made clear that a German seat meant greater German responsibility and required greater German contributions in order to fulfill these self-imposed obligations. In January 1995, for example, Kinkel supported the UN secretary general's idea of creating UN stand-by arrangements for national forces. He also supported the secretary-general's request for German participation in UN operations in Angola and Kuwait, which Kohl and Rühe denied.[63] Karl Kaiser argued that a permanent German and Japanese seat would increase the legitimacy of the Security Council because it would then better reflect the structure of the international system.[64]

For others, however, there was more damage than benefit in the German request. Hans Arnold, former German ambassador to the United Nations, deplored the fact that the initiative had silently killed the German demand for a common European seat in the Security Council. Moreover, Germany was put into the role of a petitioner. According to Arnold, it was questionable whether a change would actually strengthen the Security Council. Arnold also saw a deviation from the role of a "civilian power" that emphasized the cooperative (economic) sectors of the UN and an attempt to become a "normal power" that emphasized the interventionist (military) sectors.[65]

V

The starting point for change was international pressure; government action provided the initial domestic impetus. Party politics, and eventually public opinion, followed after a lag. Between 1990 and 1995, all parties were engaged in a collective learning process, incrementally adopting more activist positions.[66] The domestic discussion was often intensive, with the junior coalition partner FDP not always in agreement with the activist CDU/CSU and the SPD and Green parties often in opposition.

Overall, the opposition was in a weak position. The SPD had traditionally been a strong supporter of the UN. Chapter VII of the UN charter specifically allowed peace-enforcing missions. Now that Germany was asked to contribute, it was difficult for the opposition to reject outright any participation. Fundamental opposition was left to grassroots peace groups.

Intermediate positions had to be found: German policy elites had begun to distinguish among "humanitarian," "peacekeeping," and "peace enforcing" missions. The opposition repeatedly demanded that German missions be limited to humanitarian missions. Later, peacekeeping missions were also added to the list of permissible actions. In November 1992, the SPD party convention decided that Germany was to participate only in peacekeeping missions. The SPD also demanded that the constitution be amended accordingly.[67] These complicated arguments were difficult to sell to the public.

The CDU/CSU, in the meantime, had the more effective communication strategy: military missions abroad were to be allowed under a collective mandate without a change of the constitution. Unilateral missions abroad would be strictly excluded. Unanimous international demands, decisive government action, and the more effective communication strategy of the CDU/CSU prevailed.

The overwhelming majority of the CDU/CSU and its ministers in the government wanted to allow military missions within the framework of the UN, NATO, or WEU. They also wanted to allow emergency measures according to Article 51 of the UN charter. There had to be a "European option," they argued, if Germany was to be a leader and serious partner in a uniting Europe. Throughout 1991 and 1992, the CDU/CSU was willing to negotiate a compromise with the SPD that demanded a change in the constitution and a limitation to peacekeeping missions. This shows that redefinition of the German security doctrine was indeed a risky step— even its advocates wanted some safeguards.

Initially, even defense minister Volker Rühe proposed making fighting missions subject to a two-thirds majority of the Bundestag.[68] A significant number of CDU/CSU politicians, however, believed that there should be no change in the constitution in order not to limit Germany's options. This decision made compromise impossible. The supreme court decision of July 1994 clearly confirmed the CDU/CSU position, although it did make missions abroad subject to a simple majority in the Bundestag.

On June 30, 1995, the federal government decided to support NATO forces in Bosnia. Germany committed air transport capabilities, reconnaissance planes, various navy units, and additional forces if necessary could potentially be involved in fighting missions. Germany was to support only the reaction force, not the hapless UNPROFOR (United Nations Protection Force).[69] The Bundestag confirmed this decision with 386 to 258 votes (11 abstentions). Forty-five SPD members of parliament and four members of the Green Party also voted for the decision, turning against the respective party lines.[70] Without much public attention, the Bundestag had opened the door to participation in actual fighting missions.

In November 1995, NATO decided on renewed airstrikes against the Bosnian Serbs. (The first such strike had taken place on May 25, 1995). The attacks were followed up by ground troops of the Croatian–Muslim Federation. As a consequence, the Bosnian Serbs withdrew from much of the occupied territory in Serbia. In November, the warring parties in the Bosnia conflict decided upon a truce, at the end of November the signed a peace agreement in Dayton. Germany was ready to contribute to the international peace forces if all conflicting parties (including the Serbs) accepted a German contribution. After the Serbs had signaled their agreement, the cabinet decided that 4,000 German military personnel would participate. The Bundestag accepted this decision with an over-whelming majority of 543 to 107 votes (6 abstentions).[71]

The SPD had great difficulty formulating a consistent policy. On the one hand, the SPD had a long pacifist tradition, and the overwhelming majority of the "basis" of the party was pacifist. On the other hand, SPD leaders were eager to demonstrate international responsibility in the face of upcoming elections. These contradictory trends and motives resulted in deep splits within the party that had not been overcome by the end of 1995. Within the SPD, the legal interpretation of the constitution was largely undisputed: only (collective) self-defense and humanitarian missions were to be allowed.[72] Deep differences, however, existed within the party about the desirability of a change of the constitution and the form such a change might take. There were three major positions within the party.[73]

The pacifist wing—which had the smallest support in the party leadership but considerable grassroots appeal—opposed all military missions abroad and supported only humanitarian missions. It rejected the government's argument that international obligations had to be fulfilled and that Germany should not choose a *"Sonderweg."* The most prominent politicians in this wing were Heidemarie Wieczoreck-Zeul, Katrin Fuchs, and Horst Peter.

The "realist" wing was represented by most of the grand old men and the security experts in the party: Willy Brandt, Hans-Jochen Vogel, Björn Engholm, Hans-Ulrich Klose, Karsten Voigt, Norbert Gansel, Florian Gerster, Egon Bahr, and Helmut Schmidt. These politicians campaigned for a change in constitution to allow humanitarian, peacekeeping, and peace-enforcing missions under UN command. (Most of them opposed UN-sanctioned missions under NATO, WEU, or national command.) The "realist" wing mustered the overwhelming majority of the party leadership but had relatively little support among party members.

The "pragmatists"—a majority of the party—were represented by such politicians as Oskar Lafontaine, Gerhard Schröder, Rudolf Scharping, and Günter Verheugen. They supported peacekeeping operations but opposed fighting missions out of area. Many of the younger party leaders subscribed to this position, trying to broker a compromise between the party base and the grand old men in the party. Oskar Lanfontaine, however, also displayed rather pacifist preferences at times.

The SPD party convention of June 1991 adopted a compromise formulated by Björn Engholm and Oskar Lafontaine. With 230 to 179 votes, the SPD rejected UN peace-enforcing and fighting missions, but supported peacekeeping missions with the condition that the constitution was to be changed. *Der Spiegel* commented that this position lacked a sense of reality: "With their vote, the comrades block a decision about German UN missions, because neither the CDU/CSU nor the FDP would support a change in the constitution limited to peacekeeping missions."[74]

In June 1992, the SPD put forward a bill to change the constitution. Germany's contribution would be limited to nonfighting peacekeeping missions under UN and OSCE command, and only professional soldiers with light arms would be allowed to participate.[75] The government, of course, did not accept this proposal, well knowing that the SPD was caught in a dilemma.[76] On the one hand, the SPD could try to stop all missions until the constitution was changed, which entailed the risk that it would also endanger missions it supported in principle. On the other hand, it ran the risk of sanctioning a change in military practice without an accompanying change of the constitution, if it did not oppose government policies.

Subsequently, Björn Engholm lobbied for "robust peacekeeping missions" (which would include self- and mission-defense), but failed to create a consensus.[77] The convention of November 1992 adopted a resolution according to which "participation in peacekeeping and humanitarian missions or for the establishment of UN security zones" would be the limit for German missions.[78] These resolutions made any constitutional compromise with the government impossible.

In June 1993, party leaders Rudolf Scharping and Günter Verheugen started a new discussion. Scharping declared that "no SPD-led government will be able to resist international obligations permanently."[79] Klose asked the party to prepare for "humanitarian missions plus X." Before a party convention, Klose demanded the go-ahead for all UN missions, Scharping wanted these missions to be conditional on achieving a two-thirds-majority in parliament.[80] Gerhard Schröder, Oskar Lafontaine, and Heidemaire Wieczorek-Zeul represented the pacifist wing. Lafontaine declared, "This is not a matter of lyrics, it is the question whether we will participate in wars or not."[81]

Although Hans-Ulrich Klose and other realists tried to make the SPD position more flexible, the 1993 party convention reconfirmed the strictly anti-interventionist party line. UN peacekeeping forces were to be allowed defensive, de-escalating measures for mission defense, but the Bundeswehr was not to participate in fighting missions or in any out-of-area missions not under UN command.[82]

The 1994 election made chancellor-candidate Rudolf Scharping more of a realist. He and other realists, such as Hans-Ulrich Klose, vice president of the Bundestag, began to advocate German participation in Bosnia.[83]

Günter Verheugen (SPD) stated that even German ground troops were conceivable in Bosnia: "Especially where Germans have incurred past debts, they have to help when they are asked."[84]

When Germany was to provide a squadron of Tornadoes to participate in air combat missions over Bosnia in 1995 in the Bundestag vote of June 30, 1945, disagreement was strong. Oskar Lafontaine and Heidemaire Wieczorek-Zeul were especially vehement in their opposition to Tornado missions, which could escalate into actual fighting missions.[85] The party leadership decided that it would support logistical and medical operations but oppose the use of Tornadoes. In the Bundestag vote of June 30, 1995, 45 realist SPD members voted with the government. To date, the SPD remains split.

Between 1990 and 1995, the FDP position moved closer toward that of the CDU/CSU. Differences with the senior governing partner mainly arose over the issue of whether a change of the constitution was necessary and whether missions without an explicit UN mandate were permissible. This put the FDP in a middle position between the CDU/CSU (with which it shared most political goals) and the SPD (with which it shared the legal interpretation).[86]

Initially, the FDP was split: a majority supported all collective missions, while a minority wanted missions abroad limited to those under UN command. The FDP also rejected UN missions without a UN mandate (for example, NATO missions according to Article 51 of the UN charter).[87] Moreover, the FDP insisted on a change of the constitution, declaring that the resolutions of the Federal Security Council of 1983 were binding. Foreign minister Genscher said that his party would not support the "break of constitutional positions held by every government to date." In addition, the FDP demanded that any UN mission be conditional on a simple majority by the legislative.[88] Genscher excused German reluctance: "Nobody should complain when Germans are pensive in matters of war and peace. I see this as a special democratic maturity of our country."[89]

In January 1993, the FDP declared that it would also support missions covered by Article 51 of the UN charter without an explicit mandate. By this time, however, the CDU/CSU position had hardened. The CDU/CSU now believed that a change was not necessary, thereby creating a severe rift in the coalition government. Foreign minister and party chairman Klaus Kinkel was in a particular dilemma because he had to present the party line and was directly confronted with international demands at the same time.[90] After the supreme court issued a preliminary opinion in 1993 and a decision in 1994, the FDP party's problems with the government line disappeared.

Klaus Kinkel began to actively support German participation in most missions to demonstrate German responsibility, solidarity, and international standing.

The Green Party, of course, which had established itself in the early 1980s as a serious political force, was the original genuinely pacifist party. The original party position consisted of a complete demilitarization of international relations, the dissolution of national forces, and the dissolution of NATO and the WEU. At the same time, the Green Party wanted to reform and strengthen collective institutions such as the UN and the CSCE. The shape and structure of the Security Council were regarded as an anachronism, and the world organization was to be made more autonomous based on a strong understanding of international law.[91]

At the time of the Persian Gulf War, the West German Green Party was not represented in the Bundestag because it had received less than 5 percent of the popular vote. The East German arm of the party, on the other hand, was present in the parliament. This fact along with the atrocities in former Yugoslavia—especially in Srebrenica and Zepa in 1995—set in motion an internal reconsideration of the pacifist party line.

The West German wing retained a strictly pacifist position throughout the Gulf War and was deeply involved in the public antiwar demonstrations. In 1992, the situation in former Yugoslavia prompted deviations from the established party position. The (East German) Bundestag members proposed a bill that would have allowed German participation in peacekeeping missions without a fighting mandate under UN command, if only professional soldiers were sent, light armament used, and if the Bundestag approved with a two-thirds majority.[92] Even this proposal was too far-reaching for the (majority) pacifist wing of the party, which rejected any participation in military missions abroad.

In 1994, the West German Greens were able to send members to the Bundestag again, among them such prominent first-generation Green politicians as Joschka Fischer. In the face of the atrocities in Srebrenica and Zepa, Joschka Fischer, Werner Schulz, Waltraud Schoppe and foreign policy spokesman Gerd Poppe demanded that Western forces stop the Serbian aggression and bring about negotiations by force. In a 12-page memorandum entitled "The Catastrophe in Bosnia and the Consequences for Our Party," Fischer advocated military protection of the UN zones. This represented a break with the pacifist and neutralist tradition of the party. As late as 1993, 90 percent of the delegates at the convention of the Green party had voted against missions. The Fischer position was not the Green majority position, but Waltraud Schoppe was able to declare that the "unconditional pacifist Petra Kelly position did not exist anymore."[93] Earlier, Fischer had also declared that NATO was an expression of German integration into the West, thus sending a pro-NATO signal in a formerly strictly anti-NATO party.[94]

By the end of 1995, the party was involved in a deep discussion: Many party leaders and members of parliament supported some types of missions abroad, while other party leaders and members of parliament, as well as a large part of the party, opposed such missions. At the party convention in December 1995, the realists proposed legitimizing military interventions to stop genocide. Though they were not able to assert their position, they received an approval rate of 38 percent.[95] At the subsequent Bundestag vote, 22 members supported German participation in the peace force in Yugoslavia, while 22 opposed it (4 abstentions).[96] The deep divisions between the realists and the pacifists were not likely to be solved anytime soon. Both wings had roughly the same strength. For the pacifists, the support of missions abroad struck at the very core of the self-conception of the Green Party; for the realists, such missions were necessary given the changed realities.

The PDS, finally, emerged as the successor to the Communist Party in East Germany and established itself as a smaller party of protest in former East Germany. It is the only party in the Bundestag that has consistently opposed any missions abroad and has kept a strictly pacifist line.[97]

Popular opinion between 1990 and 1995 underwent a similar collective learning process. Support for missions abroad grew over time, but lagged behind the government position, which in turn reflected the program of the most activist parties. The population also was considerably more skeptical on the issue of fighting missions. Moreover, the population in the new federal states—former East Germany—was decidedly more pacifist than the population in the old federal states. Finally, public opinion was highly variable, with few entrenched positions.

Public opinion (or more specifically, the absence of mass protests) throughout the Gulf War was an important factor in allowing the CDU/CSU to press for rapid change. Initially, it was hoped—or feared—that the "peace movement was experiencing a renaissance."[98] Unions, churches, the Greens, and environmental pressure groups led protests, while the SPD, the major opposition party, did not come out very strongly. In a flyer "Avoid the Ecological Disaster of the Gulf War," a number of environmental pressure groups protested against the War.[99] Four Christian peace groups cooperated.[100] Similar appeals (some signed by more than ten thousand people) were made by peace-minded physician's organizations, scientists, and unions.[101]

The demonstrations, however, were much smaller and shorter-lived than during the NATO double-track decision in the early eighties. The political heavyweights were largely missing. There was an elite consensus that the allies, who had made German unification possible, had to be supported.[102] Brandt, one of the icons of the SPD, stated that the country could not remain in the role of a paying spectator during this war. Otto Schily, one of the major figures of the peace movement in the early 1980s, stated that in "extreme cases force could be set against force as ultima ratio."[103]

The peace movement was isolated because of its sometimes anti-American undertones from a German public that was largely pro-American.[104] In an opinion poll commissioned by the left-leaning *Spiegel* and conducted by the Emnid Institute, 61 percent of Germans supported American and allied military action; only 29 percent were against it. This picture was the same in all major parties, except for the Greens. But even here, 47 percent were for the war (SPD 52 percent, FDP and CDU/CSU 81 percent). Fifty-eight percent of the population supported the stationing of German warplanes in Turkey (32 percent against); but only 43 percent were for actual combat missions (51 percent against).

Initially, even CDU/CSU politicians were cautious. German policymakers had kept in mind the country's deep divisions during the double-track decision and tried to dampen popular fears. After the beginning of allied bombings on January 17, 1991, many leading politicians—among them Helmut Kohl—expressed their deep concern before the Bundestag. During the early days of the war many German politicians issued only weak statements of support because of imminent state elections. This temporary silence left a lasting—and negative—international impression.[105]

Between 1988 and 1995 support for participation in UN missions in former West Germany rose from 36 percent to 54 percent, while that in the former East Germany remained at a lower level.

There was a clear distinction between the East and West, with the East being much more skeptical regarding military missions and (Western) military alliances. The schism was deeper than that between the supporters of various parties (except the East German PDS). Surveys that differentiate between peacekeeping and combat missions result in a higher overall agreement than those with undifferentiated questions.

There was broad overall support for German participation. However, there also was a solid majority against combat missions. Public support was strong for "humanitarian" and "peacekeeping" missions, while support for fighting missions continued to be weak. According to an Emnid survey

Table IV.1 General Agreement to UN Missions

	September 1988	August 1990	March 1992	January 1993	April 1995
old "Länder"	36	46	45	54	54
new "Länder"			26	42	29

Source: Philippi, *Bundeswehreinsätze*, 166.

Approval Ratings, Differentiated between Peacekeeping and Combat Missions

	Feb. 1991 Infas	Feb. 1992 Infas	July 1992 Infas	August 1992 Infas	Nov. 1992 Infas	Jan. 1993 Infas	Oct. 1993 Infas	March 1994 Infas
Peacekeeping	24	41	41	46	45	46		
Combat missions	8	9	12	18	14	26	32	33
Sum	32	50	53	64	59	72		

Source: Philippi, *Bundeswehreinsätze*, 168.

conducted on the occasion of the Somalia mission, 80 percent of the public supported a military protection of food transports (17 percent against), but on the other hand, 68 percent thought that soldiers should only be used to restore infrastructure like streets and wells (29 percent against). Only 42 percent supported policing by German soldiers (54 percent against) and the use of force against armed gangs (37 percent for vs. 58 percent against). Another Emnid poll taken in December 1994 showed that the German population opposed the potential Tornado missions over Bosnia with a solid 62 percent majority (for: 33 percent).[106] Between January 1995 and November 1995, the support for Tornado missions over Bosnia rose from 34 percent to 63 percent, again indicating that popular opposition to fighting missions was weakening considerably.[107]

VI

By 1995, the German policy elites and the general public had largely adjusted to the new military doctrine. Germany's military contribution to global peacekeeping, however, remained very limited, almost symbolic. Moreover, there was little indication that contribution could be increased quickly, even if Germany actively pursued this objective.

Material Obstacles

"What army for Germany?"[108] asked Hans Rühle, former chief of planning of the Bundeswehr. In accordance with the new NATO structure, the new Bundeswehr was to have three types of forces: crisis reaction forces, main defense forces, and augmentation forces.[109] The crisis reaction forces were to be standing forces specially equipped and trained for crisis prevention. They were to be composed of mobile and flexible land, air, and sea forces to be deployed within days. They would also contribute to national defense by enabling the mobilization of the main defense forces. The main defense forces had a mobilization period of weeks or months. Many of the traditional forces would be cadred reinforcements with long mobilization periods. The augmentation forces were to reinforce the main defense forces.

What was once the most formidable land army in Europe (except that of the Soviet Union) had been designed for a massive, defensive tank battle over short distances. Now, Germany was to contribute "crisis reaction forces" with a strength of approximately 50,000. Germany was to contribute approximately 25 percent of its army (including corps and divisional forces), one-third of its air force, and 40 percent of its navy. The German contingent of crisis reaction forces was to be equipped to conduct joint operations of all three forces in situations ranging from guerrilla warfare to missions against modern armies. This was to be done from battalion to division strength.[110]

It was an open question whether such forces could be operational anytime soon. The news magazine *Focus* reported that the Bundeswehr was conceivably ill equipped for international crisis operations. Especially the army, which was to provide the core of the reaction forces—25,000 personnel—was expected to have difficulties. It possessed few of the light and mobile systems that would be needed. By 1995, the army had planned for one air-mobile brigade and a special command of 600–1,000 soldiers trained for guerrilla warfare. If Germany was acquiring power projection capabilities, it was doing so very slowly and for very limited purposes.[111] Rühle estimated that the whole Bundeswehr had a potential of only 2,000–3,000 soldiers who could be sent to international fighting missions after a six-week training course.[112]

Moreover, the Bundeswehr had to restructure in the face of severe budget cuts. After unification, the relative decrease in defense expenditures had been greater in Germany than in other NATO countries.[113] Many of the initial cuts were in the area of conventional capabilities for heavy land warfare.[114] The budgetary plans for 1995 and 1996 allocated DM 47.8 bn and DM 48.4 bn to the Bundeswehr, respectively, thus cementing the deep cuts that had been made in the 1990–93 period.

Psychological Obstacles

By far the largest challenge was the existing mindset among most soldiers and the population at large. The Federal Republic had relied on a general draft to fulfill its obligation of maintaining forces of 500,000. To create acceptance for a mass army, the government had created the concept of the "citizen in uniform," coupled with "inner leadership," both of which provided for a relatively liberal army firmly integrated in society. The Bundeswehr advertised comradeship and technical expertise. It did not mention that its soldiers might have to go to war, because peace, in the words of President Heinemann, was the test case.[115] Recruits were also given the option of serving as conscientious objectors. If accepted, they had to do civil service in hospitals, homes for the elderly, or social institutions.

"Technocrats in uniform—the officers—commanded guest workers in uniform—the draftees." War was rarely discussed, although the military leadership repeatedly attempted to raise combat morale. In many commissioned officers' messes, hand-drawn posters with the following message could be seen: "What is to be done in case of war? 1. Keep calm 2. Pay your bills. 3. Run, run, run."[116] Hans Rühle explained that the Bundeswehr did not have a single soldier with combat experience and that not only recruits, but also officers up to the general's level were openly discussing whether they had sworn their oath for anything else than defense of the home territory.[117]

Many soldiers became conscientious objectors during the Gulf War. In January 1991, 22,000 men objected to service, among them 9,200 who had already served and 1,000 who were actually serving at the time. Even a few long-term volunteers were among the 1,000. (Normally, the rejection takes place at the time of recruitment.) In all of 1991, 151,000 young potential recruits rejected armed service. Even at the height of the double-track controversy, the number had only been 68,000, and during the 1968 student movement it had been 12,000.[118] By 1991, only 8 percent of the general public believed that military service was the more important contribution to society (civil service 45 percent, both equal 45 percent, don't know 2 percent).[119]

Although the Bundeswehr had managed the transition to the new doctrine, it was foreseeable that the psychological preparation of its soldiers and the creation of new traditions would take a long time. The only military leaders who had actual combat experience and could have served as models were those of the Wehrmacht. German military tradition was covered by very restrictive rules. German units could not take over the traditions of military units of the Wehrmacht or Prussia.[120] Nobody was certain how to prepare soldiers for combat missions.[121]

Quantitative Obstacles

The government had decided that the new Bundeswehr, with 340,000 personnel, would remain an army relying on the draft. Only about 40,000 professional ranks would serve in this force; the rest of the ranks would be draftees. Recruits would serve in missions abroad only on a voluntary basis. They would have to give a statement at the beginning of active service as to whether they wanted to be used in this function. This statement would be binding.[122]

Each year approximately 175,000 recruits were needed. In 1994, the annual pool of young men was 375,000, out of which 26 percent were not able to serve, 6 percent were relieved from army service because they were members of the police or similar forces, and 30 percent were conscientious objectors. Only 38 percent remained for active service. Of those, 5 percent were serving long-term, so that only 33 percent served as recruits. Overall, only 125,000 out of a required 175,000 entered service, leaving a gap of 50,000 recruits annually.[123]

In the face of these quantitative difficulties, CSU member of the Bundestag Benno Zierer demanded a professional army of 250,000. The SPD Bundestag member and former air force general Manfred Opel supported this position.[124] Sources from the defense ministry thought it possible that the German army would be reduced to 250,000 personnel by the year 2000, even if the was maintained. This would be the case, for example, if active service for recruits were reduced from 12 to 6 months.[125] An anonymous two-star general declared that 200,000 would be a functional minimum to fulfill the core objectives of the Bundeswehr. A spokesperson of a group of "critical officers" believed that a Bundeswehr of 100,000 would be feasible.[126] A study by the research service of the Bundestag came to the conclusion that a professional army would be more effective and not more expensive.[127] The legitimacy of a large army increasing in question, the defense ministry was playing for time to save the draft. But the basis of the Bundeswehr remained uncertain. The likelihood of another significant reduction in size is still substantial.

In summary, the adjustment process between 1990 and 1995 entailed a partial normalization of German military policy. Germany adjusted to international demands, dampening international criticism. The framework through which Germany and its partners viewed international peacekeeping efforts became more similar. At the same time, the German adjustments were doctrinal and symbolic rather than material. Even the new Germany was to conduct military missions only within the mandate of an international organization such as NATO or the WEU. The reluctance to use force was still higher than in other nations. The size of Germany's potential peacekeeping contingent remained small.

Thus, the paradoxical effect of the rapid adjustment in German doctrine between the years of 1990 and 1995 may have been to safeguard the core of Germany's preferences. Germany had reacted quickly to accommodate allied demands and thus shielded itself against criticism. But it also seemed clear that Germany's contributions would remain limited in quantity, and that Germany would continue to rely mostly on multilateral, nonmilitary means of ensuring security, a perfectly valid strategy, even viewed with "realist" eyes.

V

The Loss of Utopia: Germany and European Integration, 1988–1997

I have never seen that Germany pounded on the table before an important decision. It has not misused its economic strength to dominate others. Often, its leaders have stayed in the background so that others could harvest the fruits of success.

Jacques Delors[1]

I

As with military policy, Germany's foreign policy toward European integration between 1988 and 1997 underwent a considerable change that could be termed "normalization." This period includes a number of important milestones: the German EU presidency of 1988, the Treaty of Maastricht in 1992, the ratification process, the conclusion of negotiations with entry candidates in 1994, and the negotiation of the Treaty of Amsterdam of 1997. At the beginning of the period, the notion that German and European interests were literally identical was still the prevailing one among German policymakers. During the ratification of the Treaty of Maastricht, a more reflective (and somewhat more realist) German approach toward European integration emerged. Other than in the case of security policy, this process was mostly driven from within Germany rather than prompted by outside pressure. The German government upheld supranationalist aspirations as long as possible. Eventually, however, strong popular opposition, even from within the ranks of the governing parties, forced it to scale down its ambitions.

Four factors explain this process. First, other than in the case of military policy, the opinions of what constituted the desirable model of European integration were very heterogeneous among Germany's partners. Germany was the leading proponent of supranationalist integration, and it was often alone. Eventually, it settled for considerably less in the Treaty of Maastricht.

Second, German willingness to make concessions led to an overstretch of German financial, economic, and political resources. The special nature of Germany's objectives—supranational integration—prohibited the use of traditional levers of power: decisions had to be reached by consensus, and pressure tactics were largely out of the question. Germany was willing to incur high costs to make progress. It used its financial power to pay for compromises, making disproportionate concessions without being able to achieve truly supranational solutions. At the same time, Germany's financial and economic power was increasingly exhausted because of unification. Due to unrealistic expectations, the limitations of civilian power, economic strains, and asymmetric concessions, Germany found itself overcommitted after the Treaty of Maastricht.

Third, public opinion turned against the Treaty of Maastricht and provided the death knell for "idealistic supranationalism." Interestingly enough, the German public developed a differentiated and realistic picture of the benefits and costs of Europe, which differed from the "integration-at-all-costs" approach of the government. The public seemed to sense the asymmetric nature of concessions in the Treaty of Maastricht. In particular, Germans opposed monetary integration. Despite their opposition to specific aspects of Europe, opinion polls indicate that Germans continued to strongly support European integration for its overall political objectives: helping Europe continue to enjoy prosperity and peace.[2]

Fourth, the end of the East-West conflict also ended the Soviet threat to Europe, and thus a strong reason for European coherence. Centrifugal tendencies were resurfacing.[3] Some observers, mostly from the United States, see a trend toward a neorealist foreign policy environment in Europe, replete with power balancing among the European nations.[4] Some German observers have picked up this argument. In an article from 1997, Werner Link sees a "balance of power" as the ordering principle in the new Europe.[5] Gottfried Niedhard speaks of a return to power politics.[6] And the renowned historian Klaus Hildebrandt detects the principles of hegemony and counterbalancing not only in European history, but also in contemporary Europe.[7]

II

After the creation of the European Monetary System in the late 1970s and a prolonged period of "Europessimism" and "Eurosclerosis" in the early 1980s, the mid-1980s saw renewed movement toward European integration. In 1983, the EC heads of state and government issued a "solemn declaration on the European Union." In February 1984, the European Parliament passed the blueprint of a treaty on the European Union. In June of the same year, the heads of state and government of the EC charged a conference with making recommendations on the structure of a unifying Europe and a better coordination of foreign policies. Those recommendations became the foundation of the Common European Act of 1986.[8]

It was the first comprehensive revision of the original treaties of Rome and was to pave the way for economic union to take place on January 1, 1993. It also paraphrased European Political Cooperation, an instrument for the better coordination of foreign policies that had been created in 1969/70, but that had never been legally documented.[9]

Under Jacques Delors, the European Commission partially reversed its strategies by turning the attention of the member states to the actual implementation of the Common Market. Instead of promoting supranational structures, the commission pointed out the sectoral, microeconomic, and legal steps that had to be taken to implement the Common Market.[10] The "four freedoms"—freedom of movement of labor, capital, goods, and services—were to bring about a widespread liberalization, renewed economic vitality, and further integration.[11]

Despite this renewed impetus, many questioned the success of the Common Market project in particular and further European integration in general. The budget of the European Community was strained to its limits.[12] The costs of the Common Agricultural Policy continued to grow rapidly. The southern and poorer states of the community were apprehensive about the economic and social effects of liberalization and demanded an increase in social and regional funds.[13] The Federal Republic itself had contributed to the stalemate: its inflexible position on the Common Agricultural Policy and a long and difficult domestic ratification of the Common European Act had made agreement more difficult.[14]

After the signing of the act, the EC seemed to be at a standstill. During the German presidency of 1988, however, a breakthrough occurred. Germany succeeded in fostering progress on such important issues as budgetary reform, liberalization and harmonization of laws, tax harmonization, recognition of university degrees, monetary cooperation, and the liberalization of the shipping industry and the insurance industries.[15] The Federal Republic, which had shortly before been criticized by the commission for a variety of shortcomings,[16] received strong praise for its role. In July 1988, Jacques Delors declared before the European Parliament, "In the past six months of German presidency, more has been achieved than in the past ten years." Kohl received a standing ovation from the European parliament.[17]

Well into 1987, this success had seemed unlikely. The German government had to play a "two-level-game" in which it actively negotiated both international and domestic resistance.[18] The government succeeded despite international difficulties and domestic resistance for a number reasons: First, a carefully crafted package deal made the compromise interesting to all EC nations and interest groups. Second, the deal was attractive because Germany made significant financial concessions. Third, this was possible because Germany assigned a high value to any progress, even in areas that were not Germany's foremost concerns. The increasingly critical position of the German population even reinforced the government's commitment to create irreversible integration before public support for the European project waned even further. Fourth: high international expectations for the German presidency created further pressure to succeed.

In the negotiations leading to the Common European Act, Germany had outlined its position early on. 1985 had been called a "year of decision"[19] and a "year of fate" in Germany.[20] The Common Market was to be only one element in a far-reaching bundle of measures to promote European unification. Common foreign economic and security policies, the strengthening of the European Parliament, and the acceptance of majority decisions in the Council of Ministers were to be other elements of the total reform program.[21] This position reflected the supranantionalist aspect of official German policy. The government accepted and welcomed a relative decrease in German influence and autonomy for the sake of European integration. International integration and national interests were closely linked, and one could not be understood without the other. The German "national utility function" put a strong value on integration for its own sake.

Chancellor Helmut Kohl considered himself an heir to Adenauer and was often called "one of Adenauer's grandsons." He deeply believed in the idea of European unification, although he also shared a deep gratitude toward the United States, which had been so generous to Germany during his youth after World War II. Kohl assigned a high priority to the Common Market project, promising to do everything "humanly possible to make the German 1988 presidency a success."[22] Summarizing the German position, Kohl wanted the Common Market to be completed, national sovereignty to be bundled in the new Europe, national identities to be preserved, the European parliament to be strengthened, and European security policies to be better coordinated. The European Union should proceed according to a uniform plan, not leaving behind individual states or issues. Kohl opposed a "Europe a la carte."[23] In a speech before the European Parliament, foreign minister Genscher named the completion of the Common Market as the prime goal of the German presidency and demanded a stronger role for the European Parliament.[24]

The German government had set high standards for its 1988 presidency, which it could not always fulfill. Popular and interest-group opposition to Germany's "consensus-at-all-costs" approach to European policies had already begun to form—and would break out in force after the signing of the Treaty of Maastricht more than half a decade later.

In 1988, Kohl was in a weak position. Various other prominent CDU figures such as Kurt Biedenkopf, Heiner Geißler, Rita Süssmuth and Lothar Späth had even "conspired" to replace him. Kohl survived. But in this period of weakness, German ministries and interest groups had increasingly asserted themselves within the EC fora. Agriculture minister Ignaz Kiechle (CSU) opposed the reduction of wheat prices, leading a German minister to a veto in the Council of Ministers for the first time in the history of the Federal Republic. Interior minister Eduard Zimmerman (CSU) pursued a hard line by trying to make introduction of catalytic car converters mandatory within the EU. Moreover, the Bundesbank and a large part of the German business community as well as a significant share of Germany's economists continued to defend their position that economic convergence had to take place before monetary union, thus blocking the progress of the European Monetary System.[25] Germany began to lose its image as the European model nation.

In 1986 and 1987, further conflicts between the commission and Germany erupted. Although the Federal Republic had long supported the reform of agricultural policies, it had repeatedly raised national subsidies in the agricultural sector. When the commission proposed the abolishment of exchange-loss subsidies for hard-currency countries against the express position of the German chancellor and the agricultural minister, the latter spoke of an "affront" and a "declaration of war" and claimed a "right to self-defense." Members of the government also demanded a reform of the EC budget, an end to steel subsidies, and higher environmental standards in the EC. The commission, in turn, issued a number of formal complaints against the Federal Republic.[26]

The German Länder (states) criticized the Common European Act, in which they saw "degradation of the Länder to powerless provinces directed by the EC."[27] This criticism foreshadowed a later debate about the Maastricht Treaty. As a consequence, the Federal Republic did not ratify the Common European Act until December 19, 1986, a mere 12 days before the official deadline.

Along with increasing bureaucratic difficulties, popular opinion had become much more critical of the EC as an institution, while still supporting European integration as an overall idea. The widespread liberalization of the markets envisioned by the Common European Act, for example, fostered popular concerns about the lowering of food product standards in Germany. The rejection of the four-century-old purity law for German beer by the European Court created an especially lively popular discussion.

Moreover, a number of intellectuals and even some party politicians increasingly challenged the doctrine of automatic and continuing (Western) European integration. The dawning of the new European order and the first signs of far-reaching détente were being picked up by some German intellectuals. German history, the hope for reunification, and the concept of *Mitteleuropa* (Central Europe) experienced a renaissance.[28] Though these intellectual debates had no immediate significance for the political debates, the climate gradually changed. Heretofore buried ideas resurfaced in the public domain. It became possible again to seriously question the "Western Europe first" approach without being labeled a dangerous nationalist.

By early 1987, many Germans had become somewhat "tired of Europe." Despite a fundamentally sound consensus for integration, enthusiasm had been replaced by a more sober assessment. An opinion poll conducted in early 1985 showed that 41 percent of Germans believed that the European nations had not become more integrated in the past years—the highest such number since 1974. Only 34 percent of the population saw the unification of Europe to a "United States of Europe" as an especially important objective (1981: 48 percent). Twenty percent believed that the (Western) European nations would undertake great efforts to grow together; 55 percent believed that integration would be a slow process.[29]

When Germany assumed the presidency, the 1988 budget negotiations were in a deadlock. The EC members agreed that the Common Agricultural Policy should be reformed, that the structural funds should be increased, that a fourth source of revenue should be created for the EC, and that fiscal discipline should be strengthened by spending limits. They disagreed, however, about the amount of the increase of the structural funds and the level of the spending limits. At the EC summit in Copenhagen in late 1987, the heads of state and government failed to reach an agreement. German policy itself was an obstacle to progress. Germany continued to resist automatic price cuts in agriculture because state elections in the agricultural state of Schleswig-Holstein were imminent. The Copenhagen summit ended without a final communiqué. A special summit was scheduled for early February 1988, early in the German presidency.

After the Copenhagen summit, Jacques Delors complained that the European heads of state and government wanted a "Europe of mediocrity" and that they viewed the EC with the "eyes of an accountant," not seeing the big issues.[30] Despite some clashes with the EC commission, official German policy retained a strong pro-integration bias. The presidency put strong pressures on the German government. The thirtieth anniversary of the Treaty of Rome in early 1988 and the twenty-fifth anniversary of the German treaties with France added further impetus. The Europeanist Kohl, who was in a weak position at home, wanted a foreign policy success.

After majority decisions in the council, a strengthening of the European Parliament and common foreign policies—all German objectives—had turned out to be politically infeasible, German policy focused on the remaining levers for promoting integration. In a speech before the European Parliament made shortly before the Brussels summit, foreign minister Hans-Dietrich Genscher explained that the German strategy would entail progress in budgetary reform and the completion of the Common Market.[31] This was a precondition for progress toward Germany's larger goals—supranational integration and the strengthening of the European institutions.

For this purpose, the German government adopted the reform package proposed by Jacques Delors. It contained a skillfully crafted compromise. Agricultural reform steps that would not alienate French and German agricultural interests, consisting of an upper limit on wheat production at guaranteed prices and early retirement plans for farmers, were one element. The measures adopted were not far-reaching enough for Great Britain. But Margaret Thatcher unexpectedly gave in after Kohl succeeded in isolating her on the issue. Second, the income sources of the EU were raised to 1.3 percent of the GDP of the member nations. Third, the regional funds were doubled, thus dampening the concerns of the poorer nations about economic liberalization. Germany would have to finance the major share of these items. Fourth and finally, Great Britain continued to receive its financial rebate. Germany played an essential role in breaking the deadlock by committing additional funds (conservatively estimated at DM 4.9 billion in 1988 and rising to DM 11 billion in 1992).[32]

In addition to the financial reform package, the German government also promoted monetary integration against considerable domestic opposition. Germans preferred monetary stability, safeguarded by an independent Bundesbank. The German government disregarded prevailing opinion to accommodate French interest in monetary union. Having campaigned for irreversible, supranational integration, the government was in a weak position to decline such integration in the one area where Germans would have liked to retain their independence. In his speech before the European Parliament, Genscher picked up a Delors proposal of December 1987 to create a currency union and a European central bank. In February 1988, Genscher's foreign ministry issued a memorandum about the creation of a common currency. Finance minister Gerhard Stoltenberg and Bundesbank president Karl-Otto Pöhl were apprehensive, because a closer coupling of the mark and the French franc would endanger the stability of the mark. Supported by Genscher, Kohl overruled Stoltenberg.[33] At the 1988 Hanover summit, the chiefs of government commissioned a group of 16 experts to prepare proposals for a European currency union.[34]

Though the German government was widely praised by other EC nations for its presidency, this international success did not resonate in the domestic debate. Most of the topics that would dominate the debate after the Treaty of Maastricht—the rights of federal states, the preservation of monetary stability, the safeguarding of economic, social, and environmental standards, and the excessively high German financial contributions—remained contentious issues in the late 1980s, well before unification. As with the Treaty of Maastricht, what looked like a success to the Europeanist Kohl and some other states was viewed rather skeptically by the German public. Moreover, the public had a rather differentiated opinion of European diplomacy. While an overwhelming majority supported European integration, there was also the feeling that Germany made too many concessions in specific areas.

In an opinion poll, only 14 percent of those Germans interviewed thought that the Brussels summit had promoted EC integration, while 32 percent thought it had not. Only 8percent thought the summit was a success for Germany; 35 percent thought one could not say so.[35] In late 1987, two separate polls showed that the German population expected negative consequences of the Common Market for the German economy (positive: 35 percent, negative: 58 percent) but made an overall positive judgment about the Common Market (positive: 53 percent, negative: 5 percent).[36] At the same time, the European idea was alive and well. In 1986, the overwhelming majority of surveyed Germans (94 percent) listed "prevention of war" as a major goal of the European nations.[37] This differentiated judgment indicates that the German population rightly perceived the tradeoff between German economic concessions and overall political progress.

Among all interest groups, one could have expected the business community in economically strong Germany to lend the strongest support to the Common Market project. Despite its fundamentally positive attitudes, this was not the case. Only one-third of the German corporations anticipated that their competitive position and environment would change significantly after 1992 and took steps to prepare for it, as compared to 87 percent of French corporations.[38] Kohl had to lobby German businesses. In a speech before 1,800 representatives of German industry, he admonished his audience to "make clear to our employees and the public that we are planning for the Common Market of 1992."[39] Industry indifference reflected the self-confidence and export-orientation of German industry rather than an insulated position. The managing director of the German chamber of industry and commerce (DIHT) did not think that the Common Market posed any dangers for German industry. One German top corporate executive asked, "What should we prepare for? The politicians don't know themselves what will be coming."[40]

The scientific advisory council at the economics ministry opposed any monetary union that would weaken the anti-inflationary policies of the Bundesbank.[41] An opinion poll conducted by The Society for the Protection of German Savings Deposits in 1989 showed that 57 percent of Germans rejected the ideal of a common currency (only 20 percent supported it).[42] Support in the business community was significantly higher (60 percent), yet at the lower end of the European nations (e.g., France: 97 percent).[43] Germans also criticized the high net contributions to the EC budget.[44]

Germans were also sensitive to the erosion of social standards through EC directives.[45] Representatives of the Social Democratic opposition feared the social implications of the Common Market. Labor was interested in protecting the high German social standards and wage levels, because with the Common Market, competition from low-wage countries seemed imminent. Columnist Harald Schumann summarized the left position, complaining that 1992 would be a "market without a state" in which all "social and democratic progress would be sacrificed on the altar of international competitiveness."[46]

Franz Steinkühler, head of Germany's most powerful union (IG Metall/union of metalworkers) said, "The question of the social future of Europe and the creation of a European social order is given too little attention."[47] Other German politicians, such as Lothar Späth (CDU), governor of Baden-Württemberg and Kohl opponent, also warned about the social consequences of deregulation. Even President Richard von Weizsäcker cautioned the "exuberant European in the Chancellor's office" not to overemphasize the positive aspects of the Common Market while neglecting the social and political consequences. According to von Weizsäcker, deregulation could lead to an equalization of wages and social standards.[48] Likewise, environmental standards would be endangered. Kohl reacted to these concerns by promoting a "social charter" for Europe, which was subsequently blocked by Margaret Thatcher.[49]

III

Kohl had achieved some of his Europeanist goals in 1988. This partial success and the reunification of Germany set the stage for the ambitious plans to complete European unification known as the 1992 Treaty of Maastricht. Finally, Europe should benefit from an economic and monetary union, common interior policies, and common foreign policies.

Four factors were crucial for the treaty. First, the German government vigorously pursued the creation of a European Union simultaneously with German reunification. Germany wanted to leverage the concerns of its neighbors to create a truly integrated (Western) Europe. Thus, German unification was a major opportunity to anchor Germany in supranational structures and to create irreversible institutional bonds among the EC states. At the same time, European unification would neutralize omnidirectional or neutralist tendencies in Germany.

Second, as with the Common European Act and the Brussels compromise of 1988, Germany made disproportionate concessions.[50] Germany placed a high utility on any progress, even in areas that it did not perceive to be a priority—and ended up with an imbalanced treaty. Over the course of the negotiations, it reluctantly abandoned the objectives of a significant strengthening of the European Parliament and of truly integrated foreign and security policies. To Germany's chagrin, the EU nations agreed to institutional unification only for monetary policy. Moreover, abandoning the autonomy of the Bundesbank was considered a concession by many Germans. Germany also made significant financial concessions.

Third, popular attention was focused on German unification, domestic issues, and the Persian Gulf War. Popular criticism of the EU, although present, remained low during most of the negotiation of the treaty. It broke out when the outline of the treaty became apparent—at a time when it was too late to significantly influence the German negotiating position. Criticism was directed at specific features of the treaty, e.g., monetary union, not against the idea of integration itself. A larger wave of more unspecified and populist criticism followed later when the climate had heated up.[51]

Fourth and most important, France and Germany pursued similar (though not identical) objectives, thus acting as powerful promoters of the treaty. After initial attempts to delay German reunification, Mitterrand quickly switched positions and began to link German and European unification. At the extraordinary summit in Strasbourg on December 8–9, the eleven EC heads of government welcomed German unification, but also stated that German unity must be "embedded in the perspective of European integration." The EC commission quickly adopted a supportive position, too. Jacques Delors said very early that the "if" and "how" of unification were for Germany to decide. He also emphasized Germany's strong responsibility for European unification.[52]

Simultaneously, France pressed for an acceleration of the creation of a common European currency. At the summit Mitterrand proposed that a government conference prepare the second and third stages of monetary union. Initially, Kohl was reluctant because of considerable domestic opposition in Germany. Finally he agreed that a plan "covering all aspects of the economic and monetary union should be presented before April 1, 1990."[53] Kohl also declared that Germany would not demand a higher share of votes in the European Parliament after unification.

Kohl quickly adopted the position of "deepening first," seeing monetary union as a lever to promote the German objectives of the strengthening of the European Parliament and the creation of common foreign policies. He suggested the promotion of political integration to President Mitterrand. Mitterrand and Kohl wrote a letter to the president of the council before the extraordinary EC summit in Dublin in April 1990, urging the council to intensify preparations for the government conferences to achieve the goal of economic, monetary, and political union on January 1, 1993. These objectives were included in the final declaration.[54]

At first it seemed that the French objective of currency union and the German objective of political union would both be advanced significantly. At the regular EC summit in Dublin of June 25–26, 1990, the dates for the start of the two government conferences were set for December 13 and 14, respectively. In addition, the member states agreed upon the date for the second stage of economic and monetary union. The precursor to a European central bank was to be created on January 1, 1994. Although the

British prime minister Margaret Thatcher continued to criticize the objective of political union, maintaining that democratic legitimacy could only be based on national parliaments, she agreed to the conference and opened the way for Great Britain to join the EMS the following year.[55]

In December 1990, the government conferences began their work.[56] The initial impetus, however, grew weaker over time. Throughout the government conferences, four fundamentally different positions had to be reconciled. The prevalent German postwar notion was supranationalist, assuming that the nation-state in Europe would be superseded by an ever closer European Union. This would entail strong, democratically legitimized European institutions.[57] Far-reaching supranational integration in all areas was to take place, supported by a democratically legitimized European Parliament with far-reaching powers. Italy, Belgium, the Netherlands, and Luxembourg largely shared this position.

The French position, on the other hand, was one of a Europe of fatherlands, where the heads of government would decide in the Council of Ministers. This, of course, is the technocratic and dirigisté European structure that currently dominates high-level EU decision making. France saw (and sees) Europe as a lever to increase France's geopolitical weight, not as a structure to supersede the French state. "Closer union," to Mitterrand, would mean closer monetary union to utilize German economic potential and closer intergovernmental cooperation in security and foreign affairs to raise France's power in Europe and Europe's standing in the world. The British position emphasized intergovernmental cooperation, weak central powers, deregulation, free trade, openness to new entrants, and the maintenance of strong transatlantic ties. The main objective of the southern nations was the preservation and expansion of financial assistance through EC regional funds.

These conceptual differences inevitably proved difficult to reconcile.[58] Only half of the member states supported the cautious expansion of the rights of the European Parliament, which had been proposed by the president of the European Council in early 1991.[59] A Dutch proposal in the same direction was rejected in November.[60]

The French-German initiative for common foreign and security policies experienced only a marginally better fate. In a letter of April 1990, Kohl and Mitterrand recommended that the council "define and execute common foreign and security policies."[61] In a later letter, they specified their proposal by suggesting that the council define specific areas for the common foreign and economic policies of the community.[62] In October 1991, Mitterrand and Kohl proposed a catalogue of areas that should be designated for common foreign and security policies including relations with the Soviet Union, relations with the states of Central and Southeastern Europe, relations to the southern and eastern Mediterranean countries and relations with the United States.[63]

The French-German initiative did not succeed in prescribing mandatory areas for common foreign and security policies. Although the final Treaty of Maastricht did contain provisions for a common foreign and security policy, it merely listed general goals instead of binding procedures. If all member states agreed, specific foreign policy questions could be designated as "common actions," which could then be executed with the approval of a two-thirds majority. Both the intergovernmental nature and the veto power for individual states were preserved.[64]

As a consequence, Kohl's objective of a conditionality between political and monetary union was hollowed out.[65] The final Treaty of Maastricht fell short of German objectives. Only monetary and economic policies were to contain a truly supranational element, while foreign and interior policies were still ultimately the object of national policy.

The powers of the European Parliament were to be increased incrementally, but not as strongly as desired by the German government. The parliament was to approve the president and the new commission after their appointment by the EU member states, but it was not to be able to reject individual commissioners. In addition, the parliament was to have the final say over the discretionary EU budget, but not over the obligatory budget (e.g., agriculture). The parliament was to be consulted in legislative matters, but was not to initiate bills. Finally, the parliament was to ratify international treaties.

The sudden promise of unification in 1989–90 did not change the government's perception of the national interest. On the contrary: due to the supranationalist values that were underlying German government policy, unification had an almost counterintuitive effect. A transfer of national sovereignty to a unifying Europe would assuage international fears about united Germany, safeguard security and economic well-being, and increase Europe's weight in the world. Germany continued to be willing to transfer sovereign rights to the European Union and to live with institutional structures (council, parliament) that would give it a lesser relative weight than its economic potential or population would suggest. "The stronger Germany would become, the more a culture of restraint would become imperative."[66] Later Helmut Kohl summarized the German interest: "What is happening now in Europe is a fateful process for us Europeans, but especially for us Germans. Because of historical, geographical and geopolitical reasons, the creation of an economically, socially and most importantly politically unified Europe is more important for Germany than for any other country."[67]

In a speech before students in 1991, Helmut Kohl called the "United States of Europe" the perspective for the young European generation.[68] At the United Nations on September 25, 1991, foreign minister Genscher named European unification as the first of 12 major goals of German foreign policy, saying: "We want to develop the European Community, to which we belong as a founding member, into a European Union and eventually into the United States of Europe."[69]

The public broadly supported the official government position. Throughout late 1989 and early 1990 a large majority of Germans thought that the development of a united Europe should not be slowed (Nov. 1989: "slowed" 21 percent, "not slowed" 58 percent).[70] Throughout 1990 and 1991, when the Treaty of Maastricht took shape, public attention in Germany was focused on the process of German unification. Fifty-three percent of the German population gave priority to German unification over the completion of the Common Market.[71] This did not mean that Germans rejected further European integration, but unification took up most popular attention. In early 1990, 63 percent of Germans called German membership in the EC "a good thing," putting Germany in a middle position between the extremes of Denmark (42 percent) and the Netherlands (85 percent). The completion of the Common Market, however, was judged with a certain apprehension, reflecting fears about the erosion of high German living standards (positive: 32 percent, fears: 39 percent).[72]

In 1991, the economic disaster in the former GDR became obvious to the German public. GDP in the region was a mere third of that of 1989. Many uncompetitive businesses had to close, and unemployment skyrocketed. The government's political decision to fix the cash exchange rate of the D-mark and the GDR-mark at 1:1 and the exchange rate for savings at 1:2 considerably worsened the competitive position of East German enterprises.[73] West Germany heavily subsidized the East. Public transfers from West to East amounted to roughly $ 71 bn.[74] This caused a demand-led boom in the former West Germany that lasted until mid-1992. The underlying supply-side conditions in West Germany were not favorable, however. A wave of cost-cutting and downsizing had begun that was to fully hit the country in 1992.[75] Under these conditions, labor negotiations in early 1992 were unusually controversial.[76] The increasing number of immigrants from the former East bloc, as well as from other parts of the world, became a focus of popular concern. A number of major international developments received domestic attention, of which the most important were the Persian Gulf War and its aftermath and the situation in the Soviet Union. In light of these events, the negotiations for the Treaty of Maastricht received little and belated public interest.[77]

IV

Ratifying the Treaty of Maastricht, however, proved much more difficult than negotiating it. The years 1992–93 saw a strong upsurge of domestic criticism in Germany, which eventually forced the government to scale down its expectations for a United States of Europe. Critics in the press, the opposition, and parts of the governing CDU/CSU coalition would stress the imbalanced nature of the Treaty of Maastricht. More widespread and diffuse popular fears followed, kindled by the economic downturn in Germany, the increasing stream of immigrants and the continuing mental division between the former East and West Germanies.[78] Some policy-makers were not immune to exploiting populist sentiments. The international travails of ratification raised further doubts about the treaty.

The German government was in a defensive position. Ratification was by nature a reactive process, and public finances were too strained to allow for any new initiatives. Doubts and international setbacks further weakened the government. The Länder demanded and the supreme court imposed strict limits on the government's options in European affairs. Domestic criticism forced the government to abandon some of its ambitious European policies.

The first round of criticism came from parts of the policy elite and was specifically directed at the "imbalanced" nature of the treaty. Peter Glotz, a prominent SPD member of the Bundestag, called the Treaty of Maastricht "more of an end than a beginning."[79] Kohl conceded that the Treaty was a compromise, but also thought that it was a significant step towards the goals stated in the preamble of the German constitution, continuing a "policy that all of Kohl's predecessors since 1949 had seen as an important mission of German policy." In early 1992, Kohl often argued that a historical, "irreversible" process had been set in motion.[80]

The influential weekly news magazine *Der Spiegel* was especially critical. By late 1991, the magazine commented that Kohl must "let go of all hopes to celebrate a triumphal unification party at the conference of Maastricht. To reach any agreement, Kohl had to abandon most of his objectives."[81] After the signing, *Der Spiegel* wrote that John Major was a victor of Maastricht, because he had prevailed with his opposition to the weakening of national sovereignty. Mitterrand, too, had been a victor and had stated: "All points which France wanted included in the treaties have been included." The Spanish prime minister Felipe Gonzalez was a victor, because Kohl had abandoned his original position that no additional funds should be made available to the poorer EC countries and had granted more concessions.

Only Kohl, one of the architects of the European Union, was not perceived as a victor—not even by his own supporters.[82] Germany had failed in the following areas: coupling political and economic union, imposing fiscal discipline on the union, giving more powers to the European Parliament, and establishing a meaningful common foreign and security policy. Only the strict fiscal and economic conditions for the accession to the economic and monetary union were seen as an asset. Some progress had been made winning additional competencies for the union and increasing the democratic legitimacy of decision making. But the complexity of the decision-making process had also increased.[83] Decision-making procedures would have to be reformed further.

Even Günter Nonnenmacher from the pro-European and pro-government newspaper *Frankfurter Allgemeine Zeitung* commented that Kohl had failed 75 percent.[84] An official from the foreign ministry stated that Maastricht had to fail because "We Germans want the integration of Europe, while the French want to integrate Germany."[85] In a lead commentary, Rudolf Augstein, publisher of *Der Spiegel,* criticized Kohl's argument that Maastricht had to be concluded because a closer integration of Europe would assuage international fears about the new Germany and would strengthen Germany's foreign policy. "Foreign policy and defense have long ceased to be questions of weak German self-confidence. There is no German 'yearning' for international integration. We already feel sufficiently integrated. Of course we want to participate in sensible and sensibly negotiated projects including integration [but not at any price]."[86] In another editorial, Augstein contradicted the argument that European unification had its price. "To the contrary," he argued: "Europe *was* the price Germany paid to keep France satisfied."[87]

The German population also became increasingly critical. Asked in 1984 by the Allensbach Institute whether the creation of a united Europe should proceed faster or slower, 62 percent of the surveyed opted for "faster" and 6 percent for "slower." In 1986, 47 percent opted for "faster," 5 percent for "slower." In September 1988, the figures had changed to 34 percent versus 11 percent and in June 1990 to 16 percent versus 30 percent. By August 1992, only 13 percent of the surveyed Germans supported faster integration, while 38 percent preferred a slower process.[88]

In September 1991, the German Federation of Industries stated that economic and monetary union was not a goal that should be pursued at any price.[89] In November, the SPD issued a position paper, demanding monetary stability and independence for the European Central Bank.[90] Although the Federal Republic had been able to assert its preconditions for monetary union (an independent central bank safeguarding price stability as well as strict convergence criteria), popular fear about the loss of the D-mark was widespread.[91] By December 1991, 52 percent of the German population in the former West Germany and 38 percent in the former East Germany opposed a common European currency. Only 20 percent and 32 percent, respectively, supported it.[92] The government found itself in the defensive.[93]

In January 1992, the SPD demanded that the D-mark be retained until the ECU became a stable currency. The introduction of a European currency was not to happen automatically.[94] Some SPD members even demanded changes in the Treaty of Maastricht to better safeguard the D-mark and threatened to withhold the SPD votes necessary for the ratification of the treaty in the Bundestag.[95] Wolfgang Schäuble, chairman of the CDU/CSU members of parliament, criticized this as "shameless populism" and "uninhibited opportunism" playing to unfounded fears.[96]

Tempted by the popular trend, even members of the governing parties began to join the chorus of critical voices. Peter Gauweiler (CSU), Bavarian minister of environmental affairs, called the monetary union a "Schnapsidee." The German mark, "our country's success of the century" would be replaced by "Esperanto money." Erwin Teufel (CDU), governor of Baden-Württemberg, stated that the dissolution of the DM would require a "broad political consensus" in Germany, which he did not currently see. He demanded a postponement until the governments' conference in 1996.[97]

The alternate CSU chairman Edmund Stoiber summarized concerns about the loss of the German national identity in a larger Europe, stating that Europe had degenerated from a "matter of the heart" to an "outgrowth of the head."[98] Norbert Blüm (CDU), minister for social affairs, strongly criticized the European Court. He argued that the court had interfered in too many areas and that European law in the future should be limited to general guidelines. Fewer rather than more regulations would help to democratize and integrate Europe.[99]

By late 1992, Germany also had to cope with a number of domestic problems—the integration and economic reconstruction of the former East Germany, slowing economic growth, and an unprecedented number of asylum-seekers, which would peak at 430,000 in the same year. "Against this background the Treaty of Maastricht hit the German population unprepared. Suddenly, the Germans seemed to realize how much Brussels already determined German politics."[100] In January 1992, the percentage of Germans who believed that the German identity would be lost in a united Europe had risen to 39 percent (October 1991: 21 percent).[101]

Against this backdrop, the constitutional implications of the Treaty of Maastricht became the subject of *Bund-Länder* debate. The Länder, led by SPD-governed Northrhine-Westphalia and CDU-governed Bavaria, demanded participation in any transfer of sovereign powers to the EU. This participation was to be extended not only to the areas of traditional state prerogatives like education, police, and culture, but also to national prerogatives like foreign and economic policy. Article 24 was to be modified and state powers were to be significantly increased.[102] In early November 1992, governor Max Streibl wrote to the chancellor and gave him an ultimatum: unless the federal government fulfilled the conditions set by the Länder, Kohl "could not count on the agreement by the Bundesrat."[103]

According to Article 24 of the constitution, the federal government can transfer sovereign rights to international institutions. Article 20 states that all state power derives from the people who elect the organs of the state. Article 79, paragraph 3 provides the so-called "eternal guarantee": "A modification of this constitution, which changes the federal structure of the state, the rights of the states in the legal process or the principles of articles 1 and 20 is not allowed."[104] The legal process in the EC seemed to be in conflict with German constitutional principles. According to Article 189 of the EEC treaty, the council and commission can pass laws ("directives") that are subject to the approval of the national governments, but not the national parliaments. In the Federal Republic, however, democratic approval of legal acts is necessary according to Article 20.

Kohl, who had thrown his full prestige behind the Treaty of Maastricht, was under pressure. In the final compromise, the Länder obtained large concessions. Article 23 of the constitution was enlarged significantly. The states would have to agree to a transfer of German sovereign rights to the European Union. Any measure of the European Union affecting the constitution would have to pass a two-thirds majority in the Bundesrat. In areas touching traditional state prerogatives, the Federal Republic would be represented by a delegate of the states. Florian Gerster, minister for federal and European affairs in Rhineland-Palatinate, concluded that Maastricht was a "success story" for the states.[105] This compromise further limited the future options of the German government.

The financing of the EU became another controversial topic. FDP chairman Otto Count Lambsdorff noted that the cohesion fund would bring Europe to the limits of its financial capability. In a position paper, Ingrid Matthäus-Maier, the SPD speaker for budgetary affairs, presented 10 requests to stabilize the EC budget. It included, among others, a stabilization of German contributions, transparency of the EC budget, frugality to finance the new tasks in Eastern Europe, a stronger position for the European Court of Auditors, a limit on budgetary growth, and a cancellation of special rebates for Great Britain.[106] The CDU/CSU rejoined that the "SPD is storming open doors. It is conspicuous that the SPD has been constantly criticizing our policies for Europe. The SPD is kindling a dangerous skepticism against the necessary European integration in our population in a self-serving way."[107]

Oskar Lafontaine, SPD governor of the Saarland, demanded renegotiations on a number of issues: improvements on the rights of the European Parliament, the conclusion of the financial negotiations (the "Delors-II-package"), limitations on the future number of commissioners and members of parliament, and the conclusion of the negotiations about the widening of the European Community.[108]

Despite all its public criticism, however, the SPD leadership stood behind European integration. The demand for renegotiation was dropped within days.[109] The SPD later reconfirmed its pro-European tradition. At the party convention in May 1991 in Bremen, Heidemarie Wieczorek-Zeul had reminded the delegates that the SPD was the first party to promote supranational integration between the world wars. She criticized France and Britain for having reverted to the traditional diplomacy of nation states.[110] Unlike the SPD, the Green Party was fundamentally critical of the European Union. Party members preferred a "networking of local activities" and the "cooperation of regions," but not a supranational construct.[111]

Despite the critical debate, the Bundestag agreed to the Maastricht Treaty on December 2, 1992, with an overwhelming majority of 543:16.[112] But the ratification process was far from over. The Danish population voted against the Treaty of Maastricht on June 2, 1992 in a referendum. Since unanimity was needed for ratification, the process seemed suddenly blocked. In another referendum, the French population supported the treaty by only a narrow margin of 51.05 percent on September 20. This close result in one of the core nations was regarded more as a criticism than as a confirmation of the treaty.

On September 17, the British pound and the Italian lira dropped out of the exchange rate mechanism despite massive central bank interventions in their favor. The Spanish peseta underwent a realignment of 5 percent. European integration had been dealt a severe blow.[113] The SPD members of parliament expressed their skepticism that a common currency could be introduced without political union. They also reiterated their demand that there should be no automatism between the second and third stages of the monetary and economic union and that the Bundestag and Bundesrat had to decide about the introduction of the third stage.[114]

A little less than a year after the 1992 crisis, the markets tested the EMS again. Between July 8, 1993, and August 1, 1993, the Bundesbank had to sell DM 107 billion in support of the EMS currencies. While in 1992 mainly two currencies—the British pound and the Italian lira—depreciated against the D-mark, in 1993 the D-mark sharply appreciated against almost all EC currencies. In response, Germany requested a widening of the fluctuation margins between currencies to a single corridor allowing fluctuations of 15 percent in either direction. A French proposal to appreciate the D-mark was not accepted. On August 2, the finance ministers and central bank governors sanctioned the new approach. Only the Dutch guilder retained its narrow fluctuation margin.[115] Jürgen Pfister, chief economist of the Commerzbank AG, commented, "The idea of the EMS had been put on its head. A system of fixed, but adjustable exchange rates had mutated into a system of non-fixed exchange rates that also were not adjustable anymore."[116] Josef Joffe, columnist of the *Süddeutsche Zeitung,* summarized a prevalent sentiment: "August 2, 1993, had been the farewell to the idea of a *Kleineuropa* (core Europe)."[117]

Kohl continued to defend monetary union, inviting criticism even from public figures close to the government. Monetary union was the main lever for moving France toward political union, his big project. When Kohl's vice-press secretary cautioned him that the D-mark was the national symbol of German identity, Kohl replied harshly that then the government would have to start a new press campaign. Another of his advisors mentioned that "to contradict Kohl in European issues would be deadly." In September, the CDU/CSU members of the German parliament wrote in a position paper that there was "no doubt about the monetary union."[118]

Most CDU politicians supported Kohl publicly, but made more reserved statements privately. Finance undersecretary Horst Köhler mentioned in a small circle that only France, Belgium, Luxembourg, and the Netherlands would be fit for a monetary union by 1999. In public, finance minister Theo Waigel supported monetary union, but privately he stated that monetary union was solely Kohl's idea. Kurt Biedenkopf, governor of

Saxony and a long time rival of Kohl's within the CDU, became the first top-level CDU politician to come out openly against the European currency in March 1994, saying that he "had problems with the goal of a common currency."[119]

The German supreme court also became involved in the deliberations. Four "green" members of the European Parliament as well as Manfred Brunner (FDP), the former chief of cabinet of the German EC commissioner Martin Bangemann (FDP) appealed to the supreme court, arguing that the Treaty of Maastricht would endanger the German constitution and currency. The supreme court took the complaint seriously, issuing a detailed catalogue of 15 questions to be answered by the federal government. Among other questions, the court demanded to know whether the German parliament would still have its constitutional powers in the new Europe and whether the transfer of sovereign rights to the union level was irreversible, especially if the future European Central Bank did not preserve price stability. The foreign and finance ministers had to be present for detailed hearings.[120] All of a sudden, Germany, which had been in the vanguard of the European process, was in danger of failure.

On October 13, 1993, the court issued a judgment that approved the Treaty of Maastricht and removed the last barrier to German ratification of the treaty. The very same evening the federal government handed over its ratification document. Germany was the last state to ratify the treaty.[121]

The judges imposed strict conditions upon the European process and institutions. The democratic foundations of the European Union would have to be expanded in line with integration. The Bundestag would have to retain "substantial powers."[122] The union would not be allowed to levy financial obligations on its members without consent of these members. In addition, the federal government would remain one of the "masters of the treaty." Its agreement to the treaty would not constitute an "automatism to economic and monetary union." Each further step of integration would have to be based on the conditions which were laid down in the treaty and could have been foreseen at the time of its ratification. New EU measures would have to be agreed to by the federal government.[123] The treaty, designed for an unlimited time, could also be canceled by an appropriate legal act. If European organs used their powers in ways that were not covered by the treaty and the German ratification law, this would not be binding for Germany.[124] The court also explicitly reserved its right to examine whether the organs of the union remained within their competencies and powers. The court summarized that the Treaty of Maastricht would create a "European association of states, which would be based on the individual states and respect their national identities." The foundation of a "United States of Europe" was "not intended," according to the judges.[125]

Both the *Bund-Länder* compromise and the supreme court further limited the government's options. Plans for a political union based on supranational integration were, if not impossible, relegated to a very distant future. Evaluating the events of the past years, Edmund Stoiber, the new governor of Bavaria, remarked that "the United States of Europe had been the goal of a generation from the sixties and seventies. Europe may be dear and worthy to us, but it cannot become a fatherland to replace the national fatherland."[126]

The CSU consequently replaced the phrase "United States of Europe" with "Union of European Nations" in its party program.[127] Stoiber said that the central European state, a goal still listed in the CDU party program, was not desirable anymore. From Adenauer to Kohl, all European governments had tried to merge the German identity in a European identity. According to Stoiber, this "process was over." Stoiber also warned about the "hollowing out of the German state."[128] Even Kohl, entitled by *Der Spiegel* "the last European," canceled the phrase "United States of Europe" from his speeches in late 1993, stating that the expression could be "misunderstood." In a smaller circle, he added that "we all once started as [European] idealists."[129]

V

During and after the ratification process, the contours of a new Germany within the EU began to emerge. Like the old Federal Republic, the new Germany was fundamentally supportive of integration. Particularly in such sensitive areas as the common foreign and security policy, the strengthening of the European institutions and parliament, and the strengthening of interior policies, official support for supranational solutions was still higher than in most other European nations. At the same time, the new Germany had a more pronounced concept of national interests within the EU. Germany was becoming more "normal" in the way it defined its Europeanist ambitions. Integration at all costs was being replaced by an evaluation of the costs and benefits to Germany.

The government had three major objectives: further institutional reform and strengthening of the European Union, the widening of the EU to the north and the East, and the preservation of a "special" relationship with France. In general, the government tried to downplay any conflicts among those interests. When it became clear that Maastricht I would not include far-reaching institutional reforms, chancellor Kohl demanded in the negotiations for the treaty a clause calling for a government conference on institutional reform to start in 1996 (Maastricht II).

Constitutional limits, financial shortages, and public disenchantment had seriously limited the government's options for making another round of concessions. An increasingly skeptical German public did not help. Few of the fundamental EU conflicts of the past decade had been resolved. The overall situation had become even more complex due to the widening of the EU and the potential admission of Central and Eastern European countries. In this situation, a more explicit pursuit of national interests looked increasingly attractive.

After the ratification of the treaty, the emotional intensity of the domestic debate subsided. Whereas in the fall of 1992 47 percent of Germans feared that Germany's identity might be lost in the European Union, only 36 percent thought so in the spring of 1994.[130] The states had asserted their powers and thus been placated. The date for the creation of the Common Market passed on January 1, 1993, without revolutionary consequences for most German citizens. Only 45 percent of the proposals in the commission white book had been adopted.[131] The creation of a truly common market had not been accomplished, since the border controls had been partially replaced by domestic bureaucracy. Some core areas remained unsolved: the opening of inner-European borders and the concurrent cooperation in police matters as well as the harmonization of tax systems were still to be achieved. On January 1, 1994, the European Community became the European Union. No "big bang" accompanied this. For most Germans, this act was not much more than the creation of a new name with little impact on daily life.

The sentiment in Germany had shifted. Only 13 percent of Germans supported a centralized European state. Seventy-four percent preferred a confederation of states. These survey results were stable between 1992 and 1994, reflecting German preferences for highly decentralized ("federal") solutions. The population also opposed a common currency with a wide margin of 70 percent and preferred a reduction of German contributions to the EU budget.[132] The largest share of Germans (35 percent) wanted to retain the status of integration, while only 23 percent wanted further deepening.[133] Forty-one percent of the Germans thought that the countries of the EU had mostly contradictory interests, while 35 percent believed they had mostly common interests.[134]

These critical positions, however, did not lessen overall popular approval of the EU. It was as if the population had sensed the implicit interstate bargains hidden behind the EU structure—namely, German financial and political concessions in exchange for overall favorable security and economic conditions.[135] Forty-two percent of Germans agreed that the EU was primarily a structure to safeguard peace and freedom, whereas 32 percent thought that economic motives were dominant. Sixty-seven percent of Germans regarded it as good for the future that Germany was a member of the EU, although 32 percent said that Germany had more specific disadvantages than advantages (more advantages: 16 percent). Only 20 percent believed that Germany would be better off economically without the EU, while 50 percent did not believe this. Only 15 percent believed that the new Germany could better pursue its interests without the EU, while 70 percent thought that united Germany needed the EU to dampen fears and to show its partners that Germany was a reliable ally.[136] With the dampening of popular sentiment, political temptations to provide populist solutions decreased.

Further Institutional Reform and Deepening

The government continued to support stronger European institutions, including a strengthening of the parliament. The old motives for creating a close Western European union were given additional weight by the insight that a union that would admit additional new members would have to be reformed to remain viable. The CDU/CSU continued to favor the increase of the powers of the European parliament, the principle of majority votes in the council, the creation of a common foreign and security policy and common interior policies. A position paper mentioned that both parties were aware that in "some European states there were significant reservations" against increasing the powers of the parliament. But this should not keep Germany from striving for such powers and a uniform legal process: All laws were to be approved by the council and the parliament, and the parliament should have the full right to initiate laws.[137] The CSU position on Maastricht II was remarkably moderate and similar to the CDU. Only the expansion of EU powers was to be subject to a double majority: A majority of ministers would have to be replicated by a majority of the respective national populations.[138]

The SPD commission for European affairs largely agreed with the German government's objectives for Maastricht II, but differed in its analysis of the situation. It openly concluded that a true European Union in the form of a federal state would not be an option of the immediate future. Like the government parties, the SPD demanded the institution of a uniform legislative process, an increase of the powers of the European Parliament, and stronger cooperation in immigration, interior, environmental, and social policies. According to the SPD, however, it would not be possible to achieve policies anytime soon, since many member states would insist on the intergovernmental nature of these areas.[139]

Widening of the EU

Widening was of particular importance to Germany for two reasons. The EFTA states, the next round of members, shared Germany's general philosophies. The second round of widening to the East would also help to stabilize Central Europe. The pressures on Germany to support new entrants were strong: Germany was culturally close to Austria (one of the most likely candidates for membership) and close to the Northern European EFTA states. It shared many common interests with these states, among which assistance to the East and free trade were the most prevalent. Germany was also under strong pressure to assist the states of Central and Eastern Europe. An emphasis on widening was not new in the intellectual debate. Herbert Kremp of the conservative daily *Die Welt* had written in 1991 that "the idea to unite the industrial heartland of Europe, the West, was a form of assertion against Soviet hegemony and against the bipolar Soviet–American world directorate. . . . But the philosophy of the deepeners, core Europe, is dead. With the spreading of freedom in Eastern Europe, this idea lost its plausible motive. Pursued further, core Europe must degenerate into a European directorate over united Germany."[140]

In a 1992 speech, Willy Brandt developed similar ideas, saying that "many people became aware for the first time that Europe didn't end at the demarcation lines in the East and that we have neighbors in Central and Eastern Europe which are close to us." Brandt proposed an assistance scheme on a grand scale (like the Marshall Plan). Czechoslovakia, Poland, and Hungary could be members by the turn of the millennium. He conceded that there were worries in Brussels, but "that the EC had been founded to promote, not to hinder, the development and integration of new democracies."[141] At its 1991 party convention in Bremen, the SPD voted for a "United States of Europe" consisting of all European nations that desired to be members. Visions that placed Germany in the center of a united Europe were characterized by Peter Glotz as a "new German ideology joining the far right and the far left."[142]

Sir Ralf Dahrendorf, eminent British political scientist of German origin, mentioned in an interview that some circles in France and England regarded Kohl as the last "Westernist" among the leading German politicians.[143] The Green Party opposed the creation of a "European superpower" and demanded that a "deepening of existing structures must not hinder the opening and widening of the EU to the East."[144]

The German population also supported closer cooperation with Germany's eastern neighbors. After unification, 50 percent of those Germans surveyed in a poll stated that a united Europe should include the Soviet Union and Eastern Europe.[145] When a more specific question about the widening of the European Union was asked later, public opinion was more conservative. In an Emnid poll commissioned by *Der Spiegel* and the *Financial Times* in November 1994, only 24 percent of the surveyed Germans advocated a widening of the EU. By comparison, 42 percent of the British population advocated a widening of the EU. Widening would most likely imply higher German financial contributions to the EU and increasing industrial competition from the East. This caused concern about economic and social standards. The differing survey results can be interpreted as a conflict between general and long-term altruism on the one hand and specific and short-term self-interest on the other.[146]

The government presented deepening and widening as nonconflicting objectives. In a speech before the German Society for Foreign Affairs, Kinkel said that keeping Europe on the course of integration—in both the dimensions of deepening and widening—would remain the prime objective of German foreign policy.[147] Former foreign minister Hans-Dietrich Genscher said that the vitality of the European process was fed by two sources: deepening and widening.[148] Gerd Tebbe, a German official in the political directorate of the EC Commission wrote:

> The question of institutional reforms is of utmost importance. It is fundamental to the future political shape of the European Union and to the future of European integration. The positions of the member states diverge to a much larger extent than during the negotiations for the Common European Act or even the Treaty of Maastricht. . . . In particular the German diplomacy, which pursues deepening and widening equally, will be presented with an interesting challenge.[149]

The CDU made clear that there should not be an indefinite time span until negotiations with Central and Eastern European countries were started. In a position paper, the CDU emphasized that negotiations for EU membership of the Visegrad states should start immediately after the government conference of 1996. The CDU admitted the legitimacy of concerns that Germany would turn eastward, but played down the consequences:

"The widening to the East will make us a European inland state. . . . We remain part of the West, and our Eastern neighbors also want to be a part of the West [*sic*]."[150] Wolfgang Schäuble, leader of the CDU/CSU group in the Bundestag, said that he saw the year 2000 "as a perspective for membership." In economic matters, there could be longer adjustment periods, as there had been with Spain and Portugal.[151] Kurt Biedenkopf, the governor of Saxony, strongly demanded that Germany increase its efforts to promote the EU membership of Central European countries.[152]

The SPD was more cautious than the CDU/CSU or the FDP on the issue of widening, probably reflecting the fact that its clientele was more sensitive to social and economic issues. In 1994, the chairman of the SPD members of parliament, Hans-Ulrich Klose, had warned about the "dangerous illusion" of the market opening towards the East. The population could not bear the competition of low-wage countries and further loss of jobs.[153] The SPD called Kinkel's demands for a rapid widening of the EU "populist" and "unrealistic."[154] During a speech in Prague, SPD chairman Rudolf Scharping expressed his understanding for the desire of the Czech Republic to be accepted as a member of the union, but he also pointed to the fact that this would be a long process with considerable difficulties.[155] Overall, the SPD addressed the issue of EU membership of Central European states in vague terms, claiming that these states "must have an all-European perspective."[156]

The German convention of industry and trade demanded that the Central and Eastern European states be given a medium- and long-term strategy on how to bridge the gap until EU membership. The best way would be the increase of free trade. However, Germany should avoid creating "exaggerated hopes: After the accession of Austria and the Nordic states the EU needs some breathing space."[157]

Initially, Germany was expected to press for the early inclusion of Central and Eastern European states into the EC, but it exercised considerable restraint. Before the admission of more members, political union in (Western) Europe was to be completed. It was the Dutch EC commissioner Frans Andriesen who broke the taboo and openly asked in 1991 whether it was "high time to design the structure of a Community of the 24."[158] A short time later, British foreign minister Douglas Hurd stated that Britain wanted to see a very open and large Europe: "Who would want to say no to Sweden and Austria?"[159]

A number of "association treaties" were concluded with the EFTA states but—rightly—regarded as interim solutions by those nations. EU membership remained the objective. During the second half of 1992,

Germany increasingly lent its weight to these demands. Paradoxically, the goal was still "deepening," not "widening," of the EU.[160] After the negative Danish referendum in the summer of 1992, the German government hoped that membership negotiations with the other Scandinavian nations and Austria would increase the pressure on Denmark. At the Edinburgh summit of December 11–12, 1992, the EU nations agreed upon negotiations that were taken up on January 1, 1993.[161]

The EU nations agreed in principle on the timetable for the acceptance of the EFTA states at the Copenhagen EC summit in the summer of 1993. Poland, Hungary, and the Czech and Slovak Republics were given "a perspective to become EU members." Even Kohl came out more openly in favor of widening. In a government declaration of November 1993, he stated, "I think it would be unbearable for us Germans if the Western borders of the Czech Republic and Poland should remain the Eastern border of the political union indefinitely." Nevertheless, he remained cautious: The passage on Eastern Europe had a length of only two short paragraphs in six pages of dense text.[162] In the East, Kohl used a clearer language: When visited by the Polish prime minister in April 1994, he told his colleague that "the EU would be a torso without Poland" and promised "to use the upcoming German presidency to find useful measures for the time until Poland had become a full member."[163]

In the second half of 1994, Germany assumed the EU presidency for the first time since 1988. In an article in *Europa-Archiv,* foreign minister Kinkel summarized the German goals for the presidency as follows: a contribution to the creation of a lasting order of peace in Europe, a decisive process for bringing the Central and Eastern European states closer to the European Union, and the securing of an economically healthy European Union that was able to act politically. Kinkel mentioned deepening last.[164]

On March 1, 1994, the EU and the first round of applicants concluded negotiations for the accession of Austria, Sweden, Finland, and Norway. *Der Spiegel* commented that the first of March "was a good-bye from the Europe of the founding fathers. On this day, Europe has voted against deepening, which had been France's major goal. What could not be achieved in the Europe of the six or twelve cannot succeed with 16 members."[165] According to *Der Spiegel,* "Germany was indisputably setting the tone this time." Kinkel perceived the negotiations as an important step in the "balancing of the heretofore Southern-tilted community."[166] In a government declaration, Kinkel remarked that "the widening is an encouraging signal to the reforming democracies in Central and Eastern Europe. . . . It is clear now that a united Germany will not remain the eastern border country of the EU; it moves to its political center instead. The acceptance of the three Nordic states and of Austria is an important step to restore the balance in Europe. The German government has never identified itself with a Western or Southwestern Union; it has always declared its loyalty to all of Europe."[167]

Preservation of the "Special Relationship" with France

This increasing German support for widening had to be reconciled with the need to preserve the special German-French relationship. By late 1993, the French-German tandem had been severely burdened by currency crises in the EMS, different positions in trade disputes with the United States, and a growing French apprehension of German power in the EU. Many in France felt that Germany had become the senior partner in the relationship, which presented a problem for prestige-seeking France. Christoph Bertram wrote, "Those in France who are thinking in purely national categories must feel that Germany won first prize in the breakdown of the order of Yalta, while France had lost."[168]

Chancellor Kohl assigned a high priority to the accommodation of French interests and worries and reiterated that the fate of France and Germany was irrevocably interlinked and that an expansion of the EC to the East should not be pushed actively.[169] Germany's invitation of the heads of state of Poland, Hungary, the Czech Republic, Slovakia, Romania, and Bulgaria to the December 1994 EU summit in Essen illustrates German sensitivity on the issue. During the preparations, the chancellor's office met with resistance by EU member nations and repeatedly canceled the invitations. After much wavering, the Central and Eastern European nations finally participated in the summit. Helmut Kohl told them, "Today you are still guests. But within a reasonable time, you will be members."[170]

Despite its self-proclaimed position as "godfather and attorney of the Eastern nations," Germany showed no sign that it was willing to risk EU relations for the issue of membership. The Central European states remained optimistic in public, but privately, a Czech diplomat conceded that he did not believe in Czech membership before 2005. "Anything sooner would be wishful thinking."[171]

German caution with regard to French interests could not prevent frequent atmospheric disturbances. In 1993, *Le Monde* detected an "interest rate dictate" by the Bundesbank. Trade presented another problem—Germany was expected by the United States to check French protectionist tendencies in the negotiations of the GATT Uruguay

Round.[172] Germany's growing status in Eastern Europe and its close ties with Russia were another problem of prestige for France. *Le Monde* saw "frictions and fissures" in the bilateral relationship.[173]

French politicians had hoped to check the growing weight of Germany through its integration into Europe and superior French diplomacy. Initially, Jacques Attali had advised his government to "de-base the DM as a lead currency" through monetary union.[174] Now, more and more French observers feared that the economic union would benefit Germany most. Former French general Gallois explained, "We can now understand why Germany was so strongly promoting European unity." An internal analysis by the German foreign office took up this argument, stating that "The situation and the parameters—and thus France's weight in Europe—had changed."[175] In the summer of 1993, foreign minister Alain Juppé explained that there were "objective difficulties" in the French-German relationship.[176] Former chancellor Helmut Schmidt wrote in the Parisian weekly *Globe-Hebedo*, "French-German cooperation has been dissolving since 1989 and Helmut Kohl has done nothing to prevent this process."[177]

Both governments tried to limit the damage. In October, the German chancellor spoke to a select audience invited to the German embassy in Paris: "France and Germany have the key roles in the construction of a united Europe. The quality of the German-French relationship determines the well-being of the whole continent. Our countries have to continue to grow even closer together. They have to become the core of the united Europe."[178]

Kohl supported the French position in the GATT negotiations, which raised his prestige in France. As the first foreign politician to do so since 1919, he was invited to speak before the French senate. There, he presented a strong and emotional plea for a united Europe and was rewarded with a standing ovation.[179] Mitterrand, in turn, defended Kohl and Germany's position: Reunification would not lead to an estrangement between Germany and France, and both would continue to be at the fore in promoting grand European initiatives.[180]

By the spring of 1994, however, tensions had resurfaced. French diplomats complained about a German power play during the widening of the EU. The French ambassador to Germany, François Scheer, criticized German foreign policy strongly at a press conference. In reaction, Kinkel mentioned that he would summon Scheer to report, a process that had no precedence in French-German relations.[181]

Again, high level politicians made strong efforts to repair the damage. Kinkel and Juppé invoked the French-German "special relationship," stating that neither country wanted a loose, "British" European Union.[182]

Mitterrand praised the positive state of the French-German relations.[183] Kinkel repeated that the French-German "special relationship" was of utmost importance and would remain the central axis of Europe.[184] A few days later Kinkel was received warmly in France.[185] In July, the newly elected German president, Roman Herzog, also emphasized the special German relationship with France.[186] Mitterrand invited the German parts of the Eurocorps to participate in the parade celebrating the French national holiday on July 14. Fifty-eight percent of the French population backed his move.[187] At the parade itself, the German units received widespread applause.[188] Yet the underlying atmosphere had changed. *Le Monde* summarized the new situation: "Nowadays France needs Germany more than Germany needs France."[189]

VI

Though Germany succeeded in admitting EFTA nations into the EU during its EU presidency of 1994, progress was more limited on most other issues. A British veto stopped the French-German initiative to make Belgian prime minister Jean-Luc Dehane the new president of the EU commission, symbolizing a growing immobilization of the EU.[190] A conflict over voting rights in the European Council was papered over by a weak compromise between Britain and the more integration-minded members states.[191] Further supranational integration in police matters, a pressing issue for Germany, stalled. Germany did not succeed in passing a convention for a European police organization, EUROPOL. Britain and sovereignty-minded France opposed the transfer of sovereign rights to this organization.[192] The principle of subsidiarity led to a creeping weakening of the union. By mid-1994, the commission had limited its legal initiatives considerably. Deregulation on technical issues continued, but integration in the political areas—foreign policies, social policies, immigration, combating international crime, and increasing parliamentary powers—remained elusive.

Impatience with the unsatisfactory progress of deepening was growing in Germany. As a result, Germany began to develop new concepts to overcome the stalemate. One was the "Europe of different speeds." Kinkel asked whether the convoy should be determined by the slowest ship or whether those who wanted to proceed faster were free to do so. He added that the German preference was to have all members on board but that Germany wanted a strong European core. A limited number of EU members should proceed faster in monetary and military integration.[193] Hans Tietmeyer, president of the Bundesbank, presented a model of "concentric circles."[194] The political scientist Josef Janning claimed that Europe needed different speeds.[195]

In the fall of 1994, Wolfgang Schäuble and the CDU foreign policy expert Karl Lamers presented a paper entitled "Deliberations on European Policies." The paper supported a widening of the EU to the East. Before a widening could be undertaken, however, the existing structures in Europe had to be deepened and strengthened. Schäuble and Lamers proposed that a European "core" proceed alone, not blocked by vetoes of other nations. They also designated the members they saw fit for the core: Germany, France, Belgium, Luxembourg, and the Netherlands.[196]

The paper caused decidedly negative international and domestic reactions.[197] Former foreign minister Hans-Dietrich Genscher characterized the paper as an "attempt by the CDU/CSU to gain profile in foreign policy, a traditional domain of the FDP." He criticized the paper for excluding certain nations. The distinction between core and periphery would not lead to progress, but to "nuclear fission."[198] The SPD demanded that Helmut Kohl distance himself from the Schäuble-Lamers paper, which, according to the SPD, was "tactless."[199] Klaus Hänsch (SPD), the president of the European Parliament, remarked that "to destroy Maastricht would not create a core, only chaos." After a few days, Schäuble conceded that his terminology had been ill chosen. He had thought of a "magnet," rather than a "core." But he also defended the substance of his proposals. Hilmar Kopper, chairman of the Deutsche Bank, defended the Schäuble paper, because "it had made explicit what we all feared or knew."[200]

It is likely that the "deliberations" were an attempt of the traditional Europeanists around Helmut Kohl to formulate strategies that would allow progress in European integration. Schäuble and Lamers sketched positions that took into account the German national interest, allowed progress in Europe, and took into account domestic resistance. The "deliberations" were only semiofficial. They had been published with the letterhead of the CDU/CSU group of members of parliament but had not been voted upon by the members. The CDU/CSU group of members of parliament issued two official papers later, in June 1995. Both papers are much more moderate than the Schäuble-Lamers paper. For example, any reference to "core Europe" is missing.[201] The coauthorship of Wolfgang Schäuble is an indicator that the paper might have a trial balloon from the highest ranks of the government.[202]

It would have indeed reflected German interests: an integration of the Central and Eastern European states would increase Germany's security and benefit its economy.[203] A limitation of the economic and currency union to the "stable" states of core Europe would also have fit the preferences of Germany and many Germans, who feared that the D-mark would be weakened by the acceptance of economically weak states. Most Germans, and the Bundesbank, adhered to the so-called "crowning theory," according to which economic conditions had to be similar before a common currency could be introduced, not the other way round.[204] Finally, a core Europe would also have facilitated deepening and institutional reform, such as a strengthening of the European Parliament, again an established German interest.[205]

The Schäuble-Lamers paper may have been the last attempt to salvage the traditional German policy toward Europe. Increasingly, Germany was switching to a more "normal" interest-based policy on issues like economic and monetary union and German net contributions to the EU. Domestic opinion, along with a very real exhaustion of financial resources, contributed to this trend. In November 1996, 53 percent of all Germans were against economic and monetary union.[206] Moreover, the Federal Republic was not able to fulfill the criteria set for economic and monetary union either in 1995 or in 1996. The public deficit was markedly above the maximum rate of 3 percent. In 1995, only Ireland, Luxembourg, and—partially—Denmark fulfilled the criteria.[207] Once again, this lead to a debate about the Euro. Parts of the SPD, which was looking for campaign themes for the 1998 federal elections, but also from the CDU/CSU, strongly criticized the Euro. Kurt Biedenkopf, CDU governor of Saxony and a longtime rival of Kohl's, called the common European currency "politically unnecessary" and "economically harmful."[208] Hans Tietmeyer, president of the Bundesbank, declared in 1997 that a postponement of the currency union "would not be a catastrophe" and that a fulfillment of the criteria would not guarantee stability by itself.[209]

The proponents of economic and monetary union came mostly from the older generation of politicians. Kohl, of course, argued that economic integration was a necessary prerequisite for political union, which in turn would prevent national egotisms and their potentially devastating effects.[210] President Roman Herzog warned of "competitive devaluations, trade wars, protectionism, renationalization of economic policies, deflation and potentially depression."[211] Former chancellor Helmut Schmidt repeatedly argued for economic and monetary union and pointed toward the negative political consequences of a failure of the project.[212]

Domestic criticism had effects on official policies: the Federal Republic, represented by finance minister Theo Waigel, demanded a contractual agreement to safeguard economic stability within the union, the so-called "stability pact." In September 1996, Germany succeeded in pushing through a number of sanctions against states that would deviate from a path of solid fiscal policies. Initially, those sanctions were to happen automatically.[213] During the negotiations, however, there were considerable conflicts between the German and French sides. France did not want the sanctions to happen automatically and wanted to create a so-called "stability council." This in turn bore the potential of seriously endangering the independence of the European Central Bank. The bank, whose existence and independence was the major condition for a German participation in economic and monetary union, were to be complemented, in the words of Lionel Jospin, by a "sort of European economic government."[214] In Dublin, Germany agreed to make sanctions conditional on a 2/3 majority in the council of ministers. France, in turn, dropped their request for a stability council. The informal group that was agreed upon in march 1997 does not pose a threat to the independence of the European Central Bank.[215]

In 1997, the first round of states for economic and monetary union was informally determined, although some of the original criteria had to be bent. Despite continuing domestic criticism, the Bundestag approved Germany's participation in the economic and monetary union by an overwhelming majority of 575 to 35 votes on April 2, 1998. Only the Party for Democratic Socialism had voted against it. The conflicts between France and Germany proved enduring. In the spring of 1998, the two countries found themselves on opposite sides on the question of who would become the first president of the European Central Bank. They reached a compromise according to which the (German-backed) Dutch president Wim Duisenberg was to serve only half a term.

Germany's net payor position in the EU became a pressing topic, not only in public debate, but even in official government policy. Previously, the government had argued that Germany's net benefits from the EU in terms of security, markets, and economic stability by far exceeded its net payments. But increasingly strained public finances began to dictate a closer scrutiny of German financial contributions to the EU. Whereas the Federal Republic had been extremely generous in subsidizing EU initiatives in the early 90s, it became increasingly difficult to continue this policy. With 30 percent of the EU budget, the Federal Republic pays for a proportionate share of the gross revenues of the EU. But only a small amount of these funds is flowing back into Germany, which makes Germany by far the largest net payor. In 1995, the per capita contribution of Germany, for example, was eight times higher than that of France.[216] The finance ministers of the German Länder complained that the Federal Republic had overpaid by DM 12.7 billion in the first half of the 1990s.[217]

A blistering sore in the budget of the European Union was—and is—the Common Agricultural Policy. Farm subsidies under this program in 1995 accounted for 48.9 percent of the total EU budget. Critics had repeatedly demanded a liberalization of this policy, a step that would enable massive savings. The farm lobby so far has prevented all steps aimed at fundamental reform. A second major drain on EU finances was the regional funds, which accounted for 29.8 percent of the EU budget. Together, these programs amounted to two-thirds of the EU budget.[218] The Federal Republic was not able to lead a reform course. A cancellation of agricultural subsidies would hurt the powerful domestic farm lobby.[219] Moreover, Germany did not fully support a reform of regional subsidies, because this might have hurt the Central European entry candidates, while Germany had an interest in strengthening those economies.[220]

German finance minister Theo Waigel proposed placing a cap on national contributions. This would limit German payments, while leaving the structure of benefits roughly intact—hardly a reform course.[221] According to calculations of the finance ministry, the additional costs for this policy would have to be borne largely by Great Britain in the form of a reduced rebate.[222] Interestingly, the German concept had a similar structure to the concessions that Margaret Thatcher had asserted for Great Britain in the 1980s.

VII

The backdrop for the Amsterdam government conference on the reform of the European Union, which Germany had demanded during the negotiations on the Treaty of Maastricht, was therefore less than promising. In Articles A and B of the treaty, the governments agreed to further develop integration in the European Union. The conference lasted from March 1996 to June 1997 and produced few results. Even more than during the negotiations for the widening of the EU, it became clear that Germany would pursue a more "normal" foreign policy, one that was based on states' distinctive national interests. The "integration-at-all-costs" approach of the early 1990s was outmoded. Germany increasingly used balancing within the union to further its own interests, even at the risk of deteriorating relations with France.

There was little doubt that the EU needed to be reformed. In order to prepare for further widening, the decision-making structures of the union needed a fundamental overhaul.[223] Moreover, the loss of acceptance by EU citizens needed the be countered with a decisive democratization of procedures.[224] Moreover, the EU needed stronger capacities for defense and crisis management.[225]

The chances for such a fundamental reform were slim. The reflection group charged with preparing the conference showed that there was little consensus among the 15 EU states. It listed problems rather than solutions.[226] German under secretary of state Werner Hoyer complained about "too many national egotisms" among the other states.[227] But Germany had also lost its elan. In his government declaration on the German goals for the conference, Kohl emphasized that there could be no going back to the power politics of another era and that Germany had to be very sensitive. But he also was much more cautious with optimistic statements about the future of Europe, having given up his standard reference to the "United States of Europe" even before.[228]

The position of the Federal Republic during the conference can be labeled "moderate intergovernmental," which represented a break from the supranational aspirations of earlier times.[229] France, Great Britain, and Germany agreed that the Council should remain the decisive organ of the EU. Germany, however, wanted to strengthen majority decisions and have those decisions better reflect the represented sizes of population. At the same time, "sensitive areas" such as public finances, taxation, social policies, and industrial policies were to be excluded.[230] This showed that the Federal Republic, too, had an inconsistent reform concept. The Federal Republic's inability to achieve domestic economic reform was reflected in its policies toward the EU. At the same time, a streamlining of decision-making structures was in Germany's interest: the EU had to be able to accommodate more members. A change in the weighting of votes would better reflect Germany's position. Germany also wanted to strengthen the European Parliament (a longtime request) and the European Commission. Because Germany also accepted the European Council as the major organ, this would resemble a two-chamber system, which in turn would render decision more rather than less effective and contradict one German objective.[231]

The German position by now was rather "normal" compared to the positions of France and Great Britain. France also wanted to reform the weighing of the votes to better reflect actual potential. Foreign minister Juppé wanted to limit the number of Commissioners to 12 and widen the margin of votes between the small and the large members from 2–10 to 3–25.[232] Great Britain and Italy also proposed a limitation on the number of commissioners; Spain made a similar proposal.[233]

Subsequently, Germany modified its position and reverted to "balancing," where it teamed up with the smaller states who were afraid of losing influence. By helping them in their resistance to a fundamental reform of voting rights,[234] Germany gained clients but risked good relations with France.[235] At the special summit of Noordwijk in late May 1997, the federal government openly supported the smaller states. A German initiative helped postpone this question.[236] As an interim step, it was agreed to limit the number of commissioners to 20. This did not increase the weight of the larger states but rather reduced it, since every state was granted at least one commissioner. The entry of new members threatened the right of the large states to send a second commissioner to Brussels.

German policy was a mixture of traditional and new elements. On the one hand, the Federal Republic had always lent a special ear to the concerns of the smaller states, who, like Germany, wanted to strengthen international law as opposed to the use of power. Germany, the Benelux states, and the Scandinavian states wanted to strengthen the European Parliament; France opposed this step. Germany and the smaller states—especially Denmark, Sweden, and Finland—had a vital interest in the widening of the union, something that France, Great Britain, and Spain were rather unenthusiastic about. One group of reasons was financial—the structural and agricultural funds would experience further strains.[237] Moreover, the political elites, especially in France, were still thinking in categories of power balances and were afraid of growing German influence through admission of further Eastern states. France demanded a stronger engagement of the EU in the Mediterranean as a counterweight.[238] This "balancing within the EU" bore the potential of dividing the two most important engines of European unification, France and Germany. A common letter by Helmut Kohl and Jacques Chirac dated December 9, 1996 demonstrated the inability of the two countries to reach an agreement rather than giving the union a new impetus.[239]

The final talks about the enlargement of the EU were lengthy and conflict-ridden.[240] Shortly before the summit in December 1997, Kohl uttered doubts in the cabinet about whether the conference would lead to decisive results. Kohl mentioned that there was to be a secret vote: the outcome was far from certain.[241] The outcome of the summit was indeed limited. The EU states decided to begin entry negotiations with Poland, Hungary, the Czech Republic, Estonia, Slovenia, and Cyprus in April 1998.[242] Josef Janning hypothesized that Germany promoted widening at the cost of deeper integration (both not necessarily in the interest of France). He also saw the emergence of blocs within the EU. Germany will put itself increasingly in the role of the advocate of Central and Eastern European states; France will increasingly be involved in the Mediterranean.[243]

The smaller EU states and Germany teamed up against France on yet another issue. Those Scandinavian countries that were not members of the WEU strongly opposed the strengthening of a European defense identity, a longtime French interest. Those states counted on NATO and the United States. In the mid 1990s, France had planned to return to the military organization of NATO. To prepare for this step, France wished to strengthen the EU's security capabilities by giving the WEU independent capabilities for action.[244] The existing structures for common foreign and security policies were to be expanded. Moreover, a high commissioner for EU foreign policy was to be instituted.[245]

This was in Germany's interest to only a limited extent. First and foremost, Germany still relied on the United States for its security. The French initiative could potentially endanger U.S. engagement in Europe. Moreover, the French government was not ready to change the intergovernmental character of decision making toward a more supranational common foreign and security policy.[246] In the worst case, this would create a structure within which the European nonnuclear powers would have been dependent on the European nuclear powers. The French insistence on an independent foreign policy was demonstrated by its resumption of nuclear tests in the Pacific. It did not help to allay German concerns about the predictability of French security policy.[247] The schisms were deep— Great Britain and the smaller EU states categorically rejected the French proposals.[248]

The German–French guideline for Common Foreign and Security Policy (CFSP) of February 27, 1996 reflected a need to paper over the differences. It contained the goals of stabilizing the eastern and southern border regions of the EU, strengthening transatlantic relations, and strengthening relations with Russia and Ukraine. The clauses about the CFSP were vague and general, containing the demand for more efficient decision making and an institution that would represent the EU in external affairs.[249]

At the government conference, Germany proposed installing a high commissioner who would chair the political committee of the Common Foreign and Security Policy mechanism. This was much less than the French demanded.[250] The final solution was a defeat for France. Although a high commissioner was to be installed, his or her position would be a lower one in the hierarchy of EU organs. The chairman of the European

Council will continue to represent the EU in external affairs and determine the EU position in international organizations and conferences. Moreover, France's efforts to strengthen the WEU beyond the tasks that it had been given during the Petersberg declaration of 1992 were largely frustrated.

In summary, the Federal Republic had begun to return to a more normal "interest-based" foreign policy in the second half of the 1990s and had left the path of Europeanist orthodoxy it had followed from the early 1950s to the early 1990s. The Federal Republic did not even shy away from a political conflict with France, and coalition-building with the smaller member states. Not even a "light" version of the traditional German policy toward Europe (e.g., as proposed in the Schäuble-Lamers paper) can be detected. The Treaty of Amsterdam does have a "flexibility clause," but it is ineffective: a majority of all states and the commission must agree to a "flexibilization" of policies. Moreover, the "sensitive" areas, in which integration has already proceeded far, are exempt from "flexibilization."[251]

In French circles, traditional power-balancing arguments grew stronger.[252] In early 1999, *Le Figaro* ran the headline "Le dictat," a reference to Nazi Germany's policies at the Munich conference of 1938.[253] An article in the weekly *L'express* with the title "Is Germany Dangerous?," complained about the asymmetric power relationship between France and its eastern neighbor. Taking Central and Eastern Europe into consideration, Germany was said to have a sphere of influence of 180 million people.[254] French political scientist Yvonne Bollmann publicized certain hypotheses in her book *The German Temptation*. A change in the German postal code system from 4 to 5 digits would be an indicator that Germany planned a territorial expansion. Especially at the eastern borders and in Alsace-Lorraine, the system would allow for additional numbers.[255] Absurd as they were, those hypotheses found some recognition in the public debate.

Similar developments can be detected in German public opinion. In an article in the conservative *Frankfurter Allgemeine Zeitung*,[256] the author foresees a "natural" restitution of the old international order to a system of competing national states.[257] The French-German youth exchange programs designed by Adenauer and de Gaulle to improve relations between the neighboring nations are deemed to have failed. In a survey held in the summer of 1997, 75 percent of interviewees stated that the French-German friendship was nothing but a myth.[258]

By the late 1990s, the fabric of the EU was still holding up. But the EU increasingly looked like a conservative club that could preserve the existing state of affairs at best. Fundamental reform in decision-making procedures, democratization and strengthening of the parliament, a common defense identity, economic and fiscal reform, and widening to the East seemed unattainable. France and Great Britain continued to block efforts to strengthen the parliament. Germany was not able to push through widening, partially in consideration of French interests, but also because this step would require fundamental fiscal and economic reforms, for which Germany was not ready. Finally, Germany was skeptical about strengthening independent security capabilities if this step could lead to an alienation of the United States. The new Schröder government thus inherited a situation and a German foreign policy that had changed considerably since the early 1990s.

VI

The Return of "Balancing":
Germany and NATO
Enlargement, 1991–1997

D
ue to the breakdown of the communist system, Germany and its security partners had the opportunity (and the obligation) to create new security structures for Europe. Possible approaches and designs included NATO enlargement, the strengthening of the OSCE, the creation of the North Atlantic Cooperation Council, the Partnership for Peace, and the European Security Council, the enlargement of the WEU, the widening of the EU, and the conclusion of far-reaching association treaties for the reforming countries. In general, these approaches can be classified as "Atlanticist" (NATO enlargement), "Europeanist" (the creation of a Western European defense identity, e.g., under the auspices of the WEU), or "all-European multilateral" (OSCE, contact group for Bosnia). Many of these approaches were not mutually exclusive. A wide range of options existed. Yet the "Atlanticists" won out and NATO expanded in 1997.

The controversy over NATO enlargement provides an opportunity to study German foreign policy in an uncharted area, where no ready-made answers existed. It is thus the first opportunity to study German foreign policy in the new security environment. In essence, NATO enlargement is the expansion of a U.S.-led security alliance, which might eventually develop a stronger European pillar. It falls short of the construction of an all-European collective system of security. In addition, NATO enlargement was increasingly viewed as an adversarial act by Russia. It therefore posed a security dilemma for Germany. Two of its major security objectives—

maintaining a U.S. commitment to Europe and maintaining and building a cooperative security system for all of Europe—are potentially at odds. Power structure as explained by asymmetric vulnerabilities together with insights from the civilian-power paradigm and bureaucratic politics explain German policy well.

Vulnerabilities

An all-European cooperative security system, coupled with a defensive back-up alliance (NATO) best reflected German preferences. Germany continued to view itself as dependent on the U.S. security shield. The slow progress of a European defense identity provided a strong incentive for Germany to strengthen and redefine NATO in a way that would guarantee continued U.S. commitment to Germany's security. At the same time, the German (and Western) relationship with Russia was key to whether a cooperative or confrontational security system would arise in Europe. Germany, as the Western state most affected by Russia, therefore paid great attention to the Russian position.

Middle Power and Civilian Values

For a traditional power, the "Europeanist" alternative to NATO enlargement held considerable attraction (as repeatedly demonstrated by France). It held the potential for Germany to establish itself as the leader of a (Western) European defense union able to provide for its own defense without threatening Russia. But Germany's nontraditional values decreased its interest in such an alternative. First, alliance leadership and prestige were less important to Germany. Second, Germany's obsession with stability and peaceful change made the risks of a vigorous pursuit of the Europeanist alternative (U.S. disengagement, renationalization) more costly for Germany than they might be for another state.

Bureaucratic Politics

Germany played a crucial role in ushering in the second stage in the debate on NATO enlargement when defense minister Rühe placed the topic on the international agenda. But Germany is erroneously seen by many analysts as a nation that vigorously campaigned for enlargement. In reality, German policy was much more cautious and omnidirectional. Instances of German initiative are best explained by bureaucratic politics.

The defense and foreign ministers were given the opportunity by the chancellor's office to explore their alternative visions of the future at times when the overall situation seemed to allow this probing. The defense minister used this opportunity to campaign for enlargement. The chancellor and the foreign minister generally favored the strengthening of multilateral structures. Because of the open international situation, however, both positions coexisted without the chancellor asserting his position.

It is indicative of Germany's high (perceived) vulnerability to developments either in the United States or in Russia that the German chancellor did not start a major policy initiative personally, as he did with regard to promoting the European Union. Rather, Germany pursued an incremental and cautious course consistent with the risks it associated with any major policy change. One unnamed foreign ministry official called this approach "equilibrist," a term that fits Germany's policies remarkably well.

Between 1991 and 1997, the debate went through four phases. In the first phase (roughly from 1991 to early 1993), the West tried to increase security cooperation through various offers for bilateral association. In the second phase (from early 1993 until the Brussels NATO summit of December 1994), NATO enlargement came to dominate the debate. In the third phase, starting with the NATO summit of December 1994, a more realistic and somber assessment of NATO enlargement began to take hold, a belated evaluation that should have taken place two to three years earlier. In phase four, the NATO states agreed on the first round of enlargement in 1997.

Germany's policies in the security sphere were more low-key than in the economic or political area (EU). Germany acted as a supporter of multilateral security structures rather than as a creator. It is indicative of Germany's actual (or perceived) vulnerability and uncertainty avoidance that alternative security arrangements (and decisive German leadership) for creating an all-European system were never seriously explored.

The issue of NATO enlargement shows that the question of "German security interests" had become much more complex and that the Federal Republic was searching for a new definition of the national interest. The Federal Republic preferred a stable and democratic order in Eastern Europe, a continuing U.S. security shield, and a further development of the European Union. In this complex situation, a middle power like the Federal Republic had to look for principles of stability and consensus among the decisive powers. This, however, was a method that worked better before 1989, when the Soviet threat helped to forge a consensus in the West. After 1989, a consensus among the Western nations had become much more difficult to achieve. At the same time, Russia demanded more attention by Germany than by other Western powers. Germany found itself in a paradoxical position: at a time when its room for autonomous action had seemingly grown, a policy of consensus was more difficult—and yet more necessary—than ever.

II

The years between 1989 and 1991 were a particularly dense period of history. They included the opening of the Berlin Wall in December 1989, the unification of Germany in October 1990, the negotiation of the Conventional Forces in Europe (CFE) treaty in November 1990, the dissolution of the Warsaw Pact in April 1991, and the disintegration of the Soviet Union in December 1991. These sea changes provided the opportunity to create radically new security structures in Europe. Germany, in particular, had the opportunity to create a truly cooperative European security system for the first time since the genesis of modern Germany in 1871. By 1995, however, European security institutions constituted a maze of interlocking, partially competing, and partially complementary approaches—"Atlanticist," "Europeanist," and "all-European multilateral."[1]

All-European Multilateral Structures

With over 50 members, the OSCE is the most encompassing security institution in Europe. Originally known as the Council for Security and Cooperation in Europe (CSCE), it was created by the final declaration of Helsinki in 1975 and provided a multilateral code for East-West relations, containing agreements for the economic and political relations among states as well as for the protection of human and citizens' rights. In 1990, the (then) 34 heads of state and government of CSCE member states met in Paris to sign the "Charter of Paris for a Free Europe." At the conference in Helsinki in 1992, the CSCE created new mechanisms for conflict resolution. The CSCE became a "regional arrangement" in accordance with chapter VIII of the UN charter. This enabled the CSCE to send observers into crisis areas and to request the deployment of military forces by NATO or WEU.[2] In 1994, it was renamed Organization for Security and Cooperation in Europe (OSCE) and received a better infrastructure, including the position of a permanent secretary-general.

161

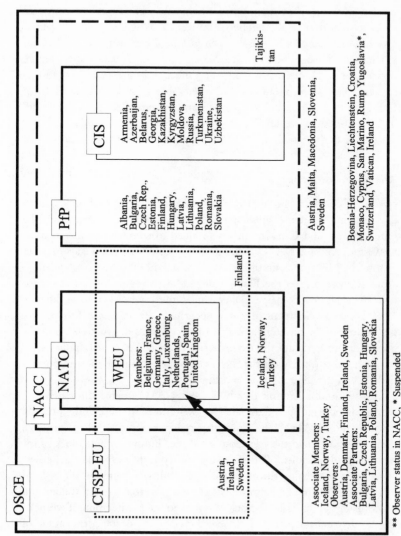

OSCE

NACC

NATO

WEU

Members:
Belgium, France,
Germany, Greece,
Italy, Luxemburg,
Netherlands,
Portugal, Spain,
United Kingdom

Iceland, Norway,
Turkey

Finland

CFSP-EU

Austria,
Ireland,
Sweden

PfP

Albania,
Bulgaria,
Czech Rep.,
Estonia,
Finland,
Hungary,
Latvia,
Lithuania,
Poland,
Romania,
Slovakia

CIS

Armenia,
Azerbaijan,
Belarus,
Georgia,
Kazakhstan,
Kyrgyzstan,
Moldova,
Russia,
Turkmenistan,
Ukraine,
Uzbekistan

Tajikis-
tan

Austria, Malta, Macedonia, Slovenia,
Sweden

Bosnia-Herzegovina, Liechtenstein, Croatia,
Monaco, Cyprus, San Marino, Rump Yugoslavia*,
Switzerland, Vatican, Ireland

Associate Members:
Iceland, Norway, Turkey
Observers:
Austria, Denmark, Finland, Ireland, Sweden
Associate Partners:
Bulgaria, Czech Republic, Estonia, Hungary,
Latvia, Lithuania, Poland, Romania, Slovakia

** Observer status in NACC, * Suspended

During the years of the breakdown of the communist system, a significant group in Germany, represented by then foreign minister Hans-Dietrich Genscher, believed that eventually the CSCE would be responsible for security in Europe, because it was the only encompassing collective system of security. With over 50 members, however, the OSCE so far has been too diverse to guarantee effective decision making. Moreover, the OSCE does not have a military infrastructure. Neither is its diplomatic infrastructure very extensive. Hopes that it would become a UN for Europe have mostly vanished. The Western states have directed more attention toward NATO.[3] However, a significant number of states, among them Russia and some CIS states, as well as some smaller and neutral Western European states, view the OSCE as the most important security arrangement in Europe.

Atlanticist Institutions

NATO, of course, is the most important "Atlanticist" institution: a collective system of defense encompassing 15 Western European states, the United States, and Canada, initially founded to counter the Soviet threat to Western Europe. NATO is the primary vehicle of U.S. engagement in Europe. In 1992, the main threat against which NATO was to safeguard— a massive attack from the East—vanished.[4] The search for new tasks for NATO began in 1989. James Baker named four potential tasks for the new NATO: the development of a new security architecture for Europe, the prevention of the proliferation of weapons of mass destruction, cooperation with the East, and the extension of cooperative security policies for the East. Baker made clear that NATO would remain the most important tie between the United States and Europe.[5]

At the London summit of July 6, 1990, NATO offered the East vastly increased cooperation and declared its intention to strengthen the political component of NATO.[6] The Copenhagen declaration of 1991 reaffirmed a decision to safeguard the common security of Europe by a network of interlocking institutions.[7] The new strategic concept of NATO acknowledged that the major threat had disappeared. Many minor threats and instabilities had emerged instead. NATO was now to safeguard welfare and peace against global risks, regional threats, and the proliferation of weapons of mass destruction. NATO still viewed itself as one of the cornerstones of a democratic and stable Europe, a transatlantic forum, a deterrent against attacks on members and the guarantor of a strategic balance in Europe. Crisis management and conflict prevention were given a new status, with defense becoming a supplementary task.[8] The concept was accepted unanimously, but NATO's original mission, which had been very specific, had been replaced with a more vague legitimization.

The heads of state and government also proposed a regular rhythm of consultations with the reforming countries through the North Atlantic Cooperation Council (NACC). The council had its origins in an October 1991 initiative by James Baker and Hans-Dietrich Genscher. It constituted itself on December 20, 1991, in Brussels.[9] It strengthened the political elements of NATO and expanded its tasks far beyond collective defense. In some areas, NATO assumed tasks that could also have been executed by the OSCE, for example in the area of verification and arms control as well as dispute resolution among reforming countries. In 1994, the NACC's activities were elevated to the next level when NATO proposed a "Partnership for Peace" (PfP) to the reforming countries, offering the possibility of even closer institutional association, including bilateral consultations, with NATO. The Partnership for Peace is a nonbinding forum for consultation and cooperation.

Europeanist Solutions

The Western European Union (WEU) and the Common Foreign and Security Policy (CFSP) of the European Union were the primary "Europeanist" structures. As opposed to all-European and Atlanticist institutions, the WEU, the Eurocorps, and the CFSP are Western European security institutions. The WEU was founded in 1948; Germany joined in 1954 at the same time it joined NATO.[10] For most of its existence, the WEU did not have its own infrastructure, since Article 4 of the WEU treaty forbids the duplication of NATO and WEU structures. Only with the renewed interest in European integration in the 1980s did the WEU become a potential candidate for a common European defense identity. In 1987, the WEU began to develop a somewhat more visible profile. In the Common European Act, the EC member states expressed their interest in a common European foreign policy and defense identity.[11] Yet there was no institutional link between the WEU and the EC/EU.

In December 1990, Helmut Kohl and François Mitterrand demanded a strengthening of the WEU and the provision of a link between the WEU and the EC. This proposal contained the potential for a future competition with NATO and a marginalization of the U.S. role in Europe—and that is how it was perceived by the United States, Great Britain, and the Netherlands. The U.S. government sent a sharp note expressing its concern.[12] At the 1991 Rome summit, George Bush asked whether the Europeans wanted to provide for their own defense—now would be the time to say so. The United States made clear that the WEU had to operate in accordance with the Atlantic alliance. This provision was integrated into the Treaty of Maastricht. The WEU was to become the security-political arm of the EU but would remain firmly integrated in the Atlantic alliance.[13] To date, however, the results have been meager.

The Eurocorps was another European initiative, presumably constituting the military core of a future European defense identity.[14] Based on an initiative by Mitterrand and Kohl, the French-German brigade was to be expanded to a multinational European corps.[15] The Eurocorps created the same problems as the proposed expansion of the WEU: The United States, Great Britain, the Netherlands, and Italy feared a competitor to NATO. The issue was resolved by placing the corps under NATO command in case of hostilities and crisis management.

III

In this network of interlocking institutions and differing approaches, German national interests were not easy to define and were the subject of considerable domestic debate. At times, German policy seemed to lack all conceptual foundations. There was a bewildering multitude of opinions, not only in the public debate, but also in the parties and even in the cabinet. The magazine *Focus* commented that there was a "Babylonian confusion."[16] David Anderson of the Aspen Institute Berlin complained that the policy of the Federal Republic was only to react to short-term trends instead of following strategic goals and assuming a leadership position.[17]

Under closer scrutiny, however, this complex debate reflected the dilemmas of a middle power in an increasingly uncertain international situation. Germany did follow its interests, but its power resources were very limited. Fundamentally, it was in Germany's interest to keep the United States in Europe, to stabilize the Central and Eastern European states, and to assist Russia.

Germany was dependent on the large powers for consensus. In the bipolar system this was easier (within the admissible range of options), since there was only one side on which a consensus had to be created. In the new environment all states were searching for new solutions. America was still Germany's most important security partner, and Germany eventually followed the gyrations of American foreign policy. At the same time, Germany was especially sensitive to developments in Russia. In the new situation, the perceptions of national interests began to diverge more widely. The Federal Republic was in the uncomfortable position of having to accommodate many different interests. A stronger foreign policy profile, under these conditions, would have meant trying to fit a square peg in a round hole.

As a nonnuclear state, Germany continued to be highly dependent on security partners. Germany was especially vulnerable to three potential developments: a breakdown of (Western) European integration, a U.S. disengagement in Europe, and adversarial developments in Russia (and Eastern Europe). In the absence of a functional European defense identity, the safeguarding of an American presence in Europe (and thus the preservation of NATO) ranked high on the scale of Germany's priorities. The preservation of European integration was of equal importance. The promotion of a European defense identity, on the other hand, was not as important as the preservation of the existing structures. The prevention of adversarial developments—such as civil strife and military adventurism in Russia—also ranked somewhat lower. Though Germany, as the Western state most affected by such developments, displayed a greater interest in Russia than its Western partners, the safeguarding of existing NATO and EU structures came first.

A 1992 RAND study found that 52 percent of Germans supported a continuation of the existing treaty system, when the name "NATO" was included in the question. Forty-six percent supported the creation of an overarching security structure including Russia and the United States, if the name "NATO" was not included in the question (27 percent supported an explicit dissolution of NATO and the creation of an overarching security system.)[18]

The model of a neutral, disarmed Germany in a system of collective security in Europe was widely discussed throughout the last years of the communist system and the period of German unification.[19] The vision could be achieved in two ways: either Germany would have to leave existing defense treaties such as NATO, or the existing treaties would have to be changed into collective systems of security instead. Egon Bahr (SPD), for example, the architect of the *Ostverträge* in the 1970s, demanded that Russia be made a NATO member.[20] In a paper published in 1998, Bahr characterized German interests as follows. First, a vital interest would be the prevention of the emergence of a threatening power in the East. A major (but not vital) interest would be maintenance of NATO and U.S. nuclear protection. Those interests should be achieved in a multilateral framework, including the strengthening of the United Nations. Power politics should eventually be replaced by the rule of law.[21] Conservative circles outside the CDU/CSU mainstream were remarkably similar in their analysis. They too wanted Germany to rely on more autonomous security policies, but they were less supportive of a multilateral approach.

German official policy never seriously considered either option.[22] Germany discounted the gains it might have made in national prestige and autonomy. Moreover, Germany placed a high value on uncertainty avoidance.[23] This conservative policy reflected the "obsession with stability and peaceful change" Hanns Maull has observed.[24] For historical or other reasons, Germany showed no desire to assume the risks associated with being a security leader. Only history can show whether this was appropriate in a particularly fluid international situation.[25]

Yet German preferences were in conflict with some of the preferences of its security partners. The United States, of course, saw NATO as the primary security mechanism. Great Britain tried to limit NATO membership. France preferred the WEU and the creation of a European defense identity. The Central European nations wanted to become members of NATO. Russia, finally, saw the OSCE as the primary forum for security in Europe.

The United States

The United States strongly supported new roles for the transatlantic security institutions. U.S.-led NATO was to be strengthened and given a new mission. There was a certain ambivalence with regard to the creation of European security institutions. Although the United States had basically supported a "European pillar" since John F. Kennedy's speech in 1963,[26] welcoming European ambitions to provide for more even burden-sharing, any attempt that would weaken NATO was viewed with suspicion. Thus, the United States strongly opposed the expansion of the WEU mandate and a coordinated European position within NATO. It also opposed the creation of the Eurocorps. Great Britain shared the U.S. position. Policymakers in Great Britain were ardent Atlanticists, avoiding every move that could weaken NATO.

Ronald Asmus et al. see common alliance interests and an expanded role for NATO on the following issues: (1) defense against a renewed hegemonic threat to Europe; (2) prevention of the return of European rivalry and the renationalization of European politics; (3) halting or slowing the spread of weapons of mass destruction and missile systems to deliver them; (4) maintaining access to Persian Gulf oil at reasonable prices; and (5) promoting an open international trade and financial system.[27] In essence, the authors propose that the United States continue its engagement and support European security and the development of a common

European identity in return for European assistance beyond Europe, especially in the Persian Gulf and with respect to the proliferation of weapons of mass destruction.[28]

Although the United States strongly supported NATO's continued existence, NATO's future mission was intensively debated in American policy circles.[29] Against the backdrop of a population that looked less willing to commit American troops to tasks abroad, one school—the majority—argued that NATO had to find new tasks to survive. Another school, a minority, believed that NATO could survive as a purely defensive alliance. The "hawks" in the United States saw a new task in counterproliferation—if need be, through military means. The Europeans, on the other hand, favored diplomatic efforts.[30] Another American interest was to expand NATO capabilities for crisis management, especially in the Persian Gulf.[31]

A third potential move to strengthen NATO was the enlargement of the alliance. American policy elites were divided on this question. Immediately after the unification of Germany, NATO expansion was not an issue. The two-plus-four treaty prohibited the stationing of allied forces on former East German territory. But as early as January 1991, Henry Kissinger wrote that "the West—and especially Western Europe—must move quickly to integrate Eastern Europe into the European Community and other Atlantic institutions (with the exception of NATO.)"[32] In the mid-1990s, advocacy of expansion became the majority opinion, but a significant minority argued that Russian concerns had to be taken more seriously.

Finally, there was also a significant minority in the United States that wanted to limit NATO to its core mission—the defense of Europe and the maintenance of an American presence in Europe. According to this view, NATO's old role was still relevant, and an enlarged role would not be supported by an increasingly skeptical American public. John Hillen wrote that: "While a slight majority of Americans (56 percent) support America's basic commitment to the Alliance, public support for the American role in NATO's Bosnian intervention peaked around 40 percent." NATO was to keep its strategic focus on collective defense and maybe undergo a limited enlargement.[33]

France

In the Atlanticist-Europeanist debate, France was the strongest champion of Europeanist approaches. Europe was increasingly to direct its own affairs, through the creation of a European political union, the strengthening of the WEU, and the Eurocorps.[34] France initially opposed the creation of the North Atlantic Cooperation Council, which expanded the mission of NATO beyond that of a defensive alliance. Initially, France did not participate in the meetings of the council. In December 1992, France also opposed NACC peacekeeping measures. France regarded the WEU and the Eurocorps as institutions that would make Europe less dependent on the United States and that would limit U.S. influence.

Since 1993, France has increasingly accepted NATO enlargement. Compromises on the Eurocorps and the WEU helped to diffuse tensions between the United States and French positions. In 1995, the French government also announced that France would cooperate more closely with NATO. The old ambivalence between keeping the United States in Europe through a defensive alliance and creating an independent European defense capability has not completely disappeared, however.

Russia

If the United States is the leading "Atlanticist" and France the leading "Europeanist" nation, Russia has maintained the position that the CSCE/OSCE is the adequate framework for constructing a collective system of security in post–Cold War Europe. Boris Yeltsin initially focused on a rapid integration with the West and the severance of ties with the Central Asian Republics. In 1991, Russia openly discussed NATO membership.[35] This brief phase of unconditional romance with Western concepts ended in 1993. In the domestic debate and in the Duma, the issue of national interests was being pressed more openly. The failed coup d'état in 1993, the electoral successes of Vladimir Zhirinovski, and continued economic and social problems have tempted even reform politicians—Yeltsin among them—to use more nationalist rhetoric. After a brief period of seeming acquiescence to NATO enlargement, Russian opposition to such a move has grown throughout 1994 and 1995. Yet in 1997 Russia agreed to one round of NATO enlargement in exchange for a special NATO-Russian security charter.

The Russian foreign policy doctrine after 1993 emphasized the strengthening of military and economic ties in the CIS and the "near abroad," thus re-establishing a Russian sphere of influence.[36] Alexander Rahr and Joachim Krause distinguish between three groups in Russia: the "Atlanticist reformers," who assign priority to integration with the West; the "Eurasianists," who see Russia in an intermediate position between East and West and hope to re-establish a Russian sphere of influence in the CIS;

and the "realists." The "realists" are not to be confused with the school of international relations bearing the same name:[37] the realists want to cooperate with the West and East, acknowledging that at times there may be objective differences. Their major goals are the establishment of stable relationships with states of the Northern Hemisphere. Russian isolation is to be avoided.[38] Unconditional Atlanticism was out of the question for Russia. The struggle was between outward-directed "realists" and "Eurasianists."

Central Europe

If Russia was torn between various geopolitical objectives, no such doubt existed in the Central European states, which clearly expressed that they belonged to the West. First, these countries' trade with Germany dwarfed all other trading relationships. Second, the traditional reservations against Germany had mostly disappeared, although some difficult restitution issues remained between Germany and the Czech Republic. Third, these nations ardently campaigned for inclusion in Western institutions to escape the "gray zone of security" in which they perceived themselves to be. At the same time, anti-Russian fears and sentiments were always avoided.[39]

The North Atlantic Cooperation Council (NACC) and the establishment of association partnerships with the WEU provided only transitory solutions. In 1991, Poland's president Lech Walesa and the Czechoslovak president Vaclav Havel mentioned that NATO could not remain closed forever. In July 1992, Ukraine demanded binding security guarantees (which only NATO could have given) in exchange for the abolishment of its nuclear weapons.[40] In August 1992, Poland presented its new defense doctrine, which contained as a major goal Poland's membership in NATO.[41] Throughout 1992, Poland's requests for NATO membership became more frequent.[42] Other countries such as Romania followed the Polish example and made clear that their goal was NATO membership.[43]

IV

From early 1993 to late 1994, the idea of NATO membership of certain Central and Eastern European countries, especially Poland, Hungary, and the Czech and Slovak Republics, gained increasing advocacy in the West. German defense minister Volker Rühe was the first Western politician to press openly for NATO membership of the Visegrad states. While France and Great Britain, as well as most Southern European nations, were opposed,

U.S. policy in this period changed from a reluctant position to ardent advocacy of widening. As a result, Central and Eastern European states were promised membership, but neither were specific candidates named nor was a timetable agreed upon. Thus the Western promises remained vague.

The "German initiative" was not really a "German" initiative. Rather, an ambivalent international situation allowed the defense ministry to express its own bureaucratic interests. Many German politicians preferred simultaneous reforms in European institutions such as the EU, WEU, and OSCE. In this context, early NATO enlargement could further German interests, but only if the West succeeded in maintaining a cooperative relationship with Russia. Defense minister Volker Rühe's initiative was consistent with the interests of the American government, which was looking to redefine NATO's mission at a time of increasing domestic pressures for the withdrawal of troops. The German foreign ministry pursued a more cautious course. And NATO enlargement was never fully embraced by Kohl, who stood in the background most of the time.

In March 1993, Rühe gave the Alastair Buchan memorial lecture at the Institute for International Strategic Studies in London. The lecture carried particular weight. Another prominent German politician, Helmut Schmidt, had used this forum to suggest changes in the West's nuclear strategy in the late 1970s, when he urged NATO to upgrade its intermediate-range nuclear capabilities in case the East would not disarm. Schmidt's lecture had had far-reaching reverberations, leading to NATO's double-track decision. In light of that precedent, Rühe's staff tried to find a topic that would live up to the occasion and came up with NATO enlargement.

Enlargement was in the defense ministry's interest for a number of reasons. It would give Germany a central role in the alliance, because Germany would become a direct partner of the new members. Restructuring in the East would also provide another mission for the ministry, thus shielding it from budgetary pressures. The defense budget had already peaked at DM 53 billion in 1991, and had subsequently been reduced to DM 52 billion in 1992. In February 1993 a further sharp reduction to DM 50 billion was announced.[44] (By 1996, the budget had dropped to DM 47 billion in nominal numbers, which entailed an even more pronounced real decline.)

In his lecture, Rühe presented a vision for the new NATO.[45] NATO was to change and engage in preventive policy in addition to its defensive mission. The relationship between the United States and Europe was to become more balanced. New members from Central Europe were to be admitted. Russia, however, was not to become a NATO member. The central passage of the speech was as follows:

The Atlantic Alliance must not become a "closed shop." I cannot see one good reason for denying future members of the European Union membership in NATO. Some nations will need a rather long period of time to meet the high economic and social standards of the European Union. Economic hurdles that present members of the EC can hardly jump across must not become insurmountable obstacles to membership in NATO. Therefore, I am asking myself whether membership in the European Union should necessarily precede accession to NATO.[46]

Foreign minister Klaus Kinkel held a different position. He did not see the "need for immediate decisions" on the issue of NATO widening. NATO was to "reconsider its policy of restraint" vis-à-vis potential Eastern applicants. Kinkel also suggested a status for the aspirants below the level of full NATO membership. Joint exercises and an enlargement of the activities of NACC could provide a solution. Moreover, an alienation of Russia and Ukraine was to be avoided.[47] Some members of the FDP opposed Rühe's proposal more strongly. Its security expert Olaf Feldmann rejected it outright. According to Feldmann, an admission of Germany's eastern neighbors into NATO would exclude the other states of the former Warsaw Pact. Instead, the CSCE should be expanded to create an all-European security architecture.[48]

In the months following his lecture in London, Rühe continued to spread his message. In his speech before the German Society for Defense Technology, he said that it was only a matter of time before such states as Poland or Hungary—an integral part of a unifying Europe—would be accepted into NATO.[49] On May 21, Rühe emphasized that NATO should accept new members. Rühe focused on the Visegrad states and was more cautious about the Baltic states, who also had declared a strong desire for NATO membership.[50]

Though Rühe explicitly excluded Russian membership in NATO, he took care to stress that a sphere of intensive security cooperation reaching from Vancouver to Vladivostock had to be created. In April, Rühe visited Russia. The German and Russian defense ministers signed a cooperation treaty that was to initiate exchanges of personnel between the two militaries. Rühe also stressed the special responsibility Germany and Russia had for security in Europe.[51]

International politics from late 1993 to late 1994 was characterized by three constants and two variables. Ardent Central and Eastern European demands for NATO membership, Rühe's continuing support, and French and British skepticism were the constant factors. The U.S. and Russian positions were the changing factors. During the months immediately following Rühe's proposals, the other Western nations were reluctant to comment or to take an explicit position. At the same time, no (Western) nation was ready to openly reject the proposals for fear of giving the impression that NATO was a club that did not care about the reforming countries. Thus Rühe found himself in the position of "lonely voice in the desert": even constant repetition of his proposals did not initiate a policy dialogue. At the same time, he was not isolated in a strict sense, since there was no official Western strategy.[52]

The highest level of government—the chancellor's office—was conspicuously uncommitted in the debate. Ultimately, the changing U.S. position allowed for a common Western approach after Rühe had placed the issue on the agenda. It is also interesting that the German position—or Rühe's initiative—was not discussed with Britain and France, which were considerably more skeptical concerning widening. Within Europe, Germany was willing to try new approaches without necessarily reconciling every step with the other European nations.

The U.S. domestic debate focused on a range of options. On the one hand, U.S. policy had a strong tradition of helping to safeguard peace and democracy; on the other it had a traditional apprehension about "entangling alliances." In December 1992, departing secretary of defense Richard Cheney proposed that some new NATO members be admitted, but clearly marked this as his personal opinion.[53] Some policy analysts demanded that Russia and Ukraine be included in the alliance.[54] Others preferred limited and early enlargement through the Central European states.[55] But ultimately, both the late Bush and early Clinton administrations concentrated on the large power relationship between the United States and Russia, particularly the issue of nuclear disarmament.

In addition, the Clinton administration gave priority to domestic issues and favored a cautious approach. The prevailing notion was that NATO enlargement should not be excluded in the long term, but that it should not be discussed at the moment. In the summer of 1993, secretary of state Warren Christopher declared that new members could be accepted by NATO at an appropriate moment. This issue, however, was not currently on the agenda.[56] In January 1994 Clinton asked why the Western nations should draw another line through Europe further to the East, thus creating new divisions.[57]

Fundamentally, however, the United States seemed open to Rühe's proposals. In April 1993, Senator Richard G. Lugar had declared that in the foreseeable future there would have to be a "new NATO" or there would be "no NATO."[58] In August 1993, Lothar Rühl reported in the German daily *Die Welt* that "Rühe's proposal is finding increasing resonance in Washington."[59] A RAND study by Ronald Asmus, Richard Kugler, and Stephen Larrabee of the same month proposed to make the Visegrad states NATO members.[60]

In Britain, reservations against NATO enlargement were markedly higher. Britain did not want to disturb the proven structure of NATO and was apprehensive of growing German influence. Throughout 1993 and 1994, enlargement was rarely discussed in Britain. Foreign secretary Douglas Hurd stated in June 1993 that "NATO enlargement could not be excluded in the long term, if the Central and Eastern European states became EU members."[61] (This position, of course, would postpone enlargement to a distant future.) A little later, defense minister Malcolm Rifkind issued a cautious but negative statement on NATO widening: "Membership of NATO involves responsibility as well as rights and cannot just be seen as a political statement of enhancing security of any individual country."[62] In September 1993, Hurd stated that NATO would not expand anytime soon.[63]

France also opposed NATO enlargement. After 1989, France had shown a strong preference for the creation of European security structures to boost French influence and to limit American influence in Europe. Initially, France did not participate in the North Atlantic Cooperation Council. In late 1992, it also denied NATO the right to plan joint missions with Eastern European nations to solve the Yugoslavia crisis. This position led to an open controversy with the United States.[64] NATO enlargement was further perceived as a strengthening of the "German bloc" in Europe. In 1993, the newly elected Balladur government cautiously revised the French position vis-à-vis NATO. A redefinition of the alliance was not categorically rejected anymore. Nevertheless, the French position remained ambiguous.[65]

After Rühe's speech, the Central and Eastern European nations became more outspoken. Hungary, which had early on given NATO permission to monitor the flight ban in Bosnia-Herzegovina from Hungarian airspace, asked for NATO support in case the Yugoslavia conflict affected Hungary. (It did not demand formal security guarantees.)[66] In July 1993, Polish defense minister Onyszkiewicz declared that Poland would discontinue the purchase of Russian defense equipment. Poland would continue to aspire to NATO membership.[67] On August 26, Onyszkiewicz demanded that NATO issue a timetable for the admission of certain Central and Eastern European states at its December summit.[68] In September, Prime Minister

Hanna Suchocka repeated this demand and declared that the Visegrad states would have to develop regional alternatives in case their concerns were not taken into account.[69] In the same month, Slovenian president Kucan declared that his country aspired to NATO membership.[70]

During a visit in Poland in late August 1993, Russian president Boris Yeltsin surprisingly declared that NATO membership was a matter for sovereign Poland to decide itself. Russia would not oppose such a decision.[71] This statement caught many Western policymakers, who had argued that a NATO enlargement would isolate Russia, by surprise. Defense minister Volker Rühe used the occasion to demand that Poland, Hungary, and the Czech Republic be given "clear perspectives" at the upcoming NATO summit.[72] NATO secretary general Manfred Wörner, who had initially been skeptical about the Rühe proposal, now supported the German defense minister.[73]

Yeltsin, however, was immediately criticized from all sides in Russia. The chairman of the Supreme Soviet security committee warned that the enlargement of NATO would have the same effect for Russia as the Treaty of Versailles had had for Germany, that is, force the country into isolation and strengthen extremist forces. Russia sent diplomatic signals to the NATO states that it would indeed see NATO enlargement as a problem and that Yeltsin's words should be taken with qualification.[74] Soon, Yeltsin revised his position in a letter to the United States, France, Great Britain, and Germany, also signaling reservations about NATO enlargement. According to Yeltsin, the two–plus–four treaty had been passed under the premise that NATO and the Soviet Union were jointly responsible for collective security in Europe.[75]

The reversal in Yeltsin's position reassured the Western skeptics of enlargement. On October 8, French foreign minister Alain Juppé openly opposed a fast enlargement of NATO.[76] At the fall meeting of the NATO defense ministers in Travemünde in late October 1993, Rühe was isolated. The Russian position grew increasingly inflexible throughout 1994. Lithuania's formal request to join NATO in January 1994 evoked sharp responses from Moscow.[77] Even the signing of the Partnership for Peace treaty framework document by foreign minister Andrei Kozyrev in June 1994 did not change this situation. In November 1994, Kozyrev signaled to the German NATO diplomat Gebhard von Moltke that Russia would view a rapid NATO enlargement as an unfriendly step that would cause a harsh reaction.[78] During a visit to the NATO summit in Brussels, Kozyrev abruptly refused to sign the readily negotiated partnership for peace treaty document between NATO and Russia. Kozyrev also criticized the final communiqué of the NATO summit for not clearly showing NATO's intentions and not excluding NATO enlargement.[79]

Ultimately, the change in the official U.S. position between 1993 and late 1994 allowed for a revision of Western policies. At the meeting of NATO defense ministers in October 1993, secretary of defense Les Aspin proposed a concept of bilateral consultations with the nations of the former Warsaw Pact and the neutral and nonaligned states of the region.[80] The concept was presented as the Partnership for Peace at the succeeding NATO summit in January 1994.[81] The United States had thus demonstrated initiative below the level of openly proposing security guarantees for the Central and Eastern European states.[82] In contrast to the NACC, PfP members were to have the option of bilateral consultations between aligned states and NATO, for example, when their security seemed threatened. Moreover, PfP was to give NATO aspirants a clear perspective on membership, while at the same time allowing for a slowdown in the debate to allow states to solve the conceptual problems affiliated with the task.

This goal, however, was not achieved. PfP remained an attempt to square the circle. Advocates of enlargement such as Rühe saw it as an important first step in NATO enlargement; opponents such as the British government saw it as a possibility to prevent full NATO membership.[83] Moreover, the Visegrad states immediately began to criticize the vagueness implied in the PfP offer.[84] The presidents of the Baltic states, worried by the electoral successes of the right-wing Russian politician Vladimir Zhirinovsky, issued a plea to NATO to fill the existing security vacuum.[85] On January 4, 1994, Lithuania formally requested acceptance as a NATO member.[86] Rühe renewed his requests, demanding that the Visegrad states be included in the North Atlantic alliance by the year 2000.[87] He also raised Polish hopes of becoming the first new NATO member,[88] and introduced a proposal for a specific timetable to the defense planning committee in September 1994.

The United States initially continued its cautious policy. Les Aspin confirmed that Partnership for Peace membership was not a ticket into NATO and did not include security guarantees.[89] In July 1994, the Senate passed the NATO Participation Act of 1994, offering far-reaching possibilities in weapons procurement to the Visegrad states. On this occasion, Under Secretary Strobe Talbott reiterated that the American administration did not share Rühe's sense of urgency and that the United States would continue its evolutionary approach to the issue of widening.[90] For a while, the administration was sending mixed signals: Clinton stated before the Polish parliament in July that full NATO membership would only be a question of time.[91] At the meeting of NATO ministers in October 1994, however, secretary of defense William Perry openly rejected Rühe's proposal for fast enlargement.[92]

Toward the end of 1994, parts of the administration veered toward a more expansionist position.[93] In late October, Clinton commissioned two working groups to analyze the options for enlargement. One was chaired by assistant secretary of state Richard Holbrooke, "the administration's leading expansionist."[94] The United States also took up consultations with its allies to explore the issue. Holbrooke announced a speech by secretary of state Warren Christopher for November 28, 1994, on the administration's position on NATO enlargement. The speech was to contain "far-ranging steps."

The change of course was caused by a number of factors. First, Clinton increasingly began to emphasize foreign policy. This new image was reinforced in 1995, when Clinton became very involved in the Bosnia crisis. Second, the Polish lobby had pressed hard for NATO enlargement, and the administration saw the new course as a possibility to enhance the Democrats' prospects in the upcoming congressional elections. A strong Republican victory in the congressional and senatorial elections reinforced this trend. Shortly after Holbrooke's announcement, however, the severe disagreements between NATO members on the further course of action in Bosnia led to the "worst crisis of NATO since the Suez-Crisis in 1956."[95] Apparently, the administration thought it too risky to open a second controversial issue, and Christopher cancelled his speech.

Germany's position was more difficult to describe than Rühe's advocacy suggested. Chancellor Kohl's was influenced by a variety of forces: Rühe's lobbying, the foreign ministry's views, and international demands and expectations, especially in the United States and Russia, all played a role. Because his personal convictions did not run as deep as on the issue of European unification, Kohl was reluctant to commit to any position or to personally start a major initiative.

Many options and alternatives were being explored in the domestic debate. The intercessions of defense minister Rühe, foreign minister Kinkel, and NATO secretary general Wörner epitomized this debate.[96] Even within the parties, the positions were not entirely clear-cut. This open process could be described as weak leadership, but it actually served German interests well. Though seen by many as the Western state that advocated NATO enlargement most ardently, Germany never really committed to any position. Given the uncertain future of Russian and American policy, Germany kept its options open, while at the same time endearing itself to the Visegrad states.

After defense minister Rühe (CDU) had made his proposal for a fast NATO enlargement with force in March 1993, different positions were staked quickly by other eminent persons inside and outside the administration. In the German coalition government, the CDU held the defense ministry, the FDP the foreign ministry. The positions of both ministers were shaped by the bureaucratic interests of their respective organizations, as well as the different philosophies of their parties. The defense ministry traditionally stood for an Atlanticist orientation and was under severe budgetary pressure. The foreign ministry, though dealing with all foreign relations, had been particularly involved in the process of European integration. Moreover, the FDP placed a somewhat higher emphasis on multilateral arrangements such as the OSCE and the UN. It was shaped by Hans-Dietrich Genscher's almost 20 years of tenure. Genscher wrote an article in mid-1992 that reflected this position well. He devoted only three short paragraphs to NATO, and two full pages to the CSCE. Genscher demanded that "The CSCE must look for new forms of collective security. It must overcome its structural weaknesses in decision-making, crisis management and conflict resolution. The crises in Yugoslavia and Nagorno-Karabak demonstrate that we need an effective instrument of crisis management and conflict resolution in Europe. The existing capabilities of the CSCE must be strengthened and made operational."[97]

NATO secretary general Wörner (a former CDU defense minister) stated that "NATO should be open to the east" without proposing any specific steps.[98] In October 1993, after Rühe had repeatedly demanded a fast NATO enlargement and the topic had been placed on the international agenda, Wörner stated that a decision on NATO enlargement was not in sight. Such an enlargement would be a multi-year-process that would have to be conducted in a way that did not alienate Russia.[99] Wörner agreed that an enlargement of NATO would strengthen European security, but at the moment there were no plans in the drawer.[100]

After the attempted a coup d'état in Russia in November 1993, former foreign minister Hans-Dietrich Genscher counseled "extreme restraint" regarding NATO enlargement.[101] Foreign minister Kinkel reiterated that the issue of enlargement would be highly sensitive. Interim solutions were to be explored.[102] Signs to the potential applicants were to be sent with "utmost care" and with a view to the situation in Russia.[103] Meeting with the Russian ambassador to Bonn, Kinkel proposed that Russia was to have a larger say in NATO. Kinkel also said that the relations of the Central and Eastern European states to the EC were more important than their relations to NATO.[104] In Warsaw, Kinkel nevertheless explained that Russia could not have a veto concerning enlargement.[105]

By mid–October 1993, press reports began to describe a behind-the-scenes tug-of-war between the defense and foreign ministry, reigned in by directives from the chancellor's office. For a while, the proponents of a collective security system had the stronger position.[106] In a speech before the Bundeswehr academy in November, Kinkel pleaded for a collective system of security in Europe. NATO was not to be expanded too early and NATO was not to create new demarcation lines within the CSCE community. The North Atlantic Cooperation Council was to be enlarged and strengthened. Neutral states were to become members, and the council was to plan joint exercises and peace missions. Russia was not to be excluded by any measure, because this would be bad for the security of even the Visegrad states.[107] In December, Kinkel reaffirmed that especially in view of the latest developments in Russia (that is, the success of nationalist Vladimir Zhirinowskij) it was important not to yield to some states' pressure for special security arrangements and to create new divisions.[108]

Chancellor Kohl maintained a low profile in most of the debate. His position was vague and changed with the circumstances. After a meeting with Hungarian prime minister Antall, Kohl stated that the process of Hungary's accession to the EU could start after 1995. Kohl also promised to present Hungary's security interests to NATO and to work toward NATO taking these interests into account.[109] At a convention of the European conservative parties in Budapest in September 1993, Kohl demanded more Western assistance and solidarity for the reforming countries. He did, however, choose EU membership instead of NATO membership as a focus of his proposals.[110] In October, Kohl stated that the Visegrad states should become "associated with NATO in an appropriate status in the long term." After a meeting with Francois Mitterrand and Edouard Balladur in December, Kohl said that an early acceptance of the Visegrad states "would not contribute to a positive development at this point."[111] Kohl also reconfirmed his strong support for Yeltsin after the electoral successes of the anti-reformers in Russia in December.[112]

The parliamentary debate was much less polarized and pronounced than the conflict between the defense and foreign ministers. Most German policymakers and analysts agreed that at some point NATO was to be expanded. They disagreed mostly about the speed of such enlargement. Moreover, the large parties (CDU/CSU and SPD) were internally divided on the issue. The proponents of fast enlargement and the proponents of slow and cautious enlargement had roughly the same strength.

Karl Lamers (CDU) cautiously supported widening, taking great care to explain the complexity of the issue and to state that there would be no simple or fast solution.[113] Alfred Dregger, the honorary chairman of the CDU/CSU group in the parliament, declared that NATO would miss its reason for existence if it refused to open to the Central and Eastern European states. The Partnership for Peace had to lead to full membership.[114] The leading CDU politicians Wolfgang Schäuble and Heiner Geißler asked for NATO security guarantees for the Central European states. Bavarian prime minister Edmund Stoiber (CSU) demanded both fast EU membership and NATO security guarantees, which were to be designed in a way so as not to alienate Russia.[115] Erwin Huber, secretary-general of the CSU, on the other hand, propagated a cautious course in order not to overstretch NATO.[116]

The SPD security expert Hans-Ulrich Klose openly advocated NATO enlargement, many others in his party opposed it.[117] SPD member Günter Verheugen wanted to strengthen collective systems of security for Europe.[118] Heidemarie Wieczorek-Zeul, SPD board member, perceived a stepwise widening of NATO as "devastating." NATO and the CSCE were to be transformed into to a system of collective security including Russia instead.[119] SPD party chairman Rudolf Scharping also opposed rapid NATO enlargement.[120]

In light of the upcoming federal elections, however, the SPD leadership increasingly assimilated official NATO policy, eager to present itself as a reliable partner. The NATO summit of 1994 threatened air strikes in Bosnia if the Serbian forces violated the cease fire. Over the following months, SPD party chairman and chancellor-candidate Scharping made clear that he would support NATO and that the SPD as a whole supported the alliance.[121] During a U.S. visit, Scharping reaffirmed that his party would act in accordance with American interests.[122]

Ultimately, the Partnership for Peace offer was not able to reign in the ambitions of the potential Central and Eastern European NATO members.[123] In April, Poland proposed joint maneuvers with NATO states. Those exercises were agreed upon by the Polish, German, and Danish defense ministers in May.[124] Poland also presented a confidential paper that included far-reaching offers to NATO.[125] The Czech Republic increased its efforts for NATO membership, often at the expense of the other Visegrad states.[126]

In June 1994, Russia signed the Partnership for Peace framework document.[127] This development gave the German expansionists—most of all, Volker Rühe—a new occasion to press their issue. Rühe demanded that

NATO be enlarged by the year 2000.[128] He also began to explore the issue of a "special relationship" with Russia that was not to include Russian veto power over NATO enlargement.[129] Rühe also reiterated his opinion that Russia could not become a member of the EU or NATO.[130] Before the 1994 meeting of the defense ministers, Rühe again demanded publicly to name the candidates for the first round of enlargement and to develop a clear timetable for enlargement.[131] The first joint maneuvers of American, German, British, Dutch, Italian, and Danish troops with Polish, Czech, Slovak, Bulgarian, Romanian, Ukrainian, and Lithuanian troops made Rühe optimistic that the Visegrad states would join NATO before the year 2000.[132]

Rühe remained as isolated at the 1994 meeting of the NATO defense ministers in Seville as he had been in Travemünde a year before. His press statement that there was "broad agreement" that the Visegrad states should be the first new members was corrected by the American secretary of defense, William Perry. According to Perry, it was too early to name candidates and NATO was to concentrate on the Partnership for Peace. Moreover, Rühe explicitly excluded Russia from NATO widening, while Perry did not want to rule out this option.[133]

Kinkel also contradicted Rühe, saying, "It can not be in the interest of the Central and Eastern European states to return to a system of blocks and confrontation in Europe as a price for membership." NATO had been justified in deciding against a timetable in Seville. Kinkel also emphasized that international structures such as NATO, the WEU, the CSCE, and the EU were to be strengthened jointly.[134] Genscher supported Kinkel publicly and stated that the widening of the EU had priority over the widening of NATO.[135]

It was characteristic of the cautious line of overall German policy that Chancellor Kohl refused to comment on the disagreement of his ministers, stating that he really preferred for ministers not to discuss the issue publicly. Foreign and security policies, according to Kohl, "were not a topic for public debates but for conversations with all actors." Therefore he would not make a public statement. Internally he would clear the matters so that everything would be correct.[136] Helmut Kohl, who was known to make many foreign policy decisions without consulting the cabinet, now allowed multiple opinions within the government. A softening of party discipline toward the end of Kohl's tenure is an insufficient explanation. By and large, Kinkel's position seems to have been closer to Kohl's, because Kinkel saw himself as an arm of Kohl, who had the ultimate say in foreign policy (Definitionskompetenz).[137] Kohl's vague position mirrored German interests and the East–West tensions. Any decisive position would weaken the middle power as long as the two main actors, the United States and Russia, could not come to an agreement.

Kohl himself had to experience the grave consequences of German indecisiveness on the occasion of the war in Chechnya. In a telephone conversation with Boris Yeltsin, Kohl signaled understanding for the Russian use of force, brutal as it was. Kohl called the conflict and the concurring violations of human rights an internal Russian matter, contradicting the position of the Federal Republic in the Bosnian crisis. Kohl said he regretted the human suffering in Chechnya and asked Russia to find an agreeable solution. But he also reassured Russia that territorial integrity was of the highest importance. Moreover, he argued against economic sanctions, which could potentially destabilize Russia. Foreign minister Kinkel made similar statements.[138]

The United States reacted with much stronger criticism and threatened the discontinuation of economic assistance to Russia. The European Council shared this criticism. The preparations for an economic agreement between the EU and Russia were suspended.[139] Kohl, who had to take Germany's especially vulnerable position into account, was isolated in the West. Chechnya showed that Germany's perception of interests and that of its Western allies could diverge where critical developments in Russia were concerned.

V

The policies of the Federal Republic between 1995 and the summer of 1997 reflect Germany's position as a middle power and its self-imposed restrictions in the choice of policy instruments. Ultimately, Germany was trying to pursue a policy of reconciliation between the United States and Russia, while remaining loyal to the United States. This policy may have been in Germany's interest, but it was difficult to execute because the weight of the Federal Republic was not large enough to influence U.S. policy. Ultimately, the asymmetric dependency of the Federal Republic on other powers, especially the United States, was the decisive factor. Despite all efforts to accommodate Russian interests, Germany eventually followed the (gyrating) U.S. policy closely.

In 1994 and 1997, the first stage of NATO enlargement was prepared and agreed upon. Two developments, in particular, were responsible for continuing caution. First, the divisions within Germany and within the Western alliance narrowed, leading to consensus on cautious NATO enlargement.[140]

The United States reverted to a more cautious position, after a brief flirtation with vigorous enlargementism, while in Germany a cautious consensus for enlargement emerged. Second, Russian opposition to the first stage of NATO enlargement was overcome. The alliance had proven its will to act during the air strikes in Bosnia and the subsequent peacekeeping missions. Many NACC countries, including Russia, participated in the peacekeeping operations, which had led to a certain amount of cooperation and confidence building.

At the NATO meeting of foreign ministers in December 1994, the members agreed in principle that NATO was to expand. In his inauguration speech, Willy Claes, the new secretary-general of NATO, made NATO enlargement his priority.[141] In October, the U.S. administration had veered toward fast enlargement and pushed the issue within NATO. This change in direction was so rapid that the German ambassador to NATO, Hermann von Richthofen, sharply criticized the U.S. government for unilaterally starting consultations with some potential applicants.[142] But the U.S. flirt with vigorous expansionism, faced with Russian opposition, was short-lived. Subsequently, the United States proposed that NATO commission a study on the "how and why" of NATO enlargement that excluded the "who and when."

The commissioning of the study was an indicator that the debate had entered a more reflective state. The "who and when" of enlargement was explicitly excluded from the mandate of the study group. Instead, basic questions about the contributions of potential new members, standardization of equipment, financial implications, and other basic issues were to be discussed. Although critics welcomed the fact that NATO was now looking at the fundamental aspects of the issue, they deplored the fact that such fundamental reflection was taking place so late, after widening had been accepted in principle.[143]

Increasing Russian opposition to widening made the U.S. government reconsider its recently found enthusiasm for rapid enlargement. Russia had welcomed the Partnership for Peace but had consistently opposed NATO enlargement. In the summer of 1994, Yeltsin, concerned that Russia be included in the political part of the G-7 summits, had accepted the PfP framework document. The U.S. policy change in favor of NATO enlargement in late 1994 caught Russia by surprise. Kozyrev argued that Russia had fallen into a trap set by the West.[144] In December, he refused to sign the individual Partnership for Peace treaty between NATO and Russia. At the CSCE summit in Budapest, Yeltsin warned of the danger of moving from a Cold War to a Cold Peace.[145] At a meeting between Kozyrev and

Christopher on January 18, 1995, Russia repeated its strong opposition to NATO enlargement. In March 1995, Richard Holbrooke partially reversed his earlier advocacy of rapid enlargement in an article in *Foreign Affairs,* explaining that there would be no list of candidates for the first round enlargement or timetables for enlargement. He also pointed to the potential difficulties of ratification in the U.S. Senate and thus put earlier U.S. pressures in perspective.[146]

In May 1995, Clinton wrote a conciliatory letter to Yeltsin that became the subject of considerable speculation among the Western allies, particularly Germany. Apparently, the letter did not exclude the option of Russian membership in NATO if Russia would sign the bilateral Partnership for Peace agreement. Though the U.S. administration repeatedly denied that the letter contained an open invitation to Russia, there was a clear shift in emphasis back to U.S.-Russian relations.[147] Holbrooke commented: "We have never said that Russia could become a NATO member. We have also never said Russia could not become a NATO member. This would at least be a theoretical option."[148] The European NATO members, on the other hand, had decidedly opposed Russian membership in NATO.[149]

In May 1995, Russia signed the individual Partnership for Peace agreement. This gave further nourishment to the idea of a special arrangement with Russia.[150] By late 1995, the U.S. administration—like its German counterpart—tried to balance the applicants' desire for NATO membership and Russia's security interests. During a trip to the Visegrad states, secretary of defense Perry expressed his confidence that Poland, the Czech Republic, Slovenia, and Hungary would be among the first new NATO members, without committing to any timetable. At the same time, he also said that Russia's security interests would have to be considered.[151]

The U.S.-Russian rapprochement on NATO enlargement had fundamentally changed the framework for German policy. Now, it was important to find a solution acceptable to all sides. Germany's position entailed the rejection of a timetable and a list of candidates for the first round of enlargement and the coupling of EU and NATO membership. The approach was generally pro-enlargement, but cautious and "equilibrist." Critical analysts who had warned earlier that an analysis of options, costs, and benefits had to precede NATO enlargement found increasing recognition.[152] With NATO having proven itself in Bosnia, the chancellor's office became less enthusiastic and stressed the legitimacy of Russia's security interests. Rühe was reined in more openly by the other members of government.

Around the time of the NATO summit in December 1994, various German politicians began to explore the idea of a linkage between a widening of NATO and the EU. Florian Gerster, the minister for federal and European affairs of Rhineland-Palatinate, proposed to solve the conflict between Russian and Central European security interests through WEU membership of the Central European states.[153] SPD leader Günter Verheugen declared that NATO and EU widening were to be parallel processes that would take "a long, long time." Moreover, he proposed a special pact between NATO and Russia.[154] CDU member of the Bundestag Karl Lamers proposed to make NATO membership conditional on membership in the EU. This, according to Lamers, would facilitate Russian agreement, because the EU was not directed against Russia.[155] Rühe, in turn, responded that a widening of the EU had to go hand in hand with a widening of NATO.[156]

Helmut Kohl assumed the role of mediator. While he made clear that Germany's position was in the West, he also tried to create understanding for Russia's situation. Kohl warned Clinton not to isolate Russia after the events in Chechnya.[157] He also conceded that Germany and the United States viewed NATO enlargement somewhat differently. In particular, Kohl opposed a definitive timetable for enlargement and argued that NATO and EU enlargement had to go hand in hand. This meant that negotiations could start in 1997 at the earliest. (In June 1995, NATO and Russia signed a document on dialogue and cooperation between NATO and Russia, which implicitly gave Russia a special role. In September 1995, NATO proposed further steps for a special relationship between NATO and Russia.)[158] Kohl reaffirmed the especially close relationship between the United states and Germany. Germany would take up the new challenges at America's side.[159]

The chancellor and the foreign minister followed largely the same course. At the thirty-second conference on defense issues in Munich, Kinkel repeated his outspoken opposition to a fast enlargement of NATO. Though Russia was not to have a veto, the strategic partnership with Russia was to be developed further—an enlargement was only conceivable as part of an overall long-term process of building a new security architecture in Europe.[160] The FDP supported this position. In February 1995, Rühe for the first time explored the idea of a strategic partnership with Russia. While he continued to oppose a Russian veto over NATO enlargement, he proposed a "contract about a strategic partnership between Russia and NATO," an idea that had been launched by the French foreign minister Alain Juppé in January 1995. Klaus Kinkel, a strong advocate of such a partnership, saw NATO and EU/WEU enlargement as parallel processes. He now also kept open the option that one would happen before the other, excluding "rigid automatisms or linkage."[161]

Rühe had been promoting a "Visegrad states first" approach since his London speech of March 1993 for pragmatic reasons. It seemed clear to him that NATO enlargement would be easier if it was limited to a few candidates in Central Europe. Any early enlargement, however limited, would serve the interests of the defense ministry better than a comprehensive reordering of the security architecture or a comprehensive enlargement later. A small enlargement would put Germany (and the defense ministry) in the center of an extended alliance and provide the ministry with a new mandate. During his visit to the Baltic states, Rühe made clear that in his eyes the Visegrad states would be the first candidates for enlargement. The Baltic states were to focus on EU membership and on security cooperation with the Nordic countries.[162]

Foreign minister Klaus Kinkel and Otto Count Lambsdorff, a prominent FDP figure and former economics minister, had said on one occasion, "Mr. Rühe mustn't say that." Kinkel said that the future security architecture in Europe was not to be built at the cost of the Baltic States. There were not to be "gray zones of security."[163] Kinkel's criticism caused the defense ministry to immediately correct Rühe's statements, explaining that Rühe did not perceive the Baltic states as second-rate candidates for NATO membership. A speaker of the ministry tried to make clear that Rühe's speech was in full accordance with the line of the federal government and the alliance. In December, the alliance was to decide over basic principles of enlargement; in a second step, countries and membership dates were to be identified.[164]

In his programmatic speech at the North Atlantic Assembly in Budapest in May 1995, Rühe demanded a fast enlargement, even without the agreement of Russia. There was to be a special relationship that took into account the security interests of Russia, but there could be no Russian veto. The only guarantee NATO could make was that there would be regular consultations so as not to surprise Russia.[165] In early September 1995, Rühe criticized Yeltsin's defense of Serbia after the bombing of Serbian positions by NATO planes. Rühe said the Russian president's language was unnecessarily confrontational.[166]

In the following months, the positions of the defense and foreign ministries began to converge. In an interview with *Der Spiegel,* Kinkel conceded that there were still conflicts between the Federal Republic and Russia. Kinkel stressed that the construction of an all-European system of security was very important, but he also mentioned that Germany could not fully support the Russian position. While Yeltsin emphasized the importance of the OSCE, Kinkel stressed that NATO was still vitally important and would have to remain at the core of Germany's security system.[167]

A similar position had been staked out by Chancellor Kohl in his speech at the North Atlantic Cooperation Council in June 1995. According to Kohl, opening NATO to the East would be a decisive contribution to European security. At the same time, Kohl stressed Russia's interests. Enlargement would have to be executed with caution, and it was not to violate the security interests of the Russian people, whom Kohl called a "great people." Cooperation between NATO and Russia was to be based on a separate and special agreement.[168]

The emerging consensus in the German government was reflected in a NATO study on the modalities of enlargement that was published in late September.[169] As was to be expected, the study did not contain the names of candidates or dates for enlargement. Moreover, the study neither contained explicit and binding conditions and criteria for NATO membership, nor did it recommend security guarantees for Russia. It emphasized that NATO forces could be placed in the new member states and that those states would have to agree with NATO's nuclear strategy. This last point was not well suited to dampen Russian fears. Gorbachev came to the fore, claiming that Russia had agreed to German unification only under the condition that NATO was not to be expanded. The two-plus-four treaty, for example, contained a clause stating that no NATO troops were to be stationed on the territory of former East Germany.[170]

Anonymous German government officials quoted by the *Frankfurter Allgemeine Zeitung* welcomed the study and identified a "clearly discernible German imprint." In particular, the study made a close connection between the widening of NATO and the EU. The official continued to comment that the process of enlargement would take approximately five years and that it was a very delicate process that would require "a high degree of equilibrism."[171] Foreign minister Kinkel confirmed this position by stating that there was to be no enlargement in 1996.[172] In an appeal before the European Council in Strasbourg, Kohl pleaded for a full integration of Russia in the new European security architecture and economy. This should include special partnerships with Russia and Ukraine.[173] Germany had returned to a cautious policy of balancing. Germany's position was in the West, but it pursued multidirectional and complex policies nevertheless.

According to political scientist Christian Hacke, the paper reflected the course of the chancellor, because it remained vague and did not oblige NATO.[174] This would delay enlargement.[175] The result, however, was another one. The Russian political elite had an opportunity to get accustomed to the idea of NATO enlargement. It had begun to accept some aspects of this process, but had always vigorously rejected a membership of the Baltic states or any other states from the territory of the former USSR.[176] Under these circumstances, it was tactically wise to allow for a consensus to form gradually, and to leave the modalities of enlargement open.

It also fit this tactic that the delegates of the NATO council offered concessions on the issue of a revision of the Conventional Forces in Europe (CFE) treaty. This treaty had included dramatic reductions in conventional force levels from the Atlantic to the Ural Mountains, which Russia had violated by its mobilization in Chechnya. At its session of September 20, 1996, the NATO council proposed a compromise by changing the definition of the territory. The NATO states thus began to make Russia offers for a potential NATO enlargement, the shape of which was not yet clearly defined.[177]

VI

During the period from late 1996 until the enlargement decision at the Madrid conference in the summer of 1997, the German policy of "balancing"—and at the same time giving the U.S. position priority—continued. Looking at the period, it becomes clear why external observers called the German policy inconsistent.[178] But taking into consideration the constraints Germany was (and is) subject to, a clear, if low-profile, strategy is discernible. German policy always had to be reconciled with the other states, most importantly the United States. Time and again, the German government had to give up some minor interest to follow the sometimes rapidly changing U.S. position. But Germany could not neglect the Russian position or that of other European states. Thus, while the impression of tactical indecisiveness or opportunism may have arisen, an encompassing concept entailing the preservation of NATO and the cooperation with and compensation of Russia can be identified. Because the Federal Republic itself was not a major power in this game, there was the constant danger that it would be pushed away from this course.

The German domestic debate was more multifaceted than Germany's official policy. But among most parties, NATO enlargement became an increasingly accepted policy goal. A group of younger Bundestag members within the governing CDU/CSU coalition warned of too many compromises with Russia and demanded a foreign policy more strongly based on moral principles.[179]

Within the Social Democrats, there were two main positions. The first faction within the SPD was much more "all-European multilateralist" and placed a higher value on good relations with Russia. Egon Bahr is representative of this faction. According to Bahr, it was imperative that Russia not be excluded—even a Russian membership in NATO was conceivable over the long term. Currently, however, NATO expansion was detrimental because it would create new points of friction and the potential for new schisms. For the Baltic states, for example, common security guarantees as proposed by Russia and NATO would be much more effective than NATO membership.[180] Hans-Dietrich Genscher, former FDP foreign minister, had a rather similar position.

Party chairman Rudolf Scharping tried to move the party position closer to the government's position to prepare the SPD for the federal elections of 1998.[181] An SPD working paper of June 16, 1997 represented a goodbye to old ideals. NATO expansion was accepted and the ultimate dissolution of the military treaties disappeared from the list of long-term goals.[182] SPD security expert Karsten Voigt had already presented a soft plan for NATO expansion in May 1995. The new members were to be members of the military organization, not just political members as proposed by France. However, there should be no lasting stationing of foreign troops or nuclear weapons on the territory of the new member states. Russia was to be closely informed about every step, and there should be a common NATO-Russia forum that would decide about certain questions, such as the monitoring of nonproliferation of some types of weapons or UN blue-helmet missions.[183] In a later article, Voigt argued that the expansion of NATO was in the best interest even of Russia because of its stabilizing effects. Moreover, the NATO decision procedures would not be weakened by such a step.[184] As the federal elections of 1997 drew closer, the SPD moved closer to the second position.

The Green Party was initially very close to the SPD faction represented by Bahr. In a 1996 paper, an SDP-Green working group including Bahr, Heidemarie Wieczorek-Zeul (SPD), Karin Fuchs (SPD), Ludger Vollmer (Green Party) and Angelika Beer (Green Party) presented a paper on security policy. The paper criticized NATO expansion and recommended a strengthening of the OSCE, which would unite the United States, Canada, Europe, and Russia in a system of collective security.[185]

But even then, members of the Green Party began to deviate from the established party philosophy of demilitarization and collective security in order to prepare for a potential participation in the federal government after the 1998 Bundestag elections. A more pragmatic line, represented by party speaker Gunda Röstel, began to emerge. The Green Party would have preferred a collective system of security. Because this opportunity had been missed, a more pragmatic line was now in order: NATO enlargement should take place, but NATO should change over time, as an all-European system of collective security that included Russia emerged. The Green Party was to promote this process. By the summer of 1997, in view of the likely participation in a coalition government, this position had become the majority position within the party.[186]

These domestic adaptations came in line with an acceleration of the pace by the U.S. administration. At the conference of the NATO defense ministers in Bergen on September 25 and 26, 1996, the U.S. secretary of defense pronounced a timetable. Negotiations were to start in 1997. At the same time, the United States offered Russia far-reaching cooperation and a strategic partnership.[187] In an election speech of October 22, Clinton also reaffirmed his commitment to NATO enlargement. The first candidates were to be named in 1997 and to be accepted by 1999. Clinton offered Russia an agreement that included regular consultations, close cooperation, and joint actions.[188] Secretary of state Warren Christopher developed the idea of an Atlantic partnership council and proposed strengthening the OSCE.[189]

The reactions in Russia were two-sided: on the one hand, there was much public posturing against NATO expansion. On the other hand, Russian officials also signaled their willingness to negotiate. In September, Russian defense minister Rodionow categorically rejected the proposals of the NATO defense ministers. Security adviser Aleksandr Lebed threatened economic sanctions and charged Germany with trying to build a new sphere of influence in Central and Eastern Europe.[190] At a meeting of the Russian cabinet of January 1, 1997, similar opinions were voiced. Russia, according to some cabinet members, was not obliged by former treaties such as START II and the KSE treaty anymore, since NATO was now threatening Russia. In the Duma, prime minister Primakov emphasized Russia's opposition to NATO expansion in any form.[191]

At the same time, there were signs of compromise. Primakov had staked out a minimalist position as early as June 1996 during the meeting of the NATO cooperation council: under no circumstances should there be integrated NATO units at Russia's border. All other items would be negotiable.[192] In early 1997, Primakov declared that NATO's actions would be judged according to NATO's readiness to make special concessions, for example in the revision of the KSE treaty. A cooperation agreement with NATO would only make sense if Russia had a voice in decisions that were of vital interest to Russia. The NATO promise not to station nuclear weapons in any new countries was a first step in the right direction. The same was true of the proposal to accept Russia as a full member in the new consultation mechanism.[193]

Der Spiegel hypothesized that it was Primakov's goal to establish Russia as a full political member in the Western community, so that Russia could exercise considerable influence even while not having membership status. Russia was to have the right to place items on the agenda in the consultative council, in which it was to be a full member. The only items to be excepted were the internal affairs of NATO and Russia. This would transform NATO into a political organization and make Russia an equal member. In negotiations with NATO secretary-general Xavier Solana, Primakov tried to make enlargement an item that was to be decided by the consultative council. Because the NATO bodies require unanimity, Russia could have blocked all decisions of the council.[194] The United States did not accept these proposals. At a meeting of the NATO foreign ministers in Brussels on February 2, 1997, Madeleine Albright confirmed that Russia was to be included in decisions, but that it could not have a veto.[195]

During the March 1997 Clinton-Yeltsin summit in Helsinki, the two sides tried to find common ground, but the fundamental issues could not be resolved. While the Russian side wished to conclude a binding international treaty that would have to be ratified by all NATO member states, the United States proposed a politically binding document or charter.[196] Clinton and Yeltsin agreed to begin negotiations that were to lead to a Start III treaty. Clinton also proposed accepting Russia into the G-7 group and revising the KSE treaty according to Russian wishes. Moreover, Clinton proposed a strengthening of the OSCE and reaffirmed the decision of the NATO council not to station nuclear weapons on the territory of the new members.[197] But in the final press conference, both sides openly admitted that the differences with respect to enlargement had not yet been resolved.[198]

The Federal Republic supported the United States, but tried to make enlargement as painless as possible for Russia. Helmut Kohl strongly advocated Russian membership in the G-7 group.[199] In April 1997, Kohl declared that Russia would participate at the next meeting in Denver as the eighth member.[200] Kohl also proposed concessions with regard to the shape of enlargement. He promised the Russian prime minister that

NATO troops would not be stationed at the Russian border.[201] Defense minister Rühe excluded an admission of the Baltic states for the time being, thereby accommodating Russian concerns. Security was to be created through an enlarged Partnership for Peace.[202] Kohl, who had been repeatedly invited to visit the Baltic states, had always declined those invitations.[203]

Overall, there was broad agreement between the United States and Germany. In February 1997, Kinkel demonstrated unity with Albright, stating that Russia had to be included in a new security system. Kinkel and Albright also opposed a Five Powers conference on the future of the European security system (the United States, France, Great Britain, Russia, Germany) as proposed by France, deciding against its closest European ally to accommodate the U.S. position.[204]

The significance of this step becomes especially clear in view of the fact that from spring to summer 1997, the strengthening of a common foreign and security policy was discussed in the context of the Amsterdam conference. In exchange for a stronger European security identity, France proposed to rejoin the military organization of NATO.

Germany also tried limit its concessions to Russia. Germany wanted to preserve NATO as a defensive treaty. A direct Russian influence on decisions within NATO was to be avoided, if possible. The short-lived U.S. proposal to create a far-reaching agreement that would have given Russia considerable influence exposed the dependency of the German position. Other European powers followed suit: the foreign ministers of Italy, Canada, and the Netherlands protested against the bilateral U.S. approach. Moreover, they argued, the number of concessions to Russia as well as the speed of the negotiations was too high.[205]

The concessions made in the Founding Act on Mutual Cooperation and Security between the North Atlantic Treaty Organization and the Russian Federation, signed by the 16 NATO heads of state and government as well as the prime minister of the Russian Federation on May 27, 1998, gave Russia a considerable influence on NATO. The charter is not a legally binding international treaty and does not give Russia a veto in NATO affairs. But it contains the creation of a permanent council between NATO and Russian foreign and defense ministers. Upon demand, the forum can also include the heads of state and government. Moreover, the charter also foresees military consultations. The heads of staff are to meet at least once per year, other military representatives once per month. The agreement contains a long list of topics with special relevance for mutual consultations with an emphasis on conflict prevention, arms control, and nonproliferation. Russia will send a representative with the rank of ambassador. A high-ranking military official with a staff will be assigned to support the ambassador. NATO also agreed not to station any nuclear weapons or large permanent troop contingents on the territory of its new members. In turn, Russia accepted that the new members were full member integrated into NATO military structures.[206]

The agreement allowed Russia a considerable de facto influence in NATO. *Der Spiegel* quoted one anonymous Kohl advisor who called the agreement a danger to NATO as a defense community. The preservation of this defense community should have been a priority of German policy. According to the advisor, Russia could exercise pressure on the smaller NATO states in its neighborhood, thereby gaining a veto via facti. Germany, however, had already accommodated the United States, so that a change of course was impossible.[207] The CDU/CSU foreign plicy coordinator Rudolf Seiters stated that there was considerable criticism among the Bundestag members. Many thought that Russia would have too large a say.[208] In the United States, too, critics warned of the dangers for NATO. In June 1998, Henry Kissinger wrote, "The so-called Founding Act between Russia and NATO . . . seeks to reconcile Russia by diluting the Atlantic Alliance into a UN-style system of collective security."[209]

Despite the considerable concessions to Russia, domestic criticism was high in Russia, too. Germany's fundamental dilemma of having to balance between many objectives therefore remained present. Boris Yeltsin had called the agreement "a great success." The NATO states had demonstrated with their signatures that they respected Russia's security concerns.[210] But former security adviser Aleksandr Lebed called the agreement a "smokescreen." The alliance had bought the right to expand through concessions, and the president had an agreement to show to his domestic opponents. But the agreement would not change the basic impotence of Russia in the face of a very powerful NATO.[211]

While fundamentally agreeing to enlargement, the Federal Republic was very concerned not to contradict any country's position openly. This, given the differences even among NATO states, was no easy feat and gave the impression of indecisiveness and weakness. The meeting of May 25, 1997, for example, clearly exposed those differences. Belgium, Luxembourg, Canada, France, Greece, Turkey, and Spain wanted to accept Slovenia and Romania in addition to the Czech Republic, Poland, and Hungary. France, in particular, promoted a "large solution" and strongly argued for the admission of at least Romania. The United States and Iceland only wanted to admit the latter three states, fearing the high costs of the large solution and an impairment of NATO's ability to act politically. The other states, including the Federal Republic, did not have a firm position.[212]

The United States had another reason to propose a small solution: any large solution would have relegated a second round of enlargement to a distant future. But despite Russia's opposition, the United States wanted to keep the door open for the Baltic states. During her visit to Lithuania on July 13, 1997, Madeleine Albright declared that Lithuania, Estonia, and Latvia had a good chance of being included in the next round. Russia, of course, reacted with heavy criticism. Foreign minister Primakov declared those plans "potentially the gravest mistake since the end of the Cold War."[213]

France had also claimed the post of supreme commander of the Mediterranean, a position that United States was not willing to give up. When it became clear that France could not get this position, it dropped its plans to rejoin the military structure of NATO.[214]

Germany's domestic debate reflected the divisions among the international community. At a meeting of the conservative heads of government, Kohl pleaded for a large solution as proposed by France. In internal deliberations, Volker Rühe was an advocate of the small American solution. In June, he made this position public. Klaus Kinkel, in turn, tried to demonstrate neutrality. The Federal Republic "would be open for any conceivable and sensible solution." The outcome was an open position. The Federal Republic made it known to the other participants of the Madrid summit that it would agree to a big solution if this found a majority, and that it would not vote against a small solution if this was the majority position.[215] At the Madrid summit of July 7 and 8, 1997, the participating states agreed to the small solution at the last possible date. The United States had pushed through its concept.

VII

Power Structure over Ideology: The Foreign Policy of the New Schröder-Fischer Government

Europe's problems cannot be solved with Germany's checkbook.

—*Gerhard Schröder*[1]

The Western alliance can be compared to a fruit basket filled with a melon, two apples, and a handful of peas.

—*Joschka Fischer*[2]

I

On October 27, 1998, the sixteen-year-long Kohl era came to an end. Gerhard Schröder, an SPD reformist, was elected chancellor in the second session of the fourteenth electoral period of the German Bundestag. The Social Democratic Party and the Green Party had formed a coalition government. Joschka Fischer of the Green Party became foreign minister, Rudolf Scharping, SPD centrist, became defense minister, and Oskar Lafontaine, SPD leftist, became finance minister.[3]

The first months of the Schröder government provide a good opportunity to study the influence of international structure and ideology on German foreign policy. Especially in security policy—Germany's policy with regard to NATO—and Germany's policy with regard to the EU, major changes seemed possible. The Green Party was a junior coalition partner with 6.7 percent of the popular vote. Yet the SPD needed the Greens to form a government—like the CDU/CSU had needed the FDP. Traditionally, the Green Party had been pacifist, supranationalist, and very critical of NATO. The Greens had argued that German forces should not be used outside Germany. A UN mandate was to be required in all cases. This position also had strong support in the SPD. Both the SPD and the Green Party were basically in favor of strengthening Europe's security capabilities. At the same time, Schröder had announced a new direction in Germany's policies toward Europe. German interests, for example in budgetary matters, were to be pursued more assertively, and not burdened by the baggage of the past.

Within a few months, international constraints made the new government follow a policy that was almost identical to that of its predecessor government. The international system and not ideology proved to be the main determinant for Germany's policy. Germany was still highly dependent on the United States for its military security and the EU for its economic security. The government therefore quickly adjusted to following the U.S. lead in NATO (as opposed to promoting a European defense identity or strengthening the OSCE or the UN), and continued its support of the existing EU structures. Stabilization and partnership with Central and Eastern European countries, though very important to Germany, were only the third priority. NATO was more important than Russia, and the existing EU was more important than the inclusion of new members.

The first months of the Schröder government showed that Germany remained a middle power in a precarious situation. The breakdown of the communist system had increased the number of variables in German diplomacy, but had given Germany little additional means to control this more complex situation. The United States, Germany's most important security partner, still often showed a leaning towards unilateral action and was slowly redefining NATO as a more activist alliance. European integration had reached a standstill. At the same time, Russia had entered the scene as an actor that could have a large impact on Germany.

The middle power Germany continued to do what it had always done best: it tried to campaign for stability, preserve the status quo, and reconcile the interests of the parties involved. In critical situations, it had to abandon its own designs in order to support the United States, on which it was still dependent for its security. Barring unforeseen events in either Russia or the United States, it is our prediction that Germany will continue to remain a force of the status quo for a long time to come.

II

In view of a potential change of government, intellectuals, the parties, and the public had begun to discuss the foundations of Germany's foreign policy and potential changes during the last years of the Kohl era. Many intellectuals demanded a reevaluation of Germany's national interests. Karl-Richard Korte, for example, called Kohl's policy a tactic of blending in with the other states, which could not be sustained because of growing domestic opposition in Germany.[4] Political scientist Christian Hacke also urged the government to pay greater attention to national interests. In Germany, he said, the term had been blurred by a veil of moral but irrational arguments for a long time. Hacke wanted Germany to examine its integration in Europe and retain only those aspects that are of advantage to Germany—not unlike France's strategy. Selective cooperation was in the national interest, he argued, but a dissolution of Germany in a future European federation was not. According to Hacke, distributional conflicts in the European Union were not signs of dissolution, but of legitimate national interests.[5] Likewise, political scientist Gregor Schöllgen demanded that Germany give up its passive background role and pursue its national interests more actively.[6]

Egon Bahr, the grand old foreign policy thinker of the SPD, provided a long analysis in January 1999. The author was markedly pleased with the emancipation of the Federal Republic. The "patronizing" would end now, he argued, and German policy would have to become normal. To submit to a "vassal-like" fear of the American allies would be wrong; German foreign and security policy should not be relegated to others. In the past, this fear had been marked by statements that there should be no German *Sonderweg*. The idea of European identity was a chimera to which Germany would have to say goodbye. Cooperation within Europe, however, was in the normal German interest.[7]

American observers saw this similarly. Former under secretary of state Robert B. Zoellick titled an article in *Internationale Politik* "Goodbye to Self-Restraint," arguing that Germany should pursue its national interests more actively.[8] Earlier, David Anderson of the Aspen Institute Berlin criticized German policy during NATO enlargement as "without concept." The Federal Republic should assume a leadership role in NATO and the EU. Germany should also pursue its own interests with less dependence on the United States.[9] Even Werner Weidenfeld, Germany's most influential political scientist and a longtime adviser of Helmut Kohl, asked whether Germany could continue with its renunciation of leadership in an increasingly complex international situation.[10]

Germany's relationship to its own troubled past seemed to have changed. In his government declaration of November 10, 1998, Gerhard Schröder spoke of the "self-confidence" of a nation that had grown up and that had no need to feel inferior or superior to anybody else. On the contrary, a faulty national self-confidence had created the German catastrophes of the twentieth century. In a talk show, Schröder declared in an open manner heretofore uncommon for German politicians that the government would act with less emotional baggage and possibly become more "German" in the future.[11] Foreign minister Fischer made similar statements: Bonn should not habitually develop tetanus if somebody in Washington coughed. According to Fischer, Germans had stood with their "hands at the seams of their slacks" for way too long.

The World War II and postwar generation of politicians, epitomized by chancellors Helmut Schmidt and Helmut Kohl, had assigned a high value to gestures of reconciliation (the postwar generation even more so than the war generation). Helmut Kohl and Francois Mitterand had celebrated the truce of November 11, 1918 in 1984 by holding hands in front of a memorial. Willy Brandt had sunk to his knees in Warsaw.[12] The commemoration of the end of the first world war is an important holiday in France: 1.4 million French soldiers had died in the first world war—much more than the 185,000 military casualties of the Second World War. Shortly after his inauguration, however, Schröder declined an invitation to participate in 1998, showing that the historical baggage had lost some of its weight.[13]

This changing perspective on history was also reflected in the public debate. In late 1998, the well-known author Martin Walser had received the peace price of the German book retailing association. In his speech on November 10, which was broadcast live, Walser complained about the political instrumentalization of Nazi crimes by others states and groups for their current purposes.[14] In the ensuing heated debate, writer Monika Maron and Klaus von Dohnanyi, former mayor of Hamburg, supported Walser's position.[15] Ignaz Bubis, chair of the German-Jewish council, accused Walser of "laying spiritual fires." Walser, he said, was the spokesman of a latent antisemitism still present in Germany.[16] Egon Bahr, in turn, supported Walser. According to Bahr, it was understandable if Walser now looked away in the face of a relentless presentation of German shame. For the future, it would have to be possible for Germany to say that even Jews could be wrong and that the state of Israel could make political mistakes. The stigma Ausschwitz should not be a burden for the normal, new German state.[17]

But what should the changes in this new and normal German state be? SPD and Green members and party commissions had deliberated upon possible changes in advance of the federal elections of 1998. Rudolf Scharping, the SPD party chairman, had led the party closer to CDU/CSU-FDP government policies to demonstrate the SPD's ability to govern.[18] Egon Bahr had presented a vision of a Europe in which NATO would ultimately be replaced by an all-European security system. Other SPD figures like Katrin Fuchs and Dieter S. Lutz supported this position and had started to discuss foreign policy issues with the members of the Green Party.[19]

At a party convention early in 1997, the SPD had passed a resolution on foreign and security policy. The resolution described NATO as an indispensable foundation of security in Europe. Yet it also claimed that changes were necessary. Europe, for example, would have to assume a larger role and speak with one voice.[20] This demand, however, is a far cry from demands to ultimately dissolve NATO, such as those outlined by Egon Bahr in 1999. Bahr tried to redefine German national interests by pointing to an analysis by Zbigniew Brzesinski claiming that disunity among Europeans in security matters was in the national interest of the United States.[21] There was no indication, however, that Bahr's analysis represented a majority position in the SPD.[22] Only the PDS, the East German successor party to the Communist regime, and parts of the Greens, representing probably 10 percent of the electorate, as well as certain intellectual circles, were outspokenly anti-American.[23] Moreover, Brzesinski's book does not conform with Bahr's interpretation. On the contrary, Brzesinski tells his countrymen that the United States would have to support European integration and will have to bear the consequences.[24]

A more moderate criticism of the United States was latent in parts of the SPD and the Green Party. These groups were of the opinion that the United States wanted to make Europe an executive arm for its own national strategy. Rudolf Augstein, editor of Der Spiegel, commented that the population of the United States needed an enemy and the United States therefore played the role of sheriff of the world. Europe was to be deputy sheriff, because the United States alone was not powerful enough. The air strikes against Kosovo were prompted by domestic considerations and were almost a "colonial war."[25]

In June 1997, a party commission of the SPD presented a discussion paper on foreign policy.[26] The commission had been staffed with politicians of the different wings of the SPD. Its recommendations, however, almost read like a program of the CDU/CSU-FDP government then in power. International interdependence, it stressed, had increased and was influencing social policy, employment, and the environment. The Federal Republic would therefore have to think and act globally.

Germany's more active role was tied to a strengthening of the United Nations to spread democracy, the rule of law, and security. A Social Democratic government would not shy away from military actions sanctioned by the United Nations. This focus on norms is more typical of a middle power than it is typical of the pacifist traditions of the SPD. The same arguments had all been heard from the CDU/CSU-FDP government.

Even with regard to NATO enlargement, the discussion paper was heavily oriented toward the policies of the CDU/CSU-FDP government. The significant SPD wing that opposed NATO enlargement in favor of an all-European system of collective security only received symbolic concessions. The NATO treaty was to remain the basis of the alliance. Enlargement would have to happen in a way that would not create new lines of conflict. If this prerequisite was fulfilled, enlargement could contribute to the stabilization of the region. There was to be a consultative agreement with Russia to include this large power in Europe and to prevent confrontation. The SPD, too, wanted to limit Russia's say in the alliance, ruling out a veto.

References to enlarging the role of the OSCE can be understood as a concession to the group around Egon Bahr, the pacifist wing of the SPD, and the potential coalition partner, the Green Party. According to these groups, the OSCE would replace NATO in the long term. Such ambitious plans, however, did not appear in the discussion paper. Only a "strengthening" of the OSCE, for example through unarmed observer missions, was proposed.

The paper also discussed Germany's dependence on the United States in security matters but emphasized that the alliance was a defensive one. Therefore Germany could only use force outside of its defensive mandate if there was a mandate of the UN or the OSCE. This demand was also directed against the American strategy of making NATO an international intervention force. Moreover, the SPD also wanted to strengthen the European pillar of the Atlantic alliance. Europe was to act jointly in international crises. The SPD's commitment to a strengthening of the CFSP and the WEU was much stronger than that of the CDU/CSU-FDP government still in power.[27] In accordance with the French proposal, a high commissioner was to represent the EU in foreign policy matters. (The result of the Amsterdam conference was much more modest. The so-called high commissioner of the EU can only act upon a mandate of the European Commission. A true high commissioner would have carried much more weight.)[28]

The program that was ultimately agreed upon at the SPD convention of December 1998 largely followed the discussion paper, but made reference to human rights. The Federal Republic was to promote its interests more strongly than before. "A peaceful, democratic and solidaric" world was said to be in the German national interest. It was the task of German foreign policy to create and strengthen violence-free ways of preventing and dealing with conflict. The respect for human rights, according to the program, was the best way to maintain peace.[29]

The doctrine of the Green Party provides a very good test case with regard to question of whether the structure of the international system or ideology ultimately determines foreign policy. The Green Party, founded in 1983 as an ecological protest party, was the original pacifist party and was also somewhat anti-American. It was closely linked with the peace movement that had sent millions to the streets in 1982 in protest against the NATO double-track decision and the stationing of Pershing II and cruise missiles on German soil.

As participation in an SPD-led coalition government became more and more likely, a lively debate ensued within the party in 1997–1998.[30] A strong faction within the Green Party demanded that Germany leave NATO. Joschka Fischer, later the foreign minister, called the Greens' first draft on the foreign and security policy of Germany an insufficient and counterproductive program if the party wanted to be part of a government. This draft spoke of an all-European security structure that would replace current military organizations. Despite Fischer's criticism, the draft received a wide majority at the party convention of March 1998. The goal of Green security policy was the long-term dissolution of the military organizations, including NATO. The UN and the OSCE were to be strengthened. The cornerstones were to be laid for a new all-European security structure based on international law, not power. National sovereignty was an outdated concept, the power to act would have to be transferred to the international community of states. The restructuring of the Bundeswehr into an "international intervention army" was to be stopped, the draft abolished, and the size of the Bundeswehr cut to 150,000.[31]

But the position of the party convention was only partially reflected in the coalition agreement of October 20, 1998. The SPD and the Green Party have reconfirmed their commitment to international organizations and supranational solutions. But the agreement does not mention the replacement of national sovereignty in security affairs by international organizations. German foreign policy is referred to as "peace policy"—a largely empty phrase.[32]

Specific goals that contradict the policy of the previous government are much harder to find. NATO is called an "indispensable pillar of European security." The presence of American troops is considered of vital importance for the security of the Federal Republic. The demand to replace NATO with an all-encompassing system of collective security in Europe does not appear in the coalition agreement—traditional security policy prevails. The OSCE and the UN are named as important pillars of security, but all measures proposed to strengthen the OSCE re nonmilitary in character. This allowed for concessions to the left wing, especially of the Green Party, while at the same time leaving NATO intact.[33]

III

If there were ever any ideological differences between the SPD-Green and the CDU/CSU-FDP governments, the no–first-strike debate and the Kosovo crisis showed that the new German government quickly accepted the international realities of a middle power in a complex situation and acted much in the same way the previous government would have acted. In other words, the new government shared the assessment of priorities of German security policy: (1) maintenance of the U.S. protective shield; (2) maintenance of the EU for economic security; and (3) stability in the East.

In the Kosovo crisis, Germany quickly followed the U.S. lead. The conflict between Serbian forces and the largely Albanian population in Kosovo had escalated throughout 1998, and there had been considerable Serbian atrocities against Albanian civilians. On September 23, 1998, the UN Security Council demanded in Resolution 1199 that both parties in the conflict stop military action and enter into a political dialogue.[34] But even this moderate resolution was not fully supported by China, whose delegate abstained from a vote. Though Russia voted for the resolution, the Russian delegate stated that this did not imply use of force.[35] In early October, the Duma voted against military action. Yeltsin ordered his foreign minister, Igor Iwanov, to do everything possible to prevent a military intervention by other powers and to give Russian support to the Yugoslav prime minister.[36]

Despite this unclear situation, the United States urged air strikes. U.S. special envoy Richard Holbrooke told Yugoslav prime minister Slobodan Milosevic during a visit that the United States and NATO were ready to strike.[37] The designated chancellor and his future foreign minister visited Washington in October 1998, before their inauguration. Even then,

Joschka Fischer later told *Der Spiegel,* Fischer had realized who ran the alliance. The possibility of implementing independent (German) views was nil.[38] Clinton sought support in threatening Serbia even without a UN mandate, but did not demand an immediate decision because of the difficult situation of the new government.[39]

A few days later, however, the U.S. administration radically changed its course. While Schröder and Fischer were on their way to meet outgoing chancellor Kohl, they were called by SPD politician Günter Verheugen. Verheugen reported that Washington now demanded immediate support for the use of force by NATO, even without a UN mandate. The chancellor and his foreign minister had fifteen minutes to decide. They decided to support the United States.[40]

During the ensuing discussion with the chancellor, the atmosphere was depressed. Kohl expressed his severe reservations about the American procedure. An intervention would alienate Russia and hurt German interests. One could not, however, ignore Germany's security dependence on the United States. According to *Der Spiegel,* Schröder told Fischer at that point that he could only take over the foreign office if he was prepared to accept the preponderance of the United States. [41]

The Bundestag debated the issue on October 16, 1998. SPD member Karsten Voigt, later under secretary of state, argued that NATO should act without a UN mandate to avert the impending humanitarian catastrophe. Some Bundestag members maintained that such unilateral action would weaken the international organizations the SPD wanted to strengthen. Voigt, however, argued that a NATO action against Serbia, even if not covered by a UN mandate and even if against the wishes of Russia, would strengthen the international organizations. NATO would be implementing a UN resolution by force—even though that resolution did not foresee the use of force.[42] Gerhard Schröder conceded that he would have preferred a fully valid UN resolution. Though NATO could not make itself dependent on the Security Council on this important issue, Schröder in principle reaffirmed the UN monopoly on power. Future defense minister Rudolf Scharping supported his predecessors.[43]

Joschka Fischer argued that the Green Party should support the resolution, but also stated that "in principle" NATO could not give itself a mandate. In this case, however, action was necessary because of exceptional circumstances and human suffering.[44] This assessment was not shared by all Green members of parliament. Ludger Vollmer, later under secretary in the foreign office, stated that he could understand the resolution, but that he could not agree with it. Together with members of parliament Winfried

Nachtwei, Kerstin Müller, and Volker Beck, he argued that the resolution should not be passed.[45]

In the ensuing Bundestag vote, there were 62 votes against the use of force and 18 abstentions. This number exceeded the number of PDS Bundestag seats. Approximately 30 Bundestag members—most likely Green and SPD, had not supported their future chancellor. SPD member Michael Müller, for example, opposed the government proposition because it would violate the UN monopoly over the use of force.[46] With the CDU, CSU, and FDP behind the proposal, however, the Bundestag supported the use of force with an overwhelming majority.

In his first government declaration of November 1998, Schröder set clear priorities. Germany would keep its commitments in the alliance and to its most important ally, the United States. The friendship between Germany and the United States would be of decisive importance. France, whose plans for a joint European defense identity had resonated in parts of the SPD, was addressed much later in the declaration.[47] Schröder's speech before the diplomatic corps on November 23, 1998 shows a similar list of priorities. Though Schröder named a stronger CFSP as one of the goals of the German EU presidency, he did not link a stronger European identity to changes in NATO structure, as did the SPD discussion paper on foreign policy. Schröder supported the status quo and a close link to the United States. Schröder's declaration was in stark contrast to SPD and Green Party papers, which contained replacement of NATO as a long-term goal. This helped Schröder to show that he was a loyal U.S. ally, something that was not necessarily clear to U.S. decision makers from the beginning.[48]

Fischer's statements, too, were in contrast to the opinion of many in his party. The conservative *Frankfurter Allgemeine Zeitung* wrote in late October 1998 that Fischer's positions would have been a reason for joy for Konrad Adenauer.[49] In August 1998, Fischer had mentioned that there would not be a Green, but only a German foreign policy.[50] After the change of government, Fischer consulted closely with former chancellor Helmut Kohl. In many interviews, Fischer reaffirmed that his policy would be characterized by continuity. The Federal Republic would have to continue to pursue its foreign policy in consensus with other states.[51] The Atlantic alliance and the European Union would remain the pillars of Germany's foreign policy.[52]

The Green foreign minister, positioned between his own "realism" and the idealism of his party members, was sitting on dynamite. Fischer grew increasingly distant from the party base and even the group of Green Bundestag members. Some of the party members saw him as a careerist and a warmonger. He was labeled a "Stresemännchen" (little Stresemann) and "The Invisible."[53] This precarious relationship with his own party may have caused him to attempt to demonstrate an independent Green identity and cause the first—and to date, the new government's only—serious conflict between Germany and the United States.

Shortly after assuming office, Fischer proposed to American secretary of state Madeleine Albright that NATO reconsider its nuclear doctrine and consider a no-first-strike policy. Fischer repeated this proposal at a meeting of NATO foreign ministers in Brussels on December 8, 1999. None of his colleagues supported him. The delegations of the nuclear powers, France, the United States, and Great Britain spoke out against such lectures on how they should use their weapons.[54] Fischer's proposal was not included in the final communiqué.[55] NATO secretary-general Xavier Solana declared shortly after the meeting that NATO would continue to need the protection of its nuclear weapons to avert threats.[56]

Yet Fischer's proposals were not without logic and could well have been in the interest of the nonnuclear power Germany. Until the dissolution of the Warsaw Pact, NATO had relied on a potential first nuclear strike to counter the East's superiority in conventional weapons. Now, with the conventional threat all but gone, a first strike was not necessary anymore to guarantee the immediate security of Germany.[57] The United States was interested in equipping NATO with the capabilities to deal with rogue states. According to *Die Zeit,* one of the U.S. objectives was to transform NATO into a global intervention force. A nuclear no-first-strike policy would counteract these objectives, but these objectives that were not necessarily shared by other European governments, with the exception of Great Britain.[58] And indeed, the SPD and the Green Party had put into their coalition agreement that they would pursue the goal of a no-first-use policy, although the agreement made no special reference to NATO.[59]

Defense minister Rudolf Scharping experienced the full criticism of the United States during his inaugural visit to Washington. To avert further damage, he distanced himself from the position of the foreign minister, declaring in a press conference with his American colleague William Cohen that Fischer's proposal was harmful.[60] To defuse Fischer's proposal and simultaneously demonstrate goodwill to his junior coalition partner, Scharping later proposed a global ban on weapons of mass destruction within the framework of the United Nations. This proposal was unrealistic and left the NATO doctrine intact.[61]

Fischer himself was eager to demonstrate his reliability within the alliance. In an interview with the *Financial Times* he declared that Germany would remain a reliable ally despite his proposal. He reiterated that there would be no discontinuities in German foreign policy. Fischer said that personally, he was no Pacifist but a supporter of NATO.[62] There are a number of potential motives for Fischer's initiative. It is likely that he wanted to make some concessions to the left wing of his party. The demand for a no-first-strike policy had been a long-standing pillar of Green security doctrine. Moreover, this demand was included in the coalition agreement and the party resolutions of the SPD. Maybe that was the reason Fischer assumed he could test the waters this way.

The Kosovo conflict shows that the foreign policy of the Schröder-Fischer government reflects the typical and long-established patterns of German foreign policy. As in the debate over NATO enlargement, the vulnerable middle power Germany tried to establish a consensus among the actors involved. Too weak itself to have a decisive influence on any of the large powers, the Federal Republic was ultimately dependent on these powers, especially the United States.

After the escalation of the conflict, NATO decided upon air strikes in March 1999. The Federal Republic participated in this action, something that would have been unthinkable a decade earlier. Germany did not simply follow the United States into a domestically motivated crisis, as Rudolf Augstein, publisher of *Der Spiegel,* hypothesized.[63] There were many valid reasons that Germany supported this action; it did not simply "yield" to American demands. As early as October 1988, under secretary of state Wolfgang Ischinger urged his American colleague Strobe Talbott to take action.[64] The German public, too, grew impatient with the suffering in Kosovo. In April, Fischer stated that the Europeans had wanted the Kosovo-intervention and that it was not an exclusively American demand.[65]

But though the goals of the United States and Germany were largely congruent, an old dilemma of German foreign policy soon resurfaced. As was the case during the discussions leading to NATO enlargement, the United States often quickly changed course without consulting with its allies. When this happened, Germany was not able to openly contradict the United States. As was the case during NATO enlargement, Germany tried to balance the interests of all actors. This policy, however, had to remain asymmetrical because of Germany's fundamental dependency on the United States.

When Jevgeny Primakov, the Russian prime minister, visited Bonn first to discuss the Kosovo crisis, German government officials were not entirely exited about this demonstration of Russian confidence. According to *Der Spiegel,* Schröder, Fischer, and Scharping unanimously agreed that Germany should not leave the impression that it would discuss matters with Russia unilaterally. The trust of the West had to be preserved by all means—there was to be no second Rapallo.[66]

The attempt to accommodate multiple interests led the red-green coalition government to repeat a typical pattern of German foreign policy—a pluralism of opinions within the government. During the discussion on NATO enlargement, foreign minister Kinkel had urged NATO to take Russia's concerns very seriously and to evaluate more Europeanist options, while defense minister Volker Rühe had argued for rapid enlargement. Under the Schröder government, the dual approach was elevated to the level of official strategy: Michael Steiner, foreign policy adviser of Gerhard Schröder, stated in April 1999 that the government would pursue a "dual strategy."[67] Gerhard Schröder later used this term in a speech before the Bundestag to describe a policy of supporting military pressure on the one hand and seeking a political solution on the other.[68] But the first part of this strategy was obviously aimed at the United States, the second part at Russia.

The chancellor and his foreign minister apparently agreed that there was only narrow room for maneuver and that the Federal Republic had to preserve the trust of its Western allies. Fischer explained that Great Britain, France, and Germany had fought over the issue of whether to recognize Slovenia and Croatia in 1991, thus replaying a constellation that had existed before World War I. Similar constellations and discussions had to be prevented.[69] Overall, Schröder pursued a somewhat more decisive course and supported the United States, while Fischer more strongly sought multilateral consensus, and tactic that he also owed to his party.

At the same time, Schröder remained firm in his statement that the Federal Republic would not send ground troops into the Kosovo.[70] During the air strikes, the chancellor reiterated the position that German troops would not participate in a ground war against the Yugoslav army and that doing so would exceed Germany's pain threshold. The domestic consensus started to slip as the military action continued. In March there was broad agreement among the German population. But a few weeks later, support for the air strikes had dropped from 64 percent to 50 percent. Now, 64 percent advocated a pause in the strikes to seek a political solution.[71]

The government campaigned for public support by collecting and disseminating information about Serbian atrocities.[72] Unmanned German reconnaissance planes were sent on surveillance missions over Kosovo.

Interviews with refugees were evaluated. In his press conferences, the German defense minister drew parallels to Germany's past. According to Scharping, a systematic genocide was happening in Kosovo.[73] At times, the reporting almost resembled propaganda from earlier European wars—atrocities against pregnant women were depicted in graphic detail.[74]

The preparation of the air strikes also showed that it was the U.S.-British tandem within the alliance that acted as initiators. In late 1999, Madeleine Albright had proposed to the White House that air strikes be used in response to a Serb massacre.[75] The British prime minister agreed to this procedure. As during the air strikes against Iraq in December 1998, both governments presented their allies with a fait accompli. Half an hour before the American president declared his readiness to strike in a speech on CNN, Blair called Schröder. Blair wanted to know if Clinton could count on Germany's support. According to his foreign policy advisers, Schröder had agreed only reluctantly.[76] This led to rising doubt as to whether the reporting was accurate.[77]

Within the government parties, the resistance against the air strikes began to rise. Former chancellor Helmut Schmidt issued grave doubts.[78] The Social Democratic mayor of Hamburg, Henning Voscherau, called the decision for NATO air strikes "wrong." Günter Verheugen had doubts about the legal basis of the attacks.[79] The governors of the new German Länder, the former GDR, were especially eager to distance themselves from the action because their electorate was traditionally more critical of NATO. Many SPD members left the party. At the special SPD party convention on April 12, Schröder ran for the position of party chair that had been left vacant by Oskar Lafontaine's resignation. He only received 75.98 percent of the votes—the second worst result since 1946. The party passed a resolution that the federal government was to seek a peaceful solution and that Germany was not to send ground troops.[80] The deployment of ground troops would have destroyed the fragile domestic consensus for air strikes. In April 1999, only 36 percent of Germans supported this option. Sixty-one percent opposed it categorically.[81]

The atmosphere was even more critical within the Green Party, which was deeply divided over the issue.[82] The pacifist wing of the party wanted to dissolve the government coalition.[83] At the special party convention in May 1999, Joschka Fischer succeeded in securing party support for the government line. The convention was accompanied by violent demonstrations. The police had to protect the delegates from militant peace activists. The foreign minister was hit by a paint bag and the impact damaged his eardrum.[84]

While Schröder did not support ground troops for a military action, he systematically prepared the German public for German peacekeeping troops in Kosovo. In an interview for the newsmagazine *Focus* in January 1999, Schröder declared his readiness to send German peacekeeping forces into Kosovo. The Federal Republic was to act in consensus with its allies.[85] Later, Schröder reiterated that it was absolutely necessary to act in consensus with the allies.[86]

On June 10, the members of the UN Security Council passed Resolution 1244. A few days before, the Serb government had agreed to withdraw its army from Kosovo. Foreign powers received authorization to move into the area and take control. The Yugoslav province was divided into five zones. A contingent of 8,500 German soldiers were deployed in the southern sector around the town of Prizren. French, Italian, British, and American forces seized power in the other sectors. In spite of its complaints, Moscow did not succeed in getting a sector of its own. To meet the Kremlin's need for an international reputation, 4,500 Russian soldiers were stationed in the French, American, and German sectors.[87]

The whole episode, once again, put the Federal Republic in the uncomfortable position of having to decide whether to support the West or Russia, without having much influence on either. Public resentment against the NATO actions was high in Russia. At the outset of the air strikes, there were violent protests before the American embassy in Moscow.[88] According to polls, 95 percent of the Russian population was against the air strikes. The Russian-Serbian friendship had a long tradition.[89] Prominent public figures also heavily criticized the strikes. General Aleksandr Lebed suggested that Russia declare the action an international aggression without a legal basis. Russia should declare Yugoslavia its sphere of interest and assist Belgrade short of entering the war.[90] Military officials declared that they were ready to defend Serbia against the Western aggression.[91]

The Russian government was aware that its economy was dependent on Western assistance. Prime minister Primakov was eager not to sever ties with the West during the crisis.[92] At the same time Boris Yeltsin was under sever pressure—there was the danger of impeachment.[93] It was difficult to say whether Yeltsin would try to use the Kosovo crisis to his advantage in this situation. In June, Russian envoy to Belgrade Viktor Chernomyrdin threatened to take action if the West continued the bombardment. Military and technological cooperation with the West and the ratification of the Salt II treaty would be stopped, and Russia, together with China and India, would oppose the strikes in the UN Security Council.[94] In April, the chairman of the Duma even declared that Russian nuclear missiles had been re-targeted to goals in the West. Shortly before, the Russian president had declared that Russia would not let itself be drawn into a war, but a statement by a parliament member once again exposed Germany's precarious position.[95] Germany, according to its priorities, acted in accordance with the United States throughout the conflict, but a growing resentment in Russia could not be in its interest.

IV

With regard to European integration, the Schröder government merely continued trends that had long gathered momentum in Kohl's era. But Schröder did enter the European scene with a certain fanfare. On many occasions, Schröder declared that Germany's policy toward Europe would now be guided more strongly by German interests and that Germany could not solve Europe's problems with the checkbook.[96] Günter Verheugen, a minister of state in the foreign ministry, announced dramatic changes. Even the widening of the EU would be endangered if Germany did not get financial relief.[97]

During his visit to Poland in November 1998, Schröder demonstrated the new style, declining to offer further financial compensation to those who had been subjected to forced labor during the Nazi era. The new chancellor also contradicted Kohl, who had promised Poland EU membership by the year 2000. Schröder made clear that he could not commit to a firm date.[98]

According to Karl Rudolf Korte, assistant professor of political science and head of the *Zentrum für angewandte Politikforschung* in Munich, Schröder challenged the Federal Republic's historically developed reason of state. Likewise, Karl Kaiser, director of the institute of the German Society for Foreign Affairs, perceives a fundamental change in German foreign policy, which has coincided with a generational change.[99] *Der Spiegel* wrote that a "cool policy of national interest" would now define the German style.[100] Publicist Werner A. Perger wrote that Schröder did not want to legitimize the European Union politically and historically, but rather through specific economic advantages.[101] The newsmagazine *Focus* detected a transformation to a policy of national interests.[102]

The European policies of the new government had three main thrusts: a reform of the EU budget, a coordination of European economic, social, and financial policies, and a strengthening of the European identity in foreign and security affairs. In all three cases, however, the structure of Germany's security interests quickly mandated a return to traditional policies.

Confronted with the danger of a disintegrating EU, Germany remained the largest contributor to the EU budget and was not able to institute rules that would treat it more equitably. Even Germany's promotion of EU widening was lackluster: Germany preferred consensus within the EU (its economic security glacis) to the acceptance of new members, even if those members were dear to Germany. Second, new finance minister Oskar Lafontaine's initiative to move the EU toward coordinated Keynesian monetary and financial policies was very short-lived and resulted in Lafontaine's resignation in the spring of 1999. And third, the European identity in foreign and security affairs quickly took a backseat to the preservation and strengthening of Germany's relationship with the United States, its most important security partner.

In his government declaration of November 10, 1998, Schröder stressed pragmatic and individual aspects of the new government's policy with regard to the European Union. The national identities of the member states would have to be preserved in the European Union. Schröder argued that a federal solution not unlike German federalism "seemed" to be the best guarantee for European integration, naming the French-German friendship as one of the pillars of the European Union. Subsequently, Schröder did not name specific institutional steps, but concentrated on specific social and economic items. Schröder wanted the EU to take a more active role in the fight against mass unemployment. An ecological tax reform, another main goal of the red-green coalition, could only succeed at the European level.[103] By addressing development of common social and economic policies, Schröder played to the left wing in his own party and to the Green Party. On these two issues, the European Union almost seemed to assume the role of an alibi for inaction at home. Schröder also defended the common currency and the independence of the European Central Bank. Schröder also addressed the potential Central European candidates for the EU, saying that Germany would pursue all opportunities for an enlargement of the EU. But at the same time, Schröder was very cautious about making a definite commitment and prepared the candidates for a longer period of waiting.[104]

The new government was not able to achieve a significant share of its reform objectives. This became clear when the objectives the government had set itself for the "Agenda 2000" were compared to the negotiation outcomes. In his government declaration, Schröder had demanded more "budgetary fairness" for Germany. This would be a difficult undertaking, but according to Schröder, the new government was firmly committed to achieving fairness.[105]

Schröder demanded fundamental changes in the Common Agricultural Policy (CAP), but also paid respect to the strong farm lobby at home. Schröder did not support a liberalization of the CAP but wanted to preserve the system of income subsidies. European farmers would have to be protected against the ruinous world market prices. Schröder proposed that the EU only provide a certain capped amount of agricultural subsidies. Amounts exceeding the base level would have to be financed by the member states. This concept, of course, was directed against France and other Mediterranean states that benefited disproportionately from agricultural funds.[106]

Among German policies toward Europe during the first half of 1999, the reform of the EU and Agenda 2000 had the highest priority. But the evolution of the negotiations made clear that despite the combative tone of the government, the fundamental framework for Germany's policies had not significantly changed. Despite its large economy, export-oriented Germany was very much dependent on preserving the EU. Foreign minister Joschka Fischer, for example, postulated a link between an enlargement of the EU and fiscal reform. In January he stated that if fiscal reform did not succeed, enlargement would imply intolerable costs, primarily in the CAP.[107] Though Schröder publicly denied such a linkage, his invitation to the meeting of the European Council of March 1999 essentially confirms its implicit existence.[108] Only by reforming its fiscal policy could the EU be saved from a deep crisis. The EU would only be prepared for further members if Agenda 2000 succeeded.

The German government was not able to significantly further any of its objectives. The negotiations of the heads of state and government in February 1999 in Bonn already showed the significant resistance of other states against reforms of the CAP, the fiscal procedures, the regional subsidies, and the German net contributor position.[109] Before the conference, German minister of agriculture Karl-Heinz Funke had proposed lowering the support prices for most agricultural products over a number of years. Among the losers would have been France, Ireland, England, and Spain. The hope of reaching a compromise along this line was destroyed quickly during the meeting. Spain's head of government, José Maria Aznar declined the proposal of the Council of Ministers outright. French president Jacques Chirac called the proposed reform of the cofinancing and lowering of support prices an "outright attack on French interests."[110]

The Petersberg meeting dampened hopes within the new government of making any significant early progress. The atmosphere was far from enthusiastic before the summit of March 1999. Unnamed government officials said that there was a low likelihood that Germany could reduce its net contribution. Even the fact that Germany had dropped the proposal of national cofinancing had not lessened French resistance. The reform of the cohesion funds was similarly unlikely.[111]

At the summit, Schröder showed himself a tough negotiator, even threatening to let the summit fail. If there was no agreement on financial reform, Schröder said he would not raise the issue again during his term of office. Germany would return to a policy of national interests. Schröder also discussed these issues with individual heads of state and government when the negotiations seemed about to fail.[112]

Despite the energy with which Schröder pursued his objectives, the summit was more of a failure than a success. According to the computations of Der Spiegel, Germany's net payor position would be lowered by only 300 million Euro. The agricultural privileges remained largely intact. The savings were mostly due to short-term patchwork solutions.[113] Nonetheless, Schröder demonstrated satisfaction at the compromise.[114]

But even within the government, there was marked criticism. State minister Verheugen said that a real reform had not taken place because of the resistance of the French government. A fast acceptance of Central European states would be impossible under these conditions.[115] Der Spiegel commented that the accession of Poland alone would more than exhaust the financial possibilities of the union.[116]

Joschka Fischer summarized the state of Europe before the Bundestag. He said that during the summit, he had realized for the first time that the states of Europe would happily and gleefully run away from each other if the Federal Republic did not assume a (financial) leadership role. Helmut Kohl, by now a simple member of the Bundestag, made an interjection. Kohl said he had been preaching for 16 years what Fischer was now saying.[117]

Another controversy captured the public attention during the first few months of the new government. Schröder had named Oskar Lafontaine the new finance minister. Lafontaine was a very influential figure in the SPD and had been a longtime governor of Saarland as well as the 1994 chancellor-candidate of the SPD. Even before he assumed office, he succeeded in prying away more responsibilities from the economics ministry for his finance ministry, leading to the resignation of the designated economics minister Jost Stollmann. Many wondered how the uneasy partnership between the reformist Schröder and his traditionalist and powerful finance minister would evolve.

Lafontaine advocated a more demand-oriented economic policy and social policies, all coordinated at the European level. Together with his chief advisor, Heiner Flassbeck, Lafontaine wanted to steer national and international economic policies away from a supply-side-oriented course to a demand-oriented Keynesian course. In his own words, Flassbeck wanted to "destroy taboos."[118] For this purpose, Lafontaine wanted to limit the independence of the European Central Bank, which was to support employment instead of watching over monetary stability.[119] Moreover, fiscal policies were to be coordinated across Europe and taxes to be harmonized. The voting procedure was to be changed from unanimity to some kind of majority voting.[120]

These demands were not entirely new. Even the Kohl government had supported a harmonization of tax policies to prevent tax flight from the Federal Republic. Other EU states with high tax rates had supported the German position. Those states also feared that the introduction of the Euro would disadvantage them.[121] Yet Lafontaine's initiative was perceived as undue interference in national domestic and economic affairs by many states. It was certainly not helped by the fact that Lafontaine represented the leftist and traditionalist part of the SPD. England categorically opposed any proposal of tax harmonization. For a brief period, the British press found a new public enemy. National sovereignty was at stake. The *Daily Mail* wrote that the British government would resist the German danger, as Lloyd George had resisted the Kaiser and Churchill had resisted Hitler. The *Guardian* saw a decisive battle ahead and even the *Financial Times* put Great Britain and Germany on a collision course.[122]

Lafontaine met with resistance not only from within the European Union but also from other industrialized nations when he proposed a system of target exchange rates and indicators for international monetary affairs. The sole supporter for this proposal was the French finance minister Dominique Strauß-Kahn.[123] One of the goals of a system of target zones for exchange rates was the exclusion of competitive devaluations. Wages were to be raised on a broad scale in line with the raise in corporate profits.[124]

Lafontaine's initiatives generated massive national and international resistance.[125] Gerhard Schröder, the party reformer, may not have been unhappy when Lafontaine surprisingly resigned in March 1999. From the beginning Schröder and Lafontaine had represented different approaches. In his government declaration, Schröder had supported the independence of the European Central Bank.[126] The French news agency AFP quoted anonymous government officials who had called Lafontaine's resignation an important victory for Schröder.[127] During a five-day trip through the EU member states in March 1999, Schröder distanced himself from his former finance minister and promised that the Federal Republic would show continuity in fiscal, monetary, and social policies.[128]

Within a short period, it became clear that the new government's designs for a stronger European identity in defense and foreign affairs remained just that: designs. As already outlined in a previous section of this chapter, the government quickly revealed its priorities by seeking a close link with the United States.

After the inauguration of the new government, high officials repeatedly stated that the Common Foreign and Security Policies had to be strengthened.[129] In January Günter Verheugen proposed that a strong, internationally respected personality become first EU high commissioner for foreign affairs. He also stressed that the European pillar within the EU had to be strengthened.[130] Wolfgang Ischinger, under secretary in the foreign office, declared that the integration of the EU and the WEU would be a priority goal of the government in the first half of 1999, when Germany would hold the chair in both organizations. The two would have to speak with one voice.[131]

Those goals bore the potential for serious conflict with the United States. The demand that Europe be able to deal with crises by itself could also be interpreted as opposition to American influence. Strengthening the European defense industry could also hurt the United States, which had become by far the largest arms exporter of the world. The United States held a monopoly-like position in many key weapons technologies within the Atlantic alliance. The German general Klaus Naumann, then chairman of NATO's military committee, saw a "yawning technological gap" between Europe and the United States.[132] The new markets in Central and Eastern Europe were one motive behind American support of NATO enlargement.[133]

Initially there were some signs that the German strategy was promising. In December 1998, France and even Great Britain did not seem disinclined to strengthen the European component, even though France had reversed its plans to rejoin into the military integration of NATO in 1997, after the United States did not cede the post of commander of NATO forces in the Mediterranean to France. Great Britain had a traditional "special" relationship with the United States and resisted any strengthening of the European identity that could endanger this relationship.

In October 1998, Tony Blair had announced in Germany that Great Britain would promote a fusion of the EU and the WEU.[134] In November, British defense minister George Robertson expressed support for a stronger European identity in a speech in Vienna.[135] The French-British summit of St. Malo created hopes that both countries would pursue the objective of a European defense identity more strongly. The defense ministers agreed to cooperate more closely to contribute to a European defense identity.[136] France, of course, hoped to loosen some of Britain's ties with the United States.[137]

The joint American–British attack on Iraq of December 16–19, 1998, showed Britain's priorities. After Iraq was accused of repeated noncompliance with the UN inspectors, the two countries decided on a joint attack. This attack had not been discussed with either the United Nations or NATO members. The British defense minister informed his colleagues when the first cruise missiles were already under way.[138]

This action had pushed hopes for a common European defense identity into the far distance. The United States had acted more or less unilaterally, supported by one European nuclear power. The French government issued a statement that it regretted the attack. Russia recalled its ambassadors from Washington and London to consultations.[139] For Germany, the typical dilemma of having to decide between two allies arose. The government quickly issued statements of support for the American–British attack. Defense minister Scharping stated that Saddam Hussein had left the allies no choice. In Brusssels, he made clear that the Federal Republic was behind the United States and Britain.[140] The Green members of parliament regretted the attack. An air strike, they said, was not the solution.[141] The federal board of the Green Party criticized the attack as illegitimate and called on the United States and Great Britain to quickly withdraw.[142] These statements, however, did not have an impact on the position of the government.

V

The SPD and the Green Party had traditionally been the parties of human rights, pacifism, and an international legal order based on the United Nations. Large parts of both parties strongly supported the position that military force could only be used with a UN or OSCE mandate. But the end of the East-West conflict had not structurally changed the functioning of the UN Security Council, which depended on consensus among its members. In the first half of the nineties, the large powers had disagreed about the right measures for keeping peace in the former Yugoslavia. Russia did not want to create a precedent for civil wars within its own territory by intervening in Yugoslavia.[143] As a consequence, the Security Council did not approve military measures. Even the UN security zones were not protected by military force—with sad results for Srebrenica.[144]

Though leading SPD and Green politicians paid the United Nations their respects, they supported NATO air strikes in Kosovo without a UN mandate, a position that would have been untenable a few years earlier. Some even argued that this action would strengthen international law. The moral motives and the seriousness of these arguments aside, it is likely that strong U.S. pressure and an interest-based policy had helped the government to move in this direction.

The issue of human rights provides another case in point. In an interview of November 1998, Fischer declared that he would pay greater attention to human rights because of what Germany had learned from its Nazi past. In particular, Germany would review its policy with respect to China. Together with his British colleague Robin Cook, Fischer proposed that the EU present regular reports on human rights. [145]In December, Fischer declared that the Federal Republic would pursue a "value-based foreign policy." The support of human rights would be in Germany's direct interest. Germany's interest in international welfare, stability, and security mandated a support of democratic governments.[146] Fischer then told columnist Josef Joffe of the *Süddeutsche Zeitung* that Germany intended to pursue a "moral foreign policy."[147]

Fischer's support of human rights was opportune for a number of reasons. The grand objective of many in the Green Party and the SPD—a strengthening of the UN and the OSCE—had proven unattainable even before the new government took power. The international support of human rights, even against the principle of national sovereignty, was a fallback position. SPD figures such as president of the Bundestag Wolgang Thierse used similar arguments.[148] In the Bundestag debate of October 16, the protection of human rights had been the main argument used to move SPD and Green members to support NATO strikes.

The case of China exemplifies that the new government was ready to relegate the human rights issue to a lower priority when specific economic interests were involved. Initially the new government had looked combative. Chinese dissident Wei Jingshei received an official invitation from the government. When the Chinese government reacted with criticism, Germany rejected it in an unusually sharp tone.[149] But when Schröder visited China in May 1999 with 33 executives of German industry, he did not broach the issue of human rights.[150] Fischer supported the rapprochement by dampening his criticism of China. An example was his speech before the EU commission on human rights in March 1999. If one had expected sharp tones from the Green president of the council of foreign ministers, one would have been disappointed. Fischer's tone remained moderate.[151]

In this analysis we argue that the actions of Germany were ultimately based on power structure and a clear idea of national interests—more or less, Germany followed the U.S. lead. However, it would be too simple to diagnose a Machiavellian instrumentalization of German foreign policy. First, the U.S. actions had a moral basis in addition to their power-political underpinnings, and second, concern for human rights was deeply embedded, not the least because of Germany's Nazi past. Also because of its position and past, however, Germany could not pursue a policy of human rights unilaterally, against its partners.

VI

The first few months of the Schröder government showed that in the perception of the government, Germany remained a middle power. If anything, the increasingly complex situation after the end of the Warsaw Pact had created a more precarious and potentially unstable situation for Germany. Germany's absolute level of security had increased, but the number of constellations that could threaten the overall stability of the European state system had also greatly increased.

Germany's newly relaxed style showed itself in the speed with which the new government reconfirmed the overall strategic analysis and design of the previous government. This confirmation of traditional interests happened despite the fact that the SPD and Green Party ideologies may have suggested other paths. Germany's list of priorities was clear. It contained: (1) a preservation of the U.S. security partnership; (2) a preservation of the European Union; and (3) stability in the East, e.g., by integrating Russia into the decision-making process or by promoting the enlargement of the EU. At any time when the relationship with the United States was at stake, Germany clearly stuck with its first preference. And when the exiting EU—Germany's economic security sphere—was at stake, Germany chose priority number two over number three.

Under Schröder, Germany was even more ready to demonstrate solidarity with the United States—even if this counteracted the European defense identity—than under Kohl. And this was the fact despite active pacifist wings in the Green Party and the SPD. Moreover, some longstanding ideas about Germany's past had been abandoned under Kohl—for example, the claim that German soldiers should not fight outside Germany or the vision that the United States of Europe would replace Germany as a fatherland at some time. This made it easier for the Schröder government to act in accordance with the allies. At times, Germany's policy may have looked indecisive. During the whole episode covered in this book, however, Germany had to juggle multiple interests, as is necessary for a middle power in Germany's position. The juggling itself was informed by a clear perspective.

Germany also used moral arguments in its foreign policy. This melange of national interests, international consensus, and moral values, however, is in the interest of a status quo-oriented middle power: in the best instance, it creates rules that are somewhat independent of the actors in the system. The specific actions of Germany, however, could almost exclusively be traced to more specific national interests and Germany's national priorities.

If the past is any indicator of the future, we should expect Germany to be the most status quo-oriented power in Europe, preserving its partnership with the United States and preserving the European Union. There will be more of the same: the NATO alliance will last, and the European Union will continue. The real test of German diplomacy would emerge if Germany were ever forced to promote a new all-European security architecture. Our analysis leaves us in doubt over whether Germany would be able to achieve this task, not because of political immaturity, but because Germany's power would simply be insufficient for such a daunting challenge.

Notes

I: Introduction

1. See, for example Philip Zelikow and Condolezza Rice, *Germany Unified and Europe Transformed—A Study in Statecraft* (Cambridge: Harvard University Press, 1995), Karl Kaiser, *Deutschlands Vereinigung: Die internationalen Aspekte* (Bergisch Gladbach: Basteil Lübbe, 1991), Richard Kiessler and Frank Elbe, *Ein runder Tisch mit scharfen Ecken: Der diplomatische Weg zur deutschen Einheit* (Baden-Baden: Nomos 1993), Michael Beschloss and Strobe Talbott, *At the Highest Levels: The Inside Story of the End of the Cold War* (Boston: Little, Brown, 1992), James A. Baker III, *The Politics of Diplomacy* (New York: G. P. Putnam & Sons, 1995), Horst Teltschik, *329 Tage: Innenansichten der Einigung,* 3rd ed. (Berlin: Siedler, 1991).
2. Thomas Kielinger and Max Otte, "Germany—the Pressured Power," *Foreign Policy* 91, no. 2 (1993): 44–62.
3. One could make the legitimate annotation that there is at least one other major perspective on international relations—the Marxist school. However, as we shall see later, the Marxist school shares a number of characteristics with the realist school that set it apart from both institutionalism and constructivsim. Moreover, it would be ironic to apply a Marxist perspective to the events that lead to its own demise. It would be more appropriate to apply this perspective when class struggle and Marxism resurfaced as significant factors in international politics.
4. This will be explored in depth in chapter 2.
5. See, for example, Henry Kissinger, *A World Restored: Metternich, Castlereagh and the Problems of Peace 1812–1822* (London: Weidenfeld and Nicolson, 1957).
6. Robert G. Gilpin, *War and Change in World Politics* (Cambridge, UK: Cambridge University Press 1981).
7. According to Waltz, "countries with great power economies have become great powers, whether or not reluctantly. Japanese and German reasons for hesitating to take the final step into the great power arena are obvious and need not be rehearsed. Yet when a country receives less attention and respect and gets its way less often than it feels it should, internal inhibitions

about becoming a great power are likely to turn into public criticism of the government for not taking its proper place in the world. Pride knows no nationality. How long can Japan and Germany live alongside other nuclear states while denying themselves nuclear capabilities." Kenneth Waltz: "The Emerging Structure of International Relations," *International Security* 18:2 (Fall 1993): 66.

8. Ibid., 64.

9. "The absence of war in Europe since 1945 has been a consequence of three structural factors: the bipolar distribution of military power on the continent; the rough military equality between the two states comprising the two poles in Europe, the United States and the Soviet Union; and the fact that each superpower was armed with a large nuclear arsenal." John J. Mearsheimer, "Back to the Future: Instability in Europe after the Cold War," *International Security* 15, no. 1 (1991): 5–56.

10. Robert O. Keohane and Joseph Nye, *Power and Interdependence: World Politics in Transition* (Boston: Little, Brown & Co., 1977), Robert O. Keohane and Stanley Hoffmann, ed., *The New European Community—Decisionmaking and Institutional Change* (Boulder: Westview Press, 1991).

11. Karl Kaiser "Außenpolititk in einer neuen Welt: der Wandel der internationalen Rahmenbedingungen" in *Die Zukunft der deutschen Außenpolitik, Arbeitspapiere zur internationalen Politik,* ed. Karl Kaiser and Hanns Maull (Bonn: Deutsche Gesellschaft für Auswärtige Politik, 1992): 9.

12. "It seems difficult to believe that Germany will accept such responsibilities and burdens without at the same time receiving a greater say in the handling of world affairs. When confronted with difficult situations, Germans—who will henceforth be as responsible for the outcome of international crises as anyone else, especially in Eastern Europe—will be as likely to impose their solutions, using their means, as any great power would be." Philip H. Gordon: "The Normalization of German Foreign Policy," *Orbis* 38, no. 2 (1994): 242.

13. Ibid., 225–226.

14. Gregor Schöllgen, *Angst vor der Macht—Die Deutschen und ihre Außenpolitik* (Berlin: Ullstein, 1993), 27–28.

15. Richard W. Smyser, "Dateline Berlin: Germany's New Vision," *Foreign Policy* 97, no. 4 (1994–95): 142–58.

16. The model for the exertion of German influence in Europe would be the American post - World War II model: "To create or to shape institutions, to initiate new approaches, to effect common policies, to place key persons in key positions, to include all who are prepared to be included, to give others their due and appropriate shares while retaining for oneself a somewhat larger but not excessive or unreasonable portion." Smyser, "Dateline Berlin," 148–9.

17. Hanns Maull, "Germany and Japan: The New Civilian Powers," *Foreign Affairs* 69, no. 5 (1990/91): 91–107. Hanns Maull, "Zivilmacht Bundesrepublik: Vierzehn Thesen für eine neue deutsche Außenpolitik," *Europa-Archiv* 47, no. 1 (1992): 269–78.

18. Maull, "Zivilmacht Bundesrepublik," 270.

19. Hans-Peter Schwarz: "Rolle und Identität der zukünftigen deutschen Außenpolitik," in *Die Zukunft der deutschen Außenpolitik, Arbeitspapiere zur Internationalen Politik,* ed. Karl Kaiser and Hanns Maull (Bonn: Deutsche Gesellschaft für Auswärtige Politik, 1992).

20. "The era Europe has entered will be qualitatively different from those it has known before, and . . . international politics of the past are not a helpful guide for predicting the patterns of the future. . . . To call the thickening web of overlapping and intersecting functional institutions anarchical is to drain the term of all but a narrowly technical meaning. Europe is, indeed, becoming recognizable as a polity, even if it is not a sovereign entity. Richard H. Ullman: *Securing Europe* (Princeton: Princeton University Press, 1991), 139, 145–6.

21. Thomas U. Berger: C*ultures of Antimilitarism—National Security in Germany and Japan* (Baltimore and London: The Johns Hopkins University Press, 1998).

22. Kissinger, *A World Restored,* 312.

23. Maull, "Vierzehn Thesen," 274–277.

24. Kielinger and Otte, "Pressured Power," 62.

25. Public Papers of the President, *The President's News Conference with Chancellor Helmut Kohl in Bonn, Germany, July 11, 1994* (Washington, D.C.: U.S. GPO, 1994), 1463.

II: A Tradition of Limited Sovereignty

1. Eberhard Kolb: *Die Weimarer Republik,* Oldenbourg Grundriß der Geschichte, vol. 16, 4th ed. (München: Oldenbourg, 1988), 46.

2. Rudolf Morsey, *Die Bundesrepublik Deutschland: Entstehung und Entwicklung bis 1969,* Oldenbourg Grundriß der Geschichte, vol. 19, 3rd ed. (München: Oldenbourg, 1995), 168.

3. Henry A. Kissinger: *A World Restored,* 312.

4. Hans-Peter Schwarz: *Die gezähmten Deutschen—von der Machtversessenheit zur Machtvergessenheit* (Stuttgart: Deutsche Verlags-Anstalt, 1985). The nouns are a listing of section titles in the book.

5. Christian Hacke: *Weltmacht wider Willen—die Außenpolitik der Bundesrepublik Deutschland* (Stuttgart: Klett-Cotta, 1988).

6. The other pillar was Germany's defense doctrine and its integration into NATO.

7. Germans called this their "basic law," since a formal constitution would have to await the reunification of the divided country.

8. Quoted in a speech by Helmut Kohl supporting the ratification of the Maastricht Treaty "Rede des Bundeskanzlers vor dem Deutschen Bundestag," *Bulletin des Presse—und Informationsamtes der Bundesregierung,* 17 December 1994, 1061–1064.

9. Timothy Garton Ash, "Germany's Choice," *Foreign Affairs* 73, no. 4 (1994): 71.

10. Frank Ninkovich, *Germany and the United States: The Transformation of the German Question Since 1945,* (New York: Twayne, 1995).

11. Morsey, *Die Bundesrepublik Deutschland,* 4.

12. "Conversation of Bevin with Stalin," in *The British Commonwealth and Europe,* vol. 3 of *Foreign Relations of the United States, 1947,* ed. Department of State (Washington, D.C.: GPO, 1972), 279.

13. "Communiqué of the Tripartite Conference of Berlin (Potsdam) 1 August 1945," in *Documents on Germany, 1944–1985,* ed. Department of State (Washington, D.C.: GPO, 1986), 63.

14. "Address by Secretary Byrnes, Stuttgart, 6 September 1946," in *Documents on Germany,* 94–96.

15. Auswärtiges Amt, ed., *Europa—Dokumente zur Frage der Europäischen Einigung* (Bonn: Auswärtiges Amt, 1953), 85.

16. "Grundgesetz der Bundesrepublik Deutschland vom 23. Mai 1949 in der Fassung vom 21. Dezember 1983 (Auszüge)," in *Aussenpolitik der Bundesrepublik Deutschland: Dokumente von 1949 bis 1994,* ed. Auswärtiges Amt (Köln: Verlag Wissenschaft und Politik, 1995), 167.

17. "The two German states [were] not regimes that created foreign policies, but foreign policies that created regimes." Karl Kaiser, *German Foreign Policy in Transition: Bonn between East and West* (Oxford: Oxford University Press, 1968).

18. Wolfgang Benz, *Die Gründung der Bundesrepublik—Von der Bizone zum souveränen Staat* (München: DTV 1989).

19. Hacke, *Weltmacht,* 49.

20. Arnulf Baring, *Im Anfang war Adenauer—Die Enstehung der Kanzlerdemokratie* (München: DTV, 1982).

21. Ibid., 86.

22. "Adenauer's erste Regierungserklärung vor dem Deutschen Bundestag, 20. September 1949," Auswärtiges Amt, ed., *Außenpolitik der Bundesrepublik Deutschland,* 170–175.

23. Ibid., 170-1.

24. "1. Sitzung vom 20.9.1949," *Verhandlungen des Deutschen Bundestages, 1. Wahlperiode, Stenographische Berichte,* 1 (1949), 29.

25. Michael Howard, "Introduction," in *Western Security: The Formative Years,* ed. Olav Riste (Oslo: Norwegian University Press, 1979), 14.

26. See, for example, Golo Mann: *Deutsche Geschichte des 19. und 20.* Jahrhunderts (Frankfurt/M.: Fischer, 1979), 1013.

27. Cited in Karl Kaiser and Klaus Becher, *Deutschland und der Irak-Konflikt: Internationale Sicherheitsverantwortung Deutschlands und Europas nach der deutschen Vereinigung* (Bonn: Europa-Union-Verlag, 1992), 9.

28. Morsey, *Die Bundesrepublik Deutschland,* 21–22.

29. "Abkommen zwischen den Alliierten Hohen Komissaren und dem Deutschen Bundeskanzler auf dem Petersberg am 22. November 1949, Niederschrift vom 23. November 1949," in *Aussenpolitik der Bundesrepublik Deutschland,* 175–177.

30. "Artikel des Europakorrespondenten der amerikanischen Zeitung Cleveland Plain Dealer über das Interview mit dem Bundeskanzler Adenauer, 4 December 1949," in *Die Konstituierung der Bundesrepublik Deutschland und der Deutschen Demokratischen Republik: 7. September bis 31. Dezember 1949,* ed. Hanns Jürgen Küsters, vol. 2 of *Dokumente aur Deutschlandpolitik: Series II* (Munich: Oldenbourg, 1996), 300–302.

31. "Memorandum Bundeskanzler Adenauers über die Sicherung des Bundesgebiets nach innen und außen, August 29, 1950," in ed. Hanns Jürgen Küsters, vol. 3 of *Dokumente zur Deutschlandpolitik: Series II* (München: Oldenbourg, 1996), 933–936.

32. "98. Sitzung vom 8.11.1951," *Verhandlungen des Deutschen Bundestages. I. Wahlperiode, Stenographische Berichte,* 5, B(1951), 3564–71.

33. *Außenpolitik der Bundesrepublik Deutschland,* 194–8.

34. Zelikow and Rice, 51, "Vertrag über die Beziehungen zwischen der Bundesrepublik und den Drei Mächten," 194–98.

35. Zeilkow and Rice, 51.

36. Hacke, Weltmacht, 72.

37. Maull, "Germany and Japan," 99–102.

38. Kaiser and Becher, *Irak-Konflikt,* 11.

39. "According to many constitutional lawyers, the constitution so far forbids Bundeswehr missions out of the NATO area. Should the constitution be changed to allow the Bundeswehr to operate in crisis areas such as the Persian Gulf or should the prohibition of out-of-area missions be maintained?" Elisabeth Noelle-Neumann and Renate Köcher, ed., *Allensbacher Jahrbuch der Demoskopie 1984–92* (München: K.G. Saur 1993), 1085.

40. Question: "The constitution states that the army is a defensive army *(Verteidigungsarmee).* Did you know that or are you hearing it for the first time?" Know: 84 percent, Hear for the first time: 16 percent. Ibid., 1064.

41. Elmar Schmähling: "Die friedfertige Armee, " *Der Spiegel,* 11 February 1991, 24.

42. Nina Philippi: *Bundeswehr-Auslandseinsätze als außen—und sicherheitspolitisches Problem des geeinten Deutschland,* (University of Trier, unpublished M.A. thesis, 1996), 54–62.

43. Bundeszentrale für politische Bildung, ed., *Grundgesetz für die Bundesrepublik Deutschland* (Bonn, Bundeszentrale für Politische Bildung, 1984).

44. Kaiser and Becher, *Irak-Konflikt,* 83–4.

45. Presse—und Informationsamt der Bundesregierung, ed., *Weißbuch 1971/71 zur Sicherheit der Bundesrepublik Deutschland und zur Entwicklung der Bundeswehr* (Bonn: Bundesdruckerei, 1970), 120–122.

46. The foreign ministry was led by Hans-Dietrich Genscher, FDP, from 1974 to 1992.

47. Opinion polls showed the broad popular support of the peace (and neutralist) movement. In 1984, 54 percent of those surveyed supported the peace movement, while 23 percent opposed it (undecided 23 percent). When confronted with the alternative, "We want to live free of fear—therefore disarm" or: "We want to live free of fear—therefore arm," 56 percent vs. 14 percent preferred the first alternative in 1983. In the same year, 56 percent of the population opposed the stationing of Pershing II and cruise missiles on German soil, while only 24 percent supported it. *Allensbacher Jahrbücher für Demoskopie, 1984–92,* 1061–4.

48. The other pillar was Germany's defense doctrine and its integration into NATO.

49. *Rede des Bundeskanzlers vor dem Deutschen Bundestag,* 1061–1064.

50. *Grundgesetz für die Bundesrepublik Deutschland,* 167.

51. Garton Ash, "Germany's Choice," 71.

52. In a speech held in Zurich, Switzerland, by Winston Churchill on September 19, 1946. "Großbritannien, Aussenpolitik, Europapläne," *Keesings Archiv der Gegenwart,* 19 September 1946, 871–872.

53. Konrad Adenauer, "Gründer für und wider den Beitritt zum Europarat," *Europa-Archiv* 5 (150): 3127–3129.

54. *Außenpolitik der Bundesrepublik Deutschland,* 40.

55. Bardo Faßbender: "Zur staatlichen Ordnung Europas nach der deutschen Einigung," *Europa-Archiv* 46, 1 (1991), 396.

56. "Aide-mémoire der Bundesregierung über die deutsch-französischen Beziehungen, November 1949," in *Die Konstituierung der Bundesrepublik und der Deutschen Demokratischen Republik: 7. September bis 31. Dezember 1949,* ed. Hanns Jürgen Küsters, vol. 2 of *Dokumente zur Deutschlandpolitik: Series II* (Munich: Oldenbourg, 1996), 237–238.

57. "Artikel des Journalisten Williams von der amerikanischen Zeitung Baltimore Sun über Äußerungen des Bundeskanzlers Adenauer, 7 November 1949," *Die Konstituierung der Bundesrepublik und der Deutschen Demokratischen Republik,* 238–240.

58. Morsey, *Die Bundesrepublik Deutschland,* 80.

59. "Note der Bundesregierung zur deutschen Friedenspolitik vom 25. März 1966," cited in Hacke, *Weltmacht,* 121–124.

60. "Regierungserklärung des Bundeskanzlers vor dem deutschen Bundestag," *Bulletin der Bundesregierung,* 18 May 1974, 593–9.

61. See C. Randall Henning: "Systemic Conflict and Regional Monetary Integration: The Case of Europe," *International Organization* 52 (Summer 1998), 537–573.

62. Hacke, *Weltmacht,* 324.

63. "Der letzte Europäer," *Der Spiegel,* 8 November 1993, 18.

64. Vorstand der SPD, ed., *Grundsatzprogramm der Sozialdemokratischen Partei Deutschlands* (Bonn: Druckhaus Deutz, 1989), 13.

65. F.D.P.-Bundesgeschäftsstelle, ed., *Liberal denken. Leistung wählen. Das Programm der F.D.P. zur Bundestagswahl 1994* (Bonn, Liberal Verlag, 1994).

66. Thomas U. Berger, *Cultures of Antimilitarism: National Security in Germany and Japan* (Baltimore and London: The Johns Hopkins University Press, 1998), 54–66.

67. "Der Brief des Bundeskanzlers and Ministerpräsident Bulganin," in *Außenpolitik der Bundesrepublik Deutschland,* 224–225.

68. *Grundgesetz für die Bundesrepublik Deutschland,* 167.

69. Arnulf Baring, *Machtwechsel: Die Ära Brandt-Scheel* (Stuttgart: Deutsche Verlagsanstalt, 1982), 203–4.

70. Ibid., 213–15.

71. Raymond L. Grathoff, *Détente and Confrontation: American-Soviet Relations from Nixon to Reagan* (Washington, D.C.: Brookings Institution, 1985).

72. See chapter IV.

73. Hacke, *Weltmacht,* 270.

74. Ibid., 265.

75. Zelikow and Rice, 26.

76. Zelikow and Rice, 30.

77. Zelikow and Rice. Teltschik, *329 Tage.* Karl Kaiser, *Deutschland's Vereinigung: Die internationalen Aspekte* (Bergisch-Gladbach: Bastei-Lübbe, 1991). Werner Weidenfeld, *Außenpolitik für die deutsche Einheit: Die Entscheidungsjahre 1989/90,* Geschichte der deutschen Einheit, vol. 4 (Stuttgart: Deutsche Verlags-Anstalt, 1998).

78. For a summary, see Karl Kaiser: "Die Einbettung des vereinten Deutschlands in Europa," in *Die Internationale Politik: Jahrbücher der Gesellschaft für Auswärtige Politik* 16 (München: Oldenbourg, 1989/90), 101–18.

79. For an account of French and British resistance to German unification see Jacques Attali, *Chronique des années 1988–1991,* vol. 3 of *Verbatim* by Jacques Attali (Paris: Fayard, 1995).

80. "Zehn-Punkte-Plan zur Überwindung der Teilung Deutschlands und Europas, vorgestellte von Helmut Kohl am 28. November 1994," *Europa-Archiv* 44, 2 (1989): D728–30.

81. "Splitter im Körper," *Der Spiegel,* January 1990, 26. See also *Allensbacher Jahrbuch der Demoskopie 1984–92,* 436.

82. Günter Gauss, "Zwei deutsche Staaten: Welcher Zukunft zugewandt?," *Die Zeit,* 20 January 1989, 14–16.

83. *Allensbacher Jahrbücher für Demoskopie, 1984–92,* 438.

84. Ronald D. Asmus: "Deutschland im Übergang—Nationales Selbstvertrauen und internationale Zurückhaltung," *Europa-Archiv* 47, 1 (1992): 205.

85. See survey results below.

86. See, for example, Wolfgang Wagner: "Die Dynamik der deutschen Wiedervereinigung—Suche nach einer Verträglichkeit für Europa," *Europa-Archiv,* 45, 1 (1990), 79.

87. "Das droht die DDR zu vernichten," *Der Spiegel,* 14 August 1989, 18.

88. Zelikow and Rice, 65.

89. "Massenexodus von Bürgern über die ungarisch-österreichisch Grenze: Ungarn öffnet seine Grenzen," *Keesings Archiv der Gegenwart,* 11 September 1989, 33744.

90. Ibid., 33745.

91. Ibid., 337444–46.

92. Ibid., 33743.

93. Zelikow and Rice, 79.

94. "Eröffnung der Generalversammlung; Abrüstungsvorschläge Bushs," *Keesings Archiv der Gegenwart,* 27 September 1989, 33812.

95. Zelikow and Rice, 86–88.

96. Kaiser, *Vereinigung,* 37.

97. "173. Sitzung vom 8.11.1989," *Verhandlungen des Deutschen Bundestages. 11. Wahlperiode, Stenographische Berichte,* 151 (1989), 1310.

98. Ibid., 13010–13017.

99. Kaiser, *Vereinigung,* p. 49.

100. "Gemeimsame Erklärung des Bundeskanzlers Helmut Kohl und des Staatspräsidenten und Generalsekretärs Michail Gorbatschow, unterzeichnet in Bonn, den 13. Juni 1989," in *Deutschlands Vereinigung: Die internationalen Aspekte,* edited by Karl Kaiser (Bergisch-Gladbach: Bastei-Lübbe, 1991), 143–148.

101. Zelikow and Rice, 94.

102. Zelikow and Rice, 159, 203–4, 223, Teltschik, *329 Tage,* 23.

103. Teltschik, *329 Tage,* 49.

104. "177. Sitzung vom 28.11.1989," *Verhandlungen des Deutschen Bundestages. 11. Wahlperiode, Stenographische Berichte,* 151 (1989): 13510–13512.

105. Ibid., 13510–1.

106. Zelikow and Rice, 176.

107. Kaiser, *Vereinigung,* 38.

108. *177. Sitzung vom 28.11.1989,* 13152–4.

109. Ibid., 13510.

110. "Zehn-Punkte-Programm Kohls zur Überwindung der deutschen Teilung," *Keesings Archiv der Gegenwart,* 28 November 1989, 33999.

111. Ibid.

112. Zelikow and Rice, 181.

113. Kaiser, *Vereinigung,* 28, 43.

114. Teltschik, *329 Tage,* 62, 65.

115. Zelikow and Rice, 169, 246.

116. Werner Weidenfeld, *Deutsche Einheit,* 312–14. Teltschik, *329 Tage,* 123.

117. Teltschik, *329 Tage,* 117.

118. Weidenfeld, *Deutsche Einheit,* 313.

119. Zelikow and Rice, 237.

120. Ibid., 246.

121. Teltschik, *329 Tage,* 159–161.

122. Ibid., 182.

123. Zelikow and Rice, 272. Kaiser, *Vereinigung,* 53.

124. Wichard Woyke, "Deutsche Wiedervereinigung," in *Handwörterbuch Internationale Politik,* 7th ed., Wichard Woyke, (Opladen: Leske-Buderich, 1998), 45.

125. Zelikow and Rice, 137.

126. Weidenfeld, *Deutsche Einheit,* 405–408.

127. Zelikow and Rice, 291

128. Zelikow and Rice, 276.

129. Teltschik, *329 Tage,* 26.

130. Ibid., 35.

131. Teltschik, *329 Tage,* 38. Zelikow and Rice, 168–170.

132. Teltschik, *329 Tage,* 26, 47.

133. Ibid., 71–74.

134. Ibid., 37.

135. Weidenfeld, *Deutsche Einheit,* 140.

136. Ibid., 145, 404.

137. Ibid., 405–7.

138. Ibid., 147.

139. Ibid., 139.

140. Zelikow and Rice, 460–2, 467.

141. Teltschik, *329 Tage,* 100–3.

142. Zelikow and Rice, 358, 372. Teltschik, *329 Tage,* 230.

143. Teltschik, *329 Tage,* 232, 234.

144. Zelikow and Rice, 480–4.

III: National Power and Influence

1. According to Waltz, states' power depends on "how they are placed on all of the following items: size of population and territory, resource endowment, economic capability, military strength, political stability and competence." Kenneth Waltz, *Theory of International Politics* (Reading, MA: Addison-Wesley Publishers, 1979), 131.

2. David A. Baldwin, "Power Analysis and World Politics: New Trends Versus Old Tendencies," *World Politics* 31 (1978/79): 161–94.

3. Klaus Knorr: *The Power of Nations* (New York: Basic Books, 1975), 3–9. For an early definition in the same vein see also Max Weber: *Wirtschaft und Gesellschaft—Grundriß der verstehenden Soziologie,* 5th (Tübingen: Mohr, 1972), 28.

4. Keohane and Nye, *Power and Interdependence,* chapters 2 and 3, 12–5.

5. Many have discounted the possibility that Germany's ideology or system may be particular attractive; others have explored it. See, for example, Fritz Stern: "Freedom and its Discontents," *Foreign Affairs* 72, no. 4 (1993): 108–25, David M. Keitly: "Shadows of Germany's Authoritarian Past," *Orbis* 38, no. 2 (1994): 207–23, Elizabeth Pond, "Germany in the New Europe," *Foreign Affairs* 71, no. 2 (1992): 114–30, Robert Gerald Livingston, "United Germany: Bigger and Better," *Foreign Policy* no. 87 (1992), 165–74, Smyser, "Dateline Berlin." Hanns Maull has embraced it fully by calling Germany (and Japan) "prototypes of a promising future." Maull, "Germany and Japan," 93.

6. Theorists argue that the importance of population and territory as a foundation of national power has declined in today's interdependent world. Richard Rosecrance: *The Rise of the Trading State: Commerce and Conquest in the Modern World* (New York: Basic Books, 1986).

7. Institut National de la Statistique et des Études des Finances, ed., *Annuaire Statistique de la France 1993* (Paris: Impr. Nat., 1993), 11.

8. Statistisches Bundesamt, ed., *Statistisches Jahrbuch für das Ausland 1995* (Wiesbaden: Metzler Poeschel, 1995), 34.

9. International comparisons of output are rendered more difficult by a number of methodological problems, the most difficult of which is the question of the appropriate exchange rate. The bar chart might overstate the size of Japan's economy somewhat, since computations were based on the 1993 exchange rate of ¥100/$.

10. Robert J. Arch and Kenneth Waltz, ed., *The Use of Force: Military Power and International Politics* (Lanham: University Press of America, 1993), 63.

11. Recently, a strong trade balance has been associated with national power by "neomercantilist" writers. For a review article see J. David Richardson: "The political economy of strategic trade policy," *International Organization* 44, no. 4 (1990): 107–35.

12. As is often lamented by U.S. "declinists," the U.S. share of total OECD output does decline, from 0.60 in 1960 to 0.43 in 1990—a long-term relative decline of almost 50 percent. The EC share is relatively stable (1960: 0.25; 1990: 0.29). The picture demonstrates that only the Japanese economy has shown solid growth relative to other OECD nations over the decades. It almost quintupled its share from 0.05 in 1960 to 0.23 in 1990.

13. "Standort Deutschland," *Der Stern,* 17 February 1994, 88.

14. "Magnet EG-Binnenmarkt," *Informationsdienst des Instituts der deutschen Wirtschaft* 18, no. 35 (1993).

15. William R. Thompson: "Long waves, technological innovation, and relative decline," *International Organization* 44, no. 1 (1990), pp. 201–33, Michael E. Porter, *The Competitive Advantage of Nations* (New York: The Free Press, 1990), see also Richard Rosecrance: "Long cycle theory and international relations," *International Organization* no. 1 (1987): 283–301.

16. "During the first decades of the century, the Universities of Berlin, Göttingen, Tübingen and München were world-famous. If one asks for the large universities of today, American names are being mentioned: Stanford, Cal-Tech, Harvard, MIT, Princeton." Konrad Seitz: "Die japanisch-amerikanische Herausforderung: Deutschlands Hochtechnologien kämpfen ums Überleben," *Aus Politik und Zeitgeschichte,* 42, no. B10–11 (1992): 13.

17. See also *Focus Extra,* 11/21/1994, 16.

18. "Arbeitskosten: stechender Lorbeer," *Informationsdienst des Instituts der deutschen Wirtschaft,* 19, no. 25 (1994).

19. "Arbeitszeit international," *Informationsdienst des Instituts der deutschen Wirtschaft,* 19, no. 30 (1994).

20. "Lohnanstieg kostet Marktanteile," *Informationsdienst des Instituts der deutschen Wirtschaft,* 19, no. 27 (1994). For a critical view of the inflexibility of the German economy see also Christian Watrin: "Germany's Economic Unification Two Years Later," *Washington, D.C.: American Institute for Contemporary German Studies Seminar Paper* no. 4 (1993), and Amity Shlaes: "Germany's Chained Economy," *Foreign Affairs* 73, no. 5 (1994): 109–25.

21. One of the main issues in the debate over American decline was the question of whether the composition of national output matters. In particular, some writers claimed that it is important for a nation to retain its industrial and manufacturing capacity and that the idea of a "service economy" would lead to low-value-added positions and low-wage jobs. Barry Bluestone and Bennet Harrisson: *The Deindustrialization of America* (New York: Basic Books, 1982). Stephen S. Cohen and John Zysman: *Manufacturing Matters: The Myth of the Post-Industrial Economy* (New York: Basic Books, 1987), 3–12. The official policy line was diametrically opposite: the composition of business would not matter and it was not an issue for national policy. Don Lavoie: *National Economic Planning: What is Left?* (Cambridge, MA.: Ballinger Publishers, 1985). President of the United States, ed., *Economic Report of the President 1984* (Washington, D.C.: Government Printing Office, 1984). See especially chapter 3, "Industrial Policy." According to this report, national power would not be affected by a shift in American economic activity from manufacturing to services.

22. Joseph Schumpeter: *The Theory of Economic Development: An Inquiry into Profits, Capital, Credit, Interest and the Business Cycle* (New York: Oxford University Press, 1961). For more recent analyses in the same vein, see James R. Kurth: "The Political Consequences of the Product Cycle," *International Organization* 33, no. 1 (1979), 1–34.

23. Porter, *Competitive Advantage,* 359–361.

24. For a discussion of the chemical industry, see Thomas L. Ilgen: "Better Living through Chemistry: The Chemical Industry in the World Economy," *International Organization* 37, no. 4 (1983): 647–80.

25. Porter, *Competitive Advantage,* 295. In addition, the United States has a strong position in the arms industry, a "timeless" business. For an analysis of the dominant U.S. position in this industry, see Ethan B. Kapstein: "America's Arms-Trade Monopoly," *Foreign Affairs* 73, no. 3 (1994), 13–20.

26. Porter, *Competitive Advantage,* 393.

27. For Japanese targeting of the computer industry, see Marie Anchordoguy: "Mastering the market: Japanese government targeting of the computer industry," *International Organization* 42, no. 3 (1988): 509–43.

28. Kaiser/Becher, *Irak-Konflikt,* 14–21.

29. In the four years of the Marshall plan, $13 bn was spent. Even in current terms, this is less than a year's support to the former East Germany. See Robert A. Packenham: *Liberal America and the Third World* (Princeton: Princeton University Press, 1973), 34.

30. Total assistance levels are hard to compile. For a comprehensive survey see Jörg M. Winterberg: *Westliche Unterstützung der Transformationsprozesse in Osteuropa* (St. Augustin: Konrad-Adenauer-Stiftung, 1994).

31. Kielinger and Otte, "Pressured Power," 52–3.

32. The Federal Republic committed DM 15 billion (roughly $10 billion) in exchange for the withdrawal of Soviet troops. "Die deutsch-russischen Beziehungen," *Internal Report by the Bundespresseamt,* May 1994 (Bonn: Bundespresseamt, 1994), 7.

33. Presse- und Informationsamt der Bundesxregierung, ed., *Europa 2000* (Bonn: Presse- und Informationsamt, 1993), 94.

34. "Ende der Spedierlaune," *Focus,* 22 July 1996, 20–3.

35. In many situations, small states with highly developed credit and tax systems may be as powerful as large nations with weak credit and tax systems over the short term, because they can mobilize a proportionately larger share of national resources for public purposes. Periods of war, for example, have often coincided with higher levels of national debt, which has helped to mobilize a country's resources for the war effort. Such a mobilization was easier in the past, when periods of public effort (mostly wars) were short. Today, smaller states may have to sustain disproportionate financial efforts much longer. In this situation, an excessive share of government economic activity might hinder entrepreneurial activity and weaken a nation in the long run. Karen A. Rasler and William R. Thompson: "Global Wars, Public Debts, and the Long Cycle," *World Politics* 35, no. 4 (1983): 489–517.

36. See M. Otte: *The United States, Japan, West Germany and Europe in the International Economy 1977–1987* (Idstein: Schulz-Kirchner Verlag, 1988). For a

detailed and early discussion of U.S. international financial and macroeconomic power see C. Fred Bergsten: *The Dilemmas of the Dollar: The Economics and Politics of United States International Monetary Policy* (New York: Council on Foreign Relations, 1975), chapters 4 and 5, C. Fred Bergsten, Etienne Davignon, and Isamu Miyazaki: *Conditions for Partnership in International Economic Management* (New York: Trilateral Commission, 1986).

37. "Heißhunger auf deutsche Anleihen," *Informationsdienst des Instituts der deutschen Wirtschaft,* 19, no. 13 (1994).

38. Henning Klodt: "Staatsverschuldung hat die Belastung der Privatwirtschaft nur aufgeschoben," *Handelsblatt,* 21 April 1992.

39. "Standort Deutschland," 96.

40. "Zwang zum Sparen," *Informationsdienst des Instituts der deutschen Wirtschaft,* 18, no. 25 (1993).

41. "West-Ost-Transfers: Anpassungs-Szenarien," *Informationsdienst des Instituts der deutschen Wirtschaft,* 19, no. 2 (1994).

42. "Steuerschätzung: Der Bund verliert im Steuerpoker," *Informationsdienst des Instituts der deutschen Wirtschaft,* 19, no. 2 (1994).

43. Knorr, *Power of Nations,* 3–9. Keohane and Nye, *Power and Interdependence,* 12–5.

44. For the prospects of European nuclear cooperation, see Karl-Heinz Kamp, *Europäische Nuklearkooperation: Chance oder Schimäre?* (Sankt Augustin: Konrad-Adenauer-Stiftung, 1995).

45. "Die Kriminalität in der Bundesrepublik Deutschland," *Bulletin des Presse- und Informationsamtes der Bundesregierung,* 25 May 1999, 289. "Flüchtlinge: jetzt geht es erst los," *Der Spiegel* 19/1999, 10 May 1999, 180–182.

46. See, for example Karl-Heinz Kamp: "Das nukleare Erbe der Sowjetunion—eine Aufgabe westlicher Sicherheitspolitik," *Europa-Archiv* 48,1 (1993), 623–32. Uwe Engelbrecht: "Moskau und die nuklearen Schlupflöcher," *General-Anzeiger,* 16 August 1994, Manfred Rowold, "Moskau wirft dem Westen Provokation vor," *Die Welt,* 18 August 1994, Marc Pitzke, "Showtime in Moskau," *Die Woche,* 25 August 1994.

47. Hanns W. Maull, "Japan und Deutschland: Die neuen Großmächte?," *Europa-Archiv* 49,1 (1994): 602–10.

48. "Isolation" must be seen in relative terms: even Japan's trade with the United States accounts for only 3.3 percent of Japan's GDP.

49. The low share of 10 percent for the U.S. in 1960 reflected the very dominant position of the U.S. economy. Both the U.S. and Germany show a long-term increase in openness, whereas Japan, after an irregularity caused by the second oil crisis, has become an even more closed economy than it was in 1960.

50. For a discussion of strategic trade policy or trade-power-interrelationships see J. David Richardson, *Political Economy,* 107–135, Benjamin J. Cohen: "The Political Economy of International Trade," *International Organization*

44, no. 2 (1990): 261–81, Paul R. Krugman, ed., *Strategic Trade Policy and the New International Economics* (Cambridge, MA.: MIT Press, 1986).

51. Small states (e.g., Latin American states) might be in a state of dependence, although size is not the only factor responsible for dependence. The counterexample is provided by the East Asian NICs (Newly Industrialized Countries). Anthony Brewer: *Marxist Theories of Imperialism* (London: Routledge & Kegan Paul, 1980), 158–61. Yun-han Chu: "State structure and economic adjustment of the East Asian newly industrializing countries," *International Organization* 43, no. 4 (1989): 647–72. Stephan Haggard concludes that "dependence appears to be a result of particular national strategies rather than a characteristic of the international system per se." Stephan Haggard: "The Newly Industrializing Countries in the International System," *World Politics* 38, no. 2 (1985/86): 343–71. Other trading advantages may derive from economies of scale and scope: if a nation can establish a dominant international position in specific sectors of the economy, it may be difficult for other nations to catch up. Skills, invested capital, and large production series will enable the leader to price its products below prices that firms in other nations would have to demand to recoup their investment. This argument dates back to Friedrich List, who applied it to the relationship of the English-German textile trade in the early nineteenth century, refuting the Ricardian argument. Friedrich List, *The National System of Political Economy* (Philadelphia: J.B. Lippincott, 1856). It has recently found renewed interest among theorists of strategic trade. See the literature on strategic trade cited in a later section.

52. *Europa 2000*, 45.

53. Alexander E. Wendt, "Anarchy is What States Make of It: The Social Construction of Power Politics," *International Organization* 46 (1992): 422–5.

54. Stephen M. Walt: *The Origins of Alliances* (Ithaca: Cornell University Press, 1987).

55. Wendt, "Anarchy," 422–5.

56. An example of U.S. suspicions toward independent German policies was Brandt's Ostpolitik. Though Nixon and Kissinger engineered a rapprochement with the Soviet Union, they were skeptical of Germany's own policies of reconciliation, which culminated in chancellor Brandt's Ostpolitik (Eastern policies). Though Ostpolitik pursued the same objectives as the Nixon-Kissinger rapprochement, the U.S. administration wanted to reserve these initiatives for itself. In the years before Brandt, the so-called "Hallstein doctrine" made the nonrecognition of the GDR an official policy for West Germany, thus greatly diminishing its means of communication with the East. Due to Brandt's leadership, Germany eventually recognized the GDR and the other territorial changes that had occurred after World War II. It incurred contractual obligations "not to violate existing borders by force." (The old Germany continued to exist as a legal

entity, though, and only ceased to exist with the final peace treaty after unification.) Brandt's initiatives relieved tensions in Central Europe and greatly improved Germany's relations with its Eastern neighbors. Nixon and Kissinger would have preferred a Germany for which the United States could speak. For detailed accounts of Brandt's Ostpolitik, see Arnulf Baring: *Machtwechsel*, William E. Griffith: *The Ostpolitik of the Federal Republic of Germany* (Cambridge, MA: MIT Press, 1978), Lawrence J. Whetten: *Germany's Ostpolitik: Relations between the Federal Republic and the Warsaw Pact Countries* (London: Oxford University Press, 1971). For U.S. policies see Raymond L. Garthoff: *Détente and* Confrontation, 108–11, and the Kissinger books cited therein.

57. See, for example, the controversies about economic coordination in the second half of the 1970s. Otte, *International Economy*, pp. 22–5. Guido Garavoglia: "From Rambouillet to Williamsburg: a Historical Assessment," in *Economic Summits and Western Decision-Making*, ed. Cesare Merlini, (London & Sydney: Croom Helm, 1985), 3.

58. "Rede des amerikanischen Präsidenten Bush in Mainz, 31. Mai 1989," *Europa Archiv* 44, 2 (1989): D356–D361.

59. Elizabeth Pond: "Die Entstehung der 'Zwei-plus-Vier,'" *Europa-Archiv* 47, 1 (1992): 619–30. Robert Blackwill: "German Unification and American Diplomacy," *New York: American Council of Germany, Occasional Paper* no. 3 (1994).

60. Initially, such a development seemed unlikely. While relations with Germany were good, a globalist "Clinton doctrine" bent on "enlarging democracy" seemed to emerge, in which the division of political responsibility among regional centers—and therefore a major independent role for Germany—played only a subordinate role. According to Charles William Maynes, in an era of rapidly spreading democracy and shrinking U.S. resources the administration had embarked on a global political strategy and a more regional economic strategy (NAFTA, Pacific basin initiative), while it should have done the opposite. In addition, it seemed that the Clinton administration was first and foremost looking toward Asia. Clinton globalism soon encountered many difficulties. Relations with Asia, for example, deteriorated. The administration's relations with Europe, however, developed positively. Charles William Maynes: "A workable Clinton doctrine," *Foreign Policy* no. 93 (1993/94): 3–22. Harry Harding: "Asia Policy on the Brink," *Foreign Policy* no. 96 (1994): 57–75.

61. For recommendations in the same vein, see also Daniel S. Hamilton: *Beyond Bonn—America and the Berlin Republic* (Washington: Carnegie Endowment for International Peace, 1994).

62. Public Papers of the President, *Interview with Foreign Journalists, July 1, 1994*, (Washington, D.C.: GPO, 1994), 1406.

63. Public Papers of the President, *The President's New Conference with Chancellor Helmut Kohl in Bonn Germany, July 11, 1994,* (Washington, D.C.: GPO, 1994), 1463.

64. ibid., p. 1466. To this author's knowledge, Thomas Kielinger and this author have first used the term "special relationship" and the idea of an active division of labor for U.S. - German relations. Kielinger and Otte, "Pressured Power," 58–61.

65. Ingo Kolboom: "Dialog mit Bauchgrimmen? Die Zukunft der deutsch-französischen Beziehungen," *Europa-Archiv* 49, 1 (1994): 257–264. See also Gordon, "Normalization," 7–10, Stanley Hoffmann, "La France dans le nouvel ordre europeén," *Politique Étrangére* 55 (1990): 504, Patrick McCarthy: *France-Germany, 1983–93: The Struggle to Cooperate* (New York: St. Martin's Press, 1993), 28.

66. Kolboom, *Dialog,* 259.

67. Napoleon I had created the Rhine union by mandating treaties among the Western German states to weaken Prussia.

68. Kolboom, "Dialog," 259. For detailed case studies on French-German cooperation in the cases of the Gulf War, the war in former Yugoslavia, assistance to Eastern Europe, and the Eurocorps, see Philip H. Gordon, *Die deutsch-französische Partnerschaft und die Atlantische Allianz,* Arbeitspapiere zur internationalen Politik der Deutschen Gesellschaft für Auswärtige Politik, vol. 28 (Bonn: Europa-Union Verlag, 1994).

69. Ibid., 69.

70. As happened during the conclusion of the Uruguay round of GATT. "Die GATT Runde muß rasch beendet werden," *Handelsblatt,* 2 December 1993. "Frankreich beansprucht eine Sonderrolle," *Die Welt,* 1 December 1993. "Kohl und Mitterrand bleiben uneins über GATT," *Frankfurter Allgemeine Zeitung,* 2 December 1993.

71. See pp. 112 ff.

72. This is in contrast to Britain, where popular opinion was more divided.

73. Luc Rosenzweig: "Un mariage de raison plutot qu'une passion folle," *Le Monde,* 23 January 1993.

74. "Eine Rose am Wischer," *Der Spiegel,* 18 July 1994, 30–2.

75. Dirk Veheyen and Christian Soe, ed., *The Germans and their Neighbors* (Boulder: Westview Press, 1993), 71, 100, 102, 352. See also "Furcht vor Deutschland," a series of articles on foreign perceptions on Germany in Neue Osnabrücker Zeitung, 31 December 1993, and a similar series in *Handelsblatt* starting in May 1993.

76. See Pond, "Germany in the New Europe," *Foreign Affairs* 71, 2 (1992): 115.

77. For Germany, widening is important to stabilize the East and should go hand in hand with deepening, while Britain might foster hopes that widening would mean the extension of the free trade area or even a dilution of the central EU powers.

78. For a thorough treatment of the topic see Celeste A. Wallander: *Mortal Friends, Best Enemies: German-Russian Cooperation after the Cold War* (Ithaca and London: Cornell University Press, 1999).

79. Smyser, "Dateline Berlin," 146–50.

80. IMF, ed., *Direction of Trade Statistics Yearbook 1995* (Washington, D.C.: International Monetary Fund, 1995), 121.

81. In a workshop on the status of the German-Russian relationship, Nikolai Pavlow stated that "Russia's relations with Germany are far more important than its relations with any other nation, including the U.S." Nikolai Pavlow: "Perspektiven der deutsch-russischen Zusammenarbeit," in *Stand und Perspektiven des Deutsch-Russischen Verhältnisses*, ed. Deutsch-Russisches Forum e.V. (Bonn: Deutsch-Russisches Forum e.V., 1993), 28–30.

82. "Bonn unterstützt den russischen Reformkurs," *Frankfurter Allgemeine Zeitung*, 7 October 1992.

83. Dietmar Ostermann: "Ein neuer Freund für den einsamen Boris Jelzin," *Frankfurter Rundschau*, 17 December 1992. Eduard Neumeier: "Mit den Deutschen geht es am besten," *Rheinischer Merkur*, 18 December 1992.

84. "Jelzin schreibt ein Buch und übergeht Mitterrand nahezu," *General-Anzeiger*, 3 May 1994.

85. Andreaj Gurko, "Das Deutschenbild der Russen," in *Deutschlandbilder in Polen und Rußland, in der Tschechoslowakei und in Ungarn*, Hanns Süssmuth, ed. (Baden-Baden: Nomos Verlagsgesellschaft, 1993), 199. In a survey conducted by RAND and the Fried-rich-Naumann-Foundation in Germany, Russia was named more often as vital to German interests than the United States (66 percent vs. 64 percent) and France (65 percent). In 1992, 60 percent named Russia, 62 percent the United States and 67 percent France. At the same time, 91 percent of the Germans still perceive the United States as Germany's most important ally. "Blick gen Osten," *Der Focus*, 6 December 1993, 11.

86. See F. Stephen Larrabee: "Moscow and the German Question," in *The Germans and their Neighbors*, ed. Dirk Verheyen and Christian Soe (Boulder, CO: Westview Press, 1993), 214–6.

87. "Streben Bonns nach Einbeziehung Russlands," *Neue Züricher Zeitung*, 12 May 1994. "Jelzin: Rußland voll in Europa integrieren," *Kölner Stadt-Anzeiger*, 12 May 1994.

88. "Boris, ich bewundere Dich," *Frankfurter Rundschau*, 22 November 1993.

89. Claus J. Duisberg: "Der Abzug der russischen Truppen aus Deutschland: eine politische und militärische Erfolgsbilanz," *Europa-Archiv* 49, 1 (1994): 461–469.

90. "Rede des russischen Präsidenten Jelzin anläßlich der Verabschiedung der russischen Streitkräfte aus Deutschland in Berlin am 31. August 1994," *Europa-Archiv* 49, 2 (1994): D559.

91. "Zwischen Bundeskanzleramt und Kreml wird ein 'rotes Telefon' geschaltet," *Kölner-Stadt-Anzeiger*, 11 May 1994.

92. "Gemeinsamer Umweltschutz," *Der Tagesspiegel*, 5 September 1994. "Deutsch-Russische Zusammenarbeit geplant," *Frankfurter Allgemeine Zeitung*, 18 August 1994. "Milch und Honig," *Der Spiegel*, 1 August 1994.

93. "Besuch russischer Generale in Deutschland," *Neue Züricher Zeitung*, 16 November 1993.

94. This position was taken, for example, by the former German foreign minister Hans-Dietrich Genscher: "Rußland verdient Vertrauen," *Frankfurter Allgemeine Zeitung*, 2 May 1994, and CDU member of parliament Karl-Heinz Hornhues: "Rußland braucht eine Sonderrolle," *Frankfurter Allgemeine Zeitung*, 11 May 1994.

95. See the analysis on pp. 108 ff.

96. "Rede des Verteidigungsministers Volker Rühe in Oxford," *Europa-Archiv* 49, 2 (1994): D4443-D448.

97. Gordon, *Deutsch-französische Partnerschaft*, 36–39.

98. "Baltische Staaten in die EU? Außenminister Kinkel will Verhandlungen vorantreiben," *Frankfurter Rundschau*, 10 March 1994. "Deutschland, die Balten und der Schirinowskij-Faktor," *Frankfurter Allgemeine Zeitung*, 9 March 1994.

99. One of the authors (Max Otte), whose father's family was among the refugees, visited his father's birthplace for the first time in 1992. It may be a hint of the new situation that he was received with utmost warmth and his hosts were almost insulted when he did not want to impose and stay overnight.

100. Hans Süssmuth: "Deutschlandbilder im Ausland," in *Deutschlandbilder in Polen und Rußland, in der Tschechoslowakei und Ungarn*, ed. Hans Süssmuth (Baden-Baden: Nomos, 1993), 20.

101. Bundespresseamt, ed., *Versöhnung, Vertrauen, gute Nachbarschaft: Die deutsch-polnischen Beziehungen*, (Bonn: Bundesdruckerei, 1994).

102. "Deutsch-Polnisches Umweltabkommen," *Frankfurter Allgemeine Zeitung*, 8 April 1994.

103. "Das deutsch-polnische Jugendwerk," in Botschaft der Republik Polen in der Bundesrepublik Deutschland [database online] (Köln: Botschaft der Republik Polen, 1997 [cited 10 August 1999]) available from *http://www.pol-bot.com/nauka_m2htm*.

104. "An der Weichsel willkommen," *Rheinischer Merkur*, 5 August 1994.

105. "Deutschlands Touristen machen Polens Grenzorte reich," *Die Welt*, 3 June 1994.

106. Russia sent a low-ranking representative, although Yeltsin had been invited.

107. By the summer of 1991, almost 50 percent on both sides had a positive picture of the other side. Hans-Adolf Jacobsen: "Polen und Deutsche" in *Deutschlandbilder in Polen und Rußland, in der Tschechoslowakei und Ungarn*, 162.

108. "Facetten der deutsch-polnischen Partnerschaft," *Neue Züricher Zeitung*, 24 July 1994.

109. In this treaty Hitler was allowed the annexation of the German-populated areas of Czechoslovakia (the Sudetenland), with over 3 million German inhabitants. After World War II, the Sudeten Germans were expelled under the harshest conditions, with about 225,000 deaths as a result of the forced transfer. They automatically lost Czech citizenship and all property. Czechoslovakia had always insisted that the Munich Treaty was invalid ex tunc (from the beginning), because was signed under duress, whereas Germany had held the position that it was invalid ex nunc (from now on). The Czechoslovak position would have legitimized the claim for far-reaching reparations, the German position may have given it some leverage in claiming compensation for expelled Germans. "Deutsch-Tschechoslowakischer-Vertrag: Die Narben der Geschichte," *Die Zeit,* 2 August 1994.

110. Between December 1989 and January 1990, President Havel repeatedly stated that "Germany can be as large as she wants to, as long as she stays democratic." He also wrote in a letter to German president Richard von Weizsäcker that the expulsion of three million Czechoslovak citizens of German ethnicity "has always struck me as a deeply immoral act, inflicting heavy damage not only on the Germans, but perhaps even more on the Czechs, both in the moral and material sense." Milan Hauner, "The Czechs and the Germans: A One-Thousand-Year-Relationship," in *The Germans and their Neighbors,* 252–4.

111. The following episode is reported about Hungary, which started the events leading to the fall of the Berlin Wall by letting East German refugees on its territory have free passage to Austria:

> At a stormy session, with Prime Minister Nemeth, Foreign Minister Gyula Horn, and Education Minister Ferenc Glatz leading the pack, the government decided to let the East Germans go to Austria and then on to West Germany. Nemeth and Horn ordered a plane to stand by and in near total secrecy they subsequently flew to Germany to see Chancellor Helmut Kohl. There, prime minister Nemeth told the Chancellor that he intended to let the East Germans have free passage to Austria. Alluding to Hungary's obligations to the Warsaw Pact, the Chancellor inquired whether Nemeth realized what the Hungarian government was doing. Nemeth barely waited for the translation before giving his affirmative reply. Now it was only a matter of agreeing on the price. "What do you want us to do?" Kohl inquired. "Nothing," said Nemeth, "It's our human duty." Kohl's eyes filled with tears.

> Ivan Volgyes: "Hungary and Germany: Two Actors in Search of a New Play," in *The Germans and their Neighbors,* 289.

112. "Bonn will Anwalt der Balten sein," *Süddeutsche Zeitung,* 10 July 1993.

113. "Bulgarien sucht Anschluß an die EG," *General-Anzeiger,* 16 January 1992.

114. "Rumänien wünscht deutsche Hilfe," *Frankfurter Allgemeine Zeitung,* 4 February 1992.

115. "Werben der Ukraine um die Gunst Bonns," *Neue Züricher Zeitung,* 6 February 1992.

116. "Beim Besuch des kasachischen Präsidenten: Bonn sagt keine Finanzhilfe zu," *Süddeutsche Zeitung,* 23 September 1992.

117. "Schewardnadse ist des Lobes voll über die deutsche Hilfe," *General-Anzeiger,* 25 June 1993.

118. "Auf dem Programm: Atomwaffen und Soldaten-Unterkünfte. Bundesvertei-digungsminister Rühe besucht die Ukraine und Kasachstan—Kiew hofft auf Bonn," *General-Anzeiger,* 16 August 1993. "Bonn schickt keine Blauhelme nach Abchasien," *Süddeutsche Zeitung,* 17 August 1993.

119. "Klagen über fehlendes Verständnis: der Außenminister Aserbaidschans zu Besuch in Bonn," *Frankfurter Allgemeine Zeitung,* 2 March 1994. "Kinkel trifft Krautscha: die Außenminister sprechen über finanzielle Hilfen für Weißrußland," *Frankfurter Allgemeine Zeitung,* 4 March 1994.

120. See the discussion by Aaron L. Friedberg, "The Future of American Power," *Political Science Quarterly* 109 (1994): 14.

121. Maull, "Germany and Japan," 95. Pond, "New Europe," 115.

122. "Völlig von der Rolle," *Der Spiegel,* 11 September 1995, 22–5.

123. Pond, "New Europe," 115.

124. Eduard Neumeier: "Mit den Deutschen geht es am besten," *Rheinischer Merkur,* 18 December 1992. Boris Kaimakow: "Das Bild des 'häßlichen Deutschen' hat sich im heutigen Rußland erschöpft," *Handelsblatt,* 27 April 1993.

125. Pond, "New Europe," 126.

126. Deutsche Bundestag. Drucksache 12/6162, "Unterstützung der Reformprozesse in den Staaten Mittel-, Südost- und Osteuropas (einschließlich der baltischen Staaten) sowie in den neuen unabhän-gigen Staaten auf dem Territorium der ehemaligen Sowjetunion," (Bonn: Bundesdruckerei, 11/12/1993), 65 ff.

127. "Wettbewerb der Rechtsordnungen in Osteuropa," *Frankfurter Allgemeine Zeitung,* 17 September 1993.

128. Gordon, *Deutsch-französische Partnerschaft,* 34.

129. "In den rauhen eurasischen Osten? Wie Deutschland dem Wunsch nach Entsendung von Lehrkräften nachkommt," *Frankfurter Allgemeine Zeitung,* 22 November 1993.

130. Arthur R. Rachwald, "Poland and Germany: From Foes to Friends?" in *The Germans and their Neighbors,* 231–249.

131. It should be noted that there is also a significant Polish population in Germany, estimated at over one million.

132. "Meinungsumschwung an der Wolga," *Die Welt,* 24 April 1992. "Irritationen beseitigt," Handelsblatt, 24 April 1992. "Nicht nur auf die Wolgarepublik starren," *Neue Zeit,* 7 July 1993.

133. "Zuspitzung der Asyldebatte; gewaltsame Angriffe und Mordanschläge gegen Ausländer," *Archiv der Gegenwart,* 23 November 1992, 37354–7.

134. Keitly, "Shadows," 207.

135. "Die Berliner Rede von Bundespräsident von Weizsäcker gegen Ausländerhaß und Fremdenfeindlichkeit," *Europa-Archiv* 47, 1 (1992): D631–3.

136. Gert Krell: "Migration und Asyl: die Weltbevölkerung zwischen Integration und Polarisierung," Hessische Stiftung Friedens- und Konfliktforschung, 8, no. 4 (1992): 14.

137. Ibid., 20–1.

IV: The Loss of Innocence

1. *Weißbuch 1971/1972 zur Sicherheit der Bundesrepublik Deutschland und zur Entwicklung der Bundeswehr* (Bonn: Presse- und Informationsamt der Bundesregierung, 1970), 24.

2. See pp. 98 ff.

3. Kaiser and Becher, *Irak-Konflikt,* 20–2.

4. Wilfried von Bredow/Thomas Jäger: "Konflikte und globale Kooperation am Ende des 20. Jahrhunderts," *Aus Politik und Zeitgeschichte,* 44, no. D26–7 (1994): 3–11. Lawrence Martin: "Nationale Sicherheit in einer neuen Weltordnung," *Europa-Archiv* 47, 1 (1992): 59–70.

5. Klaus-Dieter Wolf: "Militarisierung und Zivilisierung der internationalen Beziehungen—Situationsanalyse und Forschungsperspektiven aus politikwissenschaft-licher Sicht," in *Die Zukunft des Militärs in den Industriegesellschaften,* ed. Wilfried Karl and Thomas Nielebock, Jahrbuch für Friedens- und Konfliktforschung, vol. 18 (Baden-Baden: Nomos, 1991): 57–63.

6. "Vertrag über die abschließende Regelung in bezug auf Deutschland," ('Two-plus-four treaty'), *Bundesgesetzblatt II,* 12 September 1990, p. 1318, article 5, 1318.

7. Ibid.

8. Ibid., article 3.

9. Ibid., article 2.

10. Michael H. Haltzel: "Die Vereinigten Staaten, Europa und die Golf-Krise," *Europa-Archiv* 45, 1 (1990): 534–535.

11. "In the WEU, my colleague Stoltenberg and I have explained our position regarding the deployment of German troops. We have explained that our constitution does not allow missions by the Bundeswehr out of the treaty area. We have informed our partners, that the government together with

the opposition has begun to evaluate an amendment to the constitution. The goal is the participation of the Bundeswehr in missions that have been decided by the UN security council in accordance with the UN charter." Bericht der Bundesregierung über die Tagung der WEU und die Sitzung der EPZ zur Lage am Golf, abgegeben vom Bundesminister des Auswärtigen Hans-Dietrich Genscher, vor dem Deutschen Bundestag am 23. August 1990, in *Europa-Archiv* 46, 2 (1991): D49–52.

12. "Sitzung vom 14. January 1992," *Verhandlungen des Deutschen Bundestages. 12. Wahlperiode, Stenographischer Berichte* 155 (199): 21–4.

13. Kaiser and Becher, *Irak-Konflik,* 16.

14. William Drodziak: "Bonn Rejects to Aid U.S. Forces in the Gulf," *International Herald Tribune,* 6 September 1990.

15. "Die Deutschen an die Front," *Der Spiegel,* 4 February 1991, 19.

16. 6/91, p. 18.

17. Wolfgang Fechner: "Deutscher Beitrag zur Befreiung Kuweits: Über 17 Milliarden DM," *Europäische Sicherheit,* 4o, no. 4 (1991), 212–5. See also Kaiser and Becher, *Irak-Konflikt,* 114–7, Michael J. Inacker, *Unter Ausschluß der Öffentlichkeit? Die Deutschen in der Golfallianz* (Bonn: Bouvier, 1991).

18. Peter Riddell: "Bush presses Germany to step up international role," *Financial Times,* 19 November 1990.

19. "Only a shared sense of commitments and values will keep America in Europe beyond the Cold War. It is this sense that is endangered by the loophole approach to NATO that Germany is pursuing in a moment of crisis." Jim Hoagland: "German wobbling puts the Trans-Atlantic Partnership at Risk," *International Herald Tribune,* 31 January 1991.

20. Our world organization must be able to deal with the challenges of our times. Crisis prevention, population policies and environmental protection must be improved. . . . Germany is ready to contribute. The united Germany will assume all rights and responsibilities of the UN charter, including measures of collective security in which our forces participate. We want to change our constitution for this goal. "Rede des Außenministers Hans-Dietrich Genscher vor der 47. Vollversammlung der Vereinten Nationen am 25. September 1991," *Europa Archiv* 47, 2 (1992): D345–51.

21. Philippi, Bundeswehr, 48 (III.4), 35–60, contains an extensive discussion of the constitutional situation.

22. Inacker, *Golfallianz,* 23–31.

23. Volker Rühe: "Sinn und Auftrag der Bundeswehr im vereinten Deutschland," *Bulletin des Presse- und Informationsamtes der Bundesregierung,* 7 April 1992, 346–8.

24. "Gewachsene Instinkte," *Der Spiegel,* 18 May 1992, 27–30. "Möglichst unauffällig," *Der Spiegel,* 1 June 1992, 125–8.

25. "Nah dran am echten Krieg," *Der Spiegel,* 20 July 1992, 22–9.

26. Presseerklärung des deutschen Verteidigungsministers Volker Rühe nach der Entsendung von Einheiten zur Seeaufklärung zur Unterstützung

der Überwachung des Embargos gegen Serbien," *Europa-Archiv* 47, 2 (1992): D581.

27. "Wir wollen nicht beiseite stehen," *Der Spiegel,* 7 December 1992, 114–5.

28. "Drohung aus Washington," *Der Spiegel,* 18 January 1993, 18–20.

29. "Kohl und Kinkel vor Gericht," *Der Spiegel,* 5 April 1993, 21.

30. "Mut zum Absurden," *Der Spiegel,* 29 March 1993, 18–20.

31. "Entscheidung des Bundesgerichtshofes vom 8. April 1993 über die Teilnahme deutscher Soldaten an AWACS-Missionen," *Blätter für deutsche und internationale Politik* 48, 1 (1993): 637–40.

32. Wolfgang Wagner: "Abenteuer in Somalia," *Europa-Archiv* 49, 1 (1994): 151–60. "Feldjäger in der Wüste," *Der Spiegel,* 14 December 1992, 24–5. "Eine regelrechte Psychose," *Der Spiegel,* 21 December 1992, 18–23.

33. "Schritt für Schritt in den Krieg," *Der Spiegel,* 26 April 1993, 18.

34. "Zur Hilfe verpflichtet," *Der Spiegel,* 26 April 1993, 21.

35. "Helden in der Wüste," *Der Spiegel,* 28 June 1993, 26.

36. "Nun siegt mal schön," *Der Spiegel,* 18 July 1994, 23–8.

37. Volker Rühe, "Kein Triumphgeheul," interview, *Focus,* 18 July 1994, 22–3.

38. "Nun siegt mal schön," 23–8.

39. Ibid.

40. Ibid., 25.

41. Michael Bothe, "Rätsel aus Karlsruhe," *Der Spiegel,* 25 July 1994, 28–9.

42. "Mit Stolz," *Der Spiegel,* 15 July 1991, 26–8.

43. "Größenwahn der Generäle," *Der Spiegel,* 5 April 1992, p. 19–21.

44. "Mit Stolz," 26.

45. "Militärpolitische und militärstrategische Grundlagen und konzeptionelle Grundrichtung der Neugestaltung der Bundeswehr," *Blätter für deutsche und internationale Politik,* 37 (1992): 506–10.

46. Ibid., 507–8.

47. "Überholte Denkweise," *Der Spiegel,* 24 February 1992, 107–9.

48. Ibid., 107.

49. "Gewachsene Instinkte," 27–30.

50. "Nahe dran am echten Krieg," 22–31.

51. "Verteidigungspolitische Richtlinien für den Geschäftsbereich des Bundesministers der Verteidigung vom 26. November 1992," *Blätter für deutsche und internationale Politik* 38 (1993): 1137–51.

52. "Richtlinien," 1138.

53. "Richtlinien," 1150.

54. "Petersberger Deklaration vom 19.06.1992," in *Blätter für deutsche und internationale Politik* 37 (1992): 1020–3.

55. Bundesministerium der Verteidigung, ed., *Weißbuch 1994 zur Sicherheit der Bundesrepublik Deutschland und zur Lage und Zukunft der Bundeswehr* (Bonn: Bundesdruckerei, 1994).

56. Ibid., 42, paragraph 305.

57. Ibid., 42, paragraph 308.

58. In interviews with the author, officials within the foreign office stated that Japan's initiative caused Germany to address the topic so as not to be left behind.

59. "Rede des Bundesministers des Auswärtigen, Dr. Kinkel, am 23. September 1992 in New York," in *Aussenpolitik der Bundesrepublik Deutschland—Dokumente von 1949–1994,* ed. Auswärtiges Amt (Bonn: Auswärtiges Amt, 1995), 877.

60. "Dort spielt die Musik, Interview mit Klaus Kinkel," *Der Spiegel,* 27 September 1993, 23–4. "Mit Kinkel in der ersten Reihe," *Die Zeit,* 1 October 1993.

61. "Dokumente zur Reform des Sicherheitsrats der Vereinten Nationen," *Europa-Archiv* 48, 2 (1993): D379–96.

62. Winrich Kühne, "Erweiterung und Reform des UN-Sicherheitsrats: keine weltpolitische Nebensache," *Europa-Archiv* 49, 1 (1994), 685–92.

63. Stefan Kornelius: "Heftiger Streit um Einsatzliste—Kohl und Rühe widersetzen sich Kinkels Forderung, für eine UNO-Truppe Soldaten zu benennen," *Süddeutsche Zeitung,* 16 January 1995.

64. Karl Kaiser, "Die ständige Mitgliedschaft im Sicherheitsrat: ein berechtigtes Ziel deutscher Außenpolitik," *Europa-Archiv* 48 (1993): 533–52.

65. Hans Arnold: "Deutschlands Rolle in der UNO," *Aus Politik und Zeitgeschichte,* 44, no. B42 (1994): 34.

66. For a comprehensive presentation of the various party positions see Philippi, *Bundeswehr,* 48–156.

67. Ulrich Fastenrath: "Deutschland, Blauhelme und die Vereinten Nationen," Frankfurter Allgemeine Zeitung, 17 December 1992. Ole Diehl: "UN-Einsätze der Bundeswehr: Außenpolitische Handlungs-zwänge und innepolitischer Konsensbedarf," *Europa-Archiv* 48, 1 (1993): 219–27.

68. Volker Rühe: "Das ist keine Drohgebärde," interview, *Der Spiegel,* 20 July 1992, 32–5. Volker Rühe: "Raus aus dem Dilemma," interview, *Der Spiegel,* 21 December 1992, 21–3.

69. This raised some renewed criticism of a German special role. Marc Weller: "In Bosnien diffuser Auftrag für Blauhelme und NATO," *Frankfurter Allgemeine Zeitung,* 12 July 1995. Alan Cowell: "Germans Face Combat in the Shadow of Militarism," *International Herald Tribune,* 18 July 1995, cited in Philippi, *Bundeswehr,* 101.

70. "48. Sitzung vom 30. Juni 1995," *Verhandlungen des Deutscher Bundestages, 13. Wahlperiode, Stenographische Berichte,* 179 (1995): 4017–19.

71. "Bekenntnis zur Mitverantwortung," *Das Parlament,* 8 December 1995.

72. Philippi, *Bundeswehr,* 113

73. Ibid., 114–6.

74. "Tolerant Charakterfest," *Der Spiegel,* 23/91, pp. 20–1.

75. "KSZE-Forum für sicherheitspolitische Zusammenarbeit," *Bundestag Drucksache* 12/1995, 10 June 1992.

76. Philippi, *Bundeswehr,* 119.

77. Norbert Kostede: "Zwischen Utopie und Regierungsfähigkeit: Björn Engholms Aussagen über die Rolle der Bundeswehr verwirren die SPD," *Die Zeit,* 11 September 1992.

78. "Beschlüsse des SPD-Sonderparteitages," *Vorwärts,* 45, no. 12 (1992): 10–2.

79. "Leiser Vorbehalt," *Der Spiegel,* 30 August 1993, 21–2.

80. "Allzu forsch," *Der Spiegel,* 2 August 1993, 21–3. Hans-Ulrich Klose, "Wir müssen UNO-fähig werden," interview, *Der Spiegel,* 6 September 1993, 22–4.

81. "Vor dem Rohr," *Der Spiegel,* 13 September 1993, 22.

82. "Perspektiven einer neuen Außen- und Sicherheitspolitik," in *Protokolle des Parteitages von Wiesbaden 16.–19. November 1993,* ed. SPD-Parteivorstand (Frankfurt am Main: Union Druckerei, 1994), 978–92.

83. Hans-Ulrich Klose, "Drohpotential muß sein," interview, *Der Spiegel,* 12 December 1994, 24.

84. Günter Verheugen, "Kohls gefährlicher Sonderweg," interview, *Focus,* 25 February 1995, 24–6.

85. "Lafontaine widerspricht Scharping," *Frankfurter Allgemeine Zeitung,* 3 June 1995.

86. Philippi, *Bundeswehr,* 106–7.

87. Philippi, *Bundeswehr,* 102–5.

88. "Tolerant Charakterfest," 21.

89. Hans-Dietrich Genscher, "Ich habe Kurs gehalten," interview, *Der Spiegel,* 4 February 1991, 23.

90. Philippi, *Bundeswehr,* 107.

91. Bundesvorstand Bündnis 90/Die Grünen, ed., *Das Programm zur 1. Gesamtdeutschen Wahl, 1990,* (Bornheim: Bundesgeschäftsstelle, 1990), 18–21.

92. "Für eine Zivilisierung der internationalen Beziehungen: Politik nichtmilitärischer Konfliktlösung. Antrag der Abgeordneten Vera Wollenberger, Gerd Poppe, Werner Schulz, Dr. Wolfgang Ullmann, Konrad Weiß," *Deutscher Bundestag, Drucksache,* 12/3014, 2 July 1992.

93. "Grünes Licht für den Krieg," *Die Woche,* 11 August 1995, 6.

94. Joschka Fischer: *Risiko Deutschland: Krise und Zukunft der deutschen Politik* (Köln: Kiepenheuer und Witsch, 1994), 222.

95. "Für Antrag zu UN-Einsätzen," *Frankfurter Allgemeine Zeitung,* 11 November 1995.

96. "Streit bei den Grünen verschärft sich," *Frankfurter Allgemeine Zeitung,* 7 December 1995.

97. See, for example, "Bereich Außen- und Friedenspolitik," Infor-Brief Bundestagsgruppe PDS, 5, no. 3 (December 1995).

98. "Nie mehr Täter sein," *Der Spiegel,* 28 January 1991, 28–30.

99. "Ökokatastrophe durch Golfkrieg verhindern!," *Blätter für deutsche und internationale Politik,* 36 (1991): 167.

100. "Soldaten, geht nicht an den Golf!" resolution by four Christian peace groups, *Blätter für deutsche und internationale Politik*, 36, I (1991): 160.

101. "Den Krieg am Golf kann nur einer gewinnen: der Tod," *Blätter für deutsche und internationale Politik* 36 (1991): 104. "Kein Krieg am Golf!," *Blätter für deutsche und internationale Politik*, 36 (1991): 177–9. "Frankfurt appeal for peace in the Gulf," *Blätter für deutsche und internationale Politik*, 36 (1991): 163.

102. Text of a resolution by the "Atlantik-Brücke e.V." (Bonn) of 22.1. 1991, quoted in Kaiser and Becher, *Irak-Konflikt*, 127–8.

103. "Nie mehr Täter sein," 30.

104. Ibid., 29.

105. Kaiser and Becher, *Irak-Konflikt*, 27–30.

106. Philippi, *Bundeswehreinsätze*, 166.

107. See the various opinion polls compiled by Philippi, *Bundeswehreinsätze*, 170.

108. Hans Rühle: "Welche Armee für Deutschland," *Europa-Archiv*, 49, 1 (1994): 161–8.

109. *Weißbuch 1994*, 93, paragraph 527.

110. *Weißbuch 1994*, 95, paragraph 538.

111. Ibid., paragraph 582.

112. Ibid., 167.

113. See chapter III.

114. See chapter III, section II. See also Heinrich Fauth: "Neuer Rüstungsplan für die Bundeswehr: Minus 43, 7 Milliarden DM in 12 Haushaltsjahren," *Europäische Sicherheit* 41, no. 2 (1992): 71–4.

115. "Den Ernstfall nicht gewagt," *Der Spiegel*, 11 February 1991, 18–26.

116. Ibid., 23.

117. Hans Rühle, "Und jetzt der Krieg?" *Der Spiegel*, 24 February 1992, 108.

118. "Gewehr unterm Baum," *Der Spiegel*, 11 January 1993, 34ff.

119. *Allensbacher Jahrbücher 1984–92*, 1058.

120. Carl-Helmuth Lichel: "Gedanken zur Traditionspflege—Absage an die Generation der Gründer?," *Europäische Sicherheit* 41, no. 2 (1992): 92–6. Arthur Matyschok: "Ein Beitrag zu einer deutschen Diskussion—Tradition in der Bundeswehr," *Europäische Sicherheit* 43, no. 7 (1994): 358–61.

121. Wolf-Heinrich Krustmann: "Zukünftiges Bild des deutschen Soldaten," *Europäische Sicherheit* 44, no. 66 (1995): 914.

122. *Weißbuch 1994*, 89, paragraph 517.

123. Hans Rühle: "Welche Armee," 165. See also "Wehrpflicht am Ende," *Der Spiegel*, 8 February 1993, 36–47.

124. Manfred Opel, "Die Wehrreform der Zukunft heißt Freiwilligen-Armee," *Europäische Sicherheit* 43, no. 3 (1994): 114–6.

125. "Das hält keine Armee aus," *Der Spiegel*, 12/1993, p. 84.

125. "Wehrpflicht am Ende," 43.

126. Ibid., 45.

V: The Loss of Utopia

1. Jacques Delors, "Wir müssen Großmacht werden," interview, *Der Spiegel,* 14 October 1991, 23.

2. See opinion polls cited chapter V, section VI.

3. Werner Weidenfeld, "Die Bilanz der Europäischen Integration 1996/97," *Jahrbuch der europäischen Integration* 16 (1996/97): 16.

4. Wolfgang Wessels, "Die Europapolitik in der wissenschafttlichen Debatte," *Jahrbuch der europäischen Integration 1996/97* 16 (1996/97): 31–33.

5. Werner Link, "Die europäische Neuordnung des Mächtegleichgewichts," *Europa 2020. Szenarien einer politischen Entwicklung,* ed. Thomas Jäger and Melanie Piepenschneider (Opladen: Leske und Budrich, 1995): 31.

6. Gottfried Niedhard, Paul Junker, and Michael Richter, ed., *Deutschland in Europa—Nationale Interessen und internationale Ordnung im 20. Jahrhundert,* (Mannheim: Palatium HVS, 1997), 387.

7. Klaus Hildebrand, "Deutschland und Europa im 20. Jahrhundert," in *Deutschland in Europa—Nationale Interessen und internationale Ordnung im 20. Jahrhundert,* 394.

8. See Andrew Moravcsik, "Negotiating the Single European Act," in *The New European Community—Decisionmaking and Institutional Change,* ed. Robert O. Keohane and Stanley Hoffmann (Boulder: Westview Press, 1991), 41–85.

9. Elfriede Regelsberger, "Gemeinsame Außen- und Sicherheitspolitik," in *Die Europäische Union,* ed. Wichard Woyke and Beate Koch-Kohler, Vol. 5 of *Lexikon der Politik* (Munich: Verlag C.H. Beck, 1995), 135.

10. Kommission der EG, ed., *Vollendung des Binnenmarktes: Weißbuch der Kommission an den Europäischen Rat* (Luxembourg: Kommission der EG, 1985).

11. Paolo Ceccini, *Europa '92: Endlich ein Binnenmarkt* (Baden-Baden: Nomos Verlagsgesellschaft, 1988).

12. Thomas Läufer, "Haushaltspolitik," *Jahrbuch der Europäischen Integration* 7 (1986/87): 141–145.

13. Michael Keating, and Barry Jones, ed., *Regions in the European Community,* (Oxford: Clarendon Press, 1985).

14. Michael Garthe, "Bundesrepublik Deutschland," *Jahrbuch der Europäischen Integration* 7(1986/87): 336–345.

15. Erklärung des Außenministers Hans-Dietrich Genscher über die Resultate der deutschen EG-Präsidentschaft vor dem Europäischen Parlament, 16. Juni 1988," *Europa-Archiv* 43, 2 (1988): D440.

16. Garthe, "Bundesrepublik Deutschland," *1986/87,* 336–337.

17. "Probleme der europäischen Einigung (II)," *Europa-Archiv,* 43, 2 (1988): D438. See also Peter Hort, "Eine Bilanz der deutschen EG-Präsidentschaft," *Europa-Archiv* 43, 1 (1988): 421–428.

18. Robert D. Putnam, "Diplomacy and Domestic Politics: the Logic of Two-Level Games," *International Organization* 42 (1988): 427–460.

19. Günter Nonnenmacher, "Das Jahr der Entscheidung," *Frankfurter Allgemeine Zeitung,* 2 February 1985.

20. Horst Teltschik, "Aspekte der deutschen Außen- und Sicherheitspolitik," *Aus Politik und Zeitgeschichte* 35, no. B7–8 (1985): 13.

21. Werner Weidenfeld, "Die Bilanz der europäischen Integration 1985," *Jahrbuch der europäischen Integration* 6 (1985): 20.

22. "EG: Umschlagen ins Patt," *Der Spiegel,* 20 February 1988, 22–23.

23. "Probleme der europäischen Einigung (III)," *Europa-Archiv* 43, 2 (1988): D681.

24. "Probleme der europäischen Einigung (I)," *Europa-Archiv* 43, 2 (1988): D141.

25. Michael Garthe, "Bundesrepublik Deutschland," *Jahrbuch der Europäischen Integration* 61 (1985): 324–326.

26. Garthe, "Bundesrepublik Deutschland " 1986/87, 337.

27. Ibid., 339.

28. See, for example, Michael Stürmer, "Gibt es ein Mitteleuropa?," *Frankfurter Allgemeine Zeitung,* 21 October 1986, 1, or Karl Schlögel, "Die blockierte Vergangenheit, in Nachdenken über Mitteleuropa," *Frankfurter Allgemeine Zeitung,* 21 February 1987, Hans-Peter Schwarz, *Die Zentralmacht Europas: Deutschlands Rückkehr auf die Weltbühne* (Berlin: Siedler, 1994), 240–245.

29. Gerhard Herdegen, "Die öffentliche Meinung," *Jahrbuch der Europäischen Integration* 6 (1985): 301, 312.

30. *Financial Times,* 4 December 1987.

31. "In the following weeks and months, two major tasks have priority: the proposals of the Commission, known as Delors-Package and the completion of the Common Market. Only if we pass the Delors-Package, can we concentrate on the tasks for the future." "Rede des Außenministers Genscher über die Ziele der deutschen EU-Präsidentschaft vor dem Europäischen Parlament vom 20. Januar 1988," *Europa-Archiv* 34, 2 (1988): D150–151.

32. "Listig versteckt," *Der Spiegel,* 22 February 1988, 103–104.

33. "Noch zu früh," *Der Spiegel,* 27 June 1988, 82.

34. "Tagung des Europäischen Rates am 27. und 28. Juni 1988 in Hannover," *Europa-Archiv* 34, 2 (1988): D445–446.

35. Elisabeth Noelle-Neumann, and Gerd Gerdegen, "Die öffentliche Meinung," *Jahrbuch der Europäischen Integration* 7 (1987/88): 318.

36. Ibid., 322–323.

37. Elisabeth Noelle-Neumann, and Gerhard Herdegen, "Die öffentliche Meinung," *Jahrbuch der Europäischen Integration* 7 (1986/87): 308.

38. "Kohl wünscht sich mehr Binnenmarkt-Engagement," *Frankfurter Allgemeine Zeitung,* 16 March 1988, 13–4.

39. "Europa 1992: Die sind alle irre unterwegs," *Der Spiegel,* 9 May 1988, 26–32.

40. Ibid., p. 32.

41. "Europäische Währungsordnung," *Gutachten des wissenschaftlichen Beirats beim BMWi,* no. 61 (1989): paragraph 12.

42. "Mitteilungen und Kommentare zur Geldwertstabilität," Gemeinschaft zum Schutz der deutschen Sparer 1 (1981), 1.

43. "European Business and the ECU, Results of a Survey," *Association for the Monetary Union of Europe:* Paris, 25 October 1988.

44. Michael Garthe,"Bundesrepublik Deutschland," *Jahrbuch der Europäischen Integration* 8 (1987/88): 344. Noelle-Neumann and Herdegen, "Die öffentliche Meinung," 1987/88, 324–326.

45. "Mehr Müll, weniger Rechte," *Der Spiegel,* 20 November 1989, 138–139.

46. Harald Schumann, "Markt ohne Staat," *Der Spiegel,* 4 July 1988, 94–96.

47. "Die Hunde sind von der Kette," *Der Spiegel,* 28 November 1988, 22.

48. Ibid.

49. "Rede der britischen Premierministerin Margaret Thatcher in der europäischen Hochschule Brügge vom 20. September 1988," *Europa-Archiv* 43, 2 (1988): D683–684. Probleme der europäischen Einigung (II) 1988, D401–2. Lothar Späth, "Der Traum von Europa: I Die soziale Frage," *Der Spiegel,* 2 October 1989, 73.

50. In more traditional terms, these concessions could also be seen as a trade-off for the early recognition of Slovenia and Croatia.

51. For an account of these developments, see chapter V, section v.

52. "Die Gemeinschaft überdenkt ihr Verhältnis zu Mittel- und Osteuropa," *Frankfurter Allgemeine Zeitung,* 13 November 1989, 6.

53. "Splitter im Körper," *Der Spiegel,* 1 January 1990, 26–7. "Tagung des Europäischen Rates der Staats- und Regierungschefs am 8. und 9. Dezember 1989 in Straßburg," *Europa-Archiv* 45, 2 (1990): D10.

54. "Botschaft des Staatspräsidenten François Mitterrand und des Bundeskanzlers Helmut Kohl an den Präsidenten des Europäischen Rates der Staats- und Regierungschefs, Charles Haughey, vom 18. April 1990," *Europa-Archiv* 45, 2 (1990): D283.

55. "Probleme der Europäischen Einigung (III)," *Europa-Archiv* 45, 2 (1990): D395.

56. "Probleme der europäischen Einigung," *Europa-Archiv* 46, 2 (1991): D1.

57. Hans-Gert Pöttering, the (German) chairman of the committee on security and disarmament in the European Parliament, outlined the second objective in early 1990. Hans-Gert Pötterning, "Perspektiven für eine gemeinschaftliche Außen- und Sicherheitspolitik der EG," *Europa-Archiv* 45, 1 (1990): 341–350.

58. This dilemma was later summarized by columnist Johannes Gross: "There is a reason that the European dialogue has reached a stalemate. It is the favorite idea of our Chancellor that the continent could be unified by a stronger parliamentarization of European procedures. As much as France

and England diverge in the 'European question,' they agree that the European Union should primarily be directed and promoted by the Council of Ministers, i.e., through the cooperation of national governments. Our Federal Chancellor is elevated by the conviction that the democratic legitimacy of European politics should be increased by a strengthening of the parliament in Strasbourg; this is a credit to Kohl the idealistic democrat, it is not a credit to Kohl the real politician." Johannes Gross, "So nicht!," *Capital*, January 1995, 3.

59. "Probleme der Europäischen Einigung (II)," *Europa-Archiv* 38, 2 (1991): D361–363.

60. "Probleme der Europäischen Einigung," *Europa-Archiv* 49, 2 (1992): D89–91.

61. "Botschaft Mitterrands und Kohls," D283.

62. "Gemeinsame Botschaft des französischen Staatspräsidenten François Mitterrand und des deutschen Bundeskanzlers Helmut Kohl an den Präsidenten des Europäischen Rates der Staats- und Regierungschefs, Guilio Andreotti vom 6. Dezember 1990," in *Aussenpolitik der Bundesrepublik Deutschland*, ed. Auswärtiges Amt, 776–779.

63. Ibid., 826–829. See also Gordon, *Deutsch-Französische Partnerschaft*, 20–24.

64. On this "lowest-common-denominator-approach" to the common foreign and security policy, see also Peter Hort, "Europas Außenpolitik: Ein Fernziel," in *Europa-Archiv* 46, 1 (1991): 577–582.

65. "Die Zeit ist nicht reif," *Der Spiegel*, 14 October 1991, 18.

66. Ibid., 20.

67. "Rede des Bundeskanzlers auf dem Petersberg anläßlich des EG-Forums der deutschen Wirtschaft zum Standort Europa," *Bulletin des Presse- und Informationsamtes der Bundesregierung*, 16 October 1992, 1042.

68. "Zukunftsperspektiven der jungen Generation auf dem Weg ins vereinte Europa," *Bulletin des Presse- und Informationsamtes der Bundesregierung*, 16 October 1992, 1061.

69. "Rede des Außenministers Hans-Dietrich Genscher vor der 47. Vollversammlung der Vereinten Nationen am 25. September 1991," *Europa-Archiv* 47, 3 (1992): D354.

70. Ibid., 284.

71. The majority of the German business and policy elites, on the other hand, gave priority to the completion of the Common Market (63 percent vs. 19 percent for reunification). On average, the EC nations gave priority to the completion of the Common Market (45 percent vs. 31 percent for reunification). Elisabeth Noelle-Neumann, and Gerhard Herdegen: "Die öffentliche Meinung," *Jahrbuch der Europäischen Integration* 9 (1989/90): 280.

72. Ibid., 279.

73. See, for example, Christian Watrin, "Deutschland: Der Preis der wirtschaftlichen Vereinigung," *Aussenwirtschaft* 48, no. 1 (1993), Heft 1, 37–48.

74. Kielinger and Otte, "Pressured Power," 46.

75. "Stellenabbau in Deutschland: Eine F.A.Z.-Umfrage," *Frankfurter Allgemeine Zeitung,* 19 December 1992, 21.

76. Anita Wolf, "Bundesrepublik Deutschland," *Jahrbuch der Europäischen Integration* 10 (1991/92): 310.

77. Ibid., 310.

78. Which later subsided again, see chapter V, section VII.

79. Peter Glotz, "Europa am Scheideweg," *Europa-Archiv* 39, 1 (1992): 503.

80. See, for example, *Probleme der Europäischen Einigung 1992,* D 89–91.

81. "Das kann die EG vergiften," *Der Spiegel,* 2 December 1991, 35.

82. "Über den Rubikon," *Der Spiegel,* 16 December 1991, 22.

83. Otto Schmuck, "Der Maastrichter Vertrag zur Europäischen Union," *Europa-Archiv* 39, 1 (1992): 97–106. Markus Jachtenfuchs, "Die EG nach Maastricht," *Europa-Archiv* 39, 1 (1992): 279. Wolfgang Wessels, "Maastricht: Ergebnisse, Bewertungen und Langzeittrends," *Integration* 15, no. 1 (1992): 2–16.

84. "Über den Rubikon," 23.

85. "Das kann die EG vergiften," 38.

86. Rudolf Augstein, "Abschied von der Mark?," *Der Spiegel,* 2 December 1991, 37.

87. Rudolf Augstein, "Wer zahlt für Europa?," *Der Spiegel,* 9 August 1999, 23.

88. These figures refer to West Germans. Former East Germans, included in the poll since 1991, are even more critical of faster integration. *Allensbacher Jahrbuch der Demoskopie 1984–92,* 1011.

89. "Wirtschafts- und Währungsunion nicht um jeden Preis," *Pressemitteilung des Bundesverbandes der deutschen Industrie,* 18 September, 1991.

90. "Zwölf Forderungen der SPD an einen europäische Währungsunion," *Presseerklärung der SPD im deutschen Bundestag,* November 22, 1991.

91. "Der Vertrag über die Europäische Union," *Europa-Archiv* 93, 2 (1992): D177–D253.

92. *Allensbacher Jahrbuch der Demoskopie 1984–1992,* 1029.

93. "Regierungserklärung Bundeskanzler Kohls über die Resultate der Tagung des Europäischen Rates der Staats- und Regierungschefs in Maastricht am 13. Dezember 1991," *Aussenpolitik der Bundesrepublik Deutschland,* 846–851.

94. "An der DM festhalten, bis der ECU wirklich stabil ist," *Sozialdemokratischer Pressedienst Wirtschaft,* 2 January, 1992.

95. "Grundgesetzänderungen für Euro-Mark gibt es nur bei Nachbesserungen," *Medienservice der SPD-Abgeordneten im Europäischen Parlament,* 2 February 1992.

96. "Erklärung Wolfgang Schäubles vor der CDU/CSU-Fraktion des Deutschen Bundestages," *Pressedienst der CDU/CSU Fraktion im Deutschen Bundestag,* 21 February 1992.

97. "Beschränkt belastbar," *Der Spiegel,* 10 February 1992, 20–2.

98. Ibid., 20.

99. Norbert Blüm, "Die leise Übermacht," *Der Spiegel,* 30 November 1992, 102–107.

100. Anita Wolf, "Bundesrepublik Deutschland," 1991/92, 310.

101. Elisabeth Noelle-Neumann, "Die öffentliche Meinung," *Jahrbuch der Europäischen Integration* 10 (1991/92): 273–81.

102. "Ja, aber," *Der Spiegel,* 23 March 1992, 68.

103. "Eine Erfolgsstory," *Der Spiegel,* 23 November 1992, 38.

104. "Das Ende des Grundgesetzes?" *Der Spiegel,* 23 March 1992, 76–80.

105. Ibid., 38. See also "Schwierige Geburt," *Kurz-Nachrichtendienst der Bundesvereinigung der Deutschen Arbeitgeberverbände,* 8 December 1992.

106. "Für ein Europa der Stabilität und finanzpolitischen Solidität: 10 Forderungen an den EG-Haushalt," *Die SPD im Deutschen Bundestag,* 21 February 1992.

107. "Europapolitische Erklärung," *Pressedienst der CDU/CSU Fraktion im deutschen Bundestag,* 21 February 1992.

108. Parteivorstand der SPD, "Erklärung zu den Verträgen von Maastricht," *Presseservice der SPD,* 9 March 1992.

109. "SPD mach Weg für Europäische Union frei," *Frankfurter Rundschau,* 10 March 1992.

110. Heidemarie Wieczorek-Zeul, "Europäische Perspektiven der SPD: Antrag auf dem Bundesparteitag der SPD in Bremen," *Presseservice der SPD,* 21 May 1991.

111. "Die Grünen gegen Maastricht," *Die Zeit,* 17 July 1992, 4.

112. Thomas Läufer, "Bundesrepublik Deutschland," *Jahrbuch der europäischen Integration* 11 (1992/93): 299–397, 301.

113. "Europäische Gemeinschaften," *Europa-Archiv* 47, 3 (1992): Z247.

114. Heidemarie Wieczorek-Zeul, "Erklärung zur Krise im EWS," *Presseservice der SPD,* 17 September 1992.

115. Deutsche Bundesbank, ed. *Annual Report 1993,* (Frankfurt/M.: Deutsche Bundesbank, 1993), 87–95.

116. Jürgen Pfister, "Ist das Europäische Währungssystem am Ende?," *Europa-Archiv* 40, 1 (1993): 714.

117. Josef Joffe, "Abschied von Kleineuropa," *Süddeutsche Zeitung,* 7 August 1993.

118. "Kein Zweifel an der Währungsunion," *CDU/CSU-Fraktion im deutschen Bundestag,* Bonn, 29 November 1993.

119. "Probleme mit der Währung," *Die Woche,* 4 March 1994.

120. "Ewiges Knirschen," *Der Spiegel,* 24 May 1993, 25–6.

121. "Das Maastricht-Urteil des Bundesverfassungsgerichts," *Europa-Archiv* 40, 2 (1993): D459.

122. Ibid., D461.

123. Ibid., D462.

124. Ibid., D467.

125. Ibid., D468.

126. "Europa ist kein Vaterland," *Der Spiegel,* 13 December 1993, 36–7.

127. "Rückzug auf die Nation?" *Der Spiegel,* 25 October 1993, 167.

128. "Der letzte Europäer," 18.

129. Ibid., 18–21.

130. Elisabeth Noelle-Neumann, "Die öffentliche Meinung," *Jahrbuch der Europäischen Integration,* 12 (1993/1994): 285–294, 289–291.

131. Hans-Eckart Scharrer, "Binnenmarktpolitik," *Jahrbuch der Europäischen Integration,* 11 (1992/93): 139.

132. Noelle-Neumann, "Öffentliche Meinung," 1993/94, 289–291.

133. "Erweitern oder vertiefen," *Der Spiegel,* 5 December 1994, 47–50.

134. Noelle-Neumann, "Öffentliche Meinung," 1993/94, 290.

135. This instinctive assessment is all the more interesting, because only 15 percent felt that they were well-informed about Europe, while 73 percent thought they were not so well informed.

136. Noelle-Neumann, "Öffentliche Meinung," 1993/1994, 288–291.

137. "Seiters: Deutsche Überlegungen zur Regierungskonferenz 1996," *CDU/CSU Presse-dienst,* 2 March 1995.

138. "Bayern legt europapolitische Position für Maastricht II fest," *Bulletin des Freisstaates Bayern,* 7 April 1995, 5.

139. "Ein europäischer Bundesstaat kommt vorerst nicht zustande: Reformkonzept der SPD zu Europa," *Frankfurter Allgemeine Zeitung,* 4 February 1995. "Eine neue Garderobe für die Dame Europa: Sechs Sozialdemokraten schneidern ein Reformkonzept," *Saarbrücker Zeitung,* 8 February 1995.

140. Cited in Peter Glotz, "Neue deutsche Ideologie," *Der Spiegel,* 30 September 1991, 62–65.

141. Willy Brandt, "Eine EG von Paris bis Wladiwostok?" Frankfurter Rundschau, 13 May 1992.

142. Glotz, "Neue deutsche Ideologie," 62.

143. "Nach Osten hin ist alles offen," interview, *Der Spiegel,* 11 January 1993, 21–23.

144. Bundesgeschäftsstelle Bündnis 90/ Die Grünen, ed., *Nur mit uns* (Bornheim: Bundesgeschäftsstelle Bündnis 90/ Die Grünen, 1994), 56.

145. Ibid., 280.

146. "Erweitern oder vertiefen," *Der Spiegel,* 5 December 1994, 47–50.

147. "Rede des Außenministers Klaus Kinkel vor der Deutschen Gesellschaft für Auswärtige Politik," *Europa-Archiv* 41, 2 (1994): D541–542.

148. "Bedenkliche Thesen," interview, *Der Spiegel,* 12 September 1994, 29–32.

149. Gerd Tebbe, "Wunsch und Wirklichkeit: Das Problem der Oster-weiterung," *Europa-Archiv* 41, 1 (1994): 393, 396.

150. "Seiters: Deutsche Überlegungen."

151. "Die D-Mark ist nicht alles," interview, *Der Spiegel,* 27 March 1995, 22–24.

152. "Westeuropa endet in Polen," interview, *Der Spiegel,* 4 July 1994, 19–20.

153. "Nur noch zweite Wahl," *Der Spiegel,* 4 July 1994, 20.

154. "Kritik an Osteuropapolitik: SPD: Außenminister Kinkels Zusagen für eine rasche Osterweiterung sind populistisch," *Neue Zeit,* 25 May 1994.

155. "Europäische Perspektiven in den neunziger Jahren, Rede Rudolf Scharpings in Prag," *Presseservice der SPD,* 6 April 1994.

156. "Zehn Forderungen an die deutsche Ratspräsidentschaft der EU," *Presseservice der SPD,* 30 April 1994.

157. "Zeit der Begehrlichkeiten vorbei," *Deutscher Industrie- und Handelstag: Informationen für Presse, Funk und Fernsehen,* 20 June 1994.

158. "Geschlossene Gesellschaft," *Der Spiegel,* 6 May 1991, 207.

159. Douglas Hurd, "Europa nicht abschotten," interview, *Der Spiegel,* 28 October 1991, 206.

160. "Zuviel auf einmal," *Der Spiegel,* 14 December 1992, 35–38.

161. Werner Weidenfeld, "Die Bilanz der europäischen Integration 1992/93," in *Jahrbuch der Europäischen Integration* 11 (1992/93): 17.

162. "Erklärung der Bundesregierung zur Sondertagung des Europäischen Rates in Brüssel," *Bulletin des Presse- und Informationsamtes der Bundesregierung,* 16 November 1993, 1101–1106.

163. "Kohl macht den EU-Beitritt Polens zu seiner Sache," *Kölner-Stadt-Anzeiger,* 15 April 1994.

164. "The regional emphasis under the German presidency should be the Central and Eastern European states, Slovenia, the Baltic countries, but also Russia and the other nations of the CIS. Those reforming democracies have a clear perspective of accession since the Copenhagen summit of last year." Klaus Kinkel, "Deutschland in Europa: Zu den Zielen der deutschen Präsidentschaft in der Europäischen Union," *Europa-Archiv* 41, 1 (1994): 335–342.

165. Ibid., 18.

166. "Neuer Machtpol in Europa," *Der Spiegel,* 7 March 1994, 18–20.

167. "Erklärung der Bundesregierung über die Erweiterungsverhandlungen der Europäischen Union," *Bulletin des Presse- und Informationsamtes der Bundesregierung,* 11 March 1994, 217–218.

168. "Der Krach am Rhein," *Die Zeit,* 25 March 1994.

169. "Balsam für eine Leiche," *Der Spiegel,* 18 October 1993, 30.

170. "Falsche Hoffnungen," *Der Spiegel,* 12 December 1994, 28–29.

171. Ibid., 29.

172. "Alles härter," *Der Spiegel,* 26 July 1993, 23.

173. "Angst vorm Koloß," *Der Spiegel,* 9 August 1993, 23.

174. Ingo Kolboom argues that French diplomacy during unification showed the willingness to accept geopolitical changes, and that attempts to "maintain the balance" were only feeble manifestations of the search for prestige within the widespread acceptance of change. Ingo Kolboom, "Die Vertreibung der Dämonen: Frankreich und das vereinte Deutschland," *Europa-Archiv* 15–16 (1991): 470–475.

175. "Angst vorm Koloß," 24.

176. "Die EG lebt gefährlich," *Der Spiegel,* 24 August 1993, 134. see also "Objektive Schwierigkeiten mit Bonn," *Die Welt,* 25 August 1993.

177. "Im Urlaubsort Chamoix antwortet Balladur dem Kanzler," *General-Anzeiger,* 12 August 1993.

178. "Gegen Lethargie und Zweifel," *Frankfurter Allgemeine Zeitung,* 8 October 1993.

179. "Neues Wir-Gefühl," *Bonner Rundschau,* 14 October 1993.

180. "Mitterrand nimmt Kohl in Schutz," *General-Anzeiger,* 17 August 1993.

181. "Bonns Außenminister verliert die Nerven," *Berliner Zeitung,* 18 March 1994. See also "Der Krach am Rhein," and "Funkstörung Bonn-Paris," *Frankfurter Rundschau,* 24 March 1994.

182. "Bonn und Paris wollen kein 'britisches' Europa," *General-Anzeiger,* 23 March 1994.

183. "Mitterrand lobt Verhältnis zu Bonn," *Frankfurter Allgemeine Zeitung,* 22 March 1994.

184. "Bekenntnis zur Freundschaft," *Frankfurter Rundschau,* 21 March 1994.

185. "Kinkel wurde als ein guter Freund gefeiert," *General-Anzeiger,* 25 March 1994.

186. "Herzog betont besonderes Verhältnis zu Frankreich," *Die Welt,* 7 August 1994.

187. "Deutsche bei Festparade in Paris herzlich willkommen," *Westdeutsche Allgemeine Zeitung,* 12 July 1994.

188. "Beifall für deutsche Soldaten auf dem Champs-Elysées, Mitterrand: Ein wichtiger Schritt in die Zukunft," *Süddeutsche Zeitung,* 15 July 1994.

189. "Die EG lebt gefährlich," 135.

190. "Nur noch zweite Wahl," 16–18.

191. "Zwischenentscheidung vor der EU-Reform," *Parlamentarisch-politischer Pressedienst,* 29 March 1994.

192. "Mitteilung zu den Ergebnissen der europäischen Rates," *Presseservice der SPD,* 12 December 1994.

193. *Kinkel vor der Deutschen Gesellschaft für Auswärtige Politik,* D541–2.

194. Hans Tietmeyer, "Europäische Währungsunion und Politische Union: Das Modell mehrerer Geschwindigkeiten," *Europa-Archiv* 44, 1 (1994): 457–460.

195. Josef Janning:, "Europa braucht verschiedene Geschwindigkeiten," *Europa-Archiv* 44, 1 (1994): 527–536.

196. "Germanische Rohheit," *Der Spiegel,* 12 September 1994, 28–29.

197. Ibid., 28.

198. "Bedenkliche Thesen," 29–32.

199. Rudolf Scharping, interview, Tagesthemen, Arbeitsgemeinschaft der Rundfunkanstalten Deutschlands, 1 September 1994, Heidemarie Wieczorek-Zeul, "Erklärung zu den von der CDU/CSU-Fraktion vorgelegten Vorschlägen zu einem Kerneuropa," *Presseservice der SPD,* 5 September 1994.

200. "Wer Maastricht zerschlägt, der schafft keinen Kern," *Bonner Rundschau,* 13 September 1994.

201. Josef Janning, "Bundesrepublik Deutschland," *Jahrbuch der Europäischen Integration* 14 (1995/96): 289–291.

202. Robert Toulemon, "Kerneuropa: Deutsch französische Aktionsgemeinschaft in Sicht?," *Integration* 18, no.2 (1995): 62–64.

203. Josef Janning, "Bundesrepublik Deutschland," *Jahrbuch der Europäischen Integration* 13 (1994/95): 291. Wichard Woyke, "Von der Orientierungslosigkeit zur Konzeption: Die Außenpolitik des Vereinigten Deutschland," Politische Bildung 30 (1997): 17. "Osteuropa für den Export immer wichtiger," *Frankfurter Allgemeine Zeitung,* 17 October 1996. "Osteuropa für deutsche Wirtschaft immer wichtiger," *Frankfurter Allgemeine Zeitung,* 1 October 1996.

204. "Geld stiftet noch keine Staatlichkeit, *Frankfurter Allgemeine Zeitung,* 17 May 1995. Hans Tietmeyer, "Europa: Steigende Welle oder Urknall," *Frankfurter Allgemeine Zeitung,* 5 April 1995.

205. Janning, "Bundesrepublik," 1994/95, 291. Toulemon, "Kerneuropa," 62–64.

206. Elisabeth Noelle-Neumann, "Die öffentliche Meinung," *Jahrbuch der Europäischen Integration,* 15 (1996/97): 277. Elisabeth Noelle-Neumann, "Europa hinter dem Schleier: Schlechte Information, wenig Wissen, widersprüchliche Einstellungen," *Frankfurter Allgemeine Zeitung,* 27 September 1995.

207. Janning, "Bundesrepublik," (1995/96): 290, 296. Yves-Thibault de Silguy, "Rätselraten schadet der Währungsunion," *Frankfurter Allgemeine Zeitung,* 23 May 1996.

208. Rudolf, Augstein, "Herzog: Bitte unterschätzen Sie uns nicht," *Der Spiegel,* 4 August 1997, 34–35.

209. "Diskussion um die Konvergenzkriterien zur Teilnahme an der EWWU," *Keesings Archiv der Gegegenwart,* 27 November 1997, 41601.

210. "Außen- und europapolitische Erklärung Kohls," *Keesings Archiv der Gegenwart,* 27 June 1997, 42133. "40. Jahrestag der Unterzeichnung der römischen Verträge," *Keesings Archiv der Gegenwart,* 25 March 1997, 41916.

211. Cited in Janning, "Bundesrepublik Deutschland," 1995/96, 293.

212. "Diskussion um die Konvergenzkriterien zur Teilnahme an der EWWU," 41605–6.

213. Janning, "Bundesrepublik Deutschland, 1994/95, 289.

214. Friedhelm Solms, "Deutsch-Französische Dissonanzen," *Blätter für deutsche und internationale Politik,* 42 (1997): 827–829.

215. "Gipfeltreffen in Dublin: Einigung über den Stabilitätspakt erzielt," *Keesings Archiv der Gegenwart,* 14 December 1996, 41649. Janning, "Bundesrepublik Deutschland," 1994/95, 289.

216. " Größer und billiger: Das geht nicht. Zur zukünftigen Finanzierung der Europäischen Union," *Frankfurter Allgemeine Zeitung,* 28 April 1995. Peter Hort, "Milliarden für Europa," *Frankfurter Allgenmeine Zeitung,* 27 November 1996.

217. "Größere Ausgewogenheit angestrebt," *Frankfurter Allgemeine Zeitung,* 22 July 1997.

218. Hans-Eckart Scharrer, " Finanzen/Haushalt/Steuern," in *Die Europäische Union,* ed. Wichard Woyke, and Beate Kohler-Koch, vol. 5 of *Lexikon der Politik* (Munich: Verlag C.H. Beck, 1996), 124.

219. "Die Agenda 2000 bedeutet das Aus für 40.000 Bauern," *Frankfurter Allgemeine Zeitung,* 31 March 1998.

220. Josef Janning, "Die Bundesrepublik Deutschland," *Jahrbuch der Europäischen Integration* 16 (1997/98): 314.

221. "Waigel besteht auf Entlastung für Deutschland," *Frankfurter Allgemeine Zeitung,* 14 October 1998.

222. Janning, "Die Bundesrepublik Deutschland," 1997/98, 315.

223. Werner Weidenfeld, "Ernstfall Europa: Der Kontinent brauch konzeptionelle Klarheit." *Internationale Politik* no. 1 (1995): 11.

224. Timothy Garton Ash, "Europa Denken," *Internationale Politik,* no. 9 (1995): 3–11. "Das Demokratie-Effizient-Dilemma: Die Europäische Union gerät in eine Legitimitätsfalle." *Frankfurter Allgemeine Zeitung,* 24 April 1996. Werner Weidenfeld, "Ohne Leitbild, ohne Ordnungshilfe. Europa und die europäische Einigung sind in einen Begründungsnotstand geraten," *Frankfurter Allgemeine Zeitung,* 3 November 1997.

225. Christoph Bertram, *Europa in the Balance: Securing the Peace Won in the Cold War* (Washington, D.C.: Brookings Inst., 1995). Werner Weidenfeld, "Die Bilanz der europäischen Integration. 1995/96," *Jahrbuch der Europäischen Integration* 15 (1995/96): 14.

226. Wolfgang Wessels, "Weder Vision noch Verhandlungspaket: Der Bericht der Reflexionsgruppe im integrationspolitischen Trend," *Integration* 19, no. 1 (1996): 16. Weidenfeld, "Bilanz der europäischen Integration," 1995/96, 13.

227. Werner Hoyer, "Perspektiven für die Regierungskonferenz 1996 und die europapolitische Agenda," *Integration* 18, no. 4 (1995): 190.

228. "77. Sitzung vom 7. Dezember 1995," *Verhandlungen des Deutschen Bundestages. 12. Wahlperiode, Stenographische Berichte* 181 (1995): 6711–6720.

229. Carlo Masala, "Die Debatte über die institutionelle Reform der EU," *Aussenpolitik* 48, no. 3 (1997): 229.

230. Ibid., 229–231.

231. Ibid.

232. Francoise de la Serre, and Christian Laquesne, "Frankreich," *Jahrbuch der europäischen Integration,* 16 (1996/97): 314–315. "Regierungserklärung von Michel Barnier, Staatsminister für Europaangelegenheiten vor der französischen Nationalversammlung am 13.3.1996," in *Die Reform der Europäischen Union,* ed. Mathias Jopp (Bonn: Europa Union Verlag, 1996), 151–153.

233. Standpunkte der italienischen Regierung vom 18.3.1996 (Auszüge)," in *Die Reform der Europäischen Union,* ed. Mathias Jopp (Bonn: Europa Union Verlag, 1996) 159. "Weißbuch der britischen Regierung: Eine Partnerschaft von Nationen vom 21.3.1996," in *Die Reform der Europäischen Union,* ed. Mathias Jopp (Bonn: Europa Union Verlag, 1996),172. "Ministertreffen in Noordwijk; EWI legt Jahresbericht 1996 vor," *Keesings Archiv der Gegenwart,* 4 April 1996, 41934 –41935.

234. Christian Franck, "Belgien und Luxemburg," *Jahrbuch der Europäischen Integration* 16 (1996/97): 291. Nikolaj Petersen, "Dänemark," *Jahrbuch der europäischen Integration* 16 (1996/97): 304. Timo Kivimäki, "Finnland," *Jahrbuch der europäischen Integration* 16 (1996/97): 310. Rutger Lindahl, "Schweden," *Jahrbuch der europäischen Integration* 16 (1996/97): 355. De la Serre and Lequesne, "Frankreich," 315. "Verhandlungsgrundlage der dänischen Regierung: Ein offenes Europa vom 11.12.1995 (Auszüge)," in *Die Reform der Europäischen Union,* ed. Mathias Jopp (Bonn: Europa Union Verlag, 1996), 178. "Weißbuch der irischen Regierung vom März 1996 (Auszüge)," in *Reform der Europäischen Union,* ed. Mathias Jopp (Bonn: Europa Union Verlag, 1996), 182.

235. De la Serre and Lequesne, "Frankreich," 315. Josef Janning, "Die Bundesrepublik Deutschland," *Jahrbuch der Europäischen Integration* 15 (1996/97): 294.

236. *Ministertreffen in Noordwijk: EWI legt Jahresbericht 1996 vor,* 41934–41935.

237. "Kanzlers Zweifel," *Der Spiegel,* 29 September 1997, 16.

238. De la Serre and Lequesne, "Frankreich," 313. Toulemon, "Kerneuropa," 62.

239. Masala, "Debatte," 232

240. "Gipfeltreffen in Amsterdam," *Keesings Archiv der Gegenwart,* 17 June 1997, 42116–42117.

241. "Kanzlers Zweifel," 16.

242. "EU–Gipfel in Luxemburg: Erweiterung der EU beschlossen," *Keesings Archiv der Gegenwart,* 13 December 1997, 42505.

243. Janning, "Die Bundesrepublik Deutschland," 1996/97, 301.

244. De la Serre and Lequesne, "Frankreich," 311.

245. Elfriede Regelsberger, "Gemeinsame Außen- und Sicherheitspolitik," *Jahrbuch der Europäischen Integration* 16 (1996/97): 220.

246. De la Serre and Lequesne, "Frankreich," 316.

247. Regelsberger, "Gemeinsame Außen- und Sicherheitspolitik," 211.

248. De la Serre and Lequesne, "Frankreich," 317.

249. "Deutsch-französische Leitlinien zur GASP vom 27.2.1996," in *Die Reform der Europäischen Union,* ed. Mathias Jopp (Bonn: Europa Union Verlag, 1996), 118.

250. Regelsberger, "Gemeinsame Außen- und Sicherheitspolitik," 220.

251. Josef Janning, "Dynamik in der Zwangsjacke: Flexibilität in der Europäischen Union nach Amsterdam," *Integration* 20 (1997): 286, 288.

252. Max Gallo, "Das Europa der Deutschen," *Der Spiegel,* 16 December 1996, 140–141.

253. Jacqueline Hénard, "Verrat von Osten," *Die Zeit,* 4 February 1999, 6.

254. Ibid.

255. Ibid.

256. "Geld oder Währung," *Frankfurter Allgemeine Zeitung,* 31 January 1997, 37.

257. Ibid.

258. "Umfrage: Freundschaft mit Paris nur ein Mythos," *Frankfurter Allgemeine Zeitung,* 5 July 1997, 5.

VI: The Return of "Balancing"

1. The following chart is taken from Monika Wohlfeld, "The WEU as a Complement: Not a Substitute for NATO," *Transition* 15 December 1995, 35.

2. "Helsinki Dokument 1992: Herausforderung des Wandels," *Bulletin des Presse- und Informationsamtes der Bundesregierung,* 23 July 1992, 777–808.

3. Peter Schlotter, "Die Mühen der stillen Diplomatie: Konfliktprävention und Krisenmanagement durch die OSZE," *Aus Politik und Zeitgeschichte* 46, no. B5 (1996): 27–31.

4. For comprehensive analyses of the post - Cold War development of the Atlantic Alliance see Matthias Z. Karadi, "Die Reform der Atlantischen Allianz: Bündnispolitik als Beitrag zur kooperativen Sicherheit in Europa?," *Forschungsberichte Internationale Politik,* vol.17 (Münster: Lit.Verlag, 1994).

5. James Baker, "Ein neues Europa, ein neuer Atlantizismus: Die neue Architektur für eine neue Ära, Rede vor dem Presseclub in Berlin am 12. Dezember 1989," *Europa-Archiv* 45, 2 (1990): D79–81.

6. "Londoner Erklärung," *Bulletin des Presse- und Informationsamtes der Bundesregierung,* 10 July 1990, 777–780.

7. "Kommuniqué der Ministertagung des Nordatlantikrates," *Bulletin des Presse- und Informationsamtes der Bundesregierung,* 11 June 1991, 525–529.

8. "NATO-Gipfelkonferenz in Rom," *Bulletin des Presse- und Informationsamtes der Bundesregierung,* 13 November 1991, 1033–1048.

9. "Erklärung des Nordatlantischen Kooperationsrates über Dialog, Partnerschaft und Kooperation," *Bulletin des Presse- und Informationsamtes der Bundesregierung,* 4 January 1992, 8–9.

10. Ullman, *Securing Europe,* 50–53.

11. "Artikel Dreißig der Gemeinsamen Europäischen Akte," *Bulletin der Europäischen Gemeinschaften* 19, no. 2 (1986): 129–130.

12. Gordon, "Deutsch-französische Partnerschaft," 20–25.

13. "Petersberger Erklärung vom 19. Juni 1992," 1020–1023.

14. Gordon, "Deutsch-französische Partnerschaft," 20–25.

15. "Botschaft zur Gemeinsamen Außen- und Sicherheitspolitik," *Bulletin des Presse- und Informationsamtes der Bundesregierung,* 18 October 1991, 929–931.

16. "Mit Volldampf Richtung Osten," *Focus,* 3 June 1995, 35–36.

17. David Anderson, "Außenpolitik ohne Konzept," interview, *Focus,* 3 April 1995, 20.

18. Ronald D. Asmus, "Deutschland im Übergang: Nationales Selbstvertrauen und internationale Zurückhaltung," *Europa-Archiv* 47, 1 (1992): 205.

19. See chapter IV, section III.

20. "SPD-Sicherheitsexperte Bahr: Rußland in die NATO," *dpa Pressebrief,* 4 April 1992.

21. Egon Bahr, *Deutsche Interessen: Streitschrift zu Macht, Sicherheit und Außenpolitik* (Munich: Blessing, 1998), 24–25, 138.

22. For a presentation of the debate about German interests see Michael Kreile, "Verantwortung und Interesse in der deutschen Außen- und Sicherheitspolitik," *Aus Politik und Zeitgeschichte* 46, no. B5 (1996): 3–11.

23. In game theory, the terms "uncertainty" and "risk" denote different factors. Uncertainty is the lack of knowledge about the scope of possible outcomes. Risk is a given, if potential outcomes (as well as costs and benefits) are known, but each has only a certain probability of occurring. Uncertainty is therefore more encompassing than risk.

24. See chapter I, section II.

25. See Chapter III, section IV.

26. "Rede John F. Kennedys in der Frankfurter Paulskirche am 25. Juni 1963," *Europa-Archiv* 18 (1963): D352–359.

27. Ronald D. Asmus, Robert D. Blackwill, and Stephen F. Larrabee, "Can NATO Survive?," *The Washington Quarterly* 19, no. 2 (1996): 80.

28. Ibid., 84.

29. See, for example, Stanley Kober, "The United States and the Enlargement Debate," *Transition* 1, no. 23 (1995): 6–9. Stanley R. Sloan, "NATO's Future: Beyond Collective Defense," *CRS Report for Congress* 15 September 1995. John Hillen, "Getting NATO Back to Basics," *Strategic Review* 24, no. 2 (1996): 41–50.

30. Berthold Meyer, Harald Müller, and Hans-Joachim Schmidt, "NATO 96: Bündnis im Widerspruch," *Report der Hessischen Stiftung für Friedens- und Konfliktforschung,* 12, no. 3 (1996): 34–36. Zachary Davis, and Mitchell

Reiss, U.S. *Counterproliferation Doctrine: Issues for Congres,* CRS Research Report (Washington, D.C.: GPO 1994).

31. Meyer, Müller, and Schmidt, "NATO 96," 41–45.

32. Henry Kissinger, "No Illusions about the USSR," *The Washington Post,* 22 January 1991.

33. John Hillen, "NATO Back to Basics," 43.

34. Gordon, "Deutsch-französische Partnerschaft," 20–25.

35. Alexander Rahr, and Joachim Krause, *Russia's New Foreign Policy,* Arbeitspapiere zur internationalen Politik der deutschen Gesellschaft für Auswärtige Politik, vol. 91 (Bonn: Europa Union Verlag, 1995), 16.

36. Maxim Shaskenov, "Russian Peacekeeping in the 'Near Abroad'," *Survival* 36, no. 3 (1994): 46–70, and John W. R. Lepingwell, "The Russian Military and Security Policy in the 'Near Abroad'," *Survival* 36, no. 3 (1994): 70–93.

37. See chapter I, section II.

38. Rahr and Krause, "Russia's New Foreign Policy," 9–10.

39. Ibid. 27–30.

40. "Die Ukraine will Sichereitsgarantien," *Süddeutsche Zeitung,* 9 July 1992.

41. "Mitgliedschaft in der NATO polnische Verteidigungsdoktrin," *Frankfurter Allgemeine Zeitung,* 1 August 1992. See also "The Polish Position: Excerpts from the Polish Council's NATO Report," *Transition* 1, no. 23 (1995): 41–43. Bogdan Koszel, "Polens dorniger Weg zur NATO," *Welttrends* 4, no. 10 (1996): 45–58.

42. "Polen in die NATO?," *Die Zeit,* 13 November 1992, 12.

43. "Illiescu: Rumänien sollte der NATO beitreten," *Süddeutsche Zeitung,* 2 November 1992.

44. "Anteil des Verteidigungsetats am Bundeshaushalt," *Die Welt,* 8 February 1993. "Bundesminister der Verteidigung kündigt Überprüfung der Entscheidungen zum 'Bundeswehrplan 94' an," *Stichworte zur Sicherheitspolitik* 16, no. 2 (1993): 46–61.

45. Reprinted in Volker Rühe, "Shaping Euro-Atlantic Policies: A Grand Strategy or a New Era," *Survival* 35, no. 2 (1993): 129–138.

46. Ibid., 135.

47. "Kinkel: Die NATO soll sich Mittel- und Osteuropa stärker öffnen," *Frankfurter Allgemeine Zeitung,* 6 March 1993.

48. "FDP kritisiert Rühe Vorschlag," *dpa Pressebrief,* 14 April 1993.

49. "Rühe befürwortet Erweiterung der NATO nach Osteuropa," *dpa Pressebrief,* 31 March 1993.

50. "Rühe offen für neue NATO-Mitglieder: Plädoyer für eine Strategie des euroatlantischen Raumes," *Frankfurter Allgemeine Zeitung,* 21 May 1993. "NATO als Fundament der Sicherheitsstruktur," Rede von Bundesminister Rühe vom 21.05.1993, *Stichworte zur Sicherheitspolitik* 16, no. 6 (1993): 28–30.

51. "Bundesminister Volker Rühe zu Ergebnissen seiner Gespräche in Moskau," *Stichworte zur Sicherheitspolitik* 16, no. 5 (1993): 31–32. "Deutschland und Rußland wollen militärisch eng zusammenarbeiten," *dpa Pressebrief,* 13 April 1993. "Rühe sieht gute Entwicklung der Beziehungen zu Rußland," *dpa Pressebrief,* 14 April 1993. Stefan Kornelius, "Kleine Schritte zur Erweiterung der NATO, Rühes neue Ostpolitik: Vom Militärbündnis zur Wertegemeinschaft," *Süddeutsche Zeitung,* 19 April 1993.

52. See also Karl-Heinz Kamp, "Die Frage einer 'Osterweiterung der NATO,'" *Interne Studien und Berichte der Konrad-Adenauer-Stiftung* no. 57 (1993): 8–15.

53. "Cheney für NATO-Aufnahme osteuropäischer Länder," *Süddeutsche Zeitung,* 12 December 1992.

54. Ira Louis Strauss, "Letters to the Editor," *New York Times,* 28 June 1993.

55. Jeane Kirkpatrick, "A NATO Umbrella for Eastern Europe," *Washington Post,* 8 June 1993.

56. "Auf dem Weg zu einem Gipfeltreffen der NATO," *NATO Brief* no. 4 (1993): 5.

57. Speech by President Clinton before the North Atlantic Council on 01/10/1994. For an overview of the U.S. debate see also Kober, "Enlargement Debate," 6–9.

58. "NATO Goes Out-of-Area or Out-of-Business," *Keynote Address, XIIth German-American Roundtable, Konrad-Adenauer-Stiftung,* 11 June 1993.

59. Lothar Rühl, "Ein toter Ritter in der Rüstung?," *Die Welt,* 28 August 1993.

60. Ronald D. Asmus, Richard Kugler, and Stephen F. Larrabee, *America and Europe: A New Bargain, A New NATO* (Santa Monica: Rand Cooperation, 1993). Ronald D. Asmus, Robert Blackwill, and Stephen F. Larrabee, "NATO-Expansion. The Next Steps," *Survival* 37, no. 1 (1995): 7–33.

61. "Rede Douglas Hurds vor dem politischen Ausschuß des Carlton Clubs am 30. Juni 1993," *Britische Dokumentation der britischen Botschaft Bonn,* 9 September 1993, 5.

62. *Financial Times,* 23 September 1993.

63. "Hurd: keine baldige Ausdehnung der NATO," *Süddeutsche Zeitung,* 24 September 1993.

64. "Frankreich lieferte trauriges Schauspiel für Europa," *dpa Pressebrief,* 18 December 1992.

65. "Frankreich: Für eine stärkere Zusammenarbeit," *Frankfurter Allgemeine Zeitung,* 7 January 1994.

66. "Ungarn wünscht NATO-Unterstützung," *Süddeutsche Zeitung,* 18 May 1993.

67. Thomas Urban, "Polen strebt weiter in die NATO," *Süddeutsche Zeitung,* 10 July 1993.

68. "Polen fordert Zeitplan für NATO-Beitritt," *Frankfurter Allgemeine Zeitung,* 27 August 1993.

69. "Polens Außenminister drängt auf schnellen NATO-Beitritt," *Die Welt,* 11 September 1993. See also Koszel, "Polens dorniger Weg," 45–58.

70. "Kucan: Slowenien will Mitglied in der NATO werden," *Die Welt,* 30 September 1993.

71. "Jelzin hat nichts gegen Aufnahme Polens in NATO," *Die Welt,* 26 August 1993.

72. "Tschechische Republik/Deutschland/Rühe: NATO darf keine geschlossene Gesellschaft sein," *dpa Pressebrief,* 7 October 1993.

73. "Warschau, Prag und Budapest sehen sich sicherheitspolitisch im Stich gelassen," *Handelsblatt,* 5 October 1993.

74. Kamp, "Osterweiterung," 17.

75. "Jelzin warnt NATO vor Ausweitung nach Osteuropa," *dpa Pressebrief,* 1 October 1993. "Bedenken Jelzins gegen eine Ausweitung der NATO nach Osten," *Frankfurter Allgemeine Zeitung,* 2 October 1993.

76. "Frankreich gegen schnelle Ostausweitung der NATO," *Süddeutsche Zeitung,* 8 October 1993.

77. "Moskau stemmt sich gegen Ost-Öffnung der NATO," *Die Welt,* 6 January 1994. Andreij Kozyrev, "Partnerschaft für ein geeintes, friedliches und demokratisches Europa," *Frankfurter Rundschau,* 8 January 1994.

78. *Interfax,* 3 November 1994.

79. Karl-Heinz Kamp, Zwischen Friedenspartnerschaft und Vollmitgliedschaft: Die Frage einer Osterweiterung der NATO? (Sankt Augustin: Konrad-Adenauer-Stiftung 1995), 25–30.

80. "Die NATO bietet eine 'Partnerschaft für den Frieden' an," *Frankfurter Allgemeine Zeitung,* 22 October 1993.

81. "Erklärung der Staats- und Regierungschefs des Nordatlantikpaktes, abgegeben zum Abschluß ihrer Tagung am 10. / 11. Januar 1994 in Brüssel," *Europa-Archiv* 49, 2 (1994): D 132–134. "Vereinigte Staaten: Langsamere Gangart Rußlands wegen," *Frankfurter Allgemeine Zeitung,* 7 January 1994.

82. Kurt Kister, "Washingtoner Absage an Rühe und Wörner: Die NATO nicht gleich bis an den Bug," *Süddeutsche Zeitung,* 18 December 1993.

83. Stefan Kornelius, "Die NATO verordnet sich eine lange Denkpause," *Süddeutsche Zeitung,* 23 October 1993.

84. "Polen beklagt Absage der NATO an Erweiterung," *Welt am Sonntag,* 24 October 1993. "Die Visegrader Vier auf der Suche nach einer Perspektive," *Der Tagesspiegel,* 3 November 1993. See also Vaclav Havel, "Warum die NATO Prag nicht aussperren darf," *Die Welt,* 27 November 1993. Andrzej Olechowski, "Polen und die Nordatlantische Allianz," *Frankfurter Rundschau,* 3 January 1994. Jiri Dienstbier, "Die NATO-Partnerschaft darf kein Ersatzzuckerl sein," *Frankfurter Rundschau,* 6 January 1994.

85. "NATO soll Sicherheitsvakuum füllen," *Süddeutsche Zeitung,* 17 December 1993.

86. "Litauen beantragt formell die NATO-Mitgliedschaft," *Frankfurter Allgemeine Zeitung,* 5 January 1994.

87. Jelzin warnt NATO vor Ausdehnung," *Neue Westfälische Zeitung,* 6 January 1995.

88. "Rühe raises Polish hopes," *Financial Times,* 19 July 1994.

89. "Für Osteuropa kein Ticket in die NATO," *Die Welt,* 4 December 1993.

90. Strobe Talbott, interview, CNN, 16 July 1994.

91. "NATO-Vollmitgliedschaft der Reformstaaten nur eine Frage der Zeit," *Süddeutsche Zeitung,* 8 July 1994.

92. "Amerika läßt Rühe abblitzen," *Handelsblatt,* 3 October 1994. "NATO Entry Stalled for Visegrad Countries," *Financial Times,* 1 October 1994.

93. See Kamp, *Friedenspartnerschaft,* 16–20.

94. "NATO Rumbles to the East," *U.S. News and World Report,* 21 November 1994, 68.

95. Leo Wieland, "Für Clinton ist die NATO wichtiger als Bosnien," *Frankfurter Allgemeine Zeitung,* 2 December 1994.

96. "Die NATO blickt nach Osten: Leichte Unterschiede in der Sicht von Wörner, Rühe und Kinkel," *Die Welt,* 11 September 1993.

97. Hans-Dietrich Genscher, "Eine Stabilitätsordnung für Europa," *Europäische Sicherheit* 41 (1992): 313. See also Klaus Kinkel, "Deutsche Außenpolitik bleibt Friedenspolitik," *Europäische Sicherheit* 42 (1993): 604.

98. "Wörner: NATO muß sich nach Osten öffnen," *dpa Pressebrief,* 6 October 1993.

99. "Wörner: NATO-Erweiterung nicht entscheidungsreif," *Süddeutsche Zeitung,* 7 October 1993.

100. "Die NATO blickt nach Osten."

101. Herbert Kremp, "Rückkehr zum Realismus," *Die Welt,* 6 October 1993.

102. "Kinkel und Holst: Deutliches Zeichen der NATO für Osten," *dpa Pressebrief,* 14 October 1993.

103. "Kinkel: Schwere Tage für die USA: Gespräche auch über NATO," *dpa Pressebrief,* 5 October 1993.

104. "Rußland soll mitentscheiden," *Frankfurter Allgemeine Zeitung,* 7 October 1993.

105. "Kein Vetorecht," *Frankfurter Allgemeine Zeitung,* 15 November 1993.

106. "Deutsches Doppel: Bei der Ost-Erweiterung des Bündnisses treten Genscheristen als Bremser auf," *Focus,* 11 October 1993, 30.

107. "Kinkel: NATO mit dem ganzen Osten enger vernetzen," *Süddeutsche Zeitung,* 10 November 1993.

108. "Kinkel: NATO muß mehr Sicherheit für alle bieten," *dpa Pressebrief,* 16 December 1993.

109. "Kohl unterstützt Ungarn bei Annäherung an EG und NATO," *Frankfurter Allgemeine Zeitung,* 24 June 1993.

110. "Kohl fordert Signal für EG-Anwärter in Mittel- und Osteuropa," *dpa Pressebrief,* 2 September 1993.

111. "Kohl lehnt größere NATO ab," *Frankfurter Rundschau,* 2 December 1993.

112. "Die Lava läuft noch," *Der Spiegel,* 20 December 1993, 18–20.

113. "Karl Lamers: Suche nach einer neuen Balance," *Deutsches Allgemeines Sonntagsblatt,* 24 September 1993.

114. "Kein Zwist zwischen Kohl und Rühe über NATO-Erweiterung nach Osten," *dpa Pressebrief,* 7 January 1994. "Dregger: Sicherheitsperspektive für die Staaten Ost-Mittel-Europas," *Pressedienst der CDU/CSU-Fraktion im Deutschen Bundestag,* 7 January 1994.

115. "Stoiber für Sicherheitspartnerschaft der EU mit Osteuropa," *dpa Pressebrief,* 10 January 1994.

116. "Erwin Huber: Die NATO muß handlungsfähig bleiben," *Die Welt,* 2 December 1993.

117. "Klose für Erweiterung der NATO ausgesprochen," *dpa Pressebrief,* 25 November 1994.

118. "Verheugen fordert System gemeinsamer Sicherheit für ganz Europa," *dpa Pressebrief,* 6 January 1994.

119. "Vor NATO-Gipfel: Kohl fordert klare Beitrittsperspektiven für Ost-Nachbarn: CDU und SPD einig: Derzeit keine Ost-Erweiterung," *dpa Pressebrief,* 8 January 1994.

120. "Scharping warnt vor schneller NATO-Öffnung nach Osten," *dpa Pressebrief,* 10 January 1994. "SPD-Spitze gegen sofortige NATO-Mitgliedschaft Osteuropas," *dpa Pressebrief,* 10 January 1994.

121. "Scharping korrigiert SPD-Kurs," *Süddeutsche Zeitung,* 7 February 1994.

122. "Scharping in die USA geflogen: SPD steht zum Bündnis," *dpa Pressebrief,* 10 April 1994. "Scharping bei Christopher: Bomben nicht schön, aber nötig," *dpa Pressebrief,* 11 April 1994.

123. Georg Nogradi, "Partnerschaft für den Frieden: Illusionen und Ernüchterung," *Europäische Sicherheit* 43 (1994): 242–243. Krzystof Miszczak, "Die Sicherheits-perspektiven Ostmitteleuropas: Zwischen NATO und Rußland," *Europäische Sicherheit* 43 (1994): 295–298.

124. "Polen schlägt gemeinsame Manöver vor," *Süddeutsche Zeitung,* 26 April 1994. "Gemeinsame Übungen mit Polen beschlossen," *Frankfurter Allgemeine Zeitung,* 13 May 1994.

125. "Geheimpapier: Polens Angebote an die NATO," *Die Welt,* 19 May 1994.

126. "Die Visegrad Gruppe löst sich auf: Die Tschechen meiden die Fußkranken," *Frankfurter Allgemeine Zeitung,* 26 May 1994.

127. "Die NATO und Rußland nach dem Ende des Kalten Krieges," *dpa Pressebrief,* 22 June 1994.

128. "Rühe: Erweiterung der NATO bis zum Jahr 2000," *dpa Pressebrief,* 7 June 1994.

129. "Rühe wirbt in Amerika für strategische Partnerschaft mit Rußland," *Frankfurter Allgemeine Zeitung*, 4 May 1994.

130. "Rühe: Keine Mitgliedschaft Rußlands in NATO und EU," *General Anzeiger.* 5 July 1994.

131. "Rühe: Vorzugskandidaten für die NATO-Mitgliedschaft klar benennen," *dpa Pressebrief*, 27 September 1994.

132. "Rühe sieht Visegrad-Staaten noch vor dem Jahr 2000 in der NATO," *dpa Pressebrief*, 13 September 1994.

133. "Meinungsstreit in der NATO über die Aufnahme neuer Mitglieder," *dpa Pressebrief*, 30 September 1994.

134. "Kinkel warnt vor zu rascher NATO-Erweiterung nach Osteuropa," *dpa Pressebrief*, 7 October 1994.

135. "Genscher verteidigt Kinkels Position," *dpa Pressebrief*, 7 October 1994.

136. "Kohl will sich zum Streit um Ost-Erweiterung nicht äußern," *dpa Pressebrief*, 7 October 1994.

137. "Gegen den Strom," *Der Spiegel*, 1 July 1997, 33.

138. "Der Konflikt in Tschetschenien," *Keesings Archiv der Gegenwart*, 12 January 1995, 39645.

139. Ibid.

140. Karl-Heinz Kamp, "The Folly of Rapid NATO Expansion," *Foreign Policy* no. 98 (1995): 116–129.

141. "Neuer NATO-Generalsekretär legt Schwerpunkt auf Ost-Erweiterung," *dpa Pressebrief*, 17 October 1994. "Claes hebt Rolle der Bundesrepublik in der NATO hervor," *dpa Pressebrief*, 2 May 1995.

142. "Süddeutsche Zeitung: NATO-Botschafter kritisiert USA," *dpa Pressebrief*, 30 November 1994.

143. Karl Feldmayer, "Die NATO ist ratlos," *Frankfurter Allgemeine Zeitung*, 12 January 1994.

144. Rahr and Krause, "Russia's New Foreign Policy," 20–21. Gerhard Wettig, "Entwicklung der russischen Haltung zur NATO," *Europäische Sicherheit* 43 (1994): 235–237.

145. "Schlagabtausch Clinton-Jelzin," *Die Welt*, 6 December 1994.

146. Richard C. Holbrooke, "America: A European Power," *Foreign Affairs* 74, no. 2 (1995): 38–51. Gerhard von Glinski, "Rechnung mit einer russischen Unbekannten: Wie sich Präsident Clintons Europa-Fachmann Richard Holbrooke die Erweiterung der NATO nach Osten vorstellt," *Rheinischer Merkur*, 24 February 1995.

147. "Angebot einer NATO-Mitgliedschaft Rußlands in Clintons Brief an Jelzin wohl nicht enthalten," *Frankfurter Allgemeine Zeitung*, 11 May 1995.

148. "Washington: Kanzleramt ist Inhalt des Briefes an Jelzin bekannt: NATO-Mitgliedschaft Rußlands ist eine theoretische Option," *Frankfurter Allgemeine Zeitung*, 12 May 1995.

149. "Wie weiter zwischen dem Westen und Rußland? Amerika, Europa, Bonn denken nach," *Frankfurter Allgemeine Zeitung,* 12 May 1995.

150. "Seiters: Rußlands Zustimmung um Partnerschaftsabkommen ein erster Schritt auf dem Weg zur besonderen Partnerschaft," *Pressedienst der CDU/CSU Fraktion in Deutschen Bundestag,* 31 May 1995.

151. "Perry zu Gesprächen über die NATO in Warschau," *Frankfurter Allgemeine Zeitung,* 28 May 1995. "Perry: Slowenien ist Vorbild für Mitteleuropa," *Süddeutsche Zeitung,* 19 September 1995. "Perry plädiert für NATO-Beitritt Tschechiens," *Die Welt,* 21 September 1995. "Perry: Ungarn erfüllt bald Kriterien für NATO-Beitritt," *Frankfurter Allgemeine Zeitung,* 21 September 1995. "Perry zuversichtlich," *Frankfurter Allgemeine Zeitung,* 22 September 1995.

152. See Werner Kaltefleiter, "Risiken einer Öffnung der NATO nach Osten," *Europäische Sicherheit* 42 (1993): 609–613.

153. Florian Gerster, "Der Zug nach Westen: Die Einbindung Mittelosteuropas in die Europäische Union und in die Allianz," *Europäische Sicherheit* 43 (1994): 380–382.

154. "Verheugen warnt vor sicherheitspolitischer Spaltung Europas," *dpa Presse Brief,* 30 November 1994.

155. "Lamers: NATO und EU-Mitgliedschaft koppeln," *dpa Presse Brief,* 7 December 1994.

156. "Rühe: EU-Beitritte müssen mit NATO-Erweiterung einhergehen," *dpa Presse Brief,* 22 January 1995. "Rühe: Gleiche Pflichten für EU und NATO-Mitglieder ist Ziel," *dpa Presse Brief,* 27 January 1995.

157. See also "Erklärung von Bundeskanzler Dr. Kohl zum Tschetschenienkonflikt," *Stichworte zur Sicherheitspolitik* 18, no. 2 (1995): 7–21.

158. "Dialog und Kooperation zwischen der NATO und Rußland," *Stichworte zur Sicherheitspolitik* 18 no. 7 (1995): 17–18. "NATO unterbreitet Russland Vorschläge für besondere Zusammenarbeit," *Stichworte zur Sicherheitspolitik* 18, no. 10 (1995): 42.

159. "Kohl und Clinton unterstützen Jelzin und russischen Reformkurs," *dpa Presse Brief,* 9 February 1995. "Kohl rät in Washington zur Geduld bei NATO-Erweiterung," *Frankfurter Allgemeine Zeitung,* 11 February 1995.

160. "Kinkel gegen schnelle Osterweiterung der NATO," *Die Welt,* 6 February 1995. "Die Münchner Konferenz für Sicherheitspolitik," *Stichworte zur Sicherheitspolitik* 18, no. 3 (1995): 6–22.

161. Klaus Kinkel, "Die NATO-Erweiterung: Ein Beitrag zur Gesamteuropäischen Sicherheit," *Internationale Politik* 50, no. 4 (1995): 23.

162. "Das Baltikum und die NATO: Wünsche und Wirklichkeit," *dpa Presse Brief,* 22 August 1995. See also Siegried Thalmeier, "Klare Worte an die baltischen Republiken," *Frankurter Allgemeine Zeitung,* 20 June 1995.

163. "Das darf Herr Rühe nicht tun," *Frankfurter Allgemeine Zeitung,* 24 August 1995.

164. "Hardhöhe: Kein Streit mit Auswärtigem Amt über baltische NATO-Perspektive," *dpa Presse Brief,* 24 August 1995.

165. "Verschärfung der Spannungen zwischen Moskau und der Allianz," *Keesings Archiv der Gegenwart,* 8 September 1995, 40328.

166. Ibid.

167. Klaus Kinkel, "Das hat gewisse Ängste geweckt," interview, *Der Spiegel,* 19 February 1996, 25–26.

168. "Aufstellung der Combined Joint Task Forces beschlossen; Stärkung der europäischen Verteidigunsidentität," *Keesings Archiv der Gegenwart,* 3 June 1996, 41118.

169. "NATO Issue Study on Enlargement of Alliance," (Text of Enlargement Study), *United States Information Service Wireless File,* 29 September 1995. "NATO Rationalizes its Eastward Enlargement," *Transition* 1 no. 23 (1995): 19–26.

170. See, for example, Meyer, Müller and Schmidt, "NATO 1996," 17. "Studie zur Osterweiterung; Vorschlag zur Änderung des KSE-Vertrags," *Keesings Archiv der Gegenwart,* 20 September 1995, 40377–40379.

171. "Die deutsche Handschrift ist deutlich zu erkennen: Bonn legt Wert auf eine parallele Erweiterung der NATO und der Europäischen Union," *Frankfurter Allgemeine Zeitung,* 29 September 1995.

172. "Kinkel: 1996 keine NATO-Osterweiterung," *dpa Presse Brief,* 5 December 1995.

173. "Kohl fordert vollständige Integration Rußlands in Europa," *dpa Presse Brief,* 28 September 1995.

174. "Wirre Angst," *Der Spiegel,* 21 August 1995, 32–33.

175. Christian Hacke, "Die Haltung der Bundesrepublik Deutschland zur NATO-Osterweiterung," in *Ostmitteleuropa, Russland und die Osterweiterung der NATO: Perzeptionen und Strategien im Spannungsfeld nationaler und europäischer Sicherheit,* ed. August Pradetto (Opladen: Westdeutscher Verlag, 1997), 242.

176. "Gipfeltreffen in Helsinki," 41898. Andreas Wenger, and Jeronim Perovic, "Rußlands Sicherheitspolitik vor der Neubestimmung?: Die Herausforderung der NATO-Osterweiterung," *Osteuropa* 48 (1998): 452.

177. "Studie zur Osterweiterung," 40379.

178. Anderson, "Außenpolitik ohne Konzept," 20. "Mit Volldampf in Richtung Osten," 35–36. Hacke, "Haltung," 240. Egon Bahr, and Günter Gaus, "Die Geschichte ist anders gegangen: Vom Wandel durch Annäherung zur Osterweiterung aus Hilflosigkeit," *Blätter für deutsche und internationale Politik* 42 (1997): 696.

179. "Kohls Mythos verblaßt," *Focus,* 18 March 1996, 52–54. "Erotisches Verhältnis," *Focus,* 23 September 1996, 104–105. "Harter Kinkel gewünscht," *Der Spiegel,* 17 March 1997, 15.

180. Egon Bahr, "Es wäre ein riesiger Fehler," interview, *Die Zeit,* 2 May 1997, 4.

181. "Brett vor dem Kopf," *Focus,* 2 December 1996, 41–42.

182. "Kehrwende der SPD," *Focus,* 2 June 1997, 36.

183. "Tagung der Nordatlantischen Versammlung: Frühjahrstagung der Außen-minister und des NACC," *Keesings Archiv der Gegenwart,* 31 May 1995, 40039.

184. Karsten Voigt, "Die Osterweiterung der NATO," *Aus Politik und Zeitgeschichte* 46, no. B5 (1996): 22.

185. "Brett vor dem Kopf," 42.

186. Ludger Vollmer, *Die Grünen und die Außenpolitik: Ein schwieriges Verhältnis: Eine Ideen-, Programm und Ereignisgeschichte grüner Außenpolitik* (Münster: Westfälisches Dampfboot, 1998), 540–544. Gunda Röstel, "NATO-Oster-weiterung mitgestalten," interview, *Focus,* 10 March 1997, 71. "NATO Os-terweiterung bleibt," *Focus,* 5 August 1997, 35. "Wirre Angst," 32.

187. "Diskussion um Nachfolge-Mission in Bosnien und Osterweiterung," *Keesings Archiv der Gegenwart,* 25 September 1996, 41431.

188. "Clinton zur Führungsrolle der USA in der Welt und zur Erweiterung der NATO," *Keesings Archiv der Gegenwart,* 22 October 1996, 41531–41532.

189. "NATO: Herbstagung der Außenminister," *Keesings Archiv der Gegenwart,* 10 December 1996, 41641.

190. "Diskussion um Nachfolge Mission und Osterweiterung," 41431.

191. "Russische Diskussionen über die NATO-Osterweiterung: Solana in Moskau," *Keesings Archiv der Gegenwart,* 20 January 1997, 41734.

192. "Stärkung der europäischen Verteidigungsidentität," 41118.

193. "Russische Diskussionen," 41735.

194. Ibid.

195. "Gipfeltreffen in Helsinki," *Keesings Archiv der Gegenwart,* 20 March 1997, 41898- 41900.

196. Ibid.

197. Ibid.

198. Ibid., 41903.

199. "Schach dem Bündnis: Rußland setzt bei der NATO-Osterweiterung ein lukratives Tauschgeschäft durch, und die Deutschen helfen dabei," *Focus,* 17 May 1997, 60–62. "Mit schlechtem Gewissen," *Der Spiegel,* 3 March 1997, 22–24.

200. "Kohl: Moskau wird politisch aufgewertet," *Süddeutsche Zeitung,* 18 April 1997.

201. "Solana bleibt hart," *Der Spiegel,* 27 January 1997, 16.

202. "Diskussion um Nachfolge-Mission und Osterweiterung," 41431.

203. "Deutschland als Bremser auf dem Weg nach Europa," *Der Spiegel,* 5 May 1997, 143.

204. "Über Ost-Erweiterung der NATO völlig einig," *Süddeutsche Zeitung,* 18 February 1997.

205. "Mit schlechtem Gewissen," 22–24.

206. "Grundakte über die Beziehungen Rußlands zur NATO unterzeichnet," *Keesings Archiv der Gegenwart,* 27 May 1997, 42056.

207. "Mit schlechtem Gewissen," 22–24.

208. Rudolf Seiters, "Rußland muß Teil der Sicherheitsarchitektur sein," interview, *Süddeutsche Zeitung,* 29 March 1997.

209. Henry A. Kissinger, "The Dilution of NATO," *Washington Post,* 8 June 1997.

210. Wenger and Perovic, "Neubestimmung," 453.

211. Aleksandr Lebed, "Old Enemies, New Problems," *Petersburg Times,* 2–8 June 1997.

212. "Frühjahrstreffen der Außenminister: EAPC Nachfolgeorganisation des NACC," *Keesings Archiv der Gegenwart,* 30 May 1997, 42072.

213. "NATO-Gipfelkonferenz in Madrid," *Keesings Archiv der Gegenwart,* 9 July 1997, 42175.

214. "Drei dürfen mit," *Focus,* 7 July 1997, 208–212. "Geduckt in der Furche," *Der Spiegel,* 30 June 1997, 38. *NATO-Gipfelkonferenz,* 42164.

215. "Drei dürfen mit," 208–212. "Dafür und nicht dagegen," *Der Spiegel,* 16 June 1997, 16.

VII: Power Structure over Ideology

1. "Europa mit links," *Focus,* 14 December 1998, 22.

2. "Im Teufelskreis der Gewalt," *Der Spiegel,* 15 January 1999, 136.

3. "Gerhard Schröder zum Bundeskanzler gewählt," *Bulletin des Presse- und Informationsamtes der Bundesregierung,* 29 October 1998, 877–880.

4. Karl-Rudolf Korte, "Unbefangen und gelassen: Über die außenpolitische Normalität der Berliner Republik," *Internationale Politik* 53, no. 12 (1998): 4.

5. Christian Hacke, "Die nationalen Interessen der Bundesrepublik Deutschland an der Schwelle zum 21. Jahrhundert," *Aussenpolitik* 49, no. 2 (1998): 6.

6. Gregor Schöllgen, "Die Berliner Republik als internationale Akteur: Gibt es noch eine deutsche Interessenpolitik," *Aussenpolitik* 49, no. 2 (1998): 33–37.

7. Egon Bahr, "Die 'Normalisierung' der deutschen Aussenpolitik: Mündige Partnerschaft statt bequemer Vormundschaft," *Internationale Politik* 54, no. 1 (1999): 41–42.

8. Robert B. Zoellick, "Abschied von der Selbstbeschränkung: Deutsche Aussenpolitik aus Sicht der USA," *Internationale Politik* 53, no. 12 (1998): 21–26.

9. Anderson, "Aussenpolitik ohne Konzept," 20.

10. Werner Weidenfeld, "Fragen an die Aussenpolitik der neuen Regierung," *Internationale Politik* 54, no. 1 (1999): 1–2.

11. Korte, "Unbefangen und gelassen," 10.

12. Jacqueline Hénard, "Abschied vom Ersten Weltkrieg," *Die Zeit,* 5 November 1998, 3.

13. Korte, "Unbefangen und gelassen," 7.

14. "Total Normal?" *Der Spiegel,* 30 November 1999, 40. "Martin Walsers Dankrede beim Empfang des Friedenspreises des deutschen Buchhandels in der Frankfurter Paulskirche am 11.10.1998 (Auszüge)," *Blätter für deutsche und internationale Politik* 44 (1999):118–119.

15. Klaus von Dohnanyi, "Eine Friedensrede: Martin Walsers notwendige Klage," *Frankfurter Allgemeine Zeitung,* 14 November 1998.

16. Bahr, "Normalisierung der deutschen Aussenpolitik," 41. "Ignaz Bubis' Rede bei der Berliner Gedenkfeier zum 9. November, (Auszüge)," *Blätter für deutsche und internationale Politik* 44 (1999): 119–120. Ignatz Bubis, "Moral verjährt nicht: Ignatz Bubis über die Auschwitz Debatte und seine Auseinandersetzung mit Martin Walser und Klaus von Dohnanyi," interview, *Der Spiegel,* 30 November 1998, 52.

17. Bahr, "Normalisierung der deutschen Aussenpolitik," 41–43.

18. Korte, "Unbefangen und gelassen," 5.

19. See chapter V, section VI.

20. Sozialdemokratische Aussenpolitik im Übergang zum 21. Jahrhundert: Diskussionspapier der Schwerpunktkommission Außen- und Sicherheitspolitik für den Kongreß am 18.6.1997 in Bonn," in Sozialdemokratische Partei Deutschlands: Programmatisches [database online] (Bonn: Bundesvorstand der SPD, 1999 [cited 10 August 1999]); available from http://www.spd.de/aktuell/aussen.htm.

21. Zbigniew Brzesinski, *Die einzige Weltmacht: Amerikas Strategie der Vorherrschaft* (Weinheim and Berlin: Beltz/Quadriga, 1997).

22. Bahr, "Die Normalisierung der deutschen Aussenpolitik," 46–48.

23. Richard Herzinger, "Feindbild Rambo," *Die Zeit,* 20 May 1999, 4.

24. Brzesinksi, *Die einzige Weltmacht,* 109, 114.

25. Rudolf Augstein, "Arroganz der Macht," *Der Spiegel,* 3 May 1999, 24.

26. "Sozialdemokratische Aussenpolitik im Übergang zum 21. Jahrhundert."

27. "Deutsch-französische Leitlinien zur GASP vom 27.2.1996," 118.

28. See chapter 4, section 7.

29. "Leitantrag zur Außen-, Sicherheits- und Entwicklungspolitik: Beschlüsse des Parteitages von Hannover 2.–4. Dezember 1997," in Sozialdemokratische Partei Deutschlands: Programmatisches [database online] (Bonn, Bundesvorstand der SPD, 1999 [cited 10 August 1999]); available from http://www.spd.de/archiv/events/hannover97/aussen–1.htm.

30. Wolfgang Rudzio, *Das politische System der Bundesrepublik Deutschland,* 4th ed., (Opladen: Leske + Budrich, 1996), 153–154.

31. Vollmer, *Die Grünen und die Aussenpolitik,* 558–562.

32. "Koalitionsvereinbarung zwischen der Sozialdemokratischen Partei Deutschlands und Bündnis 90/Die Grünen, unterzeichnet am 20.10.1998 in Bonn, (Auszüge)," *Internationale Politik* 53, no. 12 (1998): 71–76.

33. Ibid.

34. "Weitere Kämpfe im Kosovo," *Keesings Archiv der Gegenwart,* 23 September 1998, 43070.

35. Ibid., 43072.

36. "Weitere Kämpfe im Kosovo: NATO droht mit Einsatz," *Keesings Archiv der Gegenwart,* 16 October 1998, 43115.

37. Ibid.

38. "Aus freier Überzeugung," *Der Spiegel,* 19 April 1999.

39. "Aus freier Überzeugung," 26–30. Gunter Hofmann, "Wie Deutschland in den Krieg geriet," *Die Zeit,* 12 May 1999, 18.

40. Ibid. 18.

41. "Aus freier Überzeugung," 26–27.

42. "Bundestag billigt deutsche Beteiligung bei möglichem NATO-Einsatz," *Keesings Archiv der Gegenwart,* 27 October 1998, 43137–43139. "248. Sitzung vom 16.10.1998," *Stenographische Berichte des Deutschen Bundestages, 12. Wahlperiode,* 193 (1998): 23132–23135.

43. "248. Sitzung vom 16.10.1998," 23147–23150, 23135–23138.

44. Ibid., 23151.

45. Ibid., 23166- 23168.

46. Ibid., 23151.

47. "Regierungserklärung von Bundeskanzler Gerhard Schröder, abgegeben am 10.11.1998 vor dem Deutschen Bundestag in Bonn (Auszüge)," *Internationale Politik* 53, no. 12 (1998): 87.

48. Hofmann, "Wie Deutschland in den Krieg geriet," 18.

49. Eckart Lohse, "Fischers Positionen wären Adenauer Grund zur Freude," *Frankfurter Allgemeine Zeitung,* 24 October 1998.

50. Joschka Fischer, "Die Selbstbeschränkung der Macht muß Fortbestehen," *Frankfurter Allgemeine Zeitung,* 8 October 1998.

51. Joschka Fischer, "Wir wollen keine Soli tanzen," interview, *Der Spiegel,* 23 November 1999, 86.

52. Joschka Fischer, "Ein Realo sieht die Welt," interview, *Die Zeit,* 12 November 1998, 2.

53. "Weltpolitik in Bielefeld," *Der Spiegel,* 10 May 1999, 24.

54. "Hände von der Hosennaht," 23. "Fischer will auf die Präsemz der Amerikaner in Europa nicht verzichten," *Frankfurter Allgemeine Zeitung,* 9 December 1998.

55. "Fischer will auf die Präsenz der Amerikaner nicht verzichten."

56. "Kernwaffen bleiben für die NATO wichtig," *Frankfurter Allgemeine Zeitung,* 4 December 1998.

57. Constanze Stelzenmüller, "Kein Sonderweg," *Die Zeit,* 26 November 1998, 5.

58. Ibid.

59. "Fischers Störfeuer," *Focus,* 30 November 1998, 100.

60. Ibid.

61. Rudolf Scharping, "Am Ende zählt nur Realismus: Verteidigungsminister Scharping warnt vor einer Provokation der NATO durch nationale Alleingänge," interview, *Focus,* 30 November 1998, 102.

62. "Deutschland NATO Fischer," *RTRG0943,* 28 January 1999.

63. Rudolf Augstein, "Madeleines Krieg," Der Spiegel, 31 May 1999, 27.

64. Hofmann, "Wie Deutschland in den Krieg geriet," 17.

65. Joschka Fischer, "Serbien gehört zu Europa," Interview *Die Zeit,* 15 April 1999, 3.

66. "Ich darf nicht wackeln," *Der Spiegel,* 3 May 1999, 27.

67. "Aus freier Überzeugung."

68. "Rede des Bundeskanzlers vor dem deutschen Bundestag vom 6. Mai 1999," *Bulletin des Presse- und Informationsamt der Bundesregierung,* 6 May 1999, 249.

69. "Serbien gehört zu Europa," 3.

70. Albright deutet eine Änderung der Nato-Strategie an," *Süddeutsche Zeitung,* 6 April 1999. "Fertiger Plan für den Bodenkrieg," *Der Spiegel,* 26 April 1999, 153.

71. "Ich darf nicht wackeln," 23. "Da bröckelt was," *Der Spiegel,* 3 May 1999, 22. Christoph Dieckmann, "Friedenskind, hilflos mittendrin," *Die Zeit,* 29 April 1999, 9.

72. "Ihr kommt nie wieder," *Der Spiegel,* 12 April 1999, 176.

73. "Ich darf nicht wackeln," 27.

74. Rudolf Scharping, "Wir kommen unserem Ziel näher," interview, *Der Spiegel,* 26 April 1999, 26.

75. Hofmann, "Wie Deutschland in den Krieg geriet," 17

76. Ibid.

77. "Da bröckelt etwas," 25.

78. "Kritik am Kosovo-Einsatz wächst: Bei SPD und Grünen mehren sich die ablehnenden Stimmen," *Süddeutsche Zeitung,* 6 April 1999.

79. "Ich darf nicht wackeln," 27–28.

80. "SPD-Parteitag: Aufstand der Linken zum Kosovo-Konflikt gescheitert," *Die Welt,* 13 April 1999.

81. "Heftiger Hauskrach bei den Grünen," *Die Welt,* 13 April 1999.

82. "Kritik am Kosovo-Einsatz wächst." "Ich darf nicht wackeln," 23.

83. "Grüne zwischen Koalitionsräson und Kriegsverweigerung," *Der Focus,* 19 April 1999, 22 –23.

84. "D-Day in Bielefeld," *Der Spiegel,* 17 May 1999, 28–29. "Mann im Strickrock," *Der Spiegel,* 17 May 1999, 30.

85. "Deutschland Kosovo," *AP0068,* 24 January 1999.
    AP 0068

86. Deutschland Bundestag Kosovo," *RTRG6782,* 24 February 1999. Gerhard Schröder, "Ich bin kein Kriegskanzler: Bundeskanzler Gerhard Schröder über Weiterungen im Krieg gegen Milosevic, die Rolle der Deutschen

beim Nato-Einsatz und den Sonderparteitag der SPD," interview, *Der Spiegel*, 12 April 1999, 32.

87. "Keimzelle eines Großalbanien," *Der Spiegel*, 21 June 1999, 157.

88. Michael Thumann, "Der Bär grollt," Die Zeit, 31 March 1999, 4.

89. Roy A., Medwedjew, "Ein hartes Njet zur NATO," *Die Zeit*, 20 May 1999, 11.

90. Aleksandr Lebed, "Gefüttert, gestreichelt, geschlagen: General Aleksandr Lebed über Rußlands Verhältnis zu den Serben und Amerikanern," interview, *Der Spiegel*, 5 April 1999, 160.

91. Medwedjew, "Ein hartes Njet," 11.

92. "Moskau will Beziehungen zum Westen nicht gefährden," *Frankfurter Allgemeine Zeitung*, 29 March 1999.

93. "Ein Fall für die Feuerwehr," *Der Spiegel*, 17 May 1999, 262.

94. Viktor Tschernomyrdin, "Nah am Abgrund," *Die Zeit*, 2 June 1999, 7.

95. "Jelzin warnt die NATO vor dem Einsatz von Bodentruppen im Kosovo," *Frankfurter Allgemeine Zeitung*, 10 April 1999.

96. "Europa mit links," 20.

97. Ibid., 22.

98. "Der neue Stil," *Focus*, 16 November 1998, 26.

99. "Hände von der Hosennaht," 23. Korte, *Unbefangen und gelassen*, 6.

100. "Europa mit links," 20.

101. Werner A. Perger, "Wir unbefangenen," *Die Zeit*, 12 November 1998, 7.

102. "Der neue Stil," 22.

103. *Koalitionsvereinbarung zwischen der Sozialdemokratischen Partei Deutschlands und Bündnis 90/Die Grünen*, 71–73. "Ansprache von Bundeskanzler Gerhard Schröder beim Jahresempfang für das diplomatische Korps in Bonn, (Auszüge)," *Internationale Politik* 53, no. 12 (1998): 98.

104. "Erklärung der Bundesregierung: Vorschau auf den europäischen Rat in Wien am 11./12.12.1998 und Ausblick auf die deutsche Präsidentschaft in der ersten Jahreshälfte 1999," *Bulletin des Presse- und Informationsamtes der Bundesregierung*, 14 December 1998, 965–966.

105. Ibid.

106. *Koalitionsvereinbarung zwischen der Sozialdemokratischen Partei Deutschlands und Bündnis 90/Die Grünen*, 71–73.

107. "Fischer stellt die Agenda 2000 an die erste Stelle," *Frankfurter Allgemeine Zeitung*, 6 January 1999.

108. "Schröder fordert den erfolgreichen Abschluß der Agenda 2000," *Frankfurter Allgemeine Zeitung*, 24 March 1999.

109. "In der EU erhebliche Meinungsverschiedenheiten in fast allen Kernfragen," *Frankfurter Allgemeine Zeitung*, 27 February 1999.

110. "Teure Wahrheit," *Der Spiegel*, 22 February 1999, 180. "D EU Agenda 2000," *AFP0134*, 26 February 1999." "EU-Gipfel, Europa," *ADN0464*, 26 February 1999. "Mit mir nicht," *Der Spiegel*, 8 March 1999, 34. Peter Non-

nemacher, "Blair spricht sich für Prodi aus," *Frankfurter Allgemeine Zeitung*, 23 March 1999.

111. "Deutschland Europa Schröder Analyse," *RTRG8134*, 10 March 1999. "Bundesregierung rückt von umstrittener Kofinanzierung ab," *Frankfurter Allgemeine Zeitung*, 5 March 1999. Jürgen R. Grote, "Regionalpolitik," in *Die europäische Union*, ed. Dieter Nohlen, vol. 5 of *Lexikon der Politik*. (München: C.H. Beck, 1996), 236.

112. "Ernstfall für Schröder," *Der Spiegel*, 29 March 1999, 29. "EU–Gipfel im Agrarstreit festgefahren," *Die Welt*, 26 March 1999.

113. "EU–Gipfel im Agrarstreit festgefahren. Michael Bergius, "EU–Mitglieder loben Berliner Kompromiß," *Frankfurter Rundschau*, 27 March 1999.

114. Knut Pries, "Erfolg für Gerhard Schröder," *Frankfurter Rundschau*, 27 March 1999.

115. "EU-Kompromiß hält nicht bis 2006," *Die Welt*, 3 April 1999.

116. "Regierung. Viele Ideen, aber kein Konzept," *Der Spiegel*, 31 May 1999, 28–30.

117. "Ernstfall für Schröder," 30.

118. "Lust am Widerstand," *Der Spiegel*, 16 November 1998, 29–31.

119. "Regierungserklärung des Bundeskanzlers: Weil wir Deutschlands Kraft vertrauen," *Bulletin des Presse- und Informationsamtes der Bundesregierung*, 11 November 1998. 913.

120. "Lafontaines Handschrift," *Der Spiegel*, 18 January 1999, 17. "Eine Katze in der Hölle," *Der Spiegel*, 7 December 1998, 177.

121. "Die große Versuchung," *Focus*, 7 December 1998, 96.

122. "Eine Katze in der Hölle," 176–177.

123. "Oskar auf Werbetour," *Der Spiegel*, 16 November 1998, 26.

124. "Lust am Widerstand," 29–31.

125. "Der Weg ist falsch," *Der Spiegel*, 7 December 1998, 32–33. Thomas Hanke, and Mario Müller, "Vorsorgliche Belagerung," *Die Zeit*, 19 November 1998, 25–26.

126. "Regierungserklärung des Bundeskanzlers: Weil wir Deutschlands Kraft vertrauen," 913.

127. "D Regierung SPD," *AFP* 12 March 1999.

128. "D Regierung EU," *AFP0180*, 15 March 1999.

129. "Sicherheitspolitik der EU stärken, Brüssel 26.1.99," *Newsticker der Bundesregierung*, 27 January 1999.

130. "Die gemeinsame Aussenpolitik der europäischen Union, Rede Staatsminister/AA Günter Verheugen beim Zentrum für europäische Integrationsforschung, Bonn, 21.1.1999," in *Reden 1999* [database online] (Bonn: Auswärtiges Amt der Bundesrepublik Deutschland, 1999 [cited 20 August 1999]); available from http://www.auswaertiges-amt.de/6_archiv/index.htm.

131. "Perspektiven deutscher Außen- und Sicherheitspolitik: Vortrag von Staatssekretär/AA Wolfgang Ischinger vor dem Forum der Chefredakteure zur Sicherheitspolitik der Bundesakademie für Sicherheitspolitik, Bad Neuenahr 27.1.1999, " in Reden 1999 [database online] (Bonn: Auswärtiges Amt der Bundesrepublik Deutschland, 1999 [cited 20 August 1999]); available from http://www.auswaertiges-amt.de/6_archiv/index.htm.

132. Wolfgang Proissl, "Kein Plan, Keine Waffen: In der Außen- und Sicherheitspolitik wird Europa noch lange auf die Unterstützung der USA angewiesen sein," Die Zeit, 27 May 1999, 6.

133. David J. Louscer, Alethia H. Cook, and Victoria Barto, "The Emerging Competitive Position of US-Defence Firms in the International Market," Defense Analysis 14, no. 2 (1998): 131–132. Helmut Schmidt, "Die Nato gehört nicht Amerika," Die Zeit, 22 April 1999, 10–11.

134. "Neu Labour hat sich entschlossen, die europäischen Partner einmal angenehm zu überraschen," Frankfurter Allgemeine Zeitung, 22 October 1998.

135. "Speaking Notes of the Right Honourable George Robertson MP, Secretary of State for Defence for the Informal Conference of Defence Ministers of the EU in Vienna, 3–4 November 1998," European Foreign Affairs Review 4, no. 1 (1999): 121–123.

136. "Frankreichs kurzer Flirt mit Großbritannien," Frankfurter Allgemeine Zeitung, 23 December 1998.

137. Ibid. 94., "Ein Treffen der besonderen Art," Frankfurter Allgemeine Zeitung, 18 December 1998.

138. "Erneute militärische Aktion gegen den Irak: Die Operation Desert Fox," Keesings Archiv der Gegenwart, 19 December 1998, 43236. Ein Treffen der besonderen Art.

139. Ein Treffen der besonderen Art.

140. Ein Treffen der besonderen Art.

141. "Irak, Konflikt ist nur mit friedlichen Mitteln zu lösen," Pressemitteilung der Bundestagsfraktion Bündnis 90/ Die Grünen, 17 December.

142. "Angriffe auf den Irak einstellen," Pressemitteilung des Bundesvorstandes Bündnis 90/Die Grünen, 17 December 1998.

143. Wallander, Mortal Friend, Best Enemies, 139, 143.

144. Ibid., 135.

145. Fischer, "Ein Realo sieht die Welt," 2.

146. "Erklärung Fischers zum 50. Jahrestag der Proklamation der Allgemeinen Erklöärung der Menschenrechte," Newsticker der Bundesregierung, 9 December 1998.

147. Joschka Fischer, "Interview des Bundesministers des Auswärtigen Joschka Fischer mit der Süddeutschen Zeitung," Süddeutsche Zeitung, 27 November 1998.

148. "Fünfzig Jahre Menschenrechte, Bonn/New York," *Newsticker der Bundesregierung,* 11 December 1998.

149. "Hände von der Hosennaht," 22–24. "Bonn weist Kritik aus Peking zurück, Bonn/Peking 5.12.1998," *Newsticker der Bundesregierung,* 5 December 1998.

150. "Jetzt mache ich es gut," *Der Spiegel,* 19 July 1999, 22–25.

151. Fischer kritisiert Vorgehen gegen chinesische Dissidenten," *Frankfurter Allgemeine Zeitung,* 24 March 1999.

Bibliography

"Abkommen zwischen den Alliierten Hohen Kommissaren und dem Deutschen Bundeskanzler auf dem Petersberg am 22. November 1949, Niederschrift vom 23. November 1949." In *Aussenpolitik der Bundesrepublik Deutschland: Dokumente von 1949 bis 1994,* ed. Auswärtiges Amt. Cologne: Verlag Wissenschaft und Politik, 1995, 175–177.

Adenauer, Konrad. "Gründe für und Wider den Beitritt zum Europarat." *Europa-Archiv* 5 (1950): 3127–3129.

"Adenauers erste Regierungserklärung vor dem Deutschen Bundestag, 20. September 1949." In *Aussenpolitik der Bundesrepublik DeutschlandDokumente von 1949–1994,* ed. Auswärtiges Amt. Cologne: Verlag Wissenschaft und Politik, 1995, 170–175.

"Address by Secretary Byrnes, Stuttgart, 6 September 1946." In *Documents on Germany, 1944–1985,* ed. Department of State. Washington, D.C.: GPO, 1986, 94–96.

"Aide-mémoire der Bundesregierung über die deutsch-französischen Beziehungen, 7. November 1949." In *Die Konstituierung der Bundesrepublik Deutschland und der Deutschen Demokratischen Republik: 7. September bis 31. Dezember 1949,* ed. Hanns Küsters. Vol. 2 of *Dokumente zur Deutschlandpolitik: Series II.* Munich: Oldenbourg, 1996, 237–238.

"Albright deutet eine Änderung der Nato-Strategie an." *Süddeutsche Zeitung,* 6 April 1999.

"Alles härter." *Der Spiegel,* 26 July 1993.

"Allzu forsch." *Der Spiegel,* 2 August 1993.

"Amerika läßt Rühe abblitzen." *Handelsblatt,* 3 October 1994.

Anchordoguy, Marie. "Mastering the Market: Japanese Government Targeting of the Computer Industry." *International Organization* 42, no. 3 (1988): 509–543.

"An der DM festhalten, bis der ECU wirklich stabil ist." *Sozialdemokratischer Pressedienst Wirtschaft,* 2 January 1992.

Anderson, David. "Aussenpolitik ohne Konzept." Interview, *Focus,* 3 April 1995.

"An der Weichsel willkommen." *Rheinischer Merkur,* 5 August 1994.

"Angebot einer NATO-Mitgliedschaft Rußlands in Clintons Brief an Jelzin wohl nicht enthalten." *Frankfurter Allgemeine Zeitung,* 11 May 1995.

"Angriffe auf den Irak einstellen." *Pressemiteilung des Bundesvorstandes Bündnis 90/Die Grünen,* 17 December 1998.

"Angst vorm Koloß." *Der Spiegel,* 9 August 1993.

"Ansprache von Bundeskanzler Gerhard Schröder beim Jahresempfang für das diplomatische Korps in Bonn, (Auszüge):" *Internationale Politik* 53, no. 12 (1998): 98.

"Anteil des Verteidigungsetats am Bundeshaushalt." *Die Welt,* 8 February 1993.

"Arbeitskosten: stechender Lorbeer." *Informationsdienst des Instituts der deutschen Wirtschaft* 19, no. 25 (1994).

"Arbeitszeit international." *Informationsdienst des Instituts der deutschen Wirtschaft* 19, no.30 (1994).

Arch, Robert J. and Kenneth Waltz, ed., *The Use of Force: Military Power and International Politics.* Lanham: University Press of America, 1993.

Arnold, Hans. "Deutschlands Rolle in der UNO." *Aus Politik und Zeitgeschichte* 44, no. B42 (1994): 27–34.

"Artikel des Europakorrespondenten der amerikanischen Zeitung Cleveland über das Interview mit dem Bundeskanzler Adenauer, 4 December 1949." In *Die Konstituierung der Bundesrepublik Deutschland und der Deutschen Demokratischen Republik: 7. September bis 31.Dezember 1949,* ed. Hanns Küsters.Vol. 2 of *Dokumente zur Deutschlandpolitik: Series II.* Munich: Oldenbourg, 1996. 300–303.

"Artikel des Journalisten Williams von der amerikanischen Zeitung Baltimore Sun über Äußerungen des Bundeskanzlers Adenauer, 7 November 1949." In *Die Konstituierung der Bundesrepublik Deutschland und der Deutschen Demokratischen Republik: 7. September bis 31.Dezember 1949,* ed. Hanns Küsters.Vol. 2 of *Dokumente zur Deutschlandpolitik: Series II.* Munich: Oldenbourg 1996, 238–240.

"Artikel Dreißig der Gemeinsamen Europäischen Akte." *Bulletin der Europäischen Gemeinschaften* 19, no. 2 (1986): 129–130.

Asmus, Ronald D., Richard Kugler, and Stephen F. Larrabee. *America and Europe: A New Bargain, A New NATO.* Santa Monica: Rand Cooperation, 1993.

————. Blackwill, Robert D., and Stephen F. Larrabee. "Can NATO Survive?." *The Washington Quarterly* 19, no. 2 (1996): 79–101.

————. "Deutschland im Übergang: Nationales Selbstvertrauen und internationale Zurückhaltung." *Europa-Archiv* 47, 1 (1992): 199–211.

————. Blackwill, Robert, and Stephen F. Larrabee, "NATO-Expansion. The Next Steps." *Survival,* 37, no. 1 (1995): 7–33.

"Auf dem Programm: Atomwaffen und SoldatenUnterkünfte. BundesverteidigungsministerRühe besucht die Ukraine und Kasachstan—Kiew hofft auf Bonn." *General-Anzeiger,* 16 August 1993.

"Auf dem Weg zu einem Gipfeltreffen der NATO." *NATO Brief* no. 4 (1993): 3–6.

"Aufruf der Atlantik-Brücke e.V." In *Deutschland und der Irak-Konflikt: Internationale Sicherheitsverantwortung Deutschlands und Europa nach der deutschen Vereinigung.* Karl Kaiser and Klaus Becher. Bonn: Europa-Union-Verlag,1992, 127–128.

"Aufstellung der Combined Joint Task Forces beschlossen; Stärkung der europäischen Verteidigunsidentität." *Keesings Archiv der Gegenwart*, 3 June 1996.

Augstein, Rudolf. "Abschied von der Mark?." *Der Spiegel*, 2 December 1991.

———. "Arroganz der Macht." *Der Spiegel*, 3 May 1999.

———. "Herzog: Bitte unterschätzen Sie uns nicht." *Der Spiegel*, 4 August 1997.

———. "Madeleines Krieg," *Der Spiegel*, 31 May 1999.

———. "Wer zahlt für Europa?" *Der Spiegel*, 9 August 1990.

"Aus freier Überzeugung." *Der Spiegel*, 19 April 1999.

Auswärtiges Amt, ed. *Europa: Dokumente zur Frage der europäischen Einigung*. Bonn: Auswärtiges Amt, 1953.

"Außen- und europapolitische Erklärung Kohls." *Keesings Archiv der Gegenwart*, 27 June 1997.

Attali, Jacques. *Chronique des années 1988–1991*. Vol. 3 of *Verbatim*. Paris: Fayard, 1995.

Bahr, Egon. *Deutsche Interessen: Streitschrift zu Macht, Sicherheit und Aussenpolitik*. Munich: Blessing, 1998.

———, and Günter Gaus. "Die Geschichte ist anders gegangen:Vom Wandel durch Annäherung zur Osterweiterungaus Hilflosigkeit." *Blätter für deutsche und internationale Politik* 42 (1997): 696703.

———. "Die 'Normalisierung' der deutschen Aussenpolitik: Mündige Partnerschaft statt bequemer Vormundschaft," *Internationale Politik* 54, no. 1 (1999): 41–52.

———. "Es wäre ein riesiger Fehler." Interview, *Die Zeit*, 2 May 1997.

Baker, James A. III. "Ein neues Europa, ein neuer Atlantizismus: Die neue Architektur für eine neue Ära, Rede vor dem Presseclub in Berlin am 12. Dezember 1989." *Europa-Archiv* 45, 2 (1990): D79–81.

———. *The Politics of Diplomacy*. New York: G. P. Putnam & Sons, 1995.

Baldwin, David A. "Power Analysis and World Politics: New Trends Versus old Tendencies." *World Politics* 31 (1978/79): 161–194.

"Balsam für eine Leiche." *Der Spiegel*, 18 October 1993.

"Baltische Staaten in die EU? Aussenminister Kinkel will Verhandlungen vorantreiben." *Frankfurter Rundschau*, 10 March 94.

Baring, Arnulf. *Im Anfang war Adenauer: Die Entstehung der Kanzlerdemokratie*. Munich: DTV, 1982.

———. *Machtwechsel: Die Ära Brandt-Scheel*. Stuttgart: Deutsche Verlagsanstalt, 1982.

"Bayern legt europapolitische Position für Maastricht II fest." *Bulletin des Freisstaates Bayern*, 7 April 1995.

"Bedenken Jelzins gegen eine Ausweitung der NATO nach Osten." *Frankfurter Allgemeine Zeitung*, 2 October 1993.

"Beifall für deutsche Soldaten auf dem Champs-Elysées; Mitterrand: Ein wichtiger Schritt in die Zukunft." *Süddeutsche Zeitung*, 15 July 1994.

"Beim Besuch des kasachischen Präsidenten: Bonn sagt keine Finanzhilfe zu." *Süddeutsche Zeitung*, 23 September 1992.

"Bekenntnis zur Freundschaft." *Frankfurter Rundschau*, 21 March 1994.

"Bekenntnis zur Mitverantwortung." *Das Parlament*, 8 December 1995.

Benz, Wolfgang. *Die Gründung der Bundesrepublik: Von der Bizone zum souveränen Staat*. München: DTV, 1989.

"Bericht der Bundesregierung über die Tagung der WEU und die Sitzung der EPZ zur Lage am Golf, abgegeben vom Bundesminister des Auswärtigen Hans-Dietrich Genscher, vordem Deutschen Bundestag am 23. August 1990." *Europa-Archiv* 46, 2 (1991): D49–52.

Berger, Thomas U. *Cultures of Antimilitarism: National Security in Germany and Japan*. Baltimore and London: The Johns Hopkins University Press, 1998.

Bergius, Michael. "EU-Mitglieder loben Berliner Kompromiß." *Frankfurter Rundschau*, 27 March 1999.

Bergsten, Fred C., Etienne Davignon, and Isamu Miyazaki. *Conditions for Partnership in International Economic Management*. New York: Trilateral Commission, 1986.

———. *The Dilemmas of the Dollar: The Economics and Politics of United States International Monetary Policy*. New York: Council on Foreign Relations, 1975.

Beschloss, Michael, and Strobe Talbott. *At the Highest Levels: The Inside Story of the End of the Cold War*. Boston: Little, Brown, 1992.

"Beschlüsse des SPDSonderparteitages." *Vorwärts* 45. no. 12 (1992): 10–12.

"Beschränkt belastbar." *Der Spiegel*, 10 February 1992.

"Besuch russischer Generale in Deutschland." *Neue Züricher Zeitung*, 16 November 93.

"Bereich Außen- und Friedenspolitik." *Info-Brief Bundestagsgruppe PDS* 5, no. 3 (December 1995).

Bertram, Christoph. *Europa in the Balance: Securing the Peace Won in the Cold War*. Washington, D.C.: Brookings Institute, 1995.

Biedenkopf, Kurt. "Westeuropa endet in Polen." Interview, *Der Spiegel*, 4 July 1994.

Blackwill, Robert. "German Unification and American Diplomacy." *New York:* American Council of Germany, Occasional Paper, no. 3 (1994).

Blüm, Norbert. "Die leise Übermacht." *Der Spiegel*, 30 November 1992.

Bluestone, Barry, and Bennet Harrisson. *The Deindustrialization of America*. New York: Basic Books, 1982.

"Bonn unterstützt den russischen Reformkurs." *Frankfurter Allgemeine Zeitung*, 7 October 1992.

"Bonns Aussenminister verliert die Nerven." *Berliner Zeitung*, 18 March 1993.

"Bonn schickt keine Blauhelme nach Abchasien." *Süddeutsche Zeitung*, 17 August 1993.

"Bonn und Paris wollen kein 'britisches' Europa." *General-Anzeiger*, 23 March 1994.

"Bonn weist Kritik aus Peking zurück, Bonn/Peking 5.12.1998," *Newsticker der Bundesregierung*, 5 December 1998.

"Bonn will Anwalt der Balten sein." *Süddeutsche Zeitung,* 10 July 1993.

"Boris, ich bewundere Dich." *Frankfurter Rundschau,* 22 November 1993.

Bothe, Michael. "Rätsel aus Karlsruhe." *Der Spiegel,* 25 July 1994.

"Botschaft des Staatspräsidenten Francois Mitterrand und des Bundeskanzlers Helmut Kohlan den Präsidenten des Europäischen Rates der Staats und Regierungschefs, Charles Haughey." *Europa-Archiv* 45, 2 (1990): D283.

"Botschaft zur Gemeinsamen Außen und Sicherheitspolitik." *Bulletin des Presse- und Informationsamtes der Bundesregierung,* 18 October 1991.

Brandt, Willy. "Eine EG von Paris bis Wladiwostok?" *Frankfurter Rundschau,* 13 May 1992.

Bredow, Wilfried von, and Thomas Jäger. "Konflikte und globale Kooperation am Ende des 20. Jahrhunderts." *Aus Politik und Zeitgeschichte* 44, no. D26–27 (1994): 3–11.

"Brett vor dem Kopf." *Focus,* 2 December 1996.

Brewer, Anthony. *Marxist Theories of Imperialism.* London: Routledge and Kegan Paul, 1980.

Brzesinski, Zbigniew. *Die einzige Weltmacht: Amerikas Strategie der Vorherrschaft.* Weinheim and Berlin: Beltz/Quadriga, 1997.

Bubis, Ignatz. "Moral verjährt nicht: Ignatz Bubis über die Auschwitz Debatte und seine Auseinandersetzung mit Martin Walser und Klaus von Dohnanyi." Interview, *Der Spiegel,* 30 November 1998.

"Bulgarien sucht Anschluß an die EG." *General-Anzeiger,* 16 January 1992.

Bundesgeschäftsstelle Bündnis 90/ Die Grünen, ed. *Nur mit uns.* Bornheim: Bundesgeschäftsstelle Bündnis 90/ Die Grünen, 1994.

Bundesminister der Verteidigung kündigt Überprüfung der Entscheidungen zum 'Bundeswehrplan 94' an." *Stichworte zur Sicherheitspolitik* 16, no. 2 (1993): 46–61.

Bundesministerium der Verteidigung, ed. *Weißbuch 1994 zur Sicherheit der Bundesrepublik Deutschland und zur Lage und Zukunft der Bundeswehr.* Bonn: Bundesdruckerei, 1994.

"Bundesminister Volker Rühe zu Ergebnissen seiner Gespräche in Moskau." *Stichworte zur Sicherheitspolitik* 16, no. 5 (1993): 31–32.

Bundespresseamt, ed. *Versöhnung, Vertrauen, gute Nachbarschaft: Die deutschpolnischen Beziehungen.* Bonn: Bundesdruckerei, 1994.

"Bundesregierung rückt von umstrittener Kofinanzierung ab." *Frankfurter Allgemeine Zeitung,* 5 March 1999.

"Bundestag billigt deutsche Beteiligung bei möglichem NATO-Einsatz." *Keesings Archiv der Gegenwart,* 27 October 1998.

Bundesvorstand Bündnis 90/Die Grünen, ed. *Das Programm zur 1. Gesamtdeutschen Wahl 1990.* Bornheim: Bundesgeschäftstelle, 1990.

Ceccini, Paolo. *Europa '92: Endlich ein Binnenmarkt.* Baden Baden: Nomos Verlagsgesellschaft, 1988.

"Cheney für NATO-Aufnahme osteuropäischer Länder." *Süddeutsche Zeitung,* 12 December 1992.

Chu, Yun-han. "State Structure and Economic Adjustment of the East Asian Newly Industrializing Countries." *International Organization* 43, no. 4 (1989): 647–672.

"Claes hebt Rolle der Bundesrepublik in der NATO hervor." *dpa Pressebrief,* 2 May 1995.

"Clinton zur Führungsrolle der USA in der Welt du zur Erweiterung der NATO." *Keesings Archiv der Gegenwart,* 22 October 1996.

Cohen, Benjamin J. "The Political Economy of International Trade." *International Organization* 44, no. 2 (1990): 261–281.

Cohen, Stephen S., and John Zysman. *Manufacturing Matters: The Myth of the PostIndustrial Economy.* New York: Basic Books, 1987.

"Communiqué of the Tripartite Conference of Berlin (Potsdam) 1 August 1945." In *Documents on Germany, 1944–1985,* ed. Department of State. Washington, D.C.: GPO, 1986, 63.

"Conversation of Bevin with Stalin." In *The British Commonwelath and Europe.* Vol. 3 of *Foreign Relations of the United States, 1947,* ed. U.S. Department of State. Washington, D.C.: GPO, 1972, 279.

Cowell, Alan. "Germans Face Combat in the Shadow of Militarism." *International Herald Tribune,* 18 July 1995.

"Da bröckelt was." *Der Spiegel,* 3 May 1999.

"Dafür und nicht dagegen." *Der Spiegel,* 16 June 1997.

Dahrendorf, Ralph. "Nach Osten hin ist alles offen." Interview, *Der Spiegel,* 11 January 1993.

"Das Baltikum und die NATO: Wünsche und Wirklichkeit." *dpa Pressebrief,* 22 August 1995

"Das darf Herr Rühe nicht tun." *Frankfurter Allgemeine Zeitung,* 24 August 1995.

"Das deutschpolnische Jugendwerk." In Botschaft der Republik Polen in der BundesrepublikDeutschland [database online]. Cologne: Botschaft der Republik Polen, 1997 [cited 10August 1999]. Available from *http://www.polbot.com/nauka_m2htm.*

"Das droht die DDR zu vernichten." *Der Spiegel,* 14 August 1989.

"Das Ende des Grundgesetzes?" *Der Spiegel,* 23 March 1992.

"Das hält keine Armee aus." *Der Spiegel,* 22 March 1993.

"Das MaastrichtUrteil des Bundesverfassungsgerichts." *Europa-Archiv* 48, 2 (1993): D459–476.

"Das Urteil des Bundesverfassungsgerichts vom 12. Juli 1994." *Europa-Archiv* 49, 2 (1994):D427–431.

Davis, Zachary, and Mitchell Reiss. *U.S. Counterproliferation Doctrine: Issues for Congress,* CRS Research Report. Washington, D.C.: GPO 1994.

Delors, Jacques. "Wir müssen Großmacht werden." Interview, *Der Spiegel,* 14 October 1991.

"Den Ernstfall nicht gewagt." *Der Spiegel,* 11 February 1991.

"Den Krieg am Golf kann nur einer gewinnen—der Tod . . ." *Blätter für deutsche und internationale Politik* 36 (1991): 104.

"Der Brief des Bundeskanzlers an Ministerpräsident Bulganin." In *Aussenpolitik der Bundesrepublik Deutschland : Dokumente von 1949–1994*, ed. Auswärtiges Amt. Bonn:Verlag Wissenschaft und Politik, 1995, 224–225.

"Der letzte Europäer." *Der Spiegel,* 8 November 1993.

"Der Konflikt in Tschetschenien." *Keesings Archiv der Gegenwart*, 12 January 1995.

"Der Krach am Rhein." *Die Zeit,* 25 March 1994.

"Der neue Stil." *Focus,* 16 November 1998.

"Der Vertrag über die Europäische Union." *Europa-Archiv* 47, 2 (1992): D177–D253.

"Der Weg ist falsch." *Der Spiegel,* 7 December 1998.

"D EU Agenda 2000." *AFP0134,* 26 February 1999.

"Deutsche bei Festparade in Paris herzlich willkommen." *Westdeutsche Allgemeine Zeitung,* 12 July 1994.

Deutsche Bundesbank, ed. *Annual Report 1993.* Frankfurt/M.: Deutsche Bundesbank, 1993.

————, ed. *Annual Report 1996.* Frankfurt/M.: Deutsche Bundesbank, 1996.

Deutscher Bundestag, ed. *Drucksachen,* 1.–13. Wahlperiode. Bonn: Universitäts-Buchdruckerei, 1950–1998.

————. *Verhandlungen des Deutschen Bundestages: Stenographische Berichte,* 1.–13. Wahlperiode. Bonn: UniversitätsBuchdruckerei, 1950–1998.

"Deutsches Doppel: Bei der Ost-Erweiterung des Bündnisses treten Genscheristen als Bremser auf." *Focus,* 11 October 1993.

"Deutsch-französische Leitlinien zur GASP vom 27.2.1996. In *Die Reform der Europäischen Union*, ed. Mathias Jopp. Bonn: Europa Union Verlag, 1996, 118–120.

"Deutschland als Bremser auf dem Weg nach Europa." *Der Spiegel,* 5 May 1997.

"Deutschland Bundestag Kosovo." *RTRG6782,* 24 February 1999.

"Deutschland, die Balten und der Schirinowskij-Faktor." *Frankfurter Allgemeine Zeitung,* 9 March 1994.

"Deutschland Europa Schröder Analyse." *RTRG8134,* 10 March 1999.

"Deutschland Kosovo." *AP0068,* 24 January 1999.

"Deutschland NATO Fischer." *RTRG0943,* 28 January 1999.

"Deutschlands Touristen machen Polens Grenzorte reich." *Die Welt,* 3 June 1994.

"Deutschland und Rußland wollen militärisch eng zusammenarbeiten." *dpa Pressebrief,* 13 April 1993.

"Deutsch-Polnisches Umweltabkommen." *Frankfurter Allgemeine Zeitung,* 8 April 1994.

"Deutsch-Russische Zusammenarbeit geplant" *Frankfurter Allgemeine Zeitung,* 18 August 1994.

"Deutsch-Tschechoslowakischer-Vertrag: Die Narben der Geschichte." *Die Zeit,* 2 August 1994.

"Dialog und Kooperation zwischen der NATO und Rußland." *Stichworte zur Sicherheitspolitik* 18, no. 7 (1995): 17–18.

"Die Agenda 2000 bedeutet das Aus für 40.000 Bauern." *Frankfurter Allgemeine Zeitung,* 31 March 1998.

"Die Berliner Rede von Bundespräsident von Weizsäcker gegen Ausländerhaß und Fremdenfeindlichkeit." *Europa-Archiv* 47, 2 (1992): D631–633.

Dieckmann, Christoph. "Friedenskind, hilflos mittendrin." *Die Zeit,* 29 April 1999.

"Die deutsche Handschrift ist deutlich zu erkennen: Bonn legt Wert auf eine parallele Erweiterung der NATO und der Europäischen Union." *Frankfurter Allgemeine Zeitung,* 29 September 1995.

"Die Deutschen an die Front." *Der Spiegel,* 4 February 1991.

"Die deutschrussischen Beziehungen." *Internal Report by the Bundespresseamt,* May 1994. Bonn: Bundespresseamt, 1994.

"Die EG lebt gefährlich." *Der Spiegel,* 24 August 1993.

"Die GATT Runde muß rasch beendet werden." *Handelsblatt,* 2 December 1993.

"Die gemeinsame Aussenpolitik der europäischen Union, Rede Staatsminister/AA Günter Verheugen beim Zentrum für europäische Integrationsforschung, Bonn, 21.1.1999." In Reden 1999 [database online]. Bonn: Auswärtiges Amt der Bundesrepublik Deutschland, 1999 [cited 20 August 1999]. Available from http://www.auswaertigesamt.de/6_archiv/index.htm.

"Die Gemeinschaft überdenkt ihr Verhältnis zu Mittel- und Osteuropa." *Frankfurter Allgemeine Zeitung,* 13 November 1989.

"Die große Versuchung." *Focus,* 7 December 1998.

"Die Grünen gegen Maastricht." *Die Zeit,* 17 July 1992.

Diehl, Ole. "UN-Einsätze der Bundeswehr—Außenpolitische Handlungszwänge undinnenpolitischer Konsensbedarf." *Europa-Archiv* 48, 1 (1993): 219–227.

"Die Hunde sind von der Kette." *Der Spiegel,* 28 November 1988.

"Die Kriminalität in der Bundesrepublik Deutschland." *Bulletin des Presse- und Informationsamtes der Bundesregierung,* 25 May 1999.

"Die Lava läuft noch." *Der Spiegel,* 20 December 1993.

"Die Münchner Konferenz für Sicherheitspolitik." *Stichworte zur Sicherheitspolitik* 18, no. 3 (1995): 6–22.

"Die NATO bietet eine 'Partnerschaft für den Frieden' an." *Frankfurter Allgemeine Zeitung,* 22 October 1993.

"Die NATO blickt nach Osten: Leichte Unterschiede in der Sicht von Wörner, Rühe und Kinkel." *Die Welt,* 11 September 1993.

"Die NATO und Rußland nach dem Ende des Kalten Krieges." *dpa Pressebrief,* 22 June 1994.

Dienstbier, Jiri. "Die NATO-Partnerschaft darf kein Ersatzuckerl sein." *Frankfurter Rundschau,* 6 January 1994.

"Diskussion um Nachfolge-Mission in Bosnien und Osterweiterung." *Keesings Archiv der Gegenwart,* 25 September 1996.

"Die Ukraine will Sicherheitsgarantien." *Süddeutsche Zeitung,* 9 July 1992.

"Die sind alle irre unterwegs." *Der Spiegel,* 9 May 1988.

"Die Visegrader Vier auf der Suche nach einer Perspektive." *Der Tagesspiegel,* 3 November 1993.

"Die Visegrad Gruppe löst sich auf: Die Tschechen meiden die Fußkranken." *Frankfurter Allgemeine Zeitung,* 26 May 1994.

"Die Zeit ist nicht reif." *Der Spiegel,* 14 October 1991.

"Diskussion um die Konvergenzkriterien zur Teilnahme an der EWWU." *Keesings Archiv der Gegenwart,* 27 November 1997.

Dohnanyi, Klaus von. "Eine Friedensrede: Martin Walsers notwendige Klage." *Frankfurter Allgemeine Zeitung,* 14 November 1998.

"Dokumente zur Reform des Sicherheitsrats der Vereinten Nationen." *Europa-Archiv* 48, 2 (1993): D 379–396.

"D Regierung EU." *AFP0180,* 15 March 1999.

"D Regierung SPD." *AFP,* 12 March 1999.

"Drei dürfen mit." *Focus,* 7 July 1997.

"Dregger: Sicherheitsperspektive für die Staaten OstMittelEuropas." *Pressedienst der CDU/CSU-Fraktion im Deutschen Bundestag,* 7 January 1994.

Drodziak, William. "Bonn Rejects to Aid U.S. Forces in the Gulf." *International Herald Tribune,* 6 September 1990.

"Drohung aus Washington." *Der Spiegel,* 18 January 1993.

Duisberg, Claus J. "Der Abzug der russischen Truppen aus Deutschland: Eine politische undmilitärische Erfolgsbilanz." *Europa-Archiv* 49, 1 (1994): 461–469.

"EG: Umschlagen ins Patt." *Der Spiegel,* 20 February 1988.

"Ein europäischer Bundesstaat kommt vorerst nicht zustande: Reformkonzept der SPD zuEuropa." *Frankfurter Allgemeine Zeitung,* 4 February 1995.

"Ein Fall für die Feuerwehr." *Der Spiegel,* 17 May 1999.

"Eine neue Garderobe für die Dame Europa: Sechs Sozialdemokraten schneidern einReformkonzept." *Saarbrücker Zeitung,* 8 February 1995.

"Eine regelrechte Psychose." *Der Spiegel,* 21 December 1992.

"Eine Rose am Wischer." *Der Spiegel,* 18 July 1994.

"Ein Treffen der besonderen Art." *Frankfurter Allgemeine Zeitung,* 18 December 1998.

"Ende der Spendierlaune." *Focus,* 22 July 1996.

Engelbrecht, Uwe. "Moskau und die nuklearen Schlupflöcher." *General-Anzeiger,* 16 August 1994.

"Entscheidung des Bundesgerichtshofes vom 8. April 1993 über die Teilnahme deutscher Soldaten an AWACS-Missionen." *Blätter für deutsche und internationale Politik* 38 (1993): 637640.

"Erklärung des Aussenministers Hans-Dietrich Genscher über die Resultate der deutschen EG-Präsidentschaft vor dem Europäischen Parlament, 16 Juni 1988." *Europa-Archiv* 43, 2 (1988): D 439–443.

"Erklärung der Bundesregierung über die Erweiterungsverhandlungen der EuropäischenUnion." *Bulletin des Presse- und Informationsamtes der Bundesregierung,* 11 March 1994.

"Erklärung der Bundesregierung: Vorschau auf den europäischen Rat in Wien am 11. und 12.12.1998 und Ausblick auf die deutsche Präsidentschaft in der ersten Jahreshälfte 1999," *Bulletin des Presse- und Informationsamtes der Bundesregierung,* 14 December 1998.

"Erklärung der Bundesregierung zur Sondertagung des Europäischen Rates in Brüssel." *Bulletin des Presse- und Informationsmates der Bundesregierung,* 16 November 1993.

"Erklärung des Nordatlantischen Kooperationsrates über Dialog, Partnerschaft und Kooperation." *Bulletin des Presse- und Informationsamtes der Bundesregierung,* 4 January 1992.

"Erklärung der Staats- und Regierungschefs des Nordatlantikpaktes, abgegeben zum Abschluß ihrer Tagung am 10. / 11. Januar 1994 in Brüssel." *Europa-Archiv* 49, 2 (1994): D127–134.

"Erklärung Fischers zum 50. Jahrestag der Proklamation der Allgemeinen Erklärung der Menschenrechte." *Newsticker der Bundesregierung,* 9 December 1998.

"Erklärung von Bundeskanzler Dr. Kohl zum Tschetschenienkonflikt." *Stichworte zur Sicherheitspolitik* 18, no. 2 (1995): 7–21.

"Erklärung Wolfgang Schäubles vor der CDU/CSU-Fraktion des Deutschen Bundestages." *Pressedienst der CDU/CSU Fraktion im Deutschen Bundestag,* 21 February 1992.

"Eröffnung der Generalversammlung: Abrüstungsvorschläge Bushs." *Keesings Archiv der Gegenwart,* 27 September 1989.

"Erotisches Verhältnis." *Focus,* 23 September 1996.

"Erneute militärische Aktion gegen den Irak: Die Operation Desert Fox." *Keesings Archiv der Gegenwart,* 19 December 1998.

"Ernstfall für Schröder," *Der Spiegel,* 29 March 1999.

"Erweitern oder Vertiefen." *Der Spiegel,* 5 December 1994.

"Erwin Huber: Die NATO muß handlungsfähig bleiben." *Die Welt,* 2 December 1993.

"EU-Kompromiß hält nicht bis 2006," *Die Welt,* 3 April 1999.

"EU-Gipfel, Europa." *ADN0464,* 26 February 1999.

"EU-Gipfel im Agrarstreit festgefahren." *Die Welt,* 26 March 1999.

"EU-Gipfel in Luxemburg: Erweiterung der EU beschlossen." *Keesings Archiv der Gegenwart,* 13 December 1997.

"Europäische Gemeinschaften." *Europa-Archiv,* 47, 3 (1992): Z247–248.

"Europäische Perspektiven in den neunziger Jahren, Rede Rudolf Scharpings in Prag." *Presseservice der SPD,* 6 April 1994.

"Europäische Währungsordnung." *Gutachten des wissenschaftlichen Beirats beim Bundesministerium für Wirtschaft* no. 61 (1989).

"Europa ist kein Vaterland." *Der Spiegel,* 13 December 1993.

"Europa mit links." *Focus,* 14 December 1998.

"Europapolitische Erklärung." *Pressedienst der CDU/CSU Fraktion im deutschen Bundestag,* 21 February 1992.

"European Business and the ECU: Results of a Survey." *Association for the MonetaryUnion of Europe: Paris,* 25 October 1988.

"Ewiges Knirschen." *Der Spiegel,* 24 May 1993.

"Facetten der deutschpolnischen Partnerschaft." *Neue Züricher Zeitung,* 24 July 1994.

"Falsche Hoffnungen." *Der Spiegel,* 12 December 1994.

Fastenrath, Ulrich. "Deutschland, Blauhelme und die Vereinten Nationen." *Frankfurter Allgemeine Zeitung* 17 December 1992.

Faßbender, Bardo. "Zur staatlichen Ordnung Europas nach der deutschen Einigung." *Europa-Archiv* 46, 1 (1991): 395–404.

Fauth, Heinrich. "Neuer Rüstungsplan für die Bundeswehr: Minus 43,7 Milliarden DM in 12 Haushaltsjahren." *Europäische Sicherheit* 41, no. 2 (1992): 71–74.

F. D. P.-Bundesgeschäftsstelle, ed. *Liberal denken. Leistung wählen. Das Programm der F.D.P. zur Bundestagswahl 1994.* Bonn: Liberal Verlag, 1994.

"FDP kritisiert Rühe Vorschlag." *dpa Pressebrief,* 14 April 1993.

Fechner, Wolfgang. "Deutscher Beitrag zur Befreiung Kuwaits: Über 17 Milliarden DM." *Europäische Sicherheit* 40, no. 4 (1991): 212–215.

"Feldjäger in der Wüste." *Der Spiegel,* 14 December 1992.

Feldmayer, Karl. "Die NATO ist ratlos." *Frankfurter Allgemeine Zeitung,* 12 January 1994.

"Fertiger Plan für den Bodenkrieg." *Der Spiegel,* 26 April 1999.

Fischer, Joschka. "Die Selbstbeschränkung der Macht muß Fortbestehen," *Frankfurter Allgemeine Zeitung,* 8 October 1998.

———. "Ein Realo sieht die Welt." Interview, *Die Zeit,* 12 November 1998.

———. *Risiko Deutschland: Krise und Zukunft der deutschen Politik.* Cologne: Kiepenheuer und Witsch, 1994.

———. "Serbien gehört zu Europa." Interview *Die Zeit,* 15 April 1999.

"Fischer kritisiert Vorgehen gegen chinesische Dissidenten," *Frankfurter Allgemeine Zeitung,* 24 March 1999.

"Fischer stellt die Agenda 2000 an die erste Stelle," *Frankfurter Allgemeine Zeitung,* 6 January 1999.

"Fischer will auf die Präsenz der Amerikaner in Europa nicht verzichten." *Frankfurter Allgemeine Zeitung,* 9 December 1998.

"Fischers Störfeuer." *Focus,* 30 November 1998.

"Flüchtlinge: Jetzt geht es erst los." *Der Spiegel,* 10 May 1999.

Franck, Christian. "Belgien und Luxemburg." *Jahrbuch der Europäischen Integration* 16 (1996/97): 287–292.

"Frankfurter Appell für Frieden am Golf." *Blätter für deutsche und internationale Politik* 36 (1991): 16.

"Frankreich beansprucht eine Sonderrolle." *Die Welt,* 1 December 93.

"Frankreich: Für eine stärkere Zusammenarbeit." *Frankfurter Allgemeine Zeitung,* 7 January 1994.

"Frankreich gegen schnelle Ostausweitung der NATO." *Süddeutsche Zeitung,* 8 October 1993.

"Frankreichs kurzer Flirt mit Großbritannien." *Frankfurter Allgemeine Zeitung,* 23 December 1998.

"Frankreich lieferte trauriges Schauspiel für Europa." *dpa Pressebrief,* 18 December 1992.

Friedberg, Aaron L. "The Future of American Power." *Political Science Quarterly* 109 (1994): 1–22.

"Frühjahrstreffen der Aussenminister: EAPC Nachfolgeorganisation des NACC." *Keesings Archiv der Gegenwart,* 30 May 1997.

"Fünfzig Jahre Menschenrechte, Bonn/New York." *Newsticker der Bundesregierung,* 11 December 1998.

"Für Antrag zu UN-Einsätzen." *Frankfurter Allgemeine Zeitung,* 11 November 1995.

"Für ein Europa der Stabilität und finanzpolitischen Solidität: 10 Forderungen an den EG-Haushalt." *Die SPD im Deutschen Bundestag,* 21 February 1992.

"Für eine Zivilisierung der internationalen Beziehungen: Politik nicht-militärischer Konfliktlösung. Antrag der Abgeordneten Vera Wollenberger, Gerd Poppe, Werner Schulz, Dr. Wolfnag Ullmann, Konrad Weiß." *Deutscher Bundestag Drucksache,* 12/3015, 2 July 1992.

"Für Osteuropa kein Ticket in die NATO." *Die Welt,* 4 December 1993.

"Funkstörung Bonn-Paris." *Frankfurter Rundschau,* 24 March 1994.

Gallo, Max. "Das Europa der Deutschen." *Der Spiegel,* 16 December 1996.

Garavoglia, Guido. "From Rambouillet to Williamsburg: A Historical Assessment." In *Economic Summits and Western Decision-Making,* ed. Cesare Merlini. London and Sydney: Croom Helm, 1985.

Garthe, Michael. "Bundesrepublik Deutschland." *Jahrbuch der Europäischen Integration* 6 (1985/86): 324–345.

———. "Bundesrepublik Deutschland." *Jahrbuch der Europäischen Integration* 7 (1986/87): 336–345.

———. "Bundesrepublik Deutschland." *Jahrbuch der Europäischen Integration* 8 (1987/88): 342–350.

Garthoff, Raymond, L. *Detente and Confrontation: American-soviet Relations from Nixon to Reagan.* Washington, D.C.: Brookings Institute, 1985.

Garton Ash, Timothy. "Germany's Choice." *Foreign Affairs* 73, no. 4 (1994): 65–81.

Gauss, Günter. "Zwei deutsche Staaten: Welcher Zukunft zugewandt?." *Die Zeit,* 20 January 1989.

"Geduckt in der Furche." *Der Spiegel,* 30 June 1997.

"Gegen den Strom." *Der Spiegel,* 1 July 1997.

"Gegen Lethargie und Zweifel." *Frankfurter Allgemeine Zeitung,* 8 October 1993.

"Geheimpapier: Polens Angebote an die NATO." *Die Welt,* 19 May 1994.

"Geld oder Währung." *Frankfurter Allgemeine Zeitung,* 31 January 1997.

"Gemeinsame Botschaft des französischen Staatspräsidenten Francois Mitterrand und desdeutschen Bundeskanzlers Helmut Kohl an den Präsidenten des Europäischen Rates der Staats und Regierungschefs, Dr. Ruud Lubbers." In

Aussenpolitik der Bundesrepublik Deutschland: Dokumente von 1949 bis 1994, ed. Auswärtiges Amt. Cologne:Verlag Wissenschaft und Politik, 1995, 826–829.

"Gemeinsame Botschaft des französischen Staatspräsidenten Francois Mitterrand und des deutschen Bundeskanzlers Helmut Kohl an den Präsidenten des Europäischen Rates der Staats- und Regierungschefs, Guilio Andreotti vom 6. Dezember 1990." In *Aussenpolitik der Bundesrepublik Deutschland: Dokumente von 1949 bis 1994,* ed. Auswärtiges Amt. Cologne:Verlag Wissenschaft und Politik, 1995, 776–779.

"Gemeinsame Erklärung des Bundeskanzlers Helmut Kohl und des Staatspräsidenten und Generalsekretärs Michail Gorbatschow, unterzeichnet in Bonn, den 13 Juni 1989." In *Deutschlands Vereinigung: Die internationalen Aspekte,* ed. Karl Kaiser.Bergisch Gladbach: Bastei Lübbe, 1991, 143–148.

"Gemeinsamer Umweltschutz." *Der Tagesspiegel,* 5 September 1994.

"Gemeinsame Übungen mit Polen beschlossen." *Frankfurter Allgemeine Zeitung,* 13 May 1994.

Genscher, Hans-Dietrich. "Bedenkliche Thesen." Interview, *Der Spiegel,* 12 September 1994.

———. "Eine Stabilitätsordnung für Europa." *Europäische Sicherheit* 41 (1992): 310–317.

———. "Ich habe Kurs gehalten." Interview *Der Spiegel,* 4 February 1991.

———. "Rußland verdient Vertrauen." *Frankfurter Allgemeine Zeitung,* 2 May 1994.

"Genscher verteidigt Kinkels Position." *dpa Pressebrief,* 7 October 1994.

"Gerhard Schröder zum Bundeskanzler gewählt." *Bulletin des Presse- und Informationsamtes der Bundesregierung,* 29 October 1998.

"Germanische Rohheit." *Der Spiegel,* 12 September 1994.

Gerster, Florian. "Der Zug nach Westen: Die Einbindung Mittelosteuropas in die Europäische Union und in die Allianz." *Europäische Sicherheit* 43 (1994): 380–382.

"Geschlossene Gesellschaft." *Der Spiegel,* 6 May 1991.

"Gewachsene Instinkte." *Der Spiegel,* 18 May 1992.

"Gewehr unterm Baum." *Der Spiegel,* 11 January 1993.

Gilpin, Robert G. *War and Change in World Politics.* Cambridge: Cambridge University Press, 1981.

"Gipfeltreffen in Amsterdam," *Keesings Archiv der Gegenwart,* 17 June 1997.

"Gipfeltreffen in Dublin: Einigung über den Stabilitätspakt erzielt." *Keesings Archiv der Gegenwart,* 14 December 1996.

"Gipfeltreffen in Helsinki." *Keesings Archiv der Gegenwart,* 20 March 1997.

Glinski, Gerhard von. "Rechnung mit einer russischen Unbekannten: Wie sich Präsident Clintons Europa-Fachmann Richard Holbrooke die Erweiterung der NATO nach Osten vorstellt." *Rheinischer Merkur,* 24 February 1995.

Glotz, Peter. "Europa am Scheideweg." *Europa-Archiv* 47, 1 (1992): 503–514.

———. "Neue deutsche Ideologie." *Der Spiegel,* 30 September 1991.

Gordon, Philip H. *Die deutsch-französische Partnerschaft und die Atlantische Allianz*. Arbeitspapiere zur Internationalen Politik derDeutschen Gesellschaft für Auswärtige Politik, Vol. 82. Bonn: Europa-Union Verlag, 1994.

———. "The Normalization of German Foreign Policy." *Orbis* 38, no. 2 (1994): 225–243.

Griffith, William E. *The Ostpolitik of the Federal Republic of Germany*. Cambridge, MA: MIT Press, 1978.

"Größenwahn der Generäle." *Der Spiegel*, 5 April 1992.

"Größere Ausgewogenheit angestrebt." *Frankfurter Allgemeine Zeitung*, 22 July 1997.

"Größer und billiger: Das geht nicht. Zur zukünftigen Finanzierung der Europäischen Union." *Frankfurter Allgemeine Zeitung*, 28 April 1995.

Gross, Johannes. "So nicht!" *Capital*, January 1995.

"Großbritannien, Aussenpolitik, Europapläne." *Keesings Archiv der Gegenwart*, 19 September 1946.

Grote, Jürgen R. "Regionalpolitik." In *Die europäische Union*, ed. Dieter Nohlen, Vol. 5 of *Lexikon der Politik*. München: C. H. Beck, 1996.

"Grünes Licht für den Krieg." *Die Woche*, 11 August 1995.

"Grüne zwischen Koalitionsräson und Kriegsverweigerung." *Focus*, 19 April 1999.

"Grundakte über die Beziehungen Rußlands zur NATO unterzeichnet." *Keesings Archiv der Gegenwart*, 27 May 1997.

"Grundgesetzänderungen für Euro-Mark gibt es nur bei Nachbesserungen." *Medienservice der SPD-Abgeordneten im Europäischen Parlament*, 2 February 1992.

"Grundgesetz für die Bundesrepublik Deutschland vom 23. Mai 1949 in der Fassung vom 21. Dezember 1983 (Auszüge)." In *Aussenpolitik der Bundesrepublik Deutschland: Dokumente von 1949 bis 1994*, ed. Auswärtiges Amt. Cologne: Verlag Wissenschaft und Politik 1995, 167–169.

Gulick, Edward Vose. *Europe's Classical Balance of Power*. New York: W. W. Norton & Co., 1967.

Gurko, Andrej. "Das Deutschenbild der Russen." In *Deutschlandbilder in Polen und Rußland, in der Tschechoslowakei und in Ungarn*, ed. Hans Süssmuth. Baden-Baden: Nomos Verlagsgesellschaft, 1993.

Hacke, Christian. "Die Haltung der Bundesrepublik Deutschland zur NATOOsterweiterung." In *Ostmitteleuropa, Russland und die Osterweiterung der NATO: Perzeptionen und Strategien im Spannungsfeld nationaler und europäischer Sicherheit*, ed. August Pradetto. Opladen: Westdeutscher Verlag, 1997.

———. "Die nationalen Interessen der Bundesrepublik Deutschland an der Schwelle zum 21. Jahrhundert." *Aussenpolitik* 49, no. 2 (1998): 5–26.

———. *Weltmacht wider Willen: Die Aussenpolitik der Bundesrepublik Deutschland*. Stuttgart: Klett-Cotta, 1988.

Haggard, Stephan. "The Newly Industrializing Countries in the International System." *World Politics* 37 (1986): 343–371.

Haltzel, Michael H. "Die Vereinigten Staaten, Europa und die Golf-Krise." *Europa-Archiv* 45, 1 (1990): 533–542.

Hamilton, Daniel S. *Beyond Bonn: America and the Berlin Republic.* Washington: Carnegie Endowment for International Peace, 1994.

Hanke, Thomas, and Mario Müller. "Vorsorgliche Belagerung," *Die Zeit,* 19 November 1998.

Harding, Harry. "Asia Policy on the Brink." *Foreign Policy* no. 96 (Fall 1994): 57–75.

"Hardhöhe: Kein Streit mit Auswärtigem Amt über baltische NATO-Perspektive." *dpa Presse Brief,* 24 August 1995.

"Harter Kinkel gewünscht." *Der Spiegel,* 17 March 1997.

Hauner, Milan. "The Czechs and the Germans: A One-Thousand-Year-Relationship." In *The Germans and their Neighbors,* ed. Dirk Verheyen and Christian Soe Boulder: Westview Press, 1993.

Havel, Vaclav. "Warum die NATO Prag nicht aussperren darf." *Die Welt,* 27 November 1993.

"Heftiger Hauskrach bei den Grünen." *Die Welt,* 13 April 1999.

"Heißhunger auf deutsche Anleihen." *Informationsdienst des Instituts der deutschen Wirtschaft* 19, no. 13 (1994).

"Helden in der Wüste." *Der Spiegel,* 28 June 1993.

"Helsinki Dokument 1992: Herausforderung des Wandels." *Bulletin des Presse und-Informationsamtes der Bundesregierung,* 23 July 1992.

Hénard, Jacqueline. "Abschied vom Ersten Weltkrieg." *Die Zeit,* 5 November 1998.

———. "Verrat von Osten." *Die Zeit,* 4 February 1999.

Henning, C. Randall. "Systemic Conflict and Regional Monetary Integration: The Case of Europe." *International Organization* 52 (Summer 1998): 537–573.

Herdegen, Gerhard. "Die öffentliche Meinung." *Jahrbuch der Europäischen Integration* 6 (1985/86): 300–314.

Herzinger, Richard. "Feindbild Rambo." *Die Zeit,* 20 May 1999.

"Herzog betont besonderes Verhältnis zu Frankreich." *Die Welt,* 7 August 1994.

Hildebrand, Klaus. "Deutschland und Europa im 20. Jahrhundert." In *Deutschland in Europa: Nationale Interessen und internationale Ordnung im 20. Jahrhundert,* ed. Gottfried Niedhard, Paul Junker, and Michael Richter. Mannheim: Palatium HVS 1997.

Hillen, John. "Getting NATO Back to Basics." *Strategic Review* 24, no. 2 (1996): 41–50.

Hoagland, Jim. "German Wobbling Puts the Trans-Atlantic Partnership at Risk." *International Herald Tribune,* 31 January 1991.

Holbrooke, Richard C. "America: A European Power." *Foreign Affairs* 74, no. 2 (1995): 38–51.

Hoffmann, Stanley. "La France dans le Nouvel Ordre Europeén." *Politique Étrangére* 55 (1990): 503–512.

Hofmann, Gunter. "Wie Deutschland in den Krieg geriet." *Die Zeit,* 12 May 1999.

Hornhues, Karl-Heinz. "Rußland braucht eine Sonderrolle." *Frankfurter Allgemeine Zeitung,* 11 May 1994.

Hort, Peter. "Eine Bilanz der deutschen EG-Präsidentschaft." *Europa-Archiv,* 43, 1 (1988): 421–428.

————. "Europas Aussenpolitik: Ein Fernziel." *Europa-Archiv* 46, 1 (1991): 577–582.

————. "Milliarden für Europa." *Frankfurter Allgemeine Zeitung,* 27 November 1996.

Howard, Michael. "Introduction." In *Western Security: The Formative Years,* ed. Olav Riste. Oslo: Norwegian University Press, 1979.

Hoyer, Werner. "Perspektiven für die Regierungskonferenz 1996 und die europapolitische Agenda." *Integration* 18, no. 4 (1995): 184–222.

Hübel, Helmut. *Der zweite Golfkrieg in der internationalen Politik,* Arbeitspapiere zur internationalen Politik der deutschen Gesellschaft für Auswärtige Politik Vol. 62. Bonn: Europa Verlags-Union, 1991.

Hurd, Douglas. "Europa nicht abschotten." Interview, *Der Spiegel,* 28 October 1991.

"Hurd: Keine baldige Ausdehnung der NATO." *Süddeutsche Zeitung,* 24 September 1993.

"Ignaz Bubis' Rede bei der Berliner Gedenkfeier zum 9. November, (Auszüge)." *Blätter für deutsche und internationale Politik* 44 (1999): 119–120.

"Ihr kommt nie wieder." *Der Spiegel,* 12 April 1999.

Ilgen, Thomas L. "Better Living through Chemistry: The Chemical Industry in the World Economy." *International Organization* 37, no. 4 (1983): 647–680.

"Illiescu: Rumänien sollte der NATO beitreten." *Süddeutsche Zeitung,* 2 November 1992.

Inacker, Michael J. *Unter Ausschluß der Öffentlichkeit? Die Deutschen in der Golfallianz.* Bonn: Bouvier, 1991.

IMF, ed. *Direction of Trade Statistics Yearbook 1993.* Washington, D.C.: IMF, 1993.

————, ed. *Direction of Trade Statistics Yearbook 1995.* Washington, D.C.: IMF, 1995.

————, ed. *International Financial Statistics Yearbook 1998.* Washington, D.C.: IMF, 1998.

"Im Teufelskreis der Gewalt." *Der Spiegel,* 15 January 1999.

"Im Urlaubsort Chamoix antwortet Balladur dem Kanzler." *General-Anzeiger,* 12 August 1993.

"In den rauhen eurasischen Osten? Wie Deutschland dem Wunsch nach Entsendung von Lehrkräften nachkommt." *Frankfurter Allgemeine Zeitung,* 22 November 1993.

"In der EU erhebliche Meinungsverschiedenheiten in fast allen Kernfragen," *Frankfurter Allgemeine Zeitung,* 27 February 1999.

"Irak, Konflikt ist nur mit friedlichen Mitteln zu lösen." *Pressemitteilung der Bundestagsfraktion Bündnis 90/ Die Grünen,* 17 December.

"Irritationen beseitigt." *Handelsblatt,* 24 April 1992.

Institut National de la Statistique et des Études des Finances, ed. *Annuaire Statistique de la France 1993.* Paris: Impr. Nat., 1993.

"Ja, aber." *Der Spiegel,* 23 March 1992.

Jachtenfuchs, Markus. "Die EG nach Maastricht." *Europa-Archiv* 47, 1 (1992): 279–287.

Jacobsen, Hans-Adolf. "Polen und Deutsche." In *Deutschlandbilder in Polen und Rußland, in der Tschechoslowakei und in Ungarn,* ed. Hans Süssmuth. Baden–Baden: Nomos Verlagsgesellschaft, 1993.

Janning, Josef. "Bundesrepublik Deutschland." *Jahrbuch der Europäischen Integration,* 13 (1994/95): 287–294.

————. "Bundesrepublik Deutschland." *Jahrbuch der Europäischen Integration,* 14 (1995/96): 289–297.

————. "Bundesrepublik Deutschland." *Jahrbuch der Europäischen Integration* 15 (1996/97) : 293–302.

————. "Bundesrepublik Deutschland." *Jahrbuch der Europäischen Integration* 16 (1997/98): 311–318.

————. "Dynamik in der Zwangsjacke : Flexibilität in der Europäischen Union nach Amsterdam." *Integration* 20, no. 4 (1997): 285–291.

————. "Europa braucht verschiedene Geschwindigkeiten." *Europa-Archiv* 49, 1(1994): 527–536.

Jelzin, Boris. "Europa ohne Trennungslinien." Interview, *Der Spiegel,* 21 June 1999.

"Jelzin hat nichts gegen Aufnahme Polens in NATO." *Die Welt,* 26 August 1993.

"Jelzin: Rußland voll in Europa integrieren." *Kölner-Stadt-Anzeiger,* 12 May 1994.

"Jelzin schreibt ein Buch und übergeht Mitterrand nahezu." *General-Anzeiger,* 3 May 1994.

"Jelzin warnt die NATO vor dem Einsatz von Bodentruppen im Kosovo." *Frankfurter Allgemeine Zeitung,* 10 April 1999.

"Jelzin warnt NATO vor Ausdehnung." *Neue Westfälische Zeitung,* 6 January 1995

"Jelzin warnt NATO vor Ausweitung nach Osteuropa." *dpa Pressebrief,* 1 October 1993.

"Jetzt mache ich es gut." *Der Spiegel,* 19 July 1999.

Joffe, Josef. "Abschied von Kleineuropa." *Süddeutsche Zeitung,* 7 August 1993.

Kaiser, Karl. "Aussenpolitik in einer neuen Welt: der Wandel der internationalen-Rahmenbedingungen." In *Die Zukunft der deutschen Aussenpolitik: Arbeitspapiere zurinternationalen Politik,* ed. Karl Kaiser and Hanns Maull. Bonn: DeutscheGesellschaft für Auswärtige Politik, 1992.

————, and Klaus Becher. *Deutschland und der Irak-Konflikt: Internationale Sicherheitsverantwortung Deutschlands und Europa nach der deutschen Vereinigung.* Bonn: Europa-Union-Verlag,1992.

————. *Deutschlands Vereinigung: Die internationalen Aspekte.* Bergisch Gladbach: Bastei Lübbe, 1991.

————. "Die Einbettung des vereinten Deutschlands in Europa." *Die Internationale Politik: Jahrbücher der Gesellschaft für Auswärtige Politik München* 16 (1989/90): 101–118.

————. "Die ständige Mitgliedschaft im Sicherheitsrat: Ein berechtigtes Ziel deutscher Aussenpolitik." *Europa-Archiv* 48, 1 (1993): 533–552.

————. *German Foreign Policy in Transition: Bonn between East and West.* Oxford: Clarendon Press, 1968.

Kaimakow, Boris. "Das Bild des 'häßlichen Deutschen' hat sich im heutigen Rußland erschöpft." *Handelsblatt,* 27 April 1993.

Kaltefleiter, Werner. "Risiken einer Öffnung der NATO nach Osten." *Europäische Sicherheit* 42 (1993): 609–613.

Kamp, KarlHeinz. "Das nukleare Erbe der Sowjetunion: Eine Aufgabe westlicher-Sicherheitspolitik." *Europa-Archiv* 48, 1 (1993): 623–632.

————. "Die Frage einer ‚Osterweiterung der NATO'," *Interne Studien und Berichte der Konrad-Adenauer-Stiftung* no. 57 (1993).

————. *Europäische Nuklearkooperation: Chance oder Schimäre?.* Sankt Augustin: Konrad-Adenauer-Stiftung, 1995.

————. "The Folly of Rapid NATO Expansion." *Foreign Policy* no. 98 (1995): 116–129.

————. *Zwischen Friedenspartnerschaft und Vollmitgliedschaft: Die Frage einer Osterweiterung der NATO?* Sankt Augustin: Konrad-Adenauer-Stiftung, 1995.

Kapstein, Ethan B. "America's Arms-Trade Monopoly." *Foreign Affairs* 73, no. 3 (1994): 13–20.

Karadi, Matthias Z. *Die Reform der Atlantischen Allianz: Bündnispolitik als Beitrag zur kooperativen Sicherheit in Europa?* Forschungsberichte Internationale Politik Vol. 17, (Münster: Lit.Verlag, 1994).

"Karl Lamers: Suche nach einer neuen Balance." *Deutsches Allgemeines Sonntagsblatt,* 24 September 1993.

Keating, Michael, and Barry Jones. ed. *Regions in the European Community.* Oxford: Clarendon Press, 1985.

"Kehrtwende der SPD." *Focus,* 2 June 1997.

"Keimzelle eines Großalbanien," *Der Spiegel,* 21 June 1999.

"Kein Krieg am Golf!" *Blätter für deutsche und internationale Politik* 36 (1991): 177–179.

"Kein Vetorecht." *Frankfurter Allgemeine Zeitung,* 15 November 1993.

"Kein Zweifel and Währungsunion." *CDU/CSU-Fraktion im Deutschen Bundestag,* 29 September 1993.

"Kein Zwist zwischen Kohl und Rühe über NATO-Erweiterung nach Osten." *dpa Pressebrief,* 7 January 1994.

Keitly, David M. "Shadows of Germany's Authoritarian Past." *Orbis* 38, no. 2 (1994): 207–223.

Keohane, Robert O., and Stanley Hoffmann. ed. *The New European Community—Decisionmaking and Institutional Change.* Boulder: Westview Press, 1991.

————, and Joseph, S. Nye. *Power and Interdependence: World Politics in Transition.* Boston: Little, Brown & Co., 1977.

"Kernwaffen bleiben für die NATO wichtig." *Frankfurter Allgemeine Zeitung,* 4 December 1998.

Kielinger, Thomas. Otte Max. "Germany: The Pressured Power," *Foreign Policy* 91, no. 2 (1993): 44–62.

Kiessler, Richard, and Frank Elbe. *Ein runder Tisch mit scharfen Ecken: Der diplomatische Weg zur deutschen Einheit.* Baden-Baden: Nomos 1993.

"Kinkel: Die NATO soll sich Mittel- und Osteuropa stärker öffnen." *Frankfurter Allgemeine Zeitung,* 6 March 1993.

Kinkel, Klaus. "Das hat gewisse Ängste geweckt." Interview, *Der Spiegel,* 19 February 1996.

———. "Deutsche Aussenpolitik bleibt Friedenspolitik." *Europäische Sicherheit* 42 (1993): 606–608.

———. "Deutschland in Europa: Zu den Zielen der deutschen Präsidentschaft in der Europäischen Union." *Europa-Archiv* 49, 1 (1994): 335–342.

———. "Die NATO-Erweiterung: Ein Beitrag zur Gesamteuropäischen Sicherheit." *Internationale Politik* 50, no. 4 (1995): 22–25.

———. "Dort spielt die Musik." Interview, *Der Spiegel,* 27 September 1993.

"Kinkel: Die NATO soll sich Mittel- und Osteuropa stärker öffnen." *Frankfurter Allgemeine Zeitung,* 6 March 1993.

"Kinkel gegen schnelle Osterweiterung der NATO." *Die Welt,* 6 February 1995.

"Kinkel: NATO mit dem ganzen Osten enger vernetzen." *Süddeutsche Zeitung,* 10 November 1993.

"Kinkel: NATO muß mehr Sicherheit für alle bieten." *dpa Pressebrief,* 16 December 1993.

"Kinkel: 1996 keine NATO-Osterweiterung." *dpa Pressebrief,* 5 December 1995.

"Kinkel: Schwere Tage für die USA: Gespräche auch über NATO." *dpa Pressebrief,* 5 October 1993.

"Kinkel trifft Krautscha: Die Aussenminister sprechen über finanzielle Hilfen für Weißrußland." *Frankfurter Allgemeine Zeitung,* 4 March 1994.

"Kinkel und Holst: Deutliches Zeichen der NATO für Osten." *dpa Pressebrief,* 14 October 1993.

"Kinkel warnt vor zu rascher NATO-Erweiterung nach Osteuropa." *dpa Pressebrief,* 7 October 1994.

"Kinkel wurde als ein guter Freund gefeiert." *General-Anzeiger,* 25 March 1994

Kirkpatrick, Jeane. "A NATO Umbrella for Eastern Europe." *The Washington Post,* 8 June 1993.

Kissinger, Henry A. *A World Restored: Metternich, Castlereagh and the Problems of Peace 1812–1822.* (London: Weidenfeld and Nicolson, 1957).

———. "No Illusions about the USSR." *The The Washington Post,* 22 January 1991.

———. "The Dillution of NATO." *The Washington Post,* 8 June 1997.

Kister, Kurt. "Washingtoner Absage an Rühe und Wörner: Die NATO nicht gleich bis an den Bug." *Süddeutsche Zeitung,* 18 December 1993.

Kivimäki, Timo. "Finnland." *Jahrbuch der europäischen Integration* 16 (1996/97): 307–312.

"Klagen über fehlendes Verständnis: Der Aussenminister Aserbaidschans zu Besuch in Bonn." *Frankfurter Allgemeine Zeitung,* 2 March 1994.

Klodt, Henning. "Staatsverschuldung hat die Belastung der Privatwirtschaft nuraufgeschoben." *Handelsblatt,* 21 April 1992.

Klose, HansUlrich. "Drohpotential muß sein." Interview, *Der Spiegel,* 12 December 1994.

————. "Wir müssen UNO-fähig werden." Interview, *Der Spiegel,* 6 September 1993.

"Klose für Erweiterung der NATO ausgesprochen." *dpa Pressebrief,* 25 November 1994.

Knorr, Klaus. *The Power of Nations.* New York: Basic Books, 1975.

"Koalitionsvereinbarung zwischen der Sozialdemokratischen Partei Deutschlands undBündnis 90/Die Grünen, unterzeichnet am 20.10.1998 in Bonn, (Auszüge)." *Internationale Politik* 53, no. 12 (1998): 67–79.

Kober, Stanley. "The United States and the Enlargement Debate." *Transition* 1, no. 23 (1995): 6–9.

"Kohl fordert Signal für EG-Anwärter in Mittel- und Osteuropa." *dpa Pressebrief,* 2 September 1993.

"Kohl fordert vollständige Integration Rußlands in Europa." *dpa Pressebrief,* 28 September 1995.

"Kohl lehnt größere NATO ab." *Frankfurter Rundschau,* 2 December 1993.

"Kohl macht den EU-Beitritt Polens zu seiner Sache." *Kölner-Stadt-Anzeiger,* 15 April 1994.

"Kohl: Moskau wird politisch aufgewertet." *Süddeutsche Zeitung,* 18 April 1997.

"Kohls Mythos verblaßt." *Focus,* 18 March 1996.

"Kohl rät in Washington zur Geduld bei NATO-Erweiterung." *Frankfurter Allgemeine Zeitung,* 11 February 1995.

"Kohl und Clinton unterstützen Jelzin und russischen Reformkurs." *dpa Pressebrief,* 9 February 1995.

"Kohl und Kinkel vor Gericht." *Der Spiegel,* 5 April 1993.

"Kohl und Mitterrand bleiben uneins über GATT." *Frankfurter Allgemeine Zeitung,* 2 December 1993.

"Kohl unterstützt Ungarn bei Annäherung an EG und NATO." *Frankfurter Allgemeine Zeitung,* 24 June 1993.

"Kohl will sich zum Streit um Ost-Erweiterung nicht äußern." *dpa Pressebrief,* 7 October 1994.

"Kohl wünscht mehr Binnenmarkt-Engagement." *Frankfurter Allgemeine Zeitung,* 16 March 1988.

Kolb, Eberhard. *Die Weimarer Republik.* Oldenbourg Grundriß der Geschichte, Vol. 16. 4th ed. Munich: Oldenbourg, 1993.

Kolboom, Ingo. "Dialog mit Bauchgrimmen? Die Zukunft der deutschfranzösischen Beziehungen." *Europa-Archiv* 49, 1 (1994): 257–264.

————. "Die Vertreibung der Dämonen: Frankreich und das vereinte Deutschland." *Europa-Archiv* 46, 1 (1991): 470–475.

Kommission der EG, ed. *Vollendung des Binnenmarktes: Weißbuch der Kommission an denEuropäischen Rat.* Luxemburg: Kommission der EG, 1985.

"Kommuniqué der Ministertagung des Nordatlantikrates." *Bulletin des Presse- und Informationsamtes der Bundesregierung,* 11 June 1991.

Kornelius, Stefan. "Heftiger Streit um Einsatzliste: Kohl und Rühe widersetzen sich KinkelsForderung, für eine UNO-Truppe Soldaten zu benennen." *Süddeutsche Zeitung,* 16 January 1995.

———. "Kleine Schritte zur Erweiterung der NATO, Rühes neue Ostpolitik: Vom Militärbündniszur Wertegemeinschaft." *Süddeutsche Zeitung,* 19 April 1993.

———. "Die NATO verordnet sich eine lange Denkpause." *Süddeutsche Zeitung,* 23 October 1993.

Korte, Karl-Rudolf. "Unbefangen und gelassen: Über die außenpolitische Normalität der Berliner Republik." *Internationale Politik* 53, no. 12 (1998): 3–12.

Kostede, Norbert. "Zwischen Utopie und Regierungsfähigkeit: Björn Engholms Aussagen über die Rolle der Bundeswehr verwirren die SPD." *Die Zeit,* 11 September 1992.

Koszel, Bogdan. "Polens dorniger Weg zur NATO." *Welttrends* 4, no. 10 (1996): 45–58.

Kozyrev, Andreij. "Partnerschaft für ein geeintes, friedliches und demokratisches Europa." *Frankfurter Rundschau,* 8 January 1994.

Kreile, Michael. "Verantwortung und Interesse in der deutschen Außen- und Sicherheitspolitik." *Aus Politik und Zeitgeschichte* 46, no. B5 (1996): 3–11.

Krell, Gert. "Migration und Asyl: Die Weltbevölkerung zwischen Integration und Polarisierung." *Hessische Stiftung Friedens- und Konfliktforschung,* 8, no.4 (1992).

Kremp, Herbert. "Rückkehr zum Realismus." *Die Welt,* 6 October 1993.

"Kritik am Kosovo-Einsatz wächst: Bei SPD und Grünen mehren sich die ablehnenden Stimmen." *Süddeutsche Zeitung,* 6 April 1999.

"Kritik an Osteuropapolitik - SPD: Aussenminister Kinkels Zusagen für eine rasche Osterweiterung sind populistisch." *Neue Zeit,* 25 May 1994.

Krugman, Paul R., ed. *Strategic Trade Policy and the New International Economics.* Cambridge, MA.: MIT Press, 1986.

Krustmann, Wolf-Heinrich. "Zukünftiges Bild des deutschen Soldaten." *Europäische Sicherheit* 43, no. 7 (1994): 358–361.

"KSZE-Forum für sicherheitspolitische Zusammenarbeit." *Bundestag Drucksache* 12/2789, 10 June 1992.

"Kucan: Slowenien will Mitglied in der NATO werden." *Die Welt,* 30 September 1993.

Kühne, Winrich. "Erweiterung und Reform des UNSicherheitsrats: Keine weltpolitischeNebensache." *Europa-Archiv* 49, 1 (1994): 685–692.

Kurth, James R. "The Political Consequences of the Product Cycle." *InternationalOrganization* 33, no.1 (1979): 1–34.

Läufer, Thomas. "Bundesrepublik Deutschland." *Jahrbuch der Europäischen Integration* 11 (1992/93): 299–307.

———. "Haushaltspolitik." *Jahrbuch der Europäischen Integration* 7 (1986/87): 141–153.

"Lafontaines Handschrift," *Der Spiegel,* 18 January 1999.

"Lafontaine widerspricht Scharping." *Frankfurter Allgemeine Zeitung,* 3 June 1995.

"Lamers: NATO und EU-Mitgliedschaft koppeln." *dpa Pressebrief,* 7 December 1994.

Larrabe, Stephen F. "Moscow and the German Question." In *The Germans and their Neighbors,* ed. Dirk Verheyen and Christian Soe. Boulder, CO: Westview Press, 1993.

Lavoie, Don. *National Economic Planning: What is Left?* Cambridge, MA: Ballinger Publishers, 1985.

Lebed, Aleksander. "Gefüttert, gestreichelt, geschlagen: General Aleksander Lebed über Rußlands Verhältnis zuden Serben und Amerikanern." Interview, *Der Spiegel,* 5 April 1999.

———. "Old Enemies, New Problems." *Petersburg Times,* 2–8 June 1997.

"Leiser Vorbehalt." *Der Spiegel,* 30 August 1993.

"Leitantrag zur Außen-, Sicherheits- und Entwicklungspolitik: Beschlüsse des Parteitages von Hannover 2.–4. Dezember 1997." In Sozialdemokratische Partei Deutschlands: Programmatisches [database online]. Bonn, Bundesvorstand der SPD, 1999 [cited 10 August 1999]. Available from http://www.spd.de/archiv/events/hannover97/aussen–1.htm.

Lepingwell, John W.R. "The Russian Military and Security Policy in the 'Near Abroad'" *Survival* 36, no. 3 (1994): 70–93.

Lichel, Carl-Helmuth. "Gedanken zur Traditionspflege: Absage an die Generation der Gründer?" *Europäische Sicherheit* 41, no. 2 (1992): 92–96.

Lindahl, Rutger. "Schweden." *Jahrbuch der europäischen Integration* 16 (1996/97): 355–360.

Link, Werner. "Die europäische Neuordnung des Mächtegleichgewichts." In *Europa 2020. Szenarien einer politischen Entwicklung,* ed. Thomas Jäger and Melanie Piepenschneider. Opladen: Leske und Budrich, 1995.

List, Friedrich. *The National System of Political Economy.* Philadelphia: J. B. Lippincott, 1856.

"Listig versteckt." *Der Spiegel,* 22 February 1988.

"Litauen beantragt formell die NATO-Mitgliedschaft." *Frankfurter Allgemeine Zeitung,* 5 January 1994.

Livingston, Robert Gerald. "United Germany: Bigger and Better." *Foreign Policy* no. 87 (1992): 165–174.

"Lohnanstieg kostet Marktanteile." *Informationsdienst des Instituts der deutschen Wirtschaft* 19, no. 27 (1994).

Lohse, Eckart. "Fischers Positionen wären Adenauer Grund zur Freude," *Frankfurter Allgemeine Zeitung,* 24 October 1998.

"Londoner Erklärung." *Bulletin des Presse- und Informationsamtes der Bundesregierung,* 10 July 1990.

Louscer, David J., Alethia H. Cook, and Victoria Barto. "The Emerging Competitive Position of USDefence Firms in the International Market." *Defense Analysis* 14, no. 2 (1998): 115–134.

"Lust am Widerstand," *Der Spiegel,* 16 November 1998.

"Magnet EG-Binnenmarkt." *Informationsdienst des Instituts der deutschen Wirtschaft* 18, no. 35 (1993).

"Mann im Strickrock." *Der Spiegel,* 17 May 1999.

Mann, Golo. *Deutsche Geschichte des 19. und 20. Jahrhunderts.* Frankfurt/M.: Fischer, 1979.

Martin, Lawrence. "Nationale Sicherheit in einer neuen Weltordnung." *Europa-Archiv* 47 (1992): 59 70.

"Martin Walsers Dankrede beim Empfang des Friedenspreises des deutschen Buchhandels in der Frankfurter Paulskirche am 11.10.1998 (Auszüge)." *Blätter für deutsche und internationale Politik* 44 (1999): 118–119.

Masala, Carlo. "Die Debatte über die institutionelle Reform der EU." *Aussenpolitik* 48, no. 3 (1997): 228–236.

"Massenexodus von DDR-Bürgern über die ungarisch-österreichische Grenze: Ungarn öffnetseine Grenzen." *Keesings Archiv der Gegenwart,* 11 September 1989.

Maull, Hanns. "Germany and Japan: The New Civilian Powers." *Foreign Affairs* 69, no. 5 (1990/91): 91–107.

———. "Japan und Deutschland: Die neuen Großmächte?" *Europa-Archiv,* 49, 1 (1994): 603–610.

———. "Zivilmacht Bundesrepublik: Vierzehn Thesen für eine neue deutsche Aussenpolitik." *Europa-Archiv* 47, 1 (1992): 269–278.

Matyschok, Arthur. "Ein Beitrag zu einer deutschen Diskussion: Tradition in der Bundeswehr." *Europäische Sicherheit* 43, no. 7 (1994): 358–361.

Maynes, Charles William. "A Workable Clinton Doctrine." *Foreign Policy* 93 (1993/94): 3–22.

McCarthy, Patrick. *France-Germany, 1983–93: The Struggle to Cooperate.* New York: St. Martin's Press, 1993.

Mearsheimer, John J. "Back to the Future: Instability in Europe after the Cold War." *International Security* 15, no. 1 (1991): 5–56.

Medwedjew, Roy A. "Ein hartes Njet zur NATO." *Die Zeit,* 20 May 1999.

"Mehr Müll, weniger Rechte." *Der Spiegel,* 20 November 1988.

"Meinungsstreit in der NATO über die Aufnahme neuer Mitglieder." *dpa Pressebrief,* 30 September 1994.

"Meinungsumschwung an der Wolga." *Die Welt,* 24 April 1992.

"Memorandum Bundeskanzler Adenauers über die Sicherung des Bundesgebietes nach innen und außen, 29 August 1950." In *Sicherheitspolitik der Bundesrepublik Deutschland: Dokumentation 1945–1977, Teil I,* ed. Klaus von Schubert. Bonn: Bundeszentrale für politische Bildung, 1977, 933–936.

Meyer, Berthold, Harald Müller, and Hans-Joachim Schmidt. "NATO 96: Bündnis im Widerspruch." *Report der Hessischen Stiftung für Friedens- und Konfliktforschung* 12, no. 3 (1996).

"Milch und Honig." *Der Spiegel,* 1 August 1994.

"Militärpolitische und militärstrategische Grundlagen und konzeptionelle Grundrichtung derNeugestaltung der Bundeswehr." *Blätter für deutsche und internationale Politik.* 3 (1992): 506–510.

"Ministertreffen in Noordwijk; EWI legt Jahresbericht 1996 vor," *Keesings Archiv der Gegenwart,* 4 April 1996.

Miszczak, Krzystof. "Die Sicherheits-perspektiven Ostmitteleuropas: Zwischen NATO undRußland." *Europäische Sicherheit* 43 (1994): 295–298.

"Mitgliedschaft in der NATO polnische Verteidigungsdoktrin." *Frankfurter Allgemeine Zeitung,* 1 August 1992.

"Mit Kinkel in der ersten Reihe." *Die Zeit,* 1 October 1993.

"Mit mir nicht." *Der Spiegel,* 8 March 1999.

"Mit schlechtem Gewissen." *Der Spiegel,* 3 March 1997.

"Mit Stolz." *Der Spiegel,* 15 July 1991.

"Mitteilung zu den Ergebnissen der europäischen Rates." *Presseservice der SPD,* 12 December 1994.

"Mitterrand nimmt Kohl in Schutz." *General-Anzeiger,* 17 August 1993.

"Mitterrand lobt Verhältnis zu Bonn." *Frankfurter Allgemeine Zeitung,* 22 March 1994.

"Möglichst unauffällig." *Der Spiegel,* 1 June 1992.

Moravcsik, Andrew. "Negotiating the Single European Act." In *The New European-Community: Decisionmaking and Institutional Change,* ed. Robert O. Keohane and Stanley Hoffmann. Boulder, CO: Westview Press, 1991.

Morsey, Rudolf. *Die Bundesrepublik Deutschland: Entstehung und Entwicklung bis 1969.* Oldenbourg Grundriß der Geschichte, Vol. 19, 3rd ed. Munich: Oldenbourg 1995.

"Moskau stemmt sich gegen Ost-Öffnung der NATO." *Die Welt,* 6 January 1994.

"Moskau will Beziehungen zum Westen nicht gefährden." *Frankfurter Allgemeine Zeitung,* 29 March 1999.

"Mut zum Absurden." *Der Spiegel,* 29 March 1993.

"Nahe dran am echten Krieg." *Der Spiegel,* 20 July 1992.

"NATO als Fundament der Sicherheitsstruktur." Rede von Bundesminister Rühe vom 21.05.1993, *Stichworte zur Sicherheitspolitik* 16, no. 6 (1993): 28–30.

"NATO Goes Out-of-Area or Out-of-Business," *Keynote Address, XIIth German-American Roundtable, Konrad-Adenauer-Stiftung,* 11 June 1993.

"NATO Entry Stalled for Visegrad Countries." *Financial Times,* 1 October 1994.

"NATO-Gipfelkonferenz in Madrid." *Keesings Archiv der Gegenwart,* 9 July 1997.

"NATO-Gipfelkonferenz in Rom." *Bulletin des Presse- und Informationsamtes der Bundesregierung,* 13 November 1991.

"NATO: Herbstagung der Aussenminister." *Keesings Archiv der Gegenwart*, 10 December 1996.

"NATO Issue Study on Enlargement of Alliance." *United States Information Service Wireless File*, 29 September 1995.

"NATO Osterweiterung bleibt." *Focus*, 5 August 1997.

"NATO Rationalizes its Eastward Enlargement." *Transition* 1, no. 23 (1995): 19–26.

"NATO Rumbles to the East." *U.S. News and World Report*, 21 November 1994.

"NATO soll Sicherheitsvakuum füllen." *Süddeutsche Zeitung*, 17 December 1993.

"NATO unterbreitet Russland Vorschläge für besondere Zusammenarbeit." *Stichworte zur Sicherheitspolitik* 18, no. 10 (1995): 42.

"NATO-Vollmitgliedschaft der Reformstaaten nur eine Frage der Zeit." *Süddeutsche Zeitung*, 8 July 1994.

"Nie mehr Täter sein." *Der Spiegel*, 28 January 1991.

"Neuer Machtpol in Europa." *Der Spiegel*, 7 March 1994.

"Neuer NATO-Generalsekretär legt Schwerpunkt auf Ost-Erweiterung." *dpa Pressebrief*, 17 October 1994.

"Neues Wir-Gefühl." *Bonner Rundschau*, 14 October 1993.

"Neu Labour hat sich entschlossen, die europäischen Partner einmal angenehm zu überraschen." *Frankfurter Allgemeine Zeitung*, 22 October 1998.

Neumeier, Eduard. "Mit den Deutschen geht es am besten." *Rheinischer Merkur*, 18 December 1992.

"Nicht nur auf die Wolgarepublik starren." *Neue Zeit*, 7 July 1993.

Niedhart, Gottfried, Paul Junker, and Michael Michael, ed. *Deutschland in Europa: Nationale Interessen und internationale Ordnung im 20. Jahrhundert*. Mannheim: Palatium HVS, 1997.

Ninkovich, Frank. *Germany and the United States: The Transformation of the German Question since 1945*. New York: Twayne, 1995.

"Noch zu früh." *Der Spiegel*, 27 June 1988.

Noelle-Neumann, Elisabeth. "Die öffentliche Meinung." *Jahrbuch der europäischen Integration*, 15 (1996/97): 275–280.

———. "Die öffentliche Meinung." *Jahrbuch der Europäischen Integration* 10 (1991/92): 273–281.

———. "Die öffentliche Meinung." *Jahrbuch der europäischen Integration* 12 (1993/94): 285–294.

———, and Gerhard Herdegen. "Die öffentliche Meinung." *Jahrbuch der Europäischen Integration* 7 (1986/87): 302–318.

———. "Die öffentliche Meinung." *Jahrbuch der Europäischen Integration* 8 (1987/88): 316–329.

———. "Die öffentliche Meinung." *Jahrbuch der Europäischen Integration* 9 (1989/90): 277–289.

———, and Renate Köcher. ed. *Allensbacher Jahrbuch der Demoskopie 1984–92*, München: K. G. Saur, 1993.

————. "Europa hinter dem Schleier: Schlechte Information, wenig Wissen, widersprüchliche Einstellungen." *Frankfurter Allgemeine Zeitung,* 27 September 1995.

Nogradi, Georg. "Partnerschaft für den Frieden: Illusionen und Ernüchterung." *Europäische Sicherheit* 43 (1994): 242–243.

Nonnenmacher, Günter. "Das Jahr der Entscheidung." *Frankfurter Allgemeine Zeitung,* 2 February 1985.

Nonnemnacher, Peter. "Blair spricht sich für Prodi aus," *Frankfurter Allgemeine Zeitung,* 23 March 1999.

"Nun siegt mal schön." *Der Spiegel,* 18 July 1994.

"Nur noch zweite Wahl." *Der Spiegel,* 4 July 1994.

"Objektive Schwierigkeiten mit Bonn." *Die Welt,* 25 August 1993.

OECD, ed. *Economic Outlook-Historical Statistics 1960–1990.* Paris: OECD 1992.

————, ed. *Economic OutlookHistorical Statistics 1960–1995.* Paris: OECD 1997.

"Ökokatastrophe durch Golfkrieg verhindern!" *Blätter für deutsche und internationale Politik* 36 (1991): 167.

Olechowski, Andrzej. "Polen und die Nordatlantische Allianz." *Frankfurter Rundschau,* 3 January 1994.

Opel, Manfred. "Die Wehrreform der Bundewehr heißt Freiwilligen-Armee." *Europäische Sicherheit* 43, no. 3 (1994): 114–116.

"Oskar auf Werbetour." *Der Spiegel,* 16 November 1998.

"Osteuropa für den Export immer wichtiger. " *Frankfurter Allgemeine Zeitung,* 17 October 1996.

"Osteuropa für deutsche Wirtschaft immer wichtiger." *Frankfurter Allgemeine Zeitung,* 1 October 1996.

Ostermann, Dietmar. "Ein neuer Freund für den einsamen Boris Jelzin." *Frankfurter Rundschau,* 17 December 1992.

Otte, Max. *The United States, Japan, West Germany and Europe in the International Economy 1977–1987.* Idstein: Schulz-Kirchner Verlag, 1988.

Packenham, Robert A. *Liberal America and the Third World.* Princeton, NJ: Princeton University Press, 1973.

Parteivorstand der SPD. "Erklärung zu den Verträgen von Maastricht." *Presseservice der SPD,* 9 March 1992.

Pavlow, Nikolai. "Perspektiven der deutsch-russischen Zusammenarbeit." In *Stand undPerspektiven des Deutsch-Russischen Verhältnisses,* ed. Deutsch-russisches Forum e.V., 1993.

Perger, Werner A. "Wir unbefangenen." *Die Zeit,* 12 November 1998.

"Perry plädiert für NATO-Beitritt Tschechiens." *Die Welt,* 21 September 1995.

"Perry: Slowenien ist Vorbild für Mitteleuropa." *Süddeutsche Zeitung,* 19 September 1995.

"Perry: Ungarn erfüllt bald Kriterien für NATO-Beitritt." *Frankfurter Allgemeine Zeitung,* 21 September 1995.

"Perry zu Gesprächen über die NATO in Warschau." *Frankfurter Allgemeine Zeitung,* 28 May 1995.

"Perry zuversichtlich." *Frankfurter Allgemeine Zeitung,* 22 September 1995.

"Perspektiven deutscher Außen- und Sicherheitspolitik: Vortrag von Staatssekretär/AA Wolfgang Ischinger vor dem Forum der Chefredakteure zur Sicherheitspolitik der Bundesakademie für Sicherheitspolitik, Bad Neuenahr 27.1.1999. " In Reden 1999 [database online]. Bonn: Auswärtiges Amt der Bundesrepublik Deutschland, 1999 [cited 20 August 1999]. Available from *http://www.auswaertiges-amt.de/6_archiv/index.htm*

"Perspektiven einer neuen Außen- und Sicherheitspolitik." In *Protokoll des Parteitages von Wiesbaden 16–19. November 1993,* ed. SPD-Parteivorstand. Frankfurt am Main: Union Druckerei, 1994.

"Petersberger Erklärung vom 19 Juni 1992." *Blätter für deutsche und internationale Politik* 37 (1992): 1020–1023.

Petersen, Nikolaj. "Dänemark." *Jahrbuch der europäischen Integration* 16 (1996/97): 303–306.

Pfister, Jürgen. "Ist das Europäische Währungssystem am Ende?" *Europa-Archiv* 48, 1 (1993): 711–717.

Philippi, Nina. *Bundeswehr-Auslandseinsätze als außen- und sicherheitspolitisches Problem des geeinten Deutschland.* University of Trier: unpublished M.A. thesis, 1996.

Pitzke, Marc. "Showtime in Moskau." *Die Woche,* 25 August 1994.

Pöttering, Hans-Gert. "Perspektiven für eine gemeinschaftliche Außen- und Sicherheitspolitik der EG." *Europa-Archiv* 45, 1 (1990): 341–350.

Podkaminer, Leon. *Country Reports: Bulgaria, Croatia, Czech Republic, Hungary, Poland, Romania, Russia, Slovakia, Slovenia, Ukraine.* Wien: Wiener Institut für internationale Wirtschaftsvergleiche, 1995.

"Polen beklagt Absage der NATO an Erweiterung." *Welt am Sonntag,* 24 October 1993.

"Polen fordert Zeitplan für NATO-Beitritt." *Frankfurter Allgemeine Zeitung,* 27 August 1993.

"Polen in die NATO?" *Die Zeit,* 13 November 1992.

"Polens Aussenminister drängt auf schnellen NATO-Beitritt." *Die Welt,* 11 September 1993.

"Polen schlägt gemeinsame Manöver vor." *Süddeutsche Zeitung,* 26 April 1994.

Pond, Elizabeth. "Die Entstehung der 'Zwei-plus-Vier'." *Europa-Archiv* 47, 1 (1992): 619–630.

Porter, Michael E. *The Competitive Advantage of Nations.* New York: The Free Press, 1990.

Presse- und Informationsamt der Bundesregierung, ed. *Europa 2000.* Bonn: Presse- und Informationsamt 1993.

———, ed. *Weißbuch 1971/1972 zur Sicherheit der Bundesrepublik Deutschland und zur Entwicklung der Bundeswehr.* Bonn: Bundesdruckerei, 1970.

"Presse-Erklärung des deutschen Verteidigungsministers Volker Rühe nach der Entsendung von Einheiten zur Seeaufklärung zur Unterstützung der Überwachung des Embargos gegen Serbien." *Europa-Archiv* 47, 2 (1992): D581.

Pries, Knut. "Erfolg für Gerhard Schröder," *Frankfurter Rundschau,* 27 March 1999.

"Probleme der europäischen Einigung (I)." *Europa-Archiv* 43, 2 (1988): D141.

"Probleme der europäischen Einigung (II)." *Europa-Archiv,* 43, 2 (1988): D438.

"Probleme der europäischen Einigung (III)." *Europa-Archiv* 43, 2 (1988): D681.

"Probleme der Europäischen Einigung (III)." *Europa-Archiv,* 45, 2 (1990): D395.

"Probleme der europäischen Einigung (I)." *Europa-Archiv* 46, 2 (1991): D1–3.

"Probleme der Europäischen Einigung (II)." *Europa-Archiv* 46, 2 (1991): D361–363.

"Probleme der Europäischen Einigung." *Europa-Archiv* 47, 2 (1992): D89–122.

"Probleme mit der Währung." *Die Woche,* 4 March 1994.

Proissl, Wolfgang. "Kein Plan, Keine Waffen: In der Außen- und Sicherheitspolitik wird Europa noch lange auf die Unterstützung der USA angewiesen sein," *Die Zeit,* 27 May 1999.

Public Papers of the President. *Interview with Foreign Journalists, July 1, 1994.* Washington, D.C.: GPO, 1994, 1406.

Public Papers of the President. *The President's News Conference with Chancellor Helmut Kohl in Bonn, Germany, July 11, 1994.* Washington, D.C.: GPO, 1994, 1463.

Putnam, Robert D. "Diplomacy and Domestic Politics: The Logic of Two-level Game." *International Organization* 42 (1988): 427–460.

Rachwald, Arthur R. "Poland and Germany: From Foes to Friends?" In *The Germans and their Neighbors,* ed. Dirk Verheyen and Christian Soe. Boulder, CO: Westview Press, 1993.

Rahr, Alexander, and Joachim Krause. *Russia's New Foreign Policy.* Arbeitspapiere zur internationalen Politik der deutschen Gesellschaft für Auswärtige Politik, Vol. 91. Bonn: Europa Union Verlag, 1995.

Rasler, Karen A., and William R. Thompson. "Global Wars, Public Debts, and the Long Cycle." *World Politics* 35, no. 4 (1983): 489–517.

"Rede der britischen Premierministerin Margaret Thatcher in der europäischen Hochschule Brügge vom 20. September 1988." *Europa-Archiv* 35, 2 (1988): D683–684.

"Rede des amerikanischen Präsidenten Bush in Mainz, 31. Mai 1989." *Europa-Archiv* 44, 2 (1989): D356–D361.

"Rede des Aussenministers Hans-Dietrich Genscher über die Ziele der deutschen EU-Präsidentschaft vor dem Europäischen Parlament vom 20. Januar 1988." *Europa-Archiv* 34, 2 (1988): D150–151.

"Rede des Aussenministers Hans-Dietrich Genscher vor der 47. Vollversammlung der Vereinten Nationen am 25. September 1991." *Europa-Archiv* 47, 3 (1992): D345–351.

"Rede des Aussenministers Klaus Kinkel vor der deutschen Gesellschaft für Auswärtige Politik." *Europa-Archiv* 49, 2 (1994): D540–544.

"Rede des Bundeskanzlers auf dem Petersberg anläßlich des EGForums der Deutschen Wirtschaft zum Standort Europa." *Bulletin des Presse- und Informationsamtes der Bundesregierung,* 16 October 1992.

"Rede des Bundeskanzlers vor dem Deutschen Bundestag." *Bulletin des Presse- und Informationsamtes der Bundesregierung,* 17 December 1994.

"Rede des Bundeskanzlers vor dem Deutschen Bundestag vom 6. Mai 1999." *Bulletin des Presse- und Informationsamtes der Bundesregierung,* 6 May 1999.

"Rede des Bundesministers des Auswärtigen, Dr. Kinkel, am 23. September 1992 in New York." In *Aussenpolitik der Bundesrepublik Deutschland: Dokumente von 1949–1994,* ed. Auswärtiges Amt. Bonn: Auswärtiges Amt 1995, 875–880.

"Rede des russischen Präsidenten Jelzin anläßlich der Verabschiedung der russischenStreitkräfte aus Deutschland in Berlin am 31. August 1994." *Europa Archiv* 49, 2(1994): D557-D560.

"Rede des Verteidigungsministers Volker Rühe in Oxford." *Europa-Archiv* 49, 2 (1994): D443–448.

"Rede Douglas Hurds vor dem politischen Ausschuß des Carlton Clubs am 30. Juni 1993." *Britische Dokumentation der britischen Botschaft Bonn,* 9 September 1993.

"Rede John F. Kennedys in der Frankfurter Paulskirche am 25. Juni 1963." *Europa-Archiv* 18 (1963): D352–359.

Regelsberger, Elfriede. "Gemeinsame Außen- und Sicherheitspolitik." *Jahrbuch der Europäischen Integration* 16 (1996/97): 215–224.

————. "Gemeinsame Außen- und Sicherheitspolitik." In *Die Europäische Union,* ed. Wichard Woyke and Beate Kohler-Koch, Vol. 5 of *Lexikon der Politik.* Munich:Verlag C. H. Beck, 1995.

"Regierungserklärung Bundeskanzler Kohls über die Resultate der Tagung des Europäischen Rates der Staats- und Regierungschefs in Maastricht am 13. Dezember 1991." In *Aussenpolitik der Bundesrepublik Deutschland-Dokumente von 1949–1994,* ed. Auswärtiges Amt. Bonn:Verlag Wissenschaft und Politik, 1995, 846–851.

"Regierungserklärung des Bundeskanzlers vor dem Deutschen Bundestag." *Bulletin des Presse- und Informationsamtes der Bundesregierung,* 18 May 1974.

"Regierungserklärung des Bundeskanzlers: Weil wir Deutschlands Kraft vertrauen," *Bulletindes Presse- und Informationsamtes der Bundesregierung,* 11 November 1998.

"Regierungserklärung von Bundeskanzler Gerhard Schröder, abgegeben am 10.11.1998 vor dem Deutschen Bundestag in Bonn (Auszüge)." *Internationale Politik* 53, no. 12 (1998): 84–91.

"Regierungserklärung von Michel Barnier, Staatsminster für Europaangelegenheiten vor der französischen Nationalversammlung am 13.3.1996." In *Die Reform der Europäischen Union,* ed. Mathias Jopp. Bonn: Europa UnionVerlag, 1996, 150–155.

"Regierung.Viele Ideen, aber kein Konzept." *Der Spiegel,* 31 May 1999.

"Resolution 1244 des UN-Sicherheitsrates vom 10. Juni 1999 (Auszüge)." *Blätter für deutsche und internationale Politik* 44 (1999): 877–881.

Richardson, David J. "The Political Economy of Strategic Trade Policy." *International Organization* 44, no. 4 (1990): 107–135.

Riddell, Peter. "Bush presses Germany to step up international role." *Financial Times,* 19 November 1990.

Röstel, Gunda. "NATO-Osterweiterung mitgestalten." Interview, *Focus,* 10 March 1997.

Rosecrance, Richard. "Long cycle theory and international relations." *International Organization,* 41, no. 2 (1987): 283–301.

———. *The Rise of the Trading State: Commerce and Conquest in the Modern World.* New York: Basic Books, 1986.

Rowold, Manfred. "Moskau wirft dem Westen Provokation vor." *Die Welt,* 18 August 1994.

"Rückzug auf die Nation?" *Der Spiegel,* 25 October 1993.

Rühe, Volker. "Das ist keine Drohgebärde." Interview, *Der Spiegel,* 20 July 1992.

———. "Kein Triumphgeheul." Interview, *Focus,* 18 July 1994.

———. "Raus aus dem Dilemma." *Der Spiegel,* 21 December 1992.

———. "Shaping Euro-Atlantic Policies: A Grand Strategy or a New Era." *Survival* 35, no. 2 (1993): 129–138.

———. "Sinn und Auftrag der Bundeswehr im vereinten Deutschland." *Bulletin des Presse und Informationsamtes der Bundesregierung,* 7 April 1992.

"Rühe befürwortet Erweiterung der NATO nach Osteuropa." *dpa Pressebrief,* 31 March 1993.

"Rühe: Erweiterung der NATO bis zum Jahr 2000." *dpa Pressebrief,* 7 June 1994.

"Rühe: EU-Beitritte müssen mit NATO-Erweiterung einhergehen." *dpa Pressebrief,* 22 January 1995.

"Rühe: Gleiche Pflichten für EU und NATO-Mitglieder ist Ziel." *dpa Pressebrief,* 27 January 1995.

"Rühe: Keine Mitgliedschaft Rußlands in NATO und EU." *General-Anzeiger,* 5 July 1994.

"Rühe offen für neue NATO-Mitglieder: Plädoyer für eine Strategie des euroatlantischen Raumes." *Frankfurter Allgemeine Zeitung,* 21 May 1993.

"Rühe raises Polish hopes." *Financial Times,* 19 July 1994.

"Rühe sieht gute Entwicklung der Beziehungen zu Rußland." *dpa Pressebrief,* 14 April 1993.

"Rühe sieht Visegrad-Staaten noch vor dem Jahr 2000 in der NATO." *dpa Pressebrief,* 13 September 1994.

"Rühe: Vorzugskandidaten für die NATO-Mitgliedschaft klar benennen." *dpa Pressebrief,* 27 September 1994.

"Rühe wirbt in Amerika für strategische Partnerschaft mit Rußland." *Frankfurter Allgemeine Zeitung,* 4 May 1994.

Rühl, Lothar. "Ein toter Ritter in der Rüstung?" *Die Welt,* 28 August 1993.

Rühle, Hans. "Und jetzt der Krieg?" *Der Spiegel,* 24 February 1992.

———. "Welche Armee für Deutschland." *Europa-Archiv* 49, 1 (1994): 161–168.

Rudzio, Wolfgang. *Das politische System der Bundesrepublik Deutschland,* 4th ed. Opladen: Leske und Budrich, 1996.

"Rumänien wünscht deutsche Hilfe." *Frankfurter Allgemeine Zeitung,* 4 February 1992.

"Russische Diskussionen über die NATOOsterweiterung: Solana in Moskau." *KeesingsArchiv der Gegenwart,* 20 January 1997.

"Rußland soll mitentscheiden." *Frankfurter Allgemeine Zeitung,* 7 October 1993.

"Schach dem Bündnis: Rußland setzt bei der NATO-Osterweiterung ein lukrativesTauschgeschäft durch, unddie Deutschen helfen dabei." *Focus,* 17 May 1997.

Schäuble, Wolfgang. "Die D-Mark ist nicht alles." Interview, *Der Spiegel,* 27 March 1995.

Scharping, Rudolf. "Am Ende zählt nur Realismus: Verteidigungsminister Scharping warnt vor einer Provokation der NATO durch nationale Alleingänge." Interview, *Focus,* 30 November 1998.

————. Interview, *Tagesthemen.* Arbeitsgemeinschaft der Rundfunkanstalten Deutschlands, 1 September 1994

————. "Wir kommen unserem Ziel näher." Interview, *Der Spiegel,* 26 April 1999.

"Scharping bei Christopher: Bomben nicht schön, aber nötig." *dpa Pressebrief,* 11 April 1994.

"Scharping in die USA geflogen: SPD steht zum Bündnis." *dpa Pressebrief,* 10 April 1994.

"Scharping korrigiert SPD-Kurs." *Süddeutsche Zeitung,* 7 February 1994.

"Scharping warnt vor schneller NATO-Öffnung nach Osten." *dpa Pressebrief,* 10 January 1994.

Scharrer, Hans-Eckart. "Binnenmarktpolitik." *Jahrbuch der Europäischen Integration* 11 (1992/93): 139–150.

————. "Finanzen/Haushalt/Steuern." In *Die Europäische Union,* ed. Wichard Woyke and Beate Kohler-Koch, Vol. 5 of *Lexikon der Politik.* Munich: Verlag C. H. Beck, 1996.

"Schewardnadse ist des Lobes voll über die deutsche Hilfe." *General-Anzeiger,* 25 June 1993.

"Schlagabtausch Clinton-Jelzin." *Die Welt,* 6 December 1994.

Schlögel, Karl. "Die blockierte Vergangenheit: Nachdenken über Mitteleuropa." *Frankfurter Allgemeine Zeitung,* 21 February 1987.

Schlotter, Peter. "Die Mühen der stillen Diplomatie: Konfliktprävention und Krisenmanagement durch die OSZE." *Aus Politik und Zeitgeschichte* 46, no. B5 (1996): 27–31.

Schmähling, Elmar. "Die friedfertige Armee." *Der Spiegel,* 11 February 1991.

Schmidt, Helmut. "Die Nato gehört nicht Amerika." *Die Zeit,* 22 April 1999.

Schmuck, Otto. "Der Maastrichter Vertrag zur Europäischen Union." *Europa-Archiv* 47, 1 (1992): 97–106.

Schöllgen, Gregor. *Angst vor der MachtDie Deutschen und ihre Aussenpolitik.* Berlin: Ullstein, 1993.

————. "Die Berliner Republik als internationale Akteur: Gibt es noch eine deutsche Interessenpolitik." *Aussenpolitik* 49, no. 2 (1998): 27–37.

"Schritt für Schritt in den Krieg." *Der Spiegel,* 26 April 1993.

Schröder, Gerhard. "Ich bin kein Kriegskanzler: Bundeskanzler Gerhard Schröder über Weiterungen im Krieg gegen Milosevic, die Rolle der Deutschen beim Nato-Einsatz und den Sonderparteitag der SPD." Interview, *Der Spiegel,* 12 April 1999.

"Schröder fordert den erfolgreichen Abschluß der Agenda 2000," *Frankfurter Allgemeine Zeitung,* 24 March 1999.

Schumann, Harald. "Markt ohne Staat." *Der Spiegel,* 4 July 1988.

Schumpeter, Joseph. *The Theory of Economic Development: An Inquiry into Profits, Capital, Credit, Interest and the Business Cycle.* New York: Oxford University Press, 1961.

Schwarz, Hans-Peter. *Die gezähmten Deutschen: Von der Machtversessenheit zur Machtvergessenheit.* Stuttgart: Deutsche Verlags-Anstalt 1985.

————. *Die Zentralmacht Europas: Deutschlands Rückkehr auf die Weltbühne.* Berlin: Siedler, 1994.

————. "Rolle und Identität der zukünftigen deutschen Aussenpolitik." In *Die Zukunft der deutschen Aussenpolitik, Arbeitspapiere zur internationalen Politik,* ed. Karl Kaiser and Hanns Maull. Bonn: Deutsche Gesellschaft für Auswärtige Politik, 1992.

"Schwierige Geburt." *Kurz-Nachrichtendienst der Bundesvereinigung der Deutschen Arbeitgeberverbände,* 8 December 1992.

Seiters, Rudolf. "Rußland muß Teil der Sicherheitsarchitektur sein." Interview, *Süddeutsche Zeitung,* 29 March 1997.

"Seiters: Deutsche Überlegungen zur Regierungskonferenz 1996." *CDU/CSU Pressedienst,* 2 March 1995.

"Seiters: Rußlands Zustimmung um Partnerschaftsabkommen ein erster Schritt auf dem Weg zur besonderen Partnerschaft." *Pressedienst der CDU/CSU Fraktion in Deutschen Bundestag,* 31 May 1995.

Seitz, Konrad. "Die japanisch-amerikanische Herausforderung: Deutschlands Hochtechnologien kämpfen ums Überleben." *Aus Politik und Zeitgeschichte,* 42, no. B10–11 (1992): 13.

Serre, Franciose De la, Christian Laquesne. "Frankreich." *Jahrbuch der europäischen Integration,* 16 (1996/97): 313–320.

Shaskenov, Maxim. "Russian Peacekeeping in the 'Near Abroad'." *Survival* 36, no. 3 (1994): 46–70.

Shlaes, Amity. "Germany's Chained Economy." *Foreign Affairs* 73, no. 5 (1994): 109–126.

"Sicherheitspolitik der EU stärken, Brüssel 26.1.99." *Newsticker der Bundesregierung,* 27 January 1999.

Silguy, Yves-Thibault de. "Rätselraten schadet der Währungsunion." *Frankfurter Allgemeine Zeitung,* 23 May 1996.

Sloan, Stanley R. "NATO's Future: Beyond Collective Defense." *CRS Report for Congress* 15 September 1995.

Smyser, Richard W. "Dateline Berlin: Germany's New Vision." *Foreign Policy* 97, no. 4 (1994–95): 142–158.

"Solana bleibt hart." *Der Spiegel,* 27 January 1997.

"Soldaten, geht nicht an den Golf!." *Blätter für deutsche und internationale Politik* 36, 1 (1991): 160.

Solms, Friedhelm. "Deutschfranzösische Dissonanzen." *Blätter für deutsche und internationale Politik* 42 (1997): 821–829.

"Sozialdemokratische Aussenpolitik im Übergang zum 21. Jahrhundert: Diskussionspapier der Schwerpunktkommission Außen- und Sicherheitspolitik für den Kongreß am 18.6.1997 in Bonn," In Sozialdemokratische Partei Deutschlands: Programmatisches [database online]. Bonn: Bundesvorstand der SPD, 1999 [cited 10 August 1999]. Available from *http://www.spd.de/aktuell/aussen.htm.*

Späth, Lothar. "Der Traum von Europa: I Die soziale Frage." *Der Spiegel,* 2 October 1989.

"SPD macht Weg für Europäische Union frei." *Frankfurter Rundschau,* 10 March 1992.

"SPD-Sicherheitsexperte Bahr: Rußland in die NATO." *dpa Pressebrief,* 4 April 1992.

"SPD-Spitze gegen sofortige NATO-Mitgliedschaft Osteuropas." *dpa Pressebrief,* 10 January 1994.

"SPD-Parteitag: Aufstand der Linken zum Kosovo-Konflikt gescheitert." *Die Welt,* 13 April 1999.

"Speaking Notes of the Right Honourable George Robertson MP, Secretary of State for Defence for the Informal Conference of Defence Ministers of the EU in Vienna, 3–4 November 1998." *European Foreign Affairs Review* 4, no. 1 (1999): 121–123.

"Splitter im Körper." *Der Spiegel,* 1 January 1990.

"Standpunkte der italienischen Regierung vom 18.3.1996 (Auszüge):" In *Reform der Europäischen Union,* ed. Mathias Jopp. Bonn: Europa Union Verlag, 199, 156–162.

"Standort Deutschland." *Der Stern,* 17 February.

Statistisches Bundesamt, ed. *Statistisches Jahrbuch für das Ausland 1995.* Wiesbaden: Metzler Poeschel, 1995.

"Stellenabbau in Deutschland: Ein F.A.Z.-Umfrage." *Frankfurter Allgemeine Zeitung,* 19 December 1992.

Stelzenmüller, Constanze. "Kein Sonderweg," *Die Zeit,* 26 November 1998.

Stern, Fritz. "Freedom and its Discontents." *Foreign Affairs* 72, no. 4 (1993): 108–125.

"Steuerschätzung: Der Bund verliert im Steuerpoker." *Informationsdienst des Instituts der deutschen Wirtschaft* 19, no. 26 (1994).

"Stoiber für Sicherheitspartnerschaft der EU mit Osteuropa." *dpa Pressebrief*, 10 January 1994.

Strauss, Ira Louis. "Letters to the Editor." *New York Times*, 28 June 1993.

"Streben Bonns nach Einbeziehung Russlands." *Neue Züricher Zeitung*, 12 May 1994.

"Streit bei den Grünen verschärft sich." *Frankfurter Allgemeine Zeitung*, 7 December 1995.

Stürmer, Michael. "Gibt es ein Mitteleuropa?" *Frankfurter Allgemeine Zeitung*, 21 October 1986.

"Studie zur Osterweiterung; Vorschlag zur Änderung des KSE-Vertrags." *Keesings Archiv der Gegenwart*, 20 September 1995.

"Süddeutsche Zeitung: NATO-Botschafter kritisiert USA." *dpa Pressebrief*, 30 November 1994.

Süssmuth, Hans. "Deutschlandbilder im Ausland." In *Deutschlandbilder in Polen und Rußland, in der Tschechoslowakei und Ungarn,* ed. Hans Süssmuth. Baden-Baden: Nomos, 1993.

"Tagung des Europäischen Rates der Staats- und Regierungschefs am 8. und 9. Dezember 1989 in Straßburg." *Europa-Archiv* 45, 2 (1990): D1–18.

"Tagung des Europäischen Rates der Staats- und Regierungschefs am 27. Und 28. Juni 1988in Hannover." *Europa-Archiv* 43, 2 (1988): D445–446.

"Tagung der Nordatlantischen Versammlung: Frühjahrstagung der Aussenminister und des NACC." *Keesings Archiv der Gegenwart,* 31 May 1995.

Talbott, Strobe. Interview, CNN, 16 July 1994.

Tebbe, Gerd. "Wunsch und Wirklichkeit: Das Problem der Osterweiterung." *Europa-Archiv* 49, 1 (1994): 389–396.

Teltschik, Horst. "Aspekte der deutschen Außen- und Sicherheitspolitik." *Aus Politik und Zeitgeschichte* 35, no. B7–8 (1985): 3–14.

———. *329 Tage: Innenansichten der Einigung.* 3rd ed. Berlin: Siedler, 1991.

"Teure Wahrheit," *Der Spiegel,* 22 February 1999.

Thalmeier, Siegried. "Klare Worte an die baltischen Republiken." *Frankurter Allgemeine Zeitung,* 20 June 1995.

The International Institute for Strategic Studies, ed. *The Military Balance 1997–1998.*London: Brassey, 1997.

"The Polish Position: Excerpts from the Polish Council's NATO Report." *Transition* 1, no. 23 (1995): 41–43.

The President of the United States, ed. *Economic Report of the President 1984.* Washington, D.C.: Government Printing Office, 1984.

Thompson, William R. "Long Waves, Technological Innovation, and Relative Decline." *International Organization,* 44, no. 2 (1990): 201–233.

Thumann, Michael. "Der Bär grollt." *Die Zeit,* 31 March 1999.

Tietmeyer, Hans. "Europäische Währungsunion und Politische Union: Das Modell mehrerer Geschwindigkeiten." *Europa-Archiv* 49, 1 (1994): 457–460.

———. "Europa: Steigende Welle oder Urknall." *Frankfurter Allgemeine Zeitung,* 5 April 1995.

"Tolerant, Charakterfest." *Der Spiegel,* 3 June 1991.

"Total Normal?" *Der Spiegel,* 30 November 1999.

Toulemon, Robert. "Kerneuropa: Deutschfranzösische Aktionsgemeinschaft in Sicht?" *Integration,* 18, no. 2 (1995): 62–67.

"Tschechische Republik/Deutschland/Rühe: NATO darf keine geschlossene Gesellschaft sein." *dpa Pressebrief,* 7 October 1993.

Tschernomyrdin, Viktor. "Nah am Abgrund." *Die Zeit,* 2 June 1999.

"Überholte Denkweise." *Der Spiegel,* 24 February 1992.

Ullman, Richard H. *Securing Europe.* Princeton, NJ: Princeton University Press, 1991.

"Umfrage: Freundschaft mit Paris nur Mythos." *Frankfurter Allgemeine Zeitung,* 5 July 1997.

"Ungarn wünscht NATO-Unterstützung." *Süddeutsche Zeitung,* 18 May 1993.

"Unterstützung der Reformprozesse in den Staaten Mittel-, Südost- und Osteuropas(einschließlich der baltischen Staaten) sowie in den neuen unabhängigen Staaten auf dem Territorium der ehemaligen Sowjetunion." *Deutscher Bundestag, Drucksache* 12/6162, 12 November 1993.

Urban, Thomas. "Polen strebt weiter in die NATO." *Süddeutsche Zeitung,* 10 July 1993.

"Vereinigte Staaten: Langsamere Gangart Rußlands wegen." *Frankfurter Allgemeine Zeitung,* 7 January 1994.

"Verhandlungsgrundlage der dänischen Regierung: Ein offenes Europa vom 11.12.1995 (Auszüge)." In *Reformder Europäischen Union,* ed. Mathias Jopp. Bonn: Europa Union Verlag, 1996, 177–180.

Verheugen, Günter. "Kohls gefährlicher Sonderweg." Interview, *Focus,* 25 February 1995.

"Verheugen fordert System gemeinsamer Sicherheit für ganz Europa." *dpa Pressebrief,* 6 January 1994.

"Verheugen warnt vor sicherheitspolitischer Spaltung Europas." *dpa Pressebrief,* 30 November 1994.

"Verschärfung der Spannungen zwischen Moskau und der Allianz, *Keesings Archiv der Gegenwart,* 8 September 1995.

"Verteidigungspolitische Richtlinien für den Geschäftsbereich des Bundesministers der Verteidigung vom 26. November 1992." ("Defense-Political Guidelines"). *Blätter fürdeutsche und internationale Politik* 38, 1 (1993): 1137–1151.

"Vertrag über die abschließende Regelung in bezug auf Deutschland" ("Two-plus-four-treaty"). *Bundesgesetzblatt II,* 12 September 1990, article 5, 1318.

"Vertrag über die Beziehungen zwischen der Bundesrepublik Deutschland und den Drei Mächten (Deutschlandvertrag): 26.Mai 1952." In *Aussenpolitik der Bundesrepublik Deutschland: Dokumente von 1949 bis 1994,* ed. Auswärtiges Amt. Cologne: Verlag Wissenschaft und Politik, 1995, 194–197.

"Vierzigster Jahrestag der Unterzeichnung der römischen Verträge." *Keesings Archiv der Gegenwart,* 25 March 1997.

Voigt, Karsten. "Die Osterweiterung der NATO." *Aus Politik und Zeitgeschichte* 46, no. B5 (1996): 21–26.

Volgyes, Ivan. "Hungary and Germany: Two Actors in Search of a New Play." In *The Germans and their Neighbors,* ed. Dirk Verheyen and Christian Soe. Boulder, CO: Westview Press, 1993.

"Völlig von der Rolle." *Der Spiegel,* 11 September 1995.

Vollmer, Ludger. *Die Grünen und die Aussenpolitik: Ein schwieriges Verhältnis: Eine Ideen, Programm und Ereignisgeschichte grüner Aussenpolitik.* Münster: Westfälisches Dampfboot, 1998.

"Vor dem Rohr." *Der Spiegel,* 13 September 1993.

"Vor NATO-Gipfel: Kohl fordert klare Beitrittsperspektiven für Ost-Nachbarn: CDU und SPD einig: Derzeit keine Ost-Erweiterung." *dpa Pressebrief,* 8 January 1994.

Vorstand der SPD, ed. *Grundsatzprogramm der Sozialdemokratischen Partei Deutschlands.* Bonn: Druckhaus Deutz, 1989.

Wagner, Wolfgang. "Die Dynamik der deutschen Wiedervereinigung: Suche nach einer Verträglichkeit für Europa." *Europa-Archiv* 45, 1 (1990): 79–88.

"Waigel besteht auf Entlastung für Deutschland." *Frankfurter Allgemeine Zeitung,* 14 October 1998.

Wallander, Celeste A. *Mortal Friends, Best Enemies—German-Russian Cooperation after the Cold War.* Ithaca and London: Cornell University Press, 1999.

Walt, Stephen M. *The Origins of Alliances.* Ithaca: Cornell University Press, 1987.

Waltz, Kenneth. *Theory of International Politics.* Reading, MA: Addison-Wesley Publishers, 1979.

"Warschau, Prag und Budapest sehen sich sicherheitspolitisch im Stich gelassen." *Handelsblatt,* 5 October 1993.

"Washington: Kanzleramt ist Inhalt des Briefes an Jelzin bekannt: NATO-Mitgliedschaft Rußlands ist eine theoretische Option." *Frankfurter Allgemeine Zeitung,* 12 May 1995.

Watrin, Christian. "Deutschland: Der Preis der wirtschaftlichen Vereinigung." *Aussenwirtschaft* 48, no. 1 (1993): 37–48.

———. "Germany's Economic Unification Two Years Later." *Washington, D.C.: American Institute for Contemporary German Studies Seminar Paper* no. 4 (1993).

Weber, Max. *Wirtschaft und Gesellschaft: Grundriß der verstehenden Soziologie.* 5th ed. Tübingen: Mohr, 1972.

"Wehrpflicht am Ende." *Der Spiegel,* 8 February 1993.

Weidenfeld, Werner. *Aussenpolitik für die deutsche Einheit: Die Entscheidungsjahre 1989/90.* Geschichte der deutschen Einheit Vol. 4. Stuttgart: Deutsche Verlags-Anstalt, 1998.

———. "Die Bilanz der europäischen Integration 1985." *Jahrbuch der Europäischen Integration* 6 (1985): 13–28.

———. "Die Bilanz der europäischen Integration 1992/93." *Jahrbuch der Europäischen Integration* 11 (1992/3): 13–26.

———. "Die Bilanz der europäischen Integration 1995/96." *Jahrbuch der Europäischen Integration* 15 (1995/96): 13–24.

———. "Die Bilanz der Europäischen Integration 1996/97." *Jahrbuch der Europäischen Integration* 16 (1996/97): 13–26.

———. "Fragen an die Aussenpolitik der neuen Regierung." *Internationale Politik* 54, no. 1 (1999): 1–2.

———. "Ohne Leitbild, ohne Ordnungshilfe. Europa und die europäische Einigung sind in einenBegründungsnotstand geraten." *Frankfurter Allgemeine Zeitung,* 3 November 1997.

"Weißbuch der britischen Regierung: Eine Partnerschaft von Nationen, 21.3.1996." In *Reform der Europäischen Union,* ed. Mathias Jopp. Bonn: Europa UnionVerlag, 1996, 169–176.

"Weitere Kämpfe im Kosovo." *Keesings Archiv der Gegenwart,* 23 September 1998.

Weller, Marc. "In Bosnien diffuser Auftrag für Blauhelme und NATO." *Frankfurter Allgemeine Zeitung,* 12 July 1995.

"Weltpolitik in Bielefeld," *Der Spiegel,* 10 May 1999.

Wendt, Alexander E. "Anarchy is What States Make of It: The Social Construction of Power Politics." *International Organization* 46 (1992): 422–429.

Wenger, Andreas, Jeronim Perovic. "Rußlands Sicherheitspolitik vor der Neubestimmung?: Die Herausforderung der NATO-Osterweiterung," *Osteuropa* 48 (1998): 451–466.

"Werben der Ukraine um die Gunst Bonns." *Neue Züricher Zeitung,* 6 February 1992.

"Wer Maastricht zerschlägt, der schafft keinen Kern." *Bonner Rundschau,* 13 September 1994.

Wessels, Wolfgang. "Die Europapolitik in der wissenschaftlichen Debatte." *Jahrbuch derEuropäischen Integration 1996/97* 16 (1996/97): 27–38.

———. "Maastricht: Ergebnisse, Bewertungen und Langzeittrends." *Integration* 15, no. 1 (1992): 2–16.

———. "Weder Vision noch Verhandlungspaket: Der Bericht der Reflexionsgruppe im integrationspolitischen Trend." *Integration* 19, no. 1 (1996): 14–21.

"Wettbewerb der Rechtsordnungen in Osteuropa." *Frankfurter Allgemeine Zeitung,* 17 September 1993.

Wettig, Gerhard. "Entwicklung der russischen Haltung zur NATO." *Europäische Sicherheit* 43 (1994): 235–237.

Whetten, Lawrence J. *Germany's Ostpolitik: Relations between the Federal Republic and theWarsaw Pact Countries.* London: Oxford University Press, 1971.

"West-Ost-Transfers: Anpassungs-Szenarien." *Informationsdienst des Instituts der deutschenWirtschaft* 19, no. 2 (1994).

Wieczorek-Zeul, Heidemarie. "Erklärung zu den von der CDU/CSU-Fraktion vorgelegten Vorschlägen zu einem 'Kerneuropa'." *Presseservice der SPD,* 5 September 1994.

———. "Erklärung zur Krise im EWS." *Presseservice der SPD* 17 September 1992.

————. "Europäische Perspektiven der SPD, Antrag auf dem Bundesparteitag der SPD in Bremen." *Presseservice der SPD*, 21 May 1991.

Wieland, Leo. "Für Clinton ist die NATO wichtiger als Bosnien." *Frankfurter Allgemeine Zeitung*, 2 December 1994.

"Wie weiter zwischen dem Westen und Rußland? Amerika, Europa, Bonn denken nach." *Frankfurter Allgemeine Zeitung*, 12 May 1995.

Winterberg, Jörg M. *Westliche Unterstützung der Transformationsprozesse in Osteuropa.* St. Augustin: Konrad-Adenauer-Stiftung, 1994.

"Wirre Angst." *Der Spiegel*, 21 August 1995.

"Wirtschafts und- Währungsunion nicht um jeden Preis." *Pressemitteilung des Bundesverbandes der deutschen Industrie*, 18 September 1991.

"Wir wollen nicht beiseite stehen." *Der Spiegel*, 7 December 1992.

"Wörner: NATO muß sich nach Osten öffnen." *dpa Pressebrief*, 6 October 1993.

"Wörner: NATO-Erweiterung nicht entscheidungsreif." *Süddeutsche Zeitung*, 7 October 1993.

Wohlfeld, Monika. "The WEU as a Complement, Not a Substitute, for *NATO.*" *Transition* 1, no. 23 (1995): 34–36.

Wolf, Anita. "Bundesrepublik Deutschland." *Jahrbuch der europäischen Integration* 10 (1991/92): 310–320.

Wolf, Klaus-Dieter. "Militarisierung und Zivilisierung der internationalen Beziehungen: Situationsanalyse und Forschungsperspektiven aus politikwissenschaftlicher Sicht." In *Die Zukunft des Militärs in den Industriegesellschaften,* ed. Wilfried Karl and Thomas Nielebock, Jahrbuch für Friedens- und Konfliktforschung, Vol. 18. Baden-Baden: Nomos, 1991, 57–63.

Woyke, Wichard. "Deutsche Wiedervereinigung." In *Handwörterbuch Internationale Politik,* 7th ed., ed. Wichard Woyke. Opladen: Leske und Budrich, 1998.

————. "Von der Orientierungslosigkeit zur Konzeption: Die Aussenpolitik des Vereinigten Deutschland." *Politische Bildung* 30 (1997): 9–25.

"Zehn Forderungen an die deutsche Ratspräsidentschaft der EU." *Presseservice der SPD*, 30 April 1994.

"Zehn-Punkte-Plan zur Überwindung der deutschen Teilung." *Keesings Archiv der Gegenwart*, 28 November 1989.

"Zehn-Punkte-Plan zur Überwindung der Teilung Deutschlands und Europa, vorgestellt von Helmut Kohl am 28. November 1989." *Europa-Archiv* 43, 2 (1989): D728–730.

"Zeit der Begehrlichkeiten vorbei." *Deutscher Industrie- und Handelstag: Informationen für Presse, Funk und Fernsehen*, 20 June 1994.

Zelikow, Philip, and Condolezza Rice. *Germany Unified and Europe Transformed—A Study in Statecraft.* Cambridge, MA: Harvard University Press, 1995.

Zoellick, Robert B. "Abschied von der Selbstbeschränkung: Deutsche Aussenpolitik aus Sicht der USA." *Internationale Politik* 53, no. 12 (1998): 21–26.

"Zukunftsperspektiven der jungen Generation auf dem Weg ins vereinte Europa." *Bulletin des Presse- und Informationsamtes der Bundesregierung*, 19 November 1991.

"Zur Hilfe verpflichtet." *Der Spiegel,* 26 April 1993.

"Zuspitzung der Asyldebatte, gewaltsame Angriffe und Mordanschläge gegen Ausländer." *Archiv der Gegenwart,* 23 November 1992.

"Zuviel auf einmal." *Der Spiegel,* 14 December 1992.

"Zwang zum Sparen." *Informationsdienst des Instituts der deutschen Wirtschaft* 18, no. 25 (1993).

"Zwischen Bundeskanzleramt und Kreml wird ein 'rotes Telefon' geschaltet." *Kölner-Anzeiger,* 11 May 1994.

"Zwölf Forderungen der SPD an einen europäische Währungsunion." *Presseerklärung der SPD im deutschen Bundestag,* 22 November 1991.

Index